# Corporate Strategy for Hospitality

## Tim Knowles

Lecturer
Department of Tourism and Leisure
University of Luton

LONGMAN

Addison Wesley Longman Limited
Edinburgh Gate, Harlow,
Essex CM20 2JE, England.
*and Associated Companies throughout the world*

First published 1996
Second impression 1999

**British Library Cataloguing in Publication Data**
A catalogue entry for this title is available from the British Library.

ISBN 0–582–28167–9

**Library of Congress Cataloging-in-Publication data**
A catalog entry for this title is available from the Library of Congress.

Set by 3 in $10\frac{1}{2}/13$ Palatino

Transferred to digital print on demand 2001

Printed and bound in Great Britain by Antony Rowe Ltd, Eastbourne

# CONTENTS

# CASE STUDIES

# FOREWORD

The Hotel and Catering International Management Association (HCIMA) through its educational activities has seen a trend in recent years for hospitality students to study corporate strategy and many institutions offer modules on this subject specifically related to the hospitality industry. The topic has for many years been regarded as a core module within business schools offering Masters in Business Administration.

In considering industry needs the Association has noted the importance attached to this subject by middle and senior managers, a point contained in recent research on European hospitality management skills, commissioned by the HCIMA and undertaken by the Department of Management Studies, University of Surrey.

The HCIMA has long regarded corporate strategy as a capstone subject that brings together the multidisciplinary nature of hospitality studies and is suitable for students in the final year of their studies. Tim Knowles's book brings together those elements of corporate strategy and relates them specifically to the hospitality industry on a worldwide basis. The text throughout is illustrated by detailed industry case studies. Many of the chapters illustrate how an analysis of the wider environment can be used to identify trends within our industry. The author shows throughout the need to consider key principles in other academic disciplines in order that they can be applied to the hospitality industry on both a national and international basis.

I am confident that this book will be of value both to managers and to potential managers within the hospitality industry.

Jeremy Logie FHCIMA
Chief Executive
Hotel and Catering International Management Association

# PREFACE

The subject of strategic management is frequently described as a capstone subject, which pulls together a number of disciplines such as marketing, finance and organizational behaviour. For a number of years corporate strategy has been recognized as an integral part of business studies degrees at both undergraduate and postgraduate level. A trend in the recent past has seen this subject introduced into degrees in hospitality management. While writers have published extensively on corporate strategy, a review of the available literature shows a lack of information on corporate strategy applied to the hospitality industry. What is available tends to be contained within expensive reports, academic journals and edited textbooks, the latter suffering from the weakness of being poorly edited.

The purpose of this book is to provide the student and the practising manager with an insight into the process of strategy formulation and implementation, and to relate it to trends in the hospitality industry. Backed up by hospitality case studies from around the world this book comprises ten chapters that cover all elements of the strategic management process. Each chapter commences with clear objectives for the reader, and at the end of each chapter a summary is provided along with an extensive list of further reading material.

The hospitality industry has changed considerably over the past three decades, and in particular the issues of industry structure and concentration have implications for the strategic manager. The twin issues of development and growth have had to be addressed by both the major companies and the small independent single-unit firms. The response of both the chains and the independents is discussed in depth within this book, along with some of the factors within the wider environment affecting the industry. The book finishes with a review of some of the trends and developments likely to affect the hospitality industry over the next decade, with suggestions on how the industry might respond.

Tim Knowles

# ACKNOWLEDGEMENTS

A considerable amount of assistance was given to me in the preparation of this book. I should like to express my appreciation to all my colleagues within the Department of Management Studies, University of Surrey. In particular my thanks go to Dr Chris Cooper, Dr John Fletcher, and John Westlake.

I should also like to express my thanks for the support and encouragement received from the industry, in particular the following organizations: Barclays de Zoete Wedd; BDO Hospitality Consulting; Holiday Inn; Horwath International; Jones Lang Wootton; Kleinwort Benson Securities; Pannell Kerr Forster Associates; Salomon Brothers; Smith New Court; Touche Ross Greene Belfield Smith Division; Travel and Tourism Analyst, Economist Intelligence Unit. Thanks are also due to Sue Kitching for her courtesy, efficiency and accuracy in typing this manuscript.

# CHAPTER 1

# The concept of strategic management

**OBJECTIVES**

After reading this chapter you should be able to:
- Understand the concepts of both corporate strategy and the strategic management process.
- Identify the critical elements within the strategic management process and relate them to the service industry.
- Relate the theory of strategic management to the development, growth and decline of a number of companies within the hospitality industry in the UK, Europe and the USA.

## WHAT IS STRATEGY?

To apply the concept of strategy to an organization implies that the organization's managers try to allocate resources, establish policies and procedures, assign responsibilities and give direction to the organization. They do this by using a consistent pattern of decisions that reflect a previously defined corporate mission and set of objectives.

The purpose of strategic management at all levels is to assist the leadership of an organization in helping it to adapt continually to its changing environment, so that it can enjoy a strong, growing and long life. The fundamental task is to enable the organization to adapt to meet changing opportunities and threats, and so strategic management is an important part of the organization's planning system. The subject of planning will be considered in Chapter 2, along with the environment within which the hospitality firm operates.

The business environment within which hospitality firms operate has become increasingly uncertain in recent years, and so the ability to anticipate problems is very valuable. The successful firm is the one that can live with uncertainty and incorporate it within its decision-making process. All firms make strategic decisions, but they can be taken carefully or negligently, deliberately or haphazardly, or systematically. The systematic approach to decision making lies at the heart of the strategic management process.

Organizations have got bigger and more complicated over the past 25 years. This trend has been a source of competitive advantage to some firms, but it has also caused great difficulties. It has led to a managerial information gap between the overall, corporate view of the organization and a detailed working knowledge of the business at each level. Strategic management has developed to fill this gap, with attempts to formalize and justify the decision-making process, and with the formulation of various strategy models.

Manufacturing industry has been the dominant force within economies over the last century, and so the approach of strategic management has tended to focus on production. The shift for the 1990s and beyond is towards the service industries. In a maturing hospitality industry, for a firm to survive it must be able to align itself strategically with its environment and select the appropriate strategy in order to establish a competitive advantage.

Traditional product-orientated strategic management still has a lot to offer the service sector, but the characteristics of services require a different approach to strategic management. In addition demand and supply, along with the nature of the service encounter, suggest the need to adapt the traditional product-orientated approach to the hospitality industry.

The first half of this decade was a hard time for Europe's hospitality industry. After several years of expansion in the 1980s, some of the region's leading hotel groups were left with big financial problems. Luxury chains were the first to suffer as continental Europe slipped deeper into recession. This was followed by groups covering a much broader range of hotel categories, such as France's Accor, having to reduce expenditure in response to falling income. It was clear that changes in the macroeconomic situation were reducing demand in the business and leisure segments, which in turn affected the demand for hotel accommodation in Europe.

Another issue was that of industry concentration. Between 1989 and 1992, the stock of hotel rooms in Europe belonging to publicly quoted groups grew by a fifth to 340,000 (an estimated two million rooms in Europe are offered by privately owned hotels: most of them are small and family-owned). This gives an indication of the growth in concentration of the major hotel firms in Europe. As well as borrowing heavily to expand the number of rooms, big chains also spent considerable funds renovating old hotels.

The early 1990s saw executive travel budgets reduce and property prices fall, with some groups being suffocated by debt. Two companies that illustrate this problem are the Italian hotel company Ciga and the UK-based Queens Moat Houses.

## CASE STUDY: CIGA AND QUEENS MOAT HOUSES

Ciga is an Italian hotel group owned by Fimpar, which in turn is a holding company of the Aga Khan. During the early 1990s Ciga was Europe's thirteenth largest chain, with more than 5,000 rooms. The company had 36 top-of-the-range hotels spread across the continent, including the Gritti Palace in Venice and the Imperial in Vienna. It was also in 1993 carrying around one trillion lire ($680 million) of debt, much of it built up during a spending spree in the 1980s. Unfortunately for Ciga and its creditors, the demand for five-star hotel rooms plummeted during the Gulf War in 1991, and hardly rose during the period 1992–94. As a result, Ciga lost 252 billion lire in 1992 after losing 99 billion in 1991. Sales in 1993–94 were little improved. On 21 May 1993 shares in Ciga and Fimpar were suspended on the Milan stock market after a creditor took Fimpar to court for failing to repay a $100 million loan. The company at that stage was controlled by the banks, and during 1994 was subject to speculation that it would be sold to either ITT Sheraton or Forte. Ciga was eventually sold to ITT Sheraton.

Luxury hotel groups were not the only ones with financial problems. Queens Moat Houses, a British hotel chain whose shares were also suspended during 1993–94, ran into trouble after expanding rapidly in the European market for mid-range hotels, a fiercely competitive sector. The hotel chain's problems were made worse by a management incentive scheme that backfired through lack of head office control, along with a revaluation of the company's assets. During the period 1993–94 bankers agreed on a rescue package for Queens Moat Houses, which owes £1 billion ($1.5 billion). The shares were relisted in 1995.

Both these examples illustrate how the turbulence of the wider environment can affect the well-being of the hotel industry.

## THE NATURE OF SERVICES

It is the application of strategy to the service sector, and particularly the hospitality industry, that is the focus of this book. It is therefore important to examine the nature of services. Historically businesses have considered those activities that focus on two issues:

- making customers aware of a product and its attributes;
- getting the product from the point of production to the point of consumption, sometimes referred to as **distribution channel management**.

This traditional approach is embraced by non-profit and profit-making organizations. However, it does not work for service products, as exemplified in hotels and restaurants. Managers who have learned the finer points of marketing, promotion advertising and shipping of tangible products will not be able to translate that knowledge into the successful marketing of a service product such as a hotel room. There are key differences.

There is no such thing as a pure product without some element of service. There is rather a continuum of products, from the tangible to the intangible: some products can act like a service, and some services can act like a product. This mix can change for a given item. For example, a customer may buy a soft drink from a vending machine. This purchase is weighted towards the tangible end of the continuum: the emphasis is on the product, not the service. The same customer may buy the same soft drink from a full service restaurant. In this case the purchase is weighted towards the intangible end of the continuum: the emphasis is on the service, not the product. The service product itself has two distinct dimensions:

- the procedural dimension, which is the actual service function;
- the convivial dimension, or the spirit with which the service is delivered.

The procedural dimension comprises the flow of service, timeliness, accommodation of customer needs, anticipation, communication, customer feedback and supervision. The convivial dimension encompasses the attitude of those delivering the service, which is indicated by body language, tone of voice, naming names, attentiveness, problem solving, guidance and selling. The role of service marketing is to make the intangible appear more tangible, and to reduce the risk associated with purchases that are predominantly intangible.

For example, all hoteliers will offer a room for the night. What is it that makes one hotel different from another? It is the intangible or service dimensions that are included. The main difference between a budget hotel and a luxury hotel is in the procedural and convivial dimensions of the service. A luxury hotel may provide concierge services or 24 hour room service (procedural), and a higher staff-to-guest ratio so that more personalized service may be given to the guests (convivial). In contrast, budget hotel guests may have to rely on front office employees for help during their stay, vending machines for late night snacks, and the restaurant down the street (procedural) for meals. While the employees at the budget hotel may be as friendly as those in the luxury hotel when providing service, the many other functions that they have to perform, and the lower staff-to-guest ratios, will cause the convivial element to decrease in importance. Thus the intangible convivial aspects remain intangible in the budget hotel, whereas the extensive convivial features provided by the luxury hotel feel tangible to the customers.

Furthermore, service improves the functionality of a product or adds a utility. This functionality or utility provides a value independent of any change in form, time, place or possession.

In considering **demand**, for a service or for a tangible product, a number of aspects need to be taken into account. Directed demand is essentially the same for either a product or a service: a customer wants, needs and has the ability to acquire either. However, service by its very nature does not entail physical possession, but rather the buyer's willingness to participate in or experience something. Also, service has two additional elements beyond those of more tangible products: the derived and the functional demand, which flow from the direct demand for the service, and together make up the indirect demand elements. For example, when someone eats at a restaurant (direct demand), the indirect derived demand will relate to the way the food is delivered. The indirect functional demand relates to flexibility, timing of product delivery, privacy, and the environment in which the service is performed.

## Service marketing mix

We can analyse the nature of services further by considering the service marketing mix. A company's marketing mix is traditionally defined as comprising the four P's: product, price, promotion and place, but this definition needs to be re-examined and redefined to encompass the unique aspects of service. The most frequently mentioned differences in attributes between services and products are intangibility, perishability, heterogeneity, and simultaneous production and consumption. Other attributes of services include the ease of duplication of a service product, the buyer's difficulty in evaluating or comparing products, and the variability of output volume. These attributes are described below.

Intangibility     A service is an experience, and not something that can be physically possessed. This intangibility creates a greater perceived risk for the customer, who has to rely on the promise of satisfaction without the opportunity to return the purchase: the greater the provider's promise to satisfy the customers' expectation, the greater the purchase risk. Intangibility affects the way that customers acquire services. Without personal experiences, they rely more heavily on word of mouth than on any other source of information, because service provides an experience that can never be exactly duplicated or replicated in the way that a product can. The quality of service as defined by customer expectation that is received from one department of an operation or during a previous visit affects the customer's evaluation of the entire operation. The challenge for the service provider such as a hotelier is in maintaining control of quality and standards, and being sure both are consistent throughout the firm.

Perishability     Unlike most tangible products, if a hotel room or a table in a restaurant is not occupied within any specific time period, the opportunity to generate revenue is lost. If a hotelier has ten rooms that are not occupied (sold) on one night, these ten rooms cannot be held in an inventory ready for sale the next night. The result of this perishability is that service-dominated businesses must be able to forecast demand and act accordingly. By understanding when patronage occurs, and using methods such as yield management, service providers can direct or redirect demand into periods of low demand to reduce the effect of perishability.

Heterogeneity

The procedural and convivial dimensions of service mean that it is characterized by variation and lack of uniformity. This lack of uniformity is further complicated by both employee and customer perceptions. Each customer brings different experiences and expectations, which affect the quality of consumption. It is the potential differences between what the customer expects and what is delivered that may create problems for the hospitality firm. Both Marriott and McDonald's have instituted extensive employee training and supervision, which is tightly controlled. This provides consistency throughout different locations around the world and during different time periods. There is thus a need to institutionalize services in an effort to maintain consistency.

Simultaneous production and consumption

The production of hospitality products does not take place until the customer requests it. Because perishability prevents hospitality firms from storing their products to await customer demand, the employee is part of the product, providing production at the same time as the customer consumes it. So if a customer has a negative experience, even if it is not the employee's fault, staff are still viewed as the cause of the problem.

Ease of duplication

The procedural aspects of service are the easiest to duplicate. The convivial aspects, which are intangible, are more difficult to replicate, and thus can be used as a means of differentiation. When a hospitality manager chooses to compete on the service component level, it is more effective to concentrate on the convivial dimension, or the spirit in which the service is given.

Difficulty of comparison

Because hospitality services are intangible, it is difficult for customers to determine their price or value, and hence it is difficult for them to make competitive comparisons. Each guest arrives at a property with his or her own set of expectations and experiences, and hospitality managers must be aware of how these ideas are arrived at. Consumers use three types of comparison when purchasing products and services:

- **search qualities**, which include attributes that a consumer can determine before a purchase;
- **experienced qualities**, or attributes that can only be evaluated after consumption;

- **credence qualities**, which are attributes that consumers may find impossible to evaluate because of lack of education or evaluative skills.

Experience and credence qualities dominate hospitality-related purchase decisions: hence consumers may rely more heavily on personal sources of information than they would for products that are more tangible.

**Variability of output**

The demand for hospitality products varies dramatically with the time of day, day of the week, period of the year, price and location. A restaurant is typically least busy early in the week, busier mid week, and busiest at the weekend. Resorts have high and low seasons at different times of the year. A restaurant at a highway location can be very slow sometimes, but exceedingly busy if a busload of tourists arrives. However, regardless of these factors, the customer expects the same level of service and consistency of quality at all times. Restaurateurs and hoteliers must balance the variability of demand with the added expense of increased production capacity, so as to maintain profitability. This variability of output requires that forecasting be accurate and that contingency plans be in place to meet unexpectedly high or low levels of demand.

Considering all these compounding problems facing hospitality firms, what can be done? How can managers overcome these obstacles? How can the myriad interrelated issues be resolved?

## SOLUTIONS: STRATEGIES AND TACTICS

We have seen that the hospitality firm operates within a complex environment, and the nature of services (as opposed to products) suggests that a different approach to the strategic management process is required. The unique attributes of services provide challenges that must be addressed when developing strategies and tactics. We can identify a number of broad solutions for hospitality managers:

- **Make the intangibles tangible.** This can involve creating product-like attributes when developing promotional campaigns: for example, samples and pictures of people enjoying themselves at a property. However, the firm should avoid showing images of people that imply a promise of satisfaction that cannot be achieved.
- **Develop a forecasting system.** This is required in order to determine when patronage occurs, by day, week and time of the year. It also helps to provide a level of service that customers expect, and it maintains consistency. In addition to identifying demand levels, it is equally important to forecast the price at which customers will buy a hospitality product. Some segments of the industry experience the 'profitless prosperity' syndrome, when demand for services is high but profit margins are low, and high volume is needed to make the operation

profitable. Managing demand – that is, moving excess demand to slower periods, pricing accordingly and evaluating policies that affect demand – will result in increased profitability: a concept known as **yield management**.

- **Emphasize training and supervision.** Procedural and convivial service training, in addition to product training, can give the firm a competitive edge. Continual assessment and communication of the convivial aspects of service to employees, particularly customer perceptions and needs, help to create a sense of job importance in the staff.
- **Reduce inconsistency.** Hospitality products tend to be inconsistent from one location to another and even within the same location. Management should try to overcome this problem by continually training staff and implementing quality controls.
- **Focus on inseparability.** Hospitality products and the delivery of those products by employees are largely inseparable in the mind of the customer. Therefore greater focus on human resources within the organization will pay dividends in increased customer satisfaction.
- **Identify target markets.** Determining target markets, or segments or niches of those markets, will help a hospitality firm to decide how it can best meet customer expectations, and so help to determine service styles and levels. In addition, decisions to add or change service offerings must be based on customer and organizational needs. The service component must help to create or keep customers and provide guest satisfaction. The addition of a service component must be significant enough to influence the decision of the customer to patronize an establishment, otherwise it may be a waste of organizational resources.

Problems create needs: customers do not purchase a product unless they have a problem to solve and believe that the purchase will provide the solution to that problem. Continual evaluation of customer needs and assessment of the organization's abilities to meet those needs is fundamental for a successful business.

All business operators, especially those in the hospitality industry, must be aware of the way that products and services differ. They must understand service attributes such as intangibility, perishability, heterogeneity, simultaneous production and consumption, ease of duplication, difficulty of comparison and variability of output, in order to assist the business. Managers must continually determine changing customer expectations and regularly evaluate how well their businesses are meeting those expectations. They must monitor not only financial objectives, but also intangible objectives such as customer perception, by quantifying these intangibles through tools such as customer surveys or comment cards. Observational techniques can also work well. Perhaps the most important strategy is for managers to stay in touch with their customers and markets.

These issues of the economic environment and financial environments, and the nature of services, will now be applied to the European hotel industry, and in particular to Forte and Accor.

## THE EUROPEAN HOTEL INDUSTRY: FORTE AND ACCOR

France's Accor and Britain's Forte are Europe's two biggest hotel groups. Though they are stronger than their rivals, they were battered by the recession of the early 1990s, but this did not stop them taking strategic decisions. Forte, in refocusing its business, during 1992 sold all but 24.8 per cent of its Gardner Merchant catering subsidiary for £402 million to a management buyout funded by venture capitalists and pension-fund managers. In January 1995 Gardner Merchant was sold in a trade sale to French company Sodexho for £730 million in what Gardner Merchant described as a **strategic alliance**. This allowed Forte to recoup its 24.8 per cent investment in the company. Forte furthered its aims in Europe recently by buying 52 motorway restaurants in France from the Accor hotel group for Ffr540 million ($102 million), and by signing a joint-venture deal with Agip of Italy to manage 18 hotels. In April 1993 Forte announced that it was cutting its dividend for the first time in 20 years: a reflection of the need to fund expansion, and a response to the poor financial performance of the European hotel industry.

Accor, whose 11 brands include the up-market Sofitel, mid-range Ibis and cut-price Formule 1 chains, during 1993 decided to respond to the poor economic and financial background. The company decided to reduce its FFr16 billion ($2.9 billion) debt by selling some non-hotel properties. Accor was also trying harder to exploit marketing and purchasing synergies between its various chains. Another approach considered in 1993–94 was to improve the performance of its Sofitel hotels with the suggestion of putting Sofitel and Air France's luxury Meridien chain into a joint holding company, which Accor would like to run. Meridien during that time was subject to takeover speculation, with either Accor or Forte being the likely buyers. Meridien was eventually bought by Forte.

With home-grown hotel chains on the defensive in Europe, foreign ones, in particular from North America, were well placed to steal a march on them. After all, quoted hotel chains account for an average of 14 per cent of the hotel rooms on offer in European Union countries, so there is plenty of room for growth. America's Hyatt chain is already building up its presence in Europe; Choice Hotels International, another American group that specializes in hotel franchising, has plans to expand. Table 1.1 illustrates the top ten hotels groups in Europe by rooms and country of ownership. Since this table was published changes have occurred, particularly the sale of Rank Hotels.

**Table 1.1 Top ten hotel groups in the EU by number of rooms, 1992**

| Company | Country of ownership | Size |
|---|---|---|
| Accor | France | 112,810 |
| Forte | UK | 36,750 |
| Louvre | France | 25,576 |
| Queens Moat Houses | UK | 21,123 |
| Ladbroke (Hilton) | UK | 15,164 |
| BIL Mount Charlotte | New Zealand | 14,170 |
| Bass (Holiday Inn) | UK | 11,944 |
| Saison (Inter-Continental) | Japan | 9,530 |
| ITT (Sheraton) | USA | 8,038 |
| Rank | UK | 6,939 |

Source: *Travel & Tourism Analyst* No. 1, 1993, The Economist Intelligence Unit

## THE CONCEPT OF MULTIPLE STAKEHOLDERS: AN INTRODUCTION

In addition to the economic and financial environment in which the European hotel industry has to operate, the strategic management process also needs to take account of the firm's stakeholders. We have already seen how Ciga's success was affected by its creditors, and Queens Moat Houses was influenced by its incentive scheme for general managers. The term **stakeholder** can be defined as any group or individual who can affect or is affected by the performance of the organization. Current and future strategies can be affected by both external and internal stakeholder pressures. Stakeholders' interests are not always consistent, and the organization will need to take account of their differing requirements in order to establish their relative importance. Two such categories of external stakeholder are shareholders and government; their influence will now be illustrated with a discussion of the Accor bid for Wagons-Lits.

No longer content to be on the outside looking in, minority shareholders in continental Europe have in recent years began to assert their influence in response to a recent spate of takeovers that have seen their rights affected and company profits reduced. The Bfr 14 billion ($406 million) bid in October 1991 from Accor for Wagons-Lits, the Franco-Belgian travel group, is a case in point. The bid valued Wagons-Lits' shares at BFr 8,650 each, a generous 25 per cent above their market price at the time. However, the price was lower than the BFr 12,500 at which Accor valued the company in June 1990, when it bought an option to buy the shares from its ally, Société Générale de Belgique (SGB). Dissatisfied minority shareholders claimed that Accor had controlled Wagons-Lits since then, together with the Caisse des Depots, a French savings institution that owned 28 per cent of Wagons-Lits. Accor and the Caisse des Depots, which has a 7 per cent stake in the French hotel group, denied cooperating, but on 4 December 1991 a judge ordered Accor to increase its bid, and to extend its offer until 19 December. Accor appealed against the ruling, which could have cost it another BFr 6 billion. Meanwhile another stakeholder, the European Commission, froze the bid on 17 December 1991, saying that it had serious doubts about the merger's impact on competition in the Union.

Though takeovers have increased substantially in Europe in the past few years, most are friendly. They are often arranged behind closed doors by a cabal of managers, bankers and lawyers. The beauty of such a system, say supporters, is that it avoids time-consuming fights and allows firms to take a long-term view. However, hotel companies operating in fast-moving global markets are already feeling the strain. Companies without supportive shareholders (i.e. Forte plc or Savoy plc) to protect them have to rely on other barriers. The European Commission wants to harmonize different defensive systems by introducing, among other things, strict timetables for bids, and by insisting that a full public offer be made for a firm if a buyer acquires more than one-third of its shares.

A further category of stakeholder is the big British and American institutional investors, who are also making European hospitality firms change their ways. The fund-management arm of Norwich Union, a British insurer, was among the shareholders who expressed their concern at Accor's Wagons-Lits bid. Fidelity, an American fund management company, has already attacked firms in Germany and elsewhere for neglecting minority investors' rights. Together with some form of EU takeover code, this changing philosophy towards corporate governance in Europe could eventually lead to a more open market for takeovers, which could have implications for the European hotel industry. It is this sort of discussion on stakeholders that can be set within the context of corporate governance within the European Union. The issue of stakeholder analysis and its importance for strategic management is considered in greater depth in later chapters of this book.

## CORPORATE GOVERNANCE IN THE EUROPEAN UNION

If corporate governance and the virtues or vices of free financial markets had been agonized over as much in 1985 as they are now, continental Europe would have ruined many of today's most popular and simplistic conclusions. These days, it is widely assumed that the monitoring of firms by close, caring banks is a better way to run things than the arm's-length institutional ownership of the USA and UK. Yet, in 1985, the free-market UK seemed to be outpacing the rest of bank-monitored Europe, which was in the throes of slow growth thanks to closed markets, protected managers and workers, and backward technology: the influence of Germany's Deutsche Bank was a case in point.

The central question in all this is: do free markets in finance and takeovers produce a healthier economy than those where regulation is tighter and shares are more closely held? One measure that can be used in considering this question is gross national product (GNP). Since 1950 growth in the USA and UK, in terms of GNP, has been the slowest, but if you measure from 1960 to 1990, the USA draws level in real GNP growth with West Germany, and then overtakes it both for 1970–90 and 1980–90. For the latest decade (1980–90) even the UK moves up the field: it and the USA both outpaced France and West Germany. France, underrated by many, has outgrown Germany throughout the period since World War II. If the figures are considered for real GNP per head, then West Germany fares better, because of its slow-growing (and latterly falling) population, than the USA, which has had millions of new immigrants. But even on real GNP per head, the UK outpaced West Germany in the 1980s.

On average, continental Europe conforms to the stereotypical comparison with the UK: more universal banks, closer links between banks and industry, more restrictive rules on shareholdings and voting rights, and far fewer hostile takeovers. As a key stakeholder the banks clearly influence the well-being, for better or worse, of firms in Europe.

Slowly, the European Union is edging towards laws that might make rules on shareholdings and takeovers more homogeneous and more liberal. But, even now, the average conceals as much as it reveals. From 1982 until 1988, French companies behaved rather as Japanese ones did: they ran free of their banks. When the 1980s began, they relied on banks for 71 per cent of their external financing and carried debts equal to 68 per cent of their assets. Suddenly this changed, prompted first by the Socialist government's nationalization of the main banks and, later, by a bout of liberalization and the revival of the Paris stock market. Bank debts were paid back and replaced with equity in a spate of fund-raising that put French firms ahead of the British as equity issuers. By 1988, bank borrowing accounted for only 53 per cent of their external financing; debt equalled only 63 per cent of their assets. Since then, however, this has gone into reverse in different ways. Companies have rushed back into debt, mainly to finance overseas acquisitions, especially in the UK and USA.

French firms arrived late at the foreign-investment auction, and paid high prices as a result. One example is hotel group Accor, which took the American Motel 6 chain off the hands of Kohlberg Kravis Roberts (which had bought it a year earlier in a leveraged buyout) for FFr7 billion. The other reversal of the 1980s was that French banks accelerated their purchases of equities. French banks had always had broad powers, but a new French Banking Act in 1984 broadened them still further. They responded by pushing hard into corporate finance, seeking to use shareholdings as a door-opener.

All the main French banks stressed that they did not want to boss firms around in the German style, nor did they want to send in managers or directors. They did not intend to underwrite other banks' loans if a firm went under; they would take part in financial rescues, but not as guarantors. What they wanted was business, not as an exclusive right but as a first option. In that way, the French banks were trying to be Japanese: to set up a community of interest between themselves and their clients.

Despite the changes of the past ten years or so, there is little sign in France of an active takeover market. Shareholding rules make hostile bids hard to win, as firms have a panoply of shares with different levels of voting rights (not dissimilar from Savoy plc). The bank stakes also stand in the way. Mutual funds (unit trusts in the UK) have become big shareholders in France, but few are run by independent groups; most are subsidiaries of banks, which in turn can influence decisions during bids. The arrival of an American-style takeover market is not impossible, but it is extremely unlikely. Nevertheless, French firms have aped many of the practices of American bidders: notably, they have shuffled assets with just as much vigour.

American critics of the $25 billion buyout of RJR Nabisco in 1988–89 lamented this treatment of a 'fine old American company', yet conveniently forgot that the company had only been formed in 1985 when RJ Reynolds merged with Nabisco Brands, which in turn had only been formed in 1981 when Nabisco merged with Standard Brands. RJR Nabisco promptly sold bits of itself to pay back its buyout debts, including Del Monte foods to the UK's Polly Peck (now defunct) and its biscuit division to a French group, BSN. That left BSN burdened with FFr14 billion of debt, which it reduced by FFr3.1 billion by selling its champagne businesses to Louis-Vuitton-Moet-Hennessy (LVMH), a French luxury-goods firm, which has interests in the French hotel market. A short while later LVMH reduced its debts by selling part of those businesses, the Lanson brand, only three months after it had bought it.

In contrast, the British way is a bit of a compromise – as you might expect. The UK had a big takeover boom in 1985–89, with plenty of bitterly fought hostile bids; but none was financed with the American-style highly leveraged junk bonds, and few bids have ended up in bankruptcy. Nevertheless, UK firms did take on much more debt in 1988–90, after almost a decade of using record profits to slim debts. As most takeovers were financed in cash, some of those debts went to pay for them. The burden of interest payments as a proportion of cash flow rose to a record 34 per cent in 1990, as these bigger debts met high nominal interest rates and fading cash flows. It was this central issue that had an effect on the UK hospitality industry during the period 1990–95. When debts became too large to bear, British firms also used debt restructuring and the bankruptcy laws.

The following list of takeovers (Barclays de Zoete Wedd, 1993) illustrates an almost 'pass the parcel' approach within the UK hospitality industry during the period 1980–92: an approach that has influenced the supply characteristics of the industry during the 1990s:

- Bass – Holiday Inn
- Ladbroke – Hilton International
- Mount Charlotte – Thistle
- Seibu Saison – Inter-Continental
- Mecca – Pleasurama
- Rank – Mecca
- New World – Ramada
- Brierley – Mount Charlotte Thistle
- Queens Moat Houses – Norfolk Capital
- THF – Crest
- Jarvis – Embassy
- *Scotts Hospitality changes brand from Holiday Inn to Marriott*

Compared with German banks, UK banks are more distant from their clients, which can make restructuring deals harder to complete. The big difference in the UK – which American opponents of takeovers look up to – is the voluntary but powerful **Takeover Code**. This, together with laws that protect minority shareholders, makes takeovers both easier and more difficult: easier in the sense that it bans Germanic tricks to limit the transfer of ownership; but more difficult by requiring an offer to be made to all shareholders at the same price, once a firm has accumulated 30 per cent of the shares. It prevents repeat bids within a year, and bans the bidder from acting undisclosed in concert with other people. Most notably, it bans firms from frustrating a bidder by crippling themselves with debt. Even so, the chief British worry is similar to the American one: that ownership of shares by uncaring institutions, and provision of debt by distant banks and capital markets, mean that the takeover is the only means of disciplining management. Only when a firm is put into play or bid for is the management's performance given any scrutiny.

## STRATEGIC MANAGEMENT PROCESS: FORTE PLC

The complexity of the strategic management process has already been illustrated by:

- the economic, financial and competitive environment within which the European hospitality industry operates;

- the concept of multiple stakeholders;
- the influence of the banks and financial institutions;
- corporate governance on a national and international basis.

This process will now be considered in relation to the changes at UK-based company Forte plc.

## Supply

For several years during the 1980s and 1990s, Forte hotels, in terms of supply, were on a long-term decline relative to their main UK competitors. In 1980 Forte had 22,500 rooms in the UK and 70,190 worldwide; at the same time Bass was creating the Crest brand, Ladbroke had only 4,800 rooms, Queens Moat Houses had only 1,250 rooms, and Mount Charlotte had 1,500 rooms. At the end of 1993 the Holiday Inn flag (Bass plc) flew over 1,788 hotels with 339,703 rooms in 56 countries. In 1993 alone there was a 3.1 per cent increase in rooms stock at Holiday Inn. Ladbroke in 1993 with the Hilton brand accounted for 159 hotels with 52,325 rooms in 46 countries. Forte's expansion progress had been sluggish by comparison. At the end of 1993, Forte operated 341 hotels with 29,618 rooms in the UK. It had 910 hotels with 85,352 rooms in 30 countries. Apart from the Crest acquisition from Bass in the late 1980s and the development of the budget hotel market, in which it is the market leader with TraveLodge, up to 1993 it had seen only marginal expansion in the previous 10–15 years.

## Demand

While Forte hotels' trading profit in the UK is estimated to have reached a peak of £143 million in 1989, it had dropped two years later to a low of £55 million. It probably won't be until 1996 that Forte hotels' profitability returns to the levels previously reached in the late 1980s. Throughout these difficult years for the company a number of critical tasks can be identified in attempting to illustrate the strategic management process at Forte plc.

## Forte plc: critical tasks

The strategic management process in relation to Forte plc can be defined as a set of decisions and actions that resulted in the formulation and implementation of plans designed to achieve the company's objectives. It comprised a number of critical tasks, as follows:

- Formulate the company's mission, including statements about its purpose, philosophy and objectives.
- Develop a company profile that reflects its internal conditions and capabilities.

- Assess the company's external environment, including both the competitive and general contextual factors.
- Identify the most desirable options by evaluating each option in the light of the company's mission.
- Select a set of long-term objectives and grand strategies that will achieve the most desirable options.
- Develop annual objectives and short-term strategies that are compatible with the selected set of long-term objectives and grand strategies.
- Implement the strategic choices by means of budgeted resource allocations, in which the matching of tasks, people, structures, technologies and reward systems is emphasized.
- Evaluate the success of the strategic process as an input for future decision making.

It is around these tasks that an analysis of Forte can be made from secondary data available on the firm. Many of these critical tasks will be discussed in greater detail within subsequent chapters of this book.

## Forte's business profile

Forte plc is the largest hotel operator in Britain, and its success can be traced through two critical points in its history. The first is the merger of Trust Houses and Forte Holdings in May 1970, which created Trusthouse Forte (THF); and the second is the adoption of a new corporate name, Forte plc, in June 1991.

The company began with the merger of two companies, Trust Houses and Forte Holdings. Trust Houses was formed in 1904 by the fourth Earl Grey. It originally started by trying to revive the traditional British inns, which were rapidly declining at the end of the nineteenth century. Over the years, the company built a firm reputation for quality and British tradition. In 1970 the company was operating 181 hotels, with 10,300 rooms. It also acquired a prominent interest in contract catering by the purchase of Lockhart Catering and eventually Gardner Merchant, by a merger in 1966. In 1970, just before the merger with Forte Holdings, it acquired a small stake in TraveLodge, a US budget hotel operation.

Carmine Monforte, or Charles Forte as he is better known, is an Italian immigrant who joined the private family business of milk bars. In 1935 he opened the second milk bar in London's Regent Street. Thus began Forte Holdings. Charles Forte progressively built a strong portfolio behind him. He began by venturing into restaurants, including the Criterion in Piccadilly Circus and the Café Royal in Mayfair; he won the contract to supply the catering for the 1951 Festival of Britain. He also diversified into airport catering at Heathrow Airport in 1955; roadside catering, with what later became the Little Chef chain; hotels, such as the Waldorf (1958),

George V, Plaza Athénée and Hôtel de la Tremoille, Paris; and Lillywhite Ltd, which is the only purchase that is not within the hospitality industry.

In 1970 Charles Forte was knighted Lord Forte of Ripley by Queen Elizabeth II. That year saw the merger of Forte Holdings with Trust Houses. The merger allowed two well-diversified companies to join in order to strengthen their position in the expanding hotel market. It did not begin in a harmonious tone, as there was a power struggle between Lord Crowther, chairman of Trust Houses, and Lord Forte. Furthermore, the company came under attack from a takeover bid by Allied Breweries Ltd. This approach was regarded favourably by Lord Crowther and his board members, but Charles Forte fought for the company's independence. He eventually prevented the takeover bid and at the same time won control over the company with the resignation of Lord Crowther.

Following the events of the takeover threat, Charles Forte and his son Rocco set out to expand the 26,000 hotel rooms already owned by THF. One of the main developments in this period is the completion of the Post Houses, which were initially started by Trust Houses. In 1977 the company made a significant acquisition of three hotel groups from J. Lyons and Company Ltd: the Strand Group of Hotels, Falcon Inns Group Hotels and Royal Hibernian Group Hotels. This greatly strengthened its position in the London market by the addition of 35 hotels.

On the international scene, THF expanded in the Middle East, Australia, Europe and the USA, although the prime target was in the latter two. In Europe, the company already owned the three best-known hotels in Paris. The company built the portfolio further in the 1970s and 1980s, the most prominent acquisitions being the Ritz Hotel in Madrid (1981) and the Hôtel des Bergues in Geneva (1986). In the USA, THF strengthened its shareholding in TraveLodge to a 79 per cent stake in 1973, a further 16 per cent in 1976, and finally the remaining 5 per cent in 1983. TraveLodge is the fourth largest operator in budget accommodation, but even this is less than half the size of the market leader. Furthermore, the TraveLodges were largely franchise operations, from which THF received only franchise and royalty fees. At this stage THF had always allowed the TraveLodges to operate as they saw fit; headquarters hardly intervened with the management of the individual units. Other operations in the USA are five Exclusive Hotels.

The Savoy Group is one company that Charles Forte had particularly wanted to own. During the period 1979–81 he took advantage of the economic recession that badly hit the Savoy Group by launching an initial bid worth £584 million. In June 1985 THF increased the value of its bid for the Savoy, and thus was able to control 70 per cent of the equity, but only 42 per cent of the votes, thanks to an archaic voting structure within the Savoy Group. However, in 1991 the two companies came to a settlement, as legal costs were running in excess of £1 million per annum. Thus in

1989 Rocco Forte and Donald Main, finance director of THF, were appointed to the board of the Savoy. This settlement was to last five years; under it, THF was not permitted to purchase any more shares than the existing 70 per cent equity and 42 per cent voting rights within the Savoy Hotel Company Ltd.

By the end of the 1980s THF owned a wide and varied portfolio of hotels and food and beverage establishments, meeting the needs of a whole range of market segments, from the most luxurious hotels and restaurants to budget roadside catering. However, THF was still well diversified only within the UK market, owning a mere handful of operations in Europe and the franchise TraveLodge operation in the USA. This was evident from the fact that the main source of profit (68 per cent) was from hotels, with 80 per cent of this generated in the UK. THF at that time was heavily dependent upon the UK market; as it hit the economic recession of the 1990s it learned from this mistake and tried to rectify it, as we shall see later in this analysis and from the following key points:

- In 1989 the five-year settlement period with Savoy began.
- In 1990 Alan Hearn was transferred to be Managing Director of Hotels.
- In 1990 Crest hotels were acquired from Bass for £300 million.
- In 1991 a rebranding exercise was undertaken on all its hotels.
- In 1991, a new corporate name was used, from THF to Forte.
- In 1992, the founder entrepreneur, Lord Forte, retired as Chairman, but retained his seat on the board as Life President.
- In 1992, as Lord Forte retired, Rocco Forte, the Chief Executive and son of the founder, added the Chairmanship to his duties.
- In 1992 two new non-executive directors – Sir Anthony Tennant and Sir Paul Girolami – were appointed to the board.
- At the end of 1992, after at least three years of gestation, Forte announced a joint venture with AgipPetroli, the Italian state oil company, involving the lease and management of 18 of its hotels.
- At the beginning of 1993 Gardner Merchant, the contract division, was sold, leaving Forte with essentially two divisions rather than three. During the same year Forte's inflight catering services were sold.
- Between 1991 and 1993, the corporate employee headcount was reduced by one-third to 1,000.
- During 1994 Forte was successful in the purchase of the Meridian chain of hotels from Air France.

## Long-term objectives

A key decision taken by the company in 1991 was to change its name from Trusthouse Forte to Forte plc, which allowed the establishment of a clear link between the company logo and its hotel products. Under its overall strategy of **building on strength** the company also launched in that year three new hotel brands and three collections:

● Forte TraveLodge, Forte Posthouse, Forte Crest;
● Forte Heritage, Forte Grand, Forte Exclusive.

Rocco Forte, chief executive of the group since 1983, led the company's comprehensive branding effort, establishing the name Forte as the umbrella brand over such diverse products as Happy Eater and the Hotel George V in Paris. By early 1992, the Forte name appeared on every Forte product and every outlet within each brand. The idea behind this approach was that:

● every outlet should perform to the exact specification of its brand;
● each brand should have its own specific identity; and
● all brands should carry the explicit endorsement of the Forte name.

This branding approach rests on faith in the principle of endorsement, establishing a network and pulling all the hotels together to create an organization of 341 hotels in the UK and over 900 worldwide. Forte's long-term objectives will see more streamlining, concentration on fewer products, and a move away from the group's heavy reliance on the UK economy, with a search for opportunities in both Western and Eastern Europe.

Its key objectives in branding were threefold: to penetrate new markets, to segment portfolios and to discipline costs. Within the UK, only one out of five adults uses hotels; with the establishment of consistency of product and level of service within each brand and collection, potential guests are able to know a little bit more about the value they would receive when staying at a Forte hotel. Equally, that same consistency will allow, through the company's central reservation system (CRS), worldwide communication and global selling of the company's hotel portfolio. Worldwide communication via CRS is an increasingly important aspect of remote selling, and the brand structure provides reassurance of consistency at a local level. In what many would see as an oversupplied market, segmenting portfolios by type of business and hotel allows the company to relate price and quality to its typical user group.

In researching specifically what customers use in terms of services in particular brands, the cost structure of Forte Posthouse was reduced, along with the introduction of a fixed price per room, and so costs were able to be related to targeted yields. In essence the company has tried to keep its approach both simple and deliverable.

Forte's brand marketing and continuing development of its central reservations facilities will hopefully achieve the key objective of recapturing its position as the main UK rooms-driven hotel company.

## Financial environment

In the year ended 31 January 1992 neither careful accounting policies nor strong management were able to rescue profits at Forte, which, like the rest of the leisure sector, had been very badly hit by recession, not just in the UK, but also in the USA and Europe. Worldwide, hotel profits for the half year were down from £93 million in the previous first half to £40 million, a point reflected in Table 1.2. Staff cuts had totalled 3,000, spread throughout all departments, and wages had been frozen for 25,000 employees. Overall, there have been £30 million of permanent cost reductions for the full year.

**Table 1.2 Net profit margin (per cent)**

|  | 31 Jan 1990 | 31 Jan 1991 | 31 Jan 1992 | 31 Jan 1993 | 31 Jan 1994 |
| --- | --- | --- | --- | --- | --- |
| Forte | 13.0 | 10.7 | 6.4 | 11.0 | 11.3 |
| Industry | 15.5 | 14.8 | 7.6 | (3.2) | 5.7 |

*Source:* Company accounts

## Political and economic environment

The company's heavy dependence on the UK hotel market, and London in particular, impacted heavily on Forte plc during the period 1990–92. The Gulf War in 1991 affected demand for accommodation at the higher market level brands of Forte Crest, Forte Grand and Forte Exclusive. This effect was worse in the capital cities, where the hotels were located and where they attracted international travellers, who virtually stopped travelling during this period. Equally, recession in both the UK and the USA (the two main markets) had a negative effect on the company at the higher market level brands, which are located mainly in London and the primary provincial cities. While both the UK and the USA saw a recovery in their economies during 1994, the lesson was clear: the company was over-dependent on the UK economy.

## Competitive environment

In considering the competitive environment over the past 10 years, Queens Moat had until 1992 been held up as a model that Forte ought to have followed. Queens Moat, the theory ran, had a strong presence in continental Europe, particularly in booming Germany, while Forte's hotels were largely concentrated in the recession-hit UK and in the USA, where competition is notoriously severe. In the UK, Queens Moat had devised a management incentive system that appeared to have protected the group from the worst effects of the recession. Then came the revelation that Queens Moat had booked as profits the revenue that it hoped to achieve from the targets it had set its managers. The group has been in financial trouble as a result, which has been something of a vindication of Forte's strategy. As recession hit Germany, Forte's concentration in the UK suddenly looked fortuitous. The outlook in London post 1994, where the group is heavily involved, is more promising than for years past. The yield per room declined by nearly a quarter between 1989 and 1992, and profits per room by a third. But, despite some increase in supply, there will be a steady recovery, helped by devaluation, and yield could be above the 1989 figures by 1995. Even in the British provinces, Forte's marketing efforts are bearing fruit. Like the group's sophisticated corporate advertising campaign, these were characteristic not so much of Rocco himself, but of the team that helped him to define and implement the company's objectives.

## Organizational environment

Forte's ability to take action quickly to contain costs was a result of the decentralization that the company had put in place in the 1980s. This key point centres around the organizational structure and design of the company. In addition, the establishment of Rocco Forte as chief executive saw a shift in style at the company, with it being run less autocratically, which raises the twin issues of the nature of leadership and its style. Rocco Forte recognized the need to streamline the magpie collection of assets into a far more focused company, concentrating on groups of branded hotels and chains of roadside restaurants. This streamlining began, appropriately, in the boardroom. The board had been dominated by Lord Forte's veteran friends, such as the octogenarian politician Lord Thorneycroft. These people have now gone, and Rocco Forte is now in sole charge. To counter criticism that he combines the roles of chairman and chief executive, he brought in as non-executive directors two of Britain's leading businessmen, Sir Paul Girolami of Glaxo and Sir Anthony Tennant, formerly of Guinness. These appointments were a first step in reorganizing the group's management structure, which still reflected the autocratic tradition built up during Lord Forte's 60-year reign. The purpose of appointing non-executive directors was to work with the board's longer-term view and ensure that the executives didn't get too blinkered.

In terms of organization, a new structure implemented in 1993 was based on the individual brands and the operating functions being classified as business units and reporting to a hotels and restaurant board. This in turn reports to the main Forte board, chaired by Rocco Forte. Supporting the business units within this new structure are the service units comprising sales and marketing, property building and design, purchasing and supplies, accounting and information technology. It is in this sense that the hotels and restaurants board is a vehicle for corporate leadership, supported by a small but stronger corporate centre.

## Mission development

Continuing the theme of organizational structure, decentralization in the mid 1980s occurred at the same time that Alfonso Giannuzzi, then managing director of the international hotels division, was appointed. The key objective for Giannuzzi was to work out how a global grouping of businesses could be operated effectively, and what philosophy and direction should be adopted. The resolution of this problem lay in the development of a mission statement with a clear focus on people, products and profits. Putting these 3 Ps into practice, however, was not so simple. The (then) Trusthouse Forte's international division alone was, and still is, bigger than most entire hotel companies. In the late 1980s the division employed 11,000 people in 22 countries and managed 14,764 rooms. The company at that time planned to expand in France, Italy, Germany and Spain, and was closely watching developments in Eastern Europe. When hiring employees, Giannuzzi looks for people who are oriented toward his 3 Ps and who are sincere, really interested, and have a passionate belief that they will be successful. The company's philosophy in the 1990s is as follows:

- to increase profitability and earnings per share each year in order to encourage investment and to improve and expand the business;
- to give complete customer satisfaction by efficient and courteous service, with value for money;
- to support managers and their staff in using personal initiative to improve the profit and quality of their operations while observing the company's policies;
- to provide good working conditions and to maintain effective communications at all levels to develop better understanding and assist decision making;
- to ensure no discrimination against sex, race, colour or creed;
- to train, develop and encourage promotion within the company based on merit and ability;
- to act with integrity and to maintain a proper sense of responsibility towards the public;
- to recognize the importance of each and every employee.

## Strategic business units

In 1994 Forte had two main businesses (strategic business units): hotels and restaurants, with hotels (its largest business) contributing an estimated 68 per cent of profits in 1994, a figure that it estimates will rise to 69.5 per cent in 1996. Within the UK, Forte accounts for around 8 per cent of total hotel rooms and is by far the dominant hotel operator in the country. It operates 7,718 rooms in London, and is the largest operator in the capital. Its hotels in the UK are the principal source of profits, contributing half of the group's profits for the year to January 1994.

## Implementation of strategy

As for strategic vision, the future shape of the group has become much clearer during the past five years. Since 1991 the company has focused on its two main businesses of hotel and restaurants. To this end a number of disposals were made. At the end of 1993, Forte's debt was still approximately £1.2 billion, despite the sale of Gardner Merchant, which brought in more than £200 million in cash. The company's disposal of its stake in Kentucky Fried Chicken, coupled with the sale of Alpha, its airport services, brought in around £270 million. With a fall in its interest charges, the company's debt was restructured, and this has allowed for capital expenditure. Throughout the recession of the early 1990s, Forte continued to invest materially in the refurbishment of its Exclusive and Grand hotels, preparing these brands for the economic recovery post 1994. Such refurbishments will allow greater than anticipated room rates in the medium term for these brands. Despite the low trading profits in 1991, Forte was clearly thinking strategically many years ahead by selling assets to concentrate on what it had determined were its core businesses.

## Product segmentation: an example

The accommodation product within the company's portfolio can be segmented further within each brand in order to reflect the needs of clients. One such segment is the conference market.

Because clients have become more demanding, and because the conference market has experienced difficult times in the early 1990s, hotel groups have attempted to reflect these issues in the design of conference departments and services, in an effort to make conference planning run smoothly. One such product is Forte's Venue Guarantee, which handles conference planning in 240 of the company's properties in the UK.

The philosophy behind Venue Guarantee is that hotel services should be easy to buy, consistent, and easy to budget. Under this system, each client is promised a faxed booking summary within 24 hours and a personal day planner indicating all charges and the basis of agreed billing. This approach is not dissimilar from Marriott Hotels and Resorts' No-Risk Meetings, which also promises a quote within 24 hours and simplifies the billing on one master account, with a no hidden extras guarantee. At Forte an executive meeting manager is assigned to each event to avoid the organizer's having to be shunted from one department to another.

## Corporate growth strategy

Forte's previously minimal presence in continental Europe has identified one central long-term objective, which is to develop its presence within the mainland European hotel industry. The company has entered two partnership deals, which not only show the general respect felt for Forte's management skills but also reveal the group's cash shortage, which prevents outright purchases. While it is a central objective to have much bigger roadside catering and hotel chains in continental Europe, opportunities for purchase will be dependent on Forte's finances. To this end, 1992 saw the announcement of a joint venture with Agip in Italy, involving 18 hotels with 2,534 rooms. The company has attempted further expansion in the European hotel market with its interest in both Meridien (confirmed in 1994) and Ciga (outbid by ITT Sheraton). In terms of travel-related catering it purchased Sogerba, the French motorway service station operator, and is therefore ideally placed to expand its TraveLodge network in France. The company also has joint ventures in the Republic of Ireland with Aer Lingus and in Spain with Repsol.

## The complexity of strategic management

As these critical tasks related to Forte indicate, strategic management involves the planning, directing, organizing and controlling of the company's strategy-related decisions and actions. In that sense it is the company's game plan. It provides a framework for management decisions, and reflects a company's awareness of how, when and where it should compete.

## THE SCOPE AND ASPECTS OF STRATEGIC MANAGEMENT

From this discussion it is clear that there are three aspects to strategic management:

- the strategy itself in terms of direction;
- the issue of excellence as related to effective performance; and
- the need for innovation in response to the need for the management of change.

It follows that accomplishing strategic management activities presumes a certain perspective on firms, the environment in which they operate and the specific strategies adopted.

Firms produce products and services for the benefit of their stakeholders, be they consumers, investors or employees. The objectives of the firm therefore need to balance the demands placed on it by these various stakeholders. From an administrative point of view such firms contain multiple business units (already referred to as **strategic business units**), traditionally coordinated by divisional or corporate headquarters.

The environment in which the firm operates is continually changing, and will therefore require analysis. Many economic, social, cultural, political and technological factors make up this wider environment. It is the strategy that aligns or matches the firm with its environment that will ensure (in part) success: hence the need for an accurate assessment of environmental forces. Such an analysis can be both economic and subjective. While the principal view of strategy is that it should improve a firm's performance and competitive position, it must also be both socially and politically rational: hence the emphasis by many hospitality companies, such as the Inter-Continental Hotels Group, on **green issues**.

It can be seen that strategic management can be viewed from a holistic point of view in relation to the firm, and is regarded by many as a key subject, drawing widely upon subjects such as human resource management, economics, marketing and financial management.

## Scope

The scope of strategic management can be considered under five key themes:

- **Management process.** The creation and change of strategies at all levels can be both formal and informal, incorporating both planning activities and the values and intuition of managers.
- **Management decisions.** Decisions made should relate to the perceived problem and its solution, and should be supported by relevant information. In addition they should be supported by other managers within the firm and be capable of implementation. The required resources must therefore be available.
- **Timescales.** Within both the process and the decision, strategic management involves the issue of timescale, be it long term or short term.
- **Structure of the organization.** The implementation of a strategy can be related to the organizational structure and the management of people. Power, whether it is centralized or decentralized, can affect managers' ability to work together within the structure.
- **Activities of the organization.** While the focus of the decision-making

process is normally directed to products, services or markets, within the issue of strategic management, growth, diversification and vertical integration should also be considered. Decisions within these areas will reflect on the firm's attitude towards its various stakeholders.

In translating these points into an effective strategy, one route to success may be through the study of excellent organizations and identifying the key attributes that contribute to their success. In this respect, eight key **attributes of excellence** have been identified (Peters and Waterman, 1982):

1 Sticking to the knitting: i.e. build on strengths or competences and stick to what you know best.
2 Close to the customer: i.e. listen to the customer and respond to his/her requirements.
3 Productivity through people: i.e. take a paternalistic view with regard to employees.
4 Autonomy and entrepreneurship: i.e. encourage initiative and practical risk taking, empowering people to make decisions about their own jobs.
5 Hands-on value driven: i.e. create a vision and core values that are almost inspirational in directing the organization.
6 Bias for action: i.e. an emphasis on tangible results through fast trial and error action in which people learn about the environment in which they operate.
7 Simple form/lean staff: i.e. decentralization with a small corporate headquarters.
8 Simultaneous loose–tight properties: i.e. encourage individual initiative and enterprise within a tight financial control regime.

## Rationality vs reality

Having defined the areas addressed by strategic management it would seem reasonable to assume that financially successful firms owe their success to one or more key features, namely the attributes of excellence identified above. The argument would then follow that if such attributes are imitated and installed in other firms, success will follow for them.

In trying to identify key attributes of success, one introduces the debate about two approaches to strategic management: **rationality** and **reality**. Some writers have suggested that rapid change and high levels of uncertainty (which are characteristic of the hospitality industry) make it impossible to forecast and therefore to prepare plans. In making this point we can highlight these two main approaches to the creation of strategy.

Rational criteria The link between objectives, plans and performance that is acceptable to stakeholders can be rationally applied by the use of analytical techniques.

In this sense such techniques identify a consistent relationship between the elements of the strategy, objectives, the capability of the firm and the demands of the environment. It is therefore a rational analysis that guides the actions of the firm. Once implemented, the plan's performance should be monitored, and corrective action taken as necessary. It is therefore the job of managers to monitor as well as to select the right plan.

**Reality testing**

An alternative view is that too much time is spent on research and analysis, which may result in paralysis of the firm. In an organization or industry where rapid change and high levels of uncertainty are a key feature, it is difficult to make plans for the future. The suggestion here is therefore that the route to the future position that the firm wishes to occupy should be through trial and error action.

**Rationality and reality: a comparison**

While the technical, rational approach prescribes the application of analytical techniques to select particular sequences of actions to achieve goals well in advance of acting, the reality testing approach creates a loop between discovery, choice and action. From trial-and-error experiments, learning or discovery occurs and a choice of action can be made. The choice of action is contained within the vision and values of the organization as a whole. The technically rational approach defines discovery in terms of the systematic gathering and analysis of the facts. Objectives, options and their evaluation constitute a need to choose, and action occurs when the plan is implemented.

## Leadership

The strategic leader must build and lead a team of managers and establish objectives. Styles will vary enormously, as will the scope of the objectives. Some leaders will be autocratic, others entrepreneurial, but just like the captain of a ship, the leader and his or her managers should be clear about where the firm is going, where they want to go and how they are going to get there. This requires an appreciation of the environment and an understanding of the firm's resources.

## Environmental fit

Strategy is largely the relationship between a firm and its environment. In this respect the positioning and relating of the firm to its environment will ensure its continued success. A firm draws from its resources within a competitive business environment and must produce products and services that can be marketed profitably. People's tastes change, the economy moves through the business cycle, and government policy changes; hence a clear awareness of environmental forces is important.

This requires an appreciation of potential and future threats and opportunities, and decisions need to be made on appropriate products, services and markets.

## Types of strategy

Strategies must be developed at several levels within the firm to ensure that they cover all organizational activities. At the corporate level, several strategic questions face the firm:

- What business should we compete in, given our strengths and weaknesses?
- Which new product markets should we enter?
- Which should we leave?
- What is the product market domain of the firm and the scope of its operations?

At the level of the strategic business unit, the strategic question is: how should we compete in the product markets in which we operate? Firms choose to produce one or more related or unrelated products or services for one or more markets or market segments. The firm itself should be structured to encompass this range of markets, and as diversity increases the structure is likely to be centred on strategic business units or divisions. A business unit strategy seeks to develop competitive advantage over other firms within the industry. At the lowest level of strategy is the functional area within business units. Each business unit has several functional areas, such as marketing, production, finance, human resources, planning and distribution. At this level, strategies are often called **functional policies**; they enable standardization and simplification of tasks. They jointly form the firm's basic operating system. It is important that functional strategies are designed and managed in a coordinated way so that they interrelate with each other and at the same time collectively allow a competitive advantage at the strategic business unit or level.

## Competitive advantage

Business strategy is all about competitive advantage. Without competitors there would be no need for strategy, for the sole purpose of strategic management is to enable the company to gain, as effectively as possible, a sustainable edge over its competitors. A firm should seek to create and sustain a clear competitive advantage. It will be successful and profitable if it can meet customer needs more effectively than its competitors do. Such customers should not be treated *en masse*, and products should be differentiated to appeal to defined market segments.

Hospitality firms are organized around particular functions, and their structure determines the cost of the product or service. Such costs must be related to the price that customers are willing to pay for the particular product, and should also be related to competitors' prices. Competitors within the hospitality industry will similarly differentiate their products, goods and services, again incurring costs in doing so.

Strategic success requires a clear understanding of the needs of the market, and its particular segments, and the satisfaction of target customers more effectively and more profitably than by competitors. Such differentiation is used to add value to a product or service.

## STRATEGIC DECISION-MAKING PROCESS: AN INTRODUCTION

Typically, strategic issues and the decision-making process have six dimensions.

Strategic issues require **top management decisions** because they overarch several areas of a firm's operations. It is in this respect that only top management has the perspective needed to understand the broad implications of such decisions.

In making such decisions there is a requirement for large amounts of the firm's **resources**. This is because they involve a substantial allocation of assets and money, and commit the firm to actions over an extended period. This decision-making process often affects the firm's long-term prosperity, typically over a five-year period.

Once a firm has committed itself to a particular strategy, its **image and competitive advantages** are usually tied to that strategy. Strategic decisions therefore have enduring effects on the firm, for better or worse.

Because of timescale such issues are **future orientated**. They therefore involve an element of forecasting in a turbulent and competitive environment, within which a firm will succeed only if it takes a proactive or anticipatory stance towards change.

Strategic issues usually have **multifunctional** or multi-business consequences. They are therefore complex and have implications for most areas of the firm. All areas of the firm will be affected by the allocations or reallocations, responsibilities and resources that result from such decisions.

Finally, there is a requirement to consider the firm's **external environment**, with the implication that the firm works within an open system affected by matters largely beyond its control. Management must therefore look beyond the internal operations of a firm.

## Levels of strategy

It follows from this discussion that the decision-making hierarchy of a firm typically contains three levels:

- corporate level,
- business level, and
- functional level.

To a large extent, attitudes at corporate level reflect the concerns of stakeholders and society. Corporate managers set objectives, formulate strategies and decide the functional areas in which the business as a whole should operate. In this sense they adopt a portfolio approach to the management of the business by developing long-term plans, typically for a five-year period.

At a business level, managers must translate the statements of direction and intent into objectives and strategies for individual business divisions or strategic business units. Business-level strategic managers determine how the firm will compete in a selected product market arena and relate its products and services to the market segment.

The functional level is composed principally of managers of product, geographic and functional areas, who develop annual objectives and short-term strategies in a range of disciplines such as finance and accounting, marketing, human resource management and operations. Their principal responsibility is to implement or execute the firm's strategic plans.

## Decision making and the link with problem solving

Implicit within this discussion on the nature and levels of strategy is the issue of decision making. Decision making is a process related to the existence of a problem, and it is often talked about in terms of problem solving. In many instances the problem situation is very complex, and can only be partially understood or controlled; therefore decisions are designed not so much to find ideal or perfect answers as to improve the problem situation.

The notion of rational decision making is hypothetical, because it assumes that the problem can be stated clearly and unambiguously. In reality, decision makers do not have all the information that they need to make optimum decisions, nor do they have a complete list of possible alternatives which can be drawn up and evaluated against the objectives. Equally, decision makers rarely have the time or inclination to search for ideal solutions. However, the rational model provides a useful framework for examining reality, and seeking explanations for how managers actually make decisions.

The central aim of the decision maker is primarily to seek to maximize his or her own satisfaction in making a decision. Equally, the manager may be working within a team and may not have been provided with all the information needed to make a perfectly objective decision. Thus, for a number of reasons, the rational decision-making model has weaknesses as far as practical application and use are concerned. Because of this, alternative theories of decision making have been developed, on the premise that in reality there is more subjectivity and irrationality in the decision-making process.

One view is that a satisfactory rather than an optimal course of action is chosen because of such factors as internal and external constraints, time pressure, lack of information, and the influence of interested parties. It could be argued that this approach is in fact rational within specified limits, and can be described as **bounded rationality**. The decision is bounded by three factors:

- the skills, habits and reflexes of the decision maker, which may no longer be conscious acts;
- the decision maker's values and motives; and
- the decision maker's knowledge of issues relevant to the job.

Another view is that decision makers are bounded by a discretionary area comprising social norms, formal rules and policies, moral and ethical norms and legal decisions. The decision maker accepts these restrictions, and perceives that certain alternatives will be judged permissible whereas other activities will be deemed illegitimate and inappropriate. Such a view extends the concept of bounded rationality to **bounded discretion**.

A third view could be described as **the science of muddling through**. This approach looks at alternative policies in terms of their various implications, without any stated predetermined objectives. Agreement is reached without clear reference to stated objectives. Such an approach tends to concentrate on options that are closely related to those already being followed, and hence results in incremental changes to the way that tasks are performed. There is incremental progress towards an optimum solution.

A final approach, described as **the mix scanning model**, reconciles the rigid formality of the rational approach with the more undisciplined approach of the incrementalists. Fundamental to this model is the ranking of objectives, and so its relevance for a particular organization will be related to the issues of strategic leadership and whether or not there are clearly stated, understood or supported objectives.

With all these models, decision making involves both information and people. While the strategic leader must develop an appropriate information system, he or she must also ensure that a good team of people have been gathered and that they are well managed. If objectives are not clearly stated and understood then decision making will be constrained. Satisfying alternatives may be chosen, or change may be accomplished gradually and incrementally with constant learning. While these may not be optimizing approaches, they may result in perfectly satisfactory decisions.

In all this discussion over decision making, two-way communication is at the heart of successful strategic management or change. Strategic leaders need to be effective communicators. The starting point of all management improvement is the opening of communications, both inside and outside the company. The strategic leader of a firm affects both strategy creation and strategy implementation, and he or she is responsible for establishing the basic direction of the organization, the communication systems and the structure. These influence the nature and style of decision making within the firm. In addition, decision making and change are affected by the personal ambitions of the strategic leader, his or her personal qualities, such as entrepreneurship and willingness to take risks, the style of management adopted, and the management systems used.

Having introduced the concept of the strategic management process and defined it in terms of both scope and content, it is clear that the decision-making process is central within strategy. A number of these points will now be highlighted, with a discussion on the developing hotel market of Eastern Germany. British brewers Bass plc, through its major subsidiary Holiday Inn, had to consider in 1992–93 its plans for expansion into the eastern part of Germany. This was not only a strategic move: a range of economic, financial, legislative and competitive factors had to be considered before the decision to invest could be made.

# CASE STUDY: BASS PLC, HOLIDAY INN

## Background

The proposal that was considered by Holiday Inn Worldwide (HIW) during 1993 was a joint venture between the company and a number of related property development companies in Germany. The development considered was a 190-room Holiday Inn core product and a 105-room Holiday Inn Express in Cottbus, situated in Eastern Germany. From the perspective of Holiday Inn the proposal met the two key strategic aims of increasing distribution in an underdeveloped region of a primary market (Germany) while introducing the Express budget hotel product into Europe, with effectively no capital investment. Equally, the project allowed Holiday Inn to define the physical and operating standards for the Express product in Germany, which would be an aid to expansion of this budget brand.

To this end a joint venture (JV) company, the Holiday Inn Brandenburg Hotel

Betriebsgesellschaft mbH, was established in Germany with GIVO München, a 100 per cent subsidiary of Instag AG, a major German developer. The joint interest was 50 per cent of the issued ordinary share capital of the JV at an investment by HIW of DM 0.5 million ($0.3 million), with no further investment required by HIW. The JV leased the two hotels in Cottbus, Germany, including the initial tenants F&F, pre-opening supplies and expenses, etc. from Deutsche Immobilien GmbH (DIG), also a subsidiary of Instag AG. GIVO guaranteed to meet any cash shortfalls arising in the JV over the period of an initial ten years of the lease, and HIW were not required to fund any such shortfalls. In giving this guarantee, Instag acknowledged that there would be shortfalls in the early years, and essentially traded the developer's profit, which increased the lease amount to such an extent that the hotel will probably not be able to generate a profit in the early years of trading. Instag and GIVO are therefore covering these shortfalls over time, in return for taking a higher development profit in 1993–94.

An HIW company on this basis intended to enter into a ten-year management contract with two five-year renewal options (though both JV partners must agree to renew). Monies due to HIW in projected fees from the management agreement, when set against the investment of DM 0.5 million ($0.3 million) in the JV, would be DM 2.9 million ($1.6 million). Management profits in 1994–95 were forecast at DM 0.2 million ($0.1 million), rising to DM 0.3 million ($0.2 million) in 1995–96. What follows in this case study is a detailed analysis of this decision to invest and how it was arrived at.

## Strategic considerations

The proposal to build a joint venture core brand and Express in Cottbus, Eastern Germany, met two major strategic objectives:

- It increased distribution in an underdeveloped region of the company's primary market (Germany).
- It introduced Holiday Inn Express (established in the USA in the early 1990s) into Europe, with limited capital investment. In doing so it enabled the company to define new-build physical and operating standards for the Express product in Germany.

Central to this strategic perspective is the objective of distribution in order to achieve market leadership in Germany. In order to achieve this, openings in the new *Länder* (counties) of Eastern Germany were required: a region where there was in the early 1990s extremely limited hotel supply (estimated 50,000 rooms). While approved openings in 1993 were in secondary sites (Jena, Glauchau, Suhl), the Cottbus development project in Eastern Germany was to be built in one of the top twelve East German cities.

The proposed joint venture structure satisfied the criteria that expansion should be through limited capital expenditure and at quantified, limited, risk to HIW. In addition, the relationship with Instag AG was strategically important, as their intention was to fund the construction of a further two or three Express hotels in major East German cities. One vehicle for East German growth, it was recognized, may be through such entrepreneurial construction and development companies who wish others to manage the hotel.

## Market overview

Cottbus is the political, cultural and economic centre of the South Brandenburg area of Germany. The city is situated south-east of Brandenburg, 180 km from Bresbau, 132 km south-east of Berlin and 115 km north-east of Dresden. The population density in 1992 had stabilized at approximately 123,000 people; and after the reforms of the municipality of Cottbus it will have 180,000 inhabitants.

According to the Office of City Development, the greater area of the city of Cottbus will triple in size in the medium term, a trend due partly to the development of new industrial areas. One reason for this is the fact that almost 800,000 people live in greater Cottbus, including areas such as Guben, Finsterwolde and Bad Liebenwerda.

In terms of transport infrastructure, Drewitz Airport will be expanded to be the future regional airport in sud-Brandenburg/Cottbus, and according to estimates a total of 40,000 flight movements per year are expected.

The percentage of unemployment in the area of Cottbus is the lowest in the whole of Brandenburg. The city is ranked second compared to other Bundeslanders.

Mainly commercial companies, predominantly retail and service companies, have settled in the area. Examples include the Dresden Bank, Deutsche Bank, Bayerische Vereinsbank, and insurance companies Allianz and Nurnberger.

The largest companies are:
- Union Bau Aktiengesellschaft (civil engineering) (2,160 employees);
- ESAG, Energie (1,550 employees);
- LBU (1,300 employees);
- Horten (350 employees);
- Hoechst;
- BASF.

Regional fairs are held in the City Hall of Cottbus, opposite the mixed use development that includes the proposed hotels. Tourist attractions are:
- the Jugendstil Theatre of Bernhard Sehring (1908);
- the *Altmarkt*, with its recently renovated baroque houses and shops;
- the 200 ha Branitzer Park, with Schloss Branitz, a land and lake pyramid, created by Hermann Furst von Puckler-Muskau (1992);
- the Sorbian Centre;
- the Spree Wald;
- The 23rd German National Garden Exhibition (1995) (*Bundesgartenschow*).

**The hotel market in Cottbus**

The current (1992–93) hotel supply in the city of Cottbus (excluding the 202-room Hotel Lausitz, closed on 15 November 1992 and where the future mixed use development site is), consists of four hotels with about 250 rooms as well as four similar hotels with 130 rooms combined. Table 1.3 shows the supply of local hotels.

According to the municipality, the number of available hotel rooms will increase from the current 380 (1 April 1993) to about 1,030 rooms in 1995. Both the city of Cottbus and the Chamber of Commerce estimate the long-term supply requirements for hotel rooms at 2,000 rooms.

Table 1.3  Hotel supply in Cottbus and the surrounding area, 1993

| Hotel | Number of rooms | Room rate (DM) 1993* | |
|---|---|---|---|
| | | Single | Double |
| Branitz | 204 | 165/199 | 206/219 |
| Lausitz | 128 | 168/178 | 178/198 |
| Maritim (Klingbeil) | 230 | Opening 1994 | |
| Sorat | 70 | Opening 1994 | |
| GWC | 62 | Opening 1995 | |
| Holiday Inn | 190 | Opening Feb 1995 | |
| Holiday Inn Express | 105 | Opening Oct 1995 | |

* Prices including breakfast and VAT

## Development proposal

Deutsche Immobilien GmbH (DIG), a subsidiary of Instag AG, owns a site in Cottbus, the former hotel Lausitz and the adjoining parking space. It is on this site that a complex is being built (1993–95) consisting of office space, municipal offices, retail space, food outlets, possibly a casino, as well as two hotels. These will be:

- a 190-room full service hotel, to be a Holiday Inn core brand. This hotel will have a 125-seat restaurant, a 60-seat Boulevard café and approximately ten, 60 m² meeting rooms. All bedrooms will have bath, radio, direct dial telephone, cable TV, minibars, trouser press and limited room service.
- A 105-room limited service hotel, to be a Holiday Inn Express. The proposed hotel will be equipped with luxury shower, TV and direct dial telephone in the rooms, and a pub-style food operation.
- 14,700 m² of government offices, 8,233 m² of commercial offices, 21,000 m² of services and commercial shops, and a 1,900 m² hall.

DIG intends to sell the total project to one institutional investor for DM 250 million ($138 million), and HIW built into the agreement a right to review and approve any sales documents using its name.

As at April 1993, 56 per cent of the total project had been leased out. The hotel and the remaining 20 per cent (shops) was to be let at a later stage. The site is situated in the city centre, and the neighbouring City Hall (1970) is under historic protection. It is surrounded by housing and office buildings of the municipality.

Horwath Consulting GmbH (HC) (February 1993) projected the key operating ratios at 1992 values for each product to be as shown in Table 1.4. The *Bundesgartenschow* (regional fair) will bring in a considerable number of leisure visitors to Cottbus in 1995 over a 180-day period. In the years thereafter the occupancy of the hotels will stabilize at 66 per cent for the core brand hotel and 69 per cent for the limited service Express hotel. In all projections the cost of payroll was calculated at the same level as experienced in the former West Germany. According to these overall figures there is no real growth included in Holiday Inn's projected revenues.

**Table 1.4 Key operating ratios**

|  | 1995 | 1996 | 1997 |
|---|---|---|---|
| **Core brand** | | | |
| Occupancy (%) | 69 | 67 | 66 |
| Average rate (DM) | 146 | 147 | 149 |
| Average rate ($) | 81 | 81 | 82 |
| **Express brand** | | | |
| Occupancy (%) | 70 | 69 | 69 |
| Average rate (DM) | 117 | 123 | 123 |
| Average rate ($) | 65 | 68 | 68 |

## The joint venture

The company structure, and the relationship between the companies involved, is complex.

GIVO München and Holiday Inns of Belgium NV established the joint venture company (JV), Holiday Inn Brandenburg Hotel Betriebsgesellschaft mbH, a private limited liability company. The share capital of the company was DM 1 million ($0.6 million). It was agreed that if the JV was sold without the benefit of the Holiday Inn brand, the name Holiday Inn would be removed from the name of the JV. The ownership structure was reviewed by HIW taxation specialists and was set up to provide the most economic taxation treatment for the foreseeable future.

At formation, an initial amount of DM 0.5 million ($0.3 million) was subscribed for share capital (both GIVO and HIW participated with 50 per cent). The remaining share capital was called in monthly tranches of DM 30 thousand ($17 thousand) over the remaining sixteen month development period. HIW prepared the necessary articles of association, shareholder's agreement and management contracts for the JV. The JV entered into two separate lease agreements, one for each hotel, with Deutsche Immobilien GmbH (DIG) for a period of ten years. The JV will have the right to renew these leases for at least two further periods of five years each, but both JV partners must agree to renew.

The JV authorized the management company to pay on its behalf from hotel revenue, on a monthly basis, all expenses (including fixed charges). In the event of a shortfall in the JV cash flows, GIVO guaranteed to fund such shortfalls by replenishing the hotel bank account. However, if GIVO pays a shortfall in any year, GIVO will be paid 50 per cent of any future cash surplus until the shortfall payment is repaid (the remaining 50 per cent cash surplus is divided equally between the shareholders). The shortfall payment made by GIVO is interest free.

The parties agreed that GIVO will provide four one-year unconditional and irrevocable letters of credit from Bayerische Hypotheken und Wechselbank AG for the first four years of the lease, in the amounts shown in Table 1.5. These are to back up GIVO's guarantee to fund all shortfalls.

Profits generated after payment of the annual lease, all taxes, insurance, the amortization of debts (there were none anticipated), capital reserve for the replacement of tenants' fixtures and fittings and equipment were to be distributed to the partners in equal shares.

**Table 1.5 GIVO letters of credit**

|  | DM ('000) | £ ('000) |
|---|---|---|
| Year 1 (part year) | 2510 | 1386 |
| Year 2 | 4320 | 2386 |
| Year 3 | 4320 | 2386 |
| Year 4 | 4364 | 2411 |

The JV agreed that the cost of the tenants' fixtures and fittings, pre-opening supplies and equipment will not exceed DM 7 million ($3.7 million) for the core brand and DM 1.5 million ($0.8 million) for the Express. These costs were included in the leasehold assets upon which the initial rent is payable.

Guarantees
An important aspect in all this is that GIVO, HIW's joint venture partner, gave an equity guarantee and a liquidity guarantee. This meant that it would guarantee that the equity capital of the JV, DM 1 million, will be maintained and that the JV will have sufficient cash to meet all its obligations. The GIVO guarantee was supported by two further guarantees:

- Instag, the parent of GIVO, provided an unconditional guarantee of GIVO's obligations, including its guarantee obligations.
- GIVO provided four one-year irrevocable and unconditional letters of credit in favour of the joint venture to secure GIVO's guarantee.

These amounts were believed to exceed anticipated shortfalls comfortably during the first four years, based on conservative operating assumptions. It was the belief of HIW that to allow the letters of credit to be discontinued after four years was a reasonably prudent decision, because it was anticipated that trading should have stabilized by then and that the European economy should have recovered from recession during the period 1993–95. Irrespective of this point, even though the letters of credit would not extend beyond the end of the fourth year, the GIVO guarantee and the Instag guarantee of GIVO's obligations would continue for the full ten-year lease term.

From a liability standpoint, it is important to appreciate that Instag acknowledged that there would be shortfalls in the early years. This was not a usual situation where an owner turns its hotel over to HIW to manage and does not attempt to hold HIW responsible if profits are not immediately forthcoming. In this case, Instag knew that the developer's profit it has taken will increase the lease amount to an extent that the hotel will probably not be able to cover it in the early years of trading. Instag and GIVO were willing to cover these shortfalls over time in return for taking a higher development profit at the start of the project.

It is also important to bear in mind that if the guarantees are not sufficient to pay all JV obligations, HIW may allow the JV to go into receivership rather than pay its obligations to the JV in such a way that the management contract relationship will force HIW to assume a lessee's liability. The lease obligation will be entirely the JV's, and if the hotels provide insufficient cash to meet the JV's obligations, Instag and GIVO have agreed to meet them. HIW will have no obligation to fund shortfalls. Moreover, any contributions made by Instag or GIVO will not be deemed to be contributions to equity, and hence HIW's 50 per cent equity interest will not be diluted.

Management contract
HIW within the contract charges management fees at a rate of 3 per cent of the adjusted gross revenue, with 1 per cent of the adjusted gross revenue to cover reservations, sales and marketing assessments. Fees are deducted by Holiday Inn, in its capacity as manager, from each hotel as an operating expense.

Technical service fees
HIW agreed to provide technical consulting services during the design and construction period, for a maximum amount of DM 0.5 million ($0.3 million). DM 250 thousand were paid on signing the JV formation documents, with the remainder to be paid in DM 15 thousand tranches per month over the course of the development period of some sixteen months. In effect Holiday Inn got its investment in the share capital of the JV back through the payment of these fees.

Financial analysis
The net present value (NPV) of the management fee stream over the first ten years is $1.1 million excluding any residual value. If a terminal value is attributed, the net present value is $1.5 million. As the investment in the ordinary share capital of the JV matches exactly the technical services fees in both amount and timing, the management fees stream always has a positive NPV.

## STRATEGIC LEADERSHIP

The strategic leader is responsible directly to the board of directors and through the board to the stakeholders in the business. The task of leadership, as well as providing the framework of values and motivation for employees, also includes the allocation of financial and other resources in order to set the overall direction. This approach enables choices to be made so that the efforts of the firm can be focused.

## Leadership style

The intended strategies of the firm will be implemented through the organizational structure. The effectiveness of the organizational structure is a major responsibility of the strategic leader. It is through his or her system of communications that managers throughout the organization are made strategically aware, which in turn ensures that the strategic leader stays informed of the changes that are taking place. Effective leadership, control and objectivity require a strong and capable leader. In addition, there must also be an opportunity for debate amongst the key executives who are responsible for both the creation and implementation of strategic change. The most effective leaders are people with ideas and vision, along with the ability to communicate and sell the vision and ideas.

Management style incorporates factors such as risk taking, autocracy, democracy, reliance on planning, willingness to change as opportunities arise and awareness of opportunities. There is no single recommended style. Different leaders behave individually, but the activity and relative success of the organization are strongly influenced by the style adopted.

We have already emphasized that strategies emerge as well as they can be formulated or prescribed. The role of the strategic leader must be examined in this context. Strategic change results from decisions taken and implemented in response to perceived opportunities or threats. The management of change therefore requires strategic awareness and learning, which implies the ability to recognize and interpret signals from the environment. While the role of planning systems is determined by the strategic leader, basically they are part of the decision-making process. However, the planning process should result in plans, objectives and strategies to which managers are committed because they have had an input, rather than in a set of plans that never gets implemented. Having said this, the major decisions fall to the strategic leader, and therefore he or she must decide upon the most appropriate planning system and manage it. If this is to happen effectively then the strategic leader must ensure that the managers feel encouraged, motivated and rewarded for acting accordingly. The strategic manager must design and manage an appropriate organization structure to ensure this.

## Risk

The attitude of the strategic leader towards risk may vary from risk taking to strong aversion to risk, and will influence the range of strategic choices available. Risk-orientated leaders prefer offensive, opportunistic strategies. Risk-averse leaders prefer defensive, safe strategies. Past strategy exerts far more influence on the strategic choices of risk-averse leaders than on those of risk-orientated leaders. Risk occurs whenever anyone must make a choice and the potential outcome involves uncertainty. The outcome of a typical decision will be dependent on several factors, such as customer reaction, levels of demand and competitor reactions. Some leaders will understand the situation better than others and partly for this reason will be happy to accept the risk involved in a particular choice. Personality also affects willingness to accept and take a particular risk. It is important that there is compatibility between a strategic leader's attitude towards risk and the demands of the industry. The following criteria are important in the decision:

- the attractiveness of each option to the decision maker;
- the extent to which he or she is prepared to accept the potential loss in each alternative;
- the estimated probabilities of success and failure;
- the degree to which the decision maker is likely to affect success or failure.

Hence in considering risk and strategic leadership in an organization, a number of factors are worth investigating.

Attitudes towards risk affect the way managers make decisions. High risk takers tend to make more rapid decisions based on less information than low risk takers, but they tend to process each piece of information more slowly. Environmental factors may prove significant; the availability and cost of finance, forecasts of market opportunities and market buoyancy, and feelings about the strengths and suitability of internal resources will all be important. Another aspect of the organization that will influence the risk taking is its overall culture, styles of leadership and reward systems.

## CULTURE AND VALUES

Strategy in an organization can only be analysed effectively and understood if one appreciates the basic culture and values that influence the key strategic elements. Strategy change cannot be implemented successfully without due regard for culture and the close relationship with strategic decision making.

Culture is an umbrella word that encompasses a whole set of implicit widely shared beliefs, traditions, values and expectations that characterize a particular group of people. The culture of an organization reflects, and can be determined by, the strength and style of the strategic leader. If the leader is strong he or she will have clear views about what should be done and how. If strategic leadership is weak, culture may centre on decision making to accomplish low-level objectives. Culture is based on communication and learning, and a strategic leader's vision must be communicated and understood. Events and changes affecting the organization also need to be communicated widely. If organizations expect their employees to care about and look after customers, they must in turn look after their staff. Internal culture will affect external relationships.

### The link between strategy and culture

It has been suggested that a typology of organizations can be formulated in relation to culture and strategy formulation. Proposed by Miles and Snow (1978), the typology distinguishes organizations in terms of their values and objectives, and different types will typically adopt particular approaches to strategy creation. Four categories have been defined:

- defenders;
- prospectors;
- analysers;
- reactors.

Defenders, prospectors and analysers are all regarded as positive organizations. Reactors must ultimately adopt one of the other three approaches or suffer long-term decline. Defenders have an emphasis on planning; prospectors have an entrepreneurial mode of strategy formulation. It has been argued that, as well as being a classification, the typology can be used to predict behaviour. For example, a defender organization, in a search for greater operating efficiency, might consider investing in the latest technology or might reject a strategy if it has high risk attached.

## Culture and styles of management

Another writer, Charles Handy, has developed an alternative classification of four categories of organization, based on cultural differences.

The **club culture** involves work divided by function or product, with decision making radiating out from the centre: the further away from the centre, the weaker the power and influence is. Decision taking is very dependent upon the abilities of managers within the inner circle.

The **role culture** is the more typical organization, as culture is built around defined jobs, rules and procedures and not personalities. As well as being designed for stability, the structure is also designed to allow for continuity and changes of personnel, and for this reason dramatic changes are less likely than more gradual ones. High efficiency is possible in this stable environment, but the structure can be slow to change and is therefore less suitable for dynamic situations.

Management in the **task culture** is concerned with the continuous and successful solution of problems, and performance is judged by the success of the outcomes. With this culture, particular problem situations are resolved by bringing together people and resources from various parts of the organization on a temporary basis. Once the problem is dealt with, the people move on to other tasks, and consequently discontinuity is a key characteristic.

The final category is the **person culture,** with the organization existing to help the individual rather than the other way round.

It is important to emphasize that the style adopted by the strategic leader can have a strong influence on the culture of the organization.

## Culture and power

A further element to this discussion is power, which can be defined as the potential or ability to do something. Consequently strategic change will be strongly influenced by the basis of power within an organization and by the power of the organization in relation to its environment. Change is brought about if the necessary resources can be harnessed and if people can be persuaded to behave in a particular way. Both these require power.

Power results in part from the structure of the organization, and it needs exercising in different ways within different cultures if it is to be used effectively. At the same time, power can be a feature of an individual manager's personality, and managers who are personally powerful will be in a position to influence change. In order to understand the reality of change in an organization and to examine how change might be managed it is important to consider where power lies, which managers are powerful, and where their sources of power are. While a visible, powerful and influential strategic leader is often a feature of an entrepreneurial organization, the nature and direction of incremental change will be influenced significantly by which managers are powerful and how they choose to exercise their power.

Managers are expected to apply power levers in ways that are acceptable to the predominant culture of the organization; at the same time, the manner in which power levers are actually used affects what happens in the organization. Power is required for change, and change results from the application of power. Hence the implementation of desired changes to strategy requires the effective use of power bases, but other strategic changes will result from the exercise of power by individual managers. It is important for the organization to monitor such activity and ensure that such emergent changes in strategies are desirable or acceptable. The ability of an organization to effect change within its environment will similarly depend on the exercise of power. A strong competitor with a very distinctive product or service and substantial market share may be more powerful than its competitors. A manufacturer who is able to influence distributors or suppliers will be similarly powerful. The issue here is relative power in relation to those other individuals, organizations and institutions upon whom an organization relies, with whom it trades or which influence it in some way.

## Determinants, aspects and levels of culture

The purpose of this discussion in examining culture is to determine what factors lead to consistently outstanding performance within a particular industry. Over the long term, firms that are the most successful are those that believe in something and in which the belief or beliefs have permeated through the whole organization: that is, they are communicated and understood. Examples could include progress via innovation and technology, or excellence in something that the customer values, such as service or delivery on time. People who build, develop and run successful firms invariably work hard to create strong cultures within their organizations. A number of key determinants of culture can be identified:

● **The environment and key success factors**: what the organization must do well if it is to be an effective competitor, and the values that the strategic leader considers important and wishes to see adopted in the organization. These should relate to the key success factors and to employee reward systems.

- **The visionaries who create the culture**. They can come from any background and could be, for example, product or service innovators who build the appropriate quality into the product, or creative marketing people who provide the slogans that make the product or brand name a household word.
- **The behaviour patterns in which the culture is manifest**. This can be evidenced by the way sales people deal with customers and the care and attention that goes into production.
- **The communication system**. It is around such a system that the culture revolves, and it determines just how aware employees are about the essential issues.

When the culture is strong, people know what is expected of them, and they understand how to act and decide in particular circumstances. There can also be a number of separate strands of the culture in any organization, be they leadership, the environment or the employees. There could be a strong power culture related to an influential strategic leader who is firmly in charge of the organization and whose values are widely understood and followed. This could be linked to a culture of market orientation, which ensures that customer needs are considered, and to a work culture if employees feel committed to the organization and wish to help achieve success.

A number of aspects comprise the culture of an organization, with their relative significance varying from industry to industry:

- Marketing orientation can be described as a consumer-orientated approach, and will reflect on the culture of the organization.
- Another important aspect of culture is the commitment to achieving acceptable levels of performance through the orientation of employees to clear targets.
- Innovation brings with it implications of perceived risk, and therefore attitudes towards risk and possible failure must be determined and risk deemed acceptable, so that a feeling of entrepreneurship is fostered.
- In addition to attitudes towards innovation, attitudes towards cost and cost reduction are also important.
- Two final aspects are commitment and loyalty to the organization, and the impact of and reaction to technological change. However, such change orientation may also conflict with a desire for continuity and consistency.

Culture can also be considered at several levels: the most visible is the physical and social environment and the outputs of the organization. This can include matters such as written communications, advertisements and the reception that visitors receive.

Values are the second level. They represent a sense of **what ought to be**, based on convictions held by certain key people. They revolve around the decision maker's values, which can be debated or questioned, and many strategies followed by organizations start in this way, reflecting the values held by the strategic leader. As decisions are proved to be successful they become common practice, and in this way the value becomes a belief and ultimately an assumption about behaviour practised by the organization. Group behaviour among members of the organization may evolve in a similar way, but this will be less tangible. It is also important to appreciate that certain organizations may state that they have particular values, but in reality these will be little more than verbal or written statements or aspirations for the future.

This consideration of culture, values and beliefs will now be related to a restaurant operation in Finland.

## CASE STUDY: SERVICE CULTURE IN THE MANAGEMENT OF A FINNISH RESTAURANT OPERATION (Haaja Institute, Finland)

It is clear from the discussion so far in this chapter that there seems to be no universal agreement on how organizational culture should be understood. This point is expanded on by Mr Kimmo Kuurma, Development Manager of Oy Center-Inn AB, Helsinki, Finland, who could identify no specific time or occasion when organizational culture had been discussed in the company. However, many aspects of culture had emerged historically, including quality, cleanliness and order, willingness to accept change, reception of customers, and attitudes towards all established procedures. These aspects, it seems, represent guidelines for all activities from customer service to internal training. In this respect, organizational culture at this particular restaurant operation could be described as **our way of doing things**, with all the underlying assumptions of accepted behaviour and attitudes that affect the action of all employees.

In a hotel or restaurant operation it is very difficult to separate organizational culture and service culture. At every level in the operation of a hospitality firm, one finds the connection between customers, quality of service and service (organizational/corporate) culture. The customer perceives culture in the atmosphere and in the attitudes of the service personnel, which reflect the whole company's way of thinking. Besides environment, it is top management that is seen as a source of service culture.

In the Center Inn restaurant, the service culture is strongly formed by the owners (the firm is operated by the Kuurma family). The restaurant's location is in the centre of Helsinki, with a concentration on the young adult dining-out market, all of which has an effect on the technology used, the delivery of service and the style of the operation. Senior management participates in the everyday work of the operation, and encourages learning both through work and through training. It is at the **moment of truth** that the service culture, leadership, training, development and interactive skills are measured, with the customer perceiving quality as the extent to which the service establishment meets his or her expectations. It is in this sense that service culture means an understanding of the interaction at the moment of truth and a common belief in the organization about the importance of customer contact.

It is employees in the front line of operation who create service quality for the customer. If one implements the idea of turning the organization pyramid upside down, this does not change the features of the organization, but it does give a chance to rethink the service culture and to work on attitudes within the organization. In reversing the organizational pyramid, management is able to concentrate its efforts on ensuring success in the front line of operations. This means stressing the issue of interaction with the customer and empowering the employee in the front line, thereby minimizing the hierarchy within the organization. Support systems are directed towards the same end because they should provide immediate help for the contact person and not form an obstacle in the service process. The Center Inn organizational chart reflects this strong belief in this service-orientated structure of focusing on the front-line contact person.

**SUMMARY**

This chapter introduced the concept of corporate strategy and set it within a strategic management process. It then went on to identify the critical elements within that strategic management process and related it to a number of companies within the hospitality industry, in the UK, Europe and the USA. It showed that a hospitality firm operates within an economic, financial and competitive environment and has to take account of a wide range of stakeholders, all of whom have interests in the organization. Such stakeholder pressures can be both external and internal. A final aspect considered was the organizational structure of the firm and the importance of the strategic leader, and his or her values and the beliefs. Overarching all this is the importance of culture, and this was related to a restaurant operation in Helsinki, Finland.

**FURTHER READING**

Anon 1991 Share and share alike: European takeovers, *The Economist*, 21 December

Anon 1991 Europe's corporate castles begin to crack: European businessmen are finding that cosy Continental-style capitalism has costs as well as benefits, *The Economist*, 30 November

Emmott, B 1991 Survey of international finance: European Communities beware simple comparisons between Britain and continental Europe, *The Economist*, 27 April

Faith, N 1993 Sweet dreams: Rocco Forte has finally emerged from the shadow of his father; is the City giving the nod to his plans for streamlining Britain's biggest hotel and catering group to fit his own vision? *The Independent*, 18 April

Gilbert, N and J Shepherd 1993 Hotel share sales stir up a storm; Suspension of trading in Queens Moat dampens hope in a sector which has been expecting better times, *The Independent*, 4 April

Foye, P J and D Lontings 1993 Accor Wagons Lits takeover: the saga continues, *International Financial Law Review*, **12**(1); 24–7

Jones, P L and S Goss Turner 1992 Creativity for hospitality managers (Forte plc). In R

Teare, D Adams and S Messenger (eds) *Managing projects in hospitality organizations*, London: Cassell, pp. 311–25

Miles, R E and C C Snow 1978 *Organizational Strategy*, New York: McGraw-Hill

Olsen, M D 1991 Strategic management in the hospitality industry: a literature review. In C P Cooper (ed.) *Progress in tourism recreation and hospitality management*, vol 3, London: Belhaven Press, pp. 215–31

Pannell Kerr Forster Associates 1995 *Eurocity report*, London: Pannell Kerr Forster Associates

Pannell Kerr Forster Associates 1995 *UK trends report*, London: Pannell Kerr Forster Associates

Pannell Kerr Forster Associates 1995 *London trends report*, London: Pannell Kerr Forster Associates

Pearce, J A and R B Robinson 1991 *Strategic management formulation, implementation and control*, 4th edn, Boston, MA: R D Irwin Inc, pp. 2–21

Peters, T J and R H Waterman 1982 *In search of excellence*, New York: Harper & Row

Pizam, A 1993 Managing cross cultural hospitality enterprises. In P Jones and A Pizam (eds) *The international hospitality industry: organizational and operational issues*, London: Pitman Publishing, pp. 205–25

Shrivastava, P 1994 *Strategic management, concepts and practices*, Cincinnati, OH: International Thomson Publishing, Chs 1 and 2

Slattery, P, G Feehely and M Savage 1994 *Quoted hotel companies: the world market 1994*, Kleinwort Benson Research, 8th Annual Review, London, pp. 119–41

Slattery, P, M Savage and G Feehely 1995 *Quoted hotel companies: the world markets 1995*, London: Kleinwort Benson Research, 9th annual review

Stacey, R D 1993 *Strategic management and organizational dynamics*, London: Pitman Publishing, pp. 1–43

Thomson, J L 1993 *Strategic management awareness and change*, 2nd edn, London: Chapman and Hall, Chs 1–3

# CHAPTER 2

# Laying the groundwork for the strategic planning process

**OBJECTIVES**

After reading this chapter you should be able to:
- Understand the process of strategic planning.
- Identify the elements and significance of the firm's general, industry and operational environment.
- Understand the techniques for environmental analysis.
- Understand the importance of formulating the firm's mission statement and objectives.

## WHAT IS STRATEGIC PLANNING?

Strategic planning is essential to survival in the hospitality industry today. It can be seen as a managerial process of developing and maintaining a viable fit between the firm's objectives and resources and its changing market opportunities. Three key aspects define the strategic planning process.

- First, the firm's businesses should be managed as an investment portfolio. The central issue here is to decide which business entities should be built, maintained, reduced or terminated. As each business has a different profit potential it does not make sense for a firm to allocate management time and funds equally to all businesses. Therefore a reallocation of resources is required appropriate to each business entity.
- The second key issue is to assess accurately the future profit potential of each business. A number of analytical scenarios of future conditions in each market need to be determined.
- The third key idea underlying planning is that of strategy. For each of its businesses, the hospitality firm must develop a **game plan** for achieving its long-term objectives. Furthermore, there is no one strategy that is optimal for all competitors in that business. Each firm must determine what makes the most sense in the light of its industry position, and its mission, objectives, opportunities and resources.

### The environment

Implicit in this discussion of strategic planning is the concept of an open system: an approach that considers the topic of environmental analysis and its effect on the organization. It can be recognized that adapting to environmental change is the essence of the strategic management process and is central to strategic planning. Five ways of modelling the environment can be identified:

- the **organizational field** model;
- the **ecological and resource dependency** model;
- the **cognitive** model;
- the **industry structure** model;
- the **era** model.

While these five approaches vary in their assumptions, in essence they all suggest that the environment influences decision making both through managerial perceptions and through the objective dimensions of industry structure. To maintain a fit between the firm and its environment, so necessary for survival and growth, strategic managers must respond to that environment. Environmental scanning is the process by which senior management become aware of events and trends outside their firm.

Firms conduct environmental analysis to identify market opportunities and threats. Such an approach also helps them to anticipate changes in highly complex and dynamic environments: by anticipating changes accurately, firms can gain competitive advantage through quick action. Environmental analysis focuses on assessing the current environment and projecting or forecasting its future state. Based on this assessment it is possible to identify opportunities, threats and external constraints on the firm. Environmental analysis also helps the firm to position itself in a continually evolving environment. It examines the consequences of a firm's strategies on the environment. Three aspects of the firm's external environment will now be considered:

- the general environment;
- the industry environment;
- the operating environment.

Each of these three areas will be discussed in the context of the tourism and hospitality industry.

## GENERAL ENVIRONMENT

The general environment comprises factors that originate beyond any single firm's operating situation: that is, economic, social, political, technological or ecological factors. Therefore it consists of:

- the natural environment or ecology of the planet;
- the international world order of economic, social and political relationships;

- the immediate economic, technological, social, cultural and political context of organizations.

It is the international world order that shapes the economic, social and political relationships between nation states. Nation states have their own unique economic, social, cultural and political institutions, processes and histories that serve as a context for business. These elements will now be discussed in greater detail and related to the hospitality industry.

## Ecological factors

Strategic planning must acknowledge the finite and limited nature of natural resources and must provide for their renewal. The value of environmental sustainability is emerging at the international level (eco-auditing, and so corporate strategic plans must aim at making firms sustainable. Even firms that do not derive products from nature, use natural resources such as fossil fuels for energy generation and the disposal of waste. It is in this respect that the firm should consider this natural environment. Perhaps one factor that forced the hospitality industry to focus on environmental issues in 1993 was the International Hotel Environment Initiative brought together by the Prince of Wales' Business Leaders' Forum. Its *Guide to best practice* brought together the collective expertise of eleven international hotel groups, controlling over a million bedrooms. The document, published in May 1993, was based on the internal environmental manual used by the Japanese-owned Inter-Continental Hotel group. Much work on environmental issues has already been undertaken in the industry, and it is contract caterer Aramark that summarizes the general approach with its message: **reduce, reuse and recycle**.

Within the hotel industry, one area of particular interest in environmental matters is **energy management**. There are approximately 500,000 rooms within the UK hotel industry, with the 30 largest hotel companies owning approximately 20 per cent of the stock while a further 10 per cent of the stock is affiliated to consortia. Energy use in the hotel sector can be divided between about 22 per cent electricity and 78 per cent fossil fuels. Energy costs (including water) average £828 per available room per year, representing approximately 2.5 per cent of total revenue in 1993. A comparison of the figures for the period 1990–93 shows that spending on energy in hotels rose by approximately 10 per cent at the same time as occupancy rates dropped. Changes in fuel prices during this period were minimal. If the figure of 500,000 rooms in the UK is multiplied by the average expenditure cost per room of £828 it would appear that energy costs within the UK hotel industry are in the region of

£400 million per year. So energy savings could represent a significant reduction in costs and an improvement in the environment.

## Economic factors

Economic factors concern the nature and direction of the economy in which a firm operates. Because consumption patterns are affected by the relative affluence of different market segments, in its strategic planning each hospitality firm must consider economic trends in the segments that affect its industry. On both a national and international level it must consider the general availability of credit, the level of disposable income and the propensity of people to spend. Interest rates, inflation rates and trends in the growth of the gross national product are all relevant factors.

The European hospitality industry is subject to a multitude of global economic influences, closely allied to political factors. The European markets are also influenced by events occurring in the other major world economies, such as Japan and the USA. The global nature of the hospitality industry ensures that trends in the global economy are just as relevant as those in domestic markets. A major determinant of hospitality sector performance in 1994–95 was the pace of global economic recovery. If one looks at real GDP growth from 1980 to 1994 (year-on-year percentage changes), the economies of the UK, Germany, Japan and the USA have been growing at different rates, and this has implications for the hospitality industry.

Until recently the potential impact of international economic forces seemed to be severely restricted, and hence was largely discounted. However, the emergence of new international power brokers has changed the focus of economic environmental forecasting. Among the most prominent of these power brokers are the European Union and the Organization of Petroleum Exporting Countries (OPEC). In addition, many countries have conducted multilateral trade negotiations in order to establish rules for international trade and conduct. These negotiations have a profound effect on almost every aspect of business activity.

All of these international forces can affect the economic well-being of the hospitality industry, for better or for worse. Consequently, firms must try to forecast the repercussions of major actions taken in both the domestic and international economic arenas. Such forecasting is a critical part of the strategic management process and feeds into the planning process. In essence, the timing and relative success of particular strategies can be influenced by economic conditions. When the economy as a whole or certain sectors of the economy are growing, demand may exist for a product or service that would not be in demand in more depressed circumstances. Similarly, the opportunity to exploit a particular strategy successfully may depend on demand that exists in growth conditions but not in recession.

## Sociocultural factors

The social and cultural environment consists of broad societal trends that affect organizations. These include demographic patterns, lifestyles, social structures, social relationships and social trends. The cultural environment of the firm emerges from shared beliefs, values, symbols and practices and is a product of the behavioural norms of the society in which the firm operates. As social attitudes change, so too does demand for various types of hotel, catering and leisure facilities. Like other forces in the general environment, social forces are dynamic, with constant change resulting from the efforts of individuals to satisfy their desires and needs by controlling and adapting to environmental factors.

One of the most profound social changes in recent years has been the entry of a large number of women into the labour market. This has not only affected the hiring and compensation policies and the resource capabilities of their employers, it has also created or greatly expanded the demand for a wide range of products and services necessitated by their absence from home. Another factor has been the increase in women executives and their specific demands for hotel accommodation, an example being the introduction of Lady Crest Rooms within Forte Crest. Key changes have also been noted in demographics, including what has been described as the **baby boom** phenomenon. There was a large increase in the birth rate in the 1950s and 1960s, and this has now swelled the ranks of young, educated, employed, urban-based adults within the economy of the 1990s. In addition, a consequence of this changing age distribution of the population has been a sharp increase in the demands made by a growing number of people over the age of 50 during the 1990s. Constrained by a different income profile, this age group category demands different services and products from the hospitality industry. This has influenced the trend in people taking second holidays, in particular short break holidays within the UK.

It is difficult to translate social change into forecasts of its effect on business. Nevertheless, informed estimates of the impact of such geographic shifts in population and changing work values can only help a firm in its attempts to formulate its plans. Sensitivity to cultural differences, in particular, is important in conducting business internationally in the hospitality industry. The major hotel companies' response to Japanese tourists within the London hotel market is a case in point. Managers involved in such an international business need to be familiar with foreign languages, business practices and customs. They must also understand local customer needs, resource availability, legal requirements and financial arrangements.

## Political and regulatory factors

The political and regulatory environment consists of legislative and electoral politics, regulations and regulatory agencies and interest group pressures. The direction and stability of political factors are a major consideration for managers in formulating corporate strategy, and it is the political factors that define the legal and regulatory parameters within which the hospitality firm must operate. As many laws and regulations are restrictive they tend to reduce the firm's profit potential, although other actions benefit and protect firms, such as patent laws, subsidies and research grants. Thus political factors may either limit or benefit the firm they influence. In addition, political activity may have a significant impact on three of the key functions that influence the environment of the firm:

- supply;
- customers;
- competition.

In terms of the customer, government demand for products and services can create, sustain, enhance or eliminate many market opportunities. Compulsory competitive tendering for catering facilities within local government is one example; such tendering has been a feature of the UK's Conservative government philosophy.

In terms of competition, government can operate as an almost unbeatable competitor in the marketplace. Thus a knowledge of government's strategies when assessing the environment can help a firm avoid unfavourable confrontation with the government as a competitor.

Within the European Union the issue of the **Social Charter** has become a highly sensitive subject, particularly on the UK political scene; it also has implications for the hospitality industry. The Social Charter is an attempt by the EU to balance the free-market ideals of 1992 with an improvement in the well-being of (chiefly) employed people. It was adopted in December 1989 by eleven out of twelve Member States. This means that the charter is not legally binding. However, the European Commission has pressed ahead with what it calls its **action plan**. which has preceded the Social Charter in terms of the Commission's short-term social policy. The Social Charter, nonetheless, contains the long-term intentions of both the Commission and eleven Member States. The Social Charter action plan covers seven basic areas:

- employment and remuneration;
- improvement of living and working conditions;
- freedom of movement;

- social protection;
- information, consultation and participation;
- equal treatment for men and women;
- health and safety protection for workers.

The hospitality industry has all too often regarded health and safety as an afterthought to matters such as food safety. This situation changed with the introduction of UK health and safety legislation on 1 January 1993.

Comparison of the original Treaty of Rome's Articles and those of the Maastricht Treaty's protocol show that the eleven have agreed to greatly broaden and extend the social objectives of the Union under what is called the **social chapter**. Under Article 117 of the Maastricht Treaty, the Union has moved from merely being agreed on the need to promote improved working conditions, to setting itself the objective of promoting proper social protection and dialogue between management and labour. The new Article 118 extends the old Article to say that, with a view to achieving the objectives of Article 117, the Union shall support and complement members states in fields such as health and safety, working conditions, information and consultation of workers, equality between men and women, and integration of persons excluded from the labour market.

Article 118 (2) allows Directives on the above issues to be adopted by qualified majority voting. It is clear that Article 118 enables the Union to introduce legislation that could radically change employment in the hospitality industry. For instance, information and consultation of workers could include provisions requiring international hotel companies such as Forte or Accor to consult workers on major business decisions. Protection or determination of employment could require the eleven to harmonize and improve the laws on, for example, notice, unfair dismissal and compensation for redundancy. Social security and social protection of workers could lead to harmonization of statutory sick pay and national insurance contributions throughout the Union. The hospitality industry is labour intensive and such moves could have cost implications. Firms are therefore greatly affected by government decisions, and continual assessment of government strategies will help individual firms to develop complementary plans that anticipate and optimize environmental opportunities.

## Technological factors

A further aspect of the general environment is that the hospitality firm should take note of technological change. To avoid obsolescence and promote innovation a firm must be aware of technological changes that might influence its industry. The technological environment influences a firm's performance through two types of change:

- changes in product or service technologies (designs, features and innovations);
- changes in process technologies.

Changes in product technology can render certain products obsolete; they can reduce demand for products, or shorten their life cycle. Changes in production processes directly influence production costs. Production process innovation can reduce the cost of manufacturing for some companies and give them a competitive advantage over others in the industry. Improvements in production processes can also affect the quality and speed of production. In the final analysis, production technologies drive competitiveness. The quasi-science of attempting to foresee advances and estimate their impact on an organization's operations is known as **technological forecasting**. Such forecasting can help to protect and improve the profitability of a firm in a growing industry. The key to the forecasting of technological advance lies in accurately predicting future technological capabilities and their impacts. A comprehensive analysis of the effect of technological changes involves study of the expected impact of these technologies on the remote environment, competitive business situation and on the business–society interface. In recent years, forecasting in this last area has warranted particular attention, particular in reference to the probable effect of technological advances on quality of life factors such as ecology and public safety.

Having identified the elements of the general environment, the next stage in the management process is one of analysis.

## ANALYSIS OF THE GENERAL ENVIRONMENT

### Opportunities

One important objective of environmental analysis is to identify opportunities and threats facing the hospitality firm. Opportunities represent potential or profitable actions, and threats are events that represent danger and risk to the firm's future. Opportunities may exist in unexploited market demand for existing products; there may be new product possibilities; it may be possible to make technological improvements in production systems that could lead to improved product quality, higher production efficiency and reduced pollution. There may be potential for cutting costs, and in addition there may be opportunities for the acquisition of new businesses.

The temporal or time-dependent opportunities must also be examined. Opportunities do not last for ever, they may arise and fade away quickly. Managers must learn to act within the 'window of opportunity'; they must be quick to grab opportunities while they last. The ability to act quickly and opportunistically is a strategic skill that needs to be developed.

## Threats

Threats are events or conditions that can potentially harm the hospitality firm's interests. They can take the form of new or restrictive regulations or the arrival of new or powerful competitors. Decline in demand for products is often a major threat to business. Other threats include harm from products and production techniques, the possibility of strikes, consumer or product boycotts, financial problems, and destruction of critical supplies. Environmental analysis should help firms to develop contingency actions to avoid or circumvent threats, and should provide general guidance for acquiring resources from the environment. It should also identify where resources may be available and how they could be obtained and it should tell managers how the firm is positioned in relation to its competitors, with respect to those resources.

While one part of the analysis examines the influences that environmental forces have on firms, the other half should focus on assessing how organizational activities affect the firm's environment. Both the human and natural environments need to be considered. Concerns over environmental degradation are becoming widespread in the hospitality industry. It is essential for managers to understand the strategic implications of the harm that organizational activities can cause to the natural environment. Most large hospitality firms have developed special analytical techniques and information systems to aid environmental analysis. Senior management receive information from this analysis as part of their strategic planning activities.

## Techniques for environmental analysis

Environmental analysis can be structured and made more manageable by using formal techniques for assessing current environmental trends and forecasting future trends. Seven techniques can be identified:

- trend extrapolation;
- econometric forecasting;
- delphi forecasting;
- strategic issues analysis;
- cross-impact matrices;
- scenario analysis; and
- system simulations.

**Trend extrapolation** uses historical changes in a variable or historical relationships between variables to identify future trends. The assumption is that historical data accurately capture the logic of changes in the variable being forecast. The technique may be used as a simple linear relationship or a more complex non-linear relationship. Trend extrapolation is useful for identifying time trends in single variables such as sales productivity, demand and cost. For instance for every £100 spent on advertising, hotel room sales may increase by £1,000.

**Econometric forecasting** uses large computer programs to predict major economic indicators. Macroeconomic variables such as gross national product, interest rates, employment rates, producer and consumer price indices, import–export and trade balance can be predicted using econometric forecasting. The statistical techniques most commonly used in such forecasting are multiple regression analysis and time series regression models. Instead of doing their own econometric forecasting, firms can simply subscribe to forecasting services to receive periodic forecasts of key economic indicators. Often they subscribe to multiple services to validate forecasts, and use the average forecast in their own strategic decision making.

**Delphi forecasting** is a qualitative forecasting technique that systematically elicits and consolidates the judgements of experts about the future. The technique, which is particularly useful when objective measures of variables to be forecast are not available, allows a consensual description of the future. The technique begins with the selection of a panel of experts from relevant fields. Panellists provide their opinions on relevant aspects of the future environment, and these opinions are circulated to all the other panellists. Reactions are gained, and a second round of opinion taking is conducted. The process of opinion polling, sharing and revision is repeated three or four times until consensus emerges. This consensus view of the future serves as the basis for the forecast.

**Strategic issues analysis** is another qualitative technique for assessing emerging strategic environmental issues. It allows broad monitoring of social, regulatory and political changes that can affect corporate performance. The technique consists of systematically monitoring these developments and identifying their impact on firms.

**Cross-impact matrices** are most useful when forecasting several interrelated variables. They acknowledge that one environmental event may increase or decrease with the occurrence of another event. The cross-impact matrix represents the influence of several related events or outcomes on each other over time. It is a simple way of keeping track of changing interactions between environmental events.

**Scenario analysis** is a technique used to forecast the occurrence of complex environmental events. It is particular useful in forecasting events in which money variables play a role. Scenarios allow the integrated consideration of these multiples or variables in explaining the emergence of future conditions. A scenario is a detailed description, if certain events occur in the future, of what their consequences will be for the hospitality firm. Scenarios describe in detail the sequence of events that could plausibly lead to a prescribed future state. They identify factors that are likely to affect the firm and they assess the implications of future conditions for corporate objectives and performance. Strategic plans and programmes that can meet environmental challenges may be explored within the scenario. Scenario analysis usually leads to the development of a best-case scenario, a worst-case scenario and the most likely scenario. Each scenario represents a different set of assumptions about external and internal factors. Scenarios may serve as a vehicle for discussing strategic plans and environmental trends. They are also useful for macro-sociological forecasting.

**Systems simulation** is a technique for examining the structural properties of industries and economic sectors, and can help in forecasting trends. Such simulations mathematically model industrial systems and consist of dozens of equations using many variables. Variables represent attributes of the industrial system, and the equations represent relationships between the variables. The simulation examines changing relationships within the industrial system, and it identifies how one set of variables and relationships changes with other sets. It also describes the optimal states of the system and involves a sensitivity analysis.

## Environmental scanning and information systems

The discussion so far has considered the general environment and some techniques available for its analysis. The process being undertaken in this respect is **environmental scanning**.

The lifeblood of any organization is information, and the analysis of environmental forces requires many types of information. Firms have developed a variety of **information systems** to generate this information, taking inputs from the firm's internal information systems in production, marketing and financial control areas. They also use a variety of outside information sources: present and potential customers; government industry analysts; academic researchers and consultants. Some of these information systems are purely manual; others use computers. The systems analyse and summarize information about customers, competitors, social and cultural trends, technological developments and regulatory changes. Strategic decision makers receive this information periodically. Successful strategic planning to secure competitive advantage depends on three aspects of the information system: speed, originality, and control. It is therefore necessary to identify the information needs of the strategic planner and exploit the key information sources available in order to design an appropriate information system.

Three types of environmental scanning systems can be found in firms: irregular, regular, and continuous. Firms with **irregular** environmental scanning systems monitor the environment through ad hoc studies. These studies focus on critical current and imminent environmental events. Staff who do these studies focus on specific events that are important to the hospitality firm, and keep track of important environmental issues, so that any surprises from a drastic environmental change can be avoided.

Firms with **regular** environmental scanning systems conduct periodic studies of selected environmental events and variables. These studies analyse how the environment will affect critical strategic decisions. These systems provide a more proactive approach to tracking the environment than the irregular scanning systems.

Firms with **continuous** environmental scanning systems have institutionalized the environmental scanning activity. They have structured data collection and processing systems and focus on a broad range of environmental variables that affect the firm's performance. Often the systems use computerized databases and analytical models.

Sometimes environmental scanning and strategic planning are integrated into a single programme, and jointly they answer central questions raised by strategic planners. Organizationally, environmental scanning is part of the strategic planning department. More recently some firms have developed competitor intelligence and analysis systems, which are dedicated to analysing the competition. Their purpose is to enable the firm to use information as a strategic resource in developing competitive advantage and more effective business strategies. Competitor information for these systems comes from a variety of conventional published and personal sources, including customers, suppliers, ex-employees of competitors, government agencies and public databases.

## INDUSTRY ENVIRONMENT

Many strategists claim that in order to start the process of strategic planning four questions need to be addressed:

- Where are we now?
- Where do we want to be?
- How are we going to get there?
- Where do we start?

It has already been shown that correct information is essential to strategic planning, but the issue here is: how does one decide whether a piece of information is critical or merely interesting? Strategic frameworks can help to answer these four questions and, in particular, help the strategic planner to focus on the most important of disciplines – **strategic thinking**. Remember that for every strategic theory represented in a framework there will be a counter-theory and so no framework can be followed prescriptively. Frameworks are useful in that they reduce the imponderable complexity of a business problem to a few simple dimensions in order to get the planning process started. The following three frameworks (discussed in greater detail in later chapters) can be used within the strategic planning process.

## General Electric's industry attractiveness matrix

This model charts the firm's competitive strengths in an industry against the industry's attractiveness. Within an industry, attractiveness includes' such factors as market size, profit margins, competition, industry growth and supplier power. Business strengths would include relative market share, management skills, product and service quality, brand image and location. The model can be used to determine which sector would offer the best investment opportunities, with the obvious point that the planner is looking for a highly attractive sector that has business strength. The general concept also has wider applications than choosing a sector: it can be used to compare the various alternative market segments that a hospitality firm or an individual property could focus upon. For example, the relative attractiveness of the conference market and a hotel's ability to serve that market can be plotted against similar criteria for the tourist market, coach tours or airline crews. This is a useful summary tool, pooling together much planning theory that can help the strategic manager in forming a clear picture of the segmentation options available to the firm and in addition which should be chosen as the best option. It can therefore be used both at company level and individual property level.

## Ansoff matrix

The setting of objectives should only be expressed in terms of products or services, and markets. Also, objectives should be set within the context of what is to be sold and to whom it is to be sold. The Ansoff matrix reduces this myriad choices to the two simple dimensions **market** and **product**, and the distinctions of **existing** and **new**. Therefore in choosing a market strategy only four choices are available:

- existing markets, existing products;
- existing markets, new products;
- new markets, existing products;
- new markets, new products.

The level of uncertainty and potential risk increases as one moves further from the market and product one understands, to an excursion into new markets and new products, which is only to be considered in the most exceptional of cases. This model is useful both in setting corporate development strategies and in planning marketing activities for individual hotels. It leads the manager to adopt a logical approach in addressing whether, for example, a hotel can sell more to its existing customers, e.g. food and beverage promotions, or whether it can develop new products for its existing market. Only when the hotel has exhausted the possibilities of selling to the existing market should it consider selling existing or new products to new markets.

The term **gap analysis** can be used to apply either to revenue or profit gaps, or to market gaps. When profits are forecast and compared with corporate financial objectives a gap is often discovered; usually the forecast profits are less than the corporate plan requires. The issue here is how to fill that gap. The gap can be divided into two distinct components. The first is an **operations gap**, which can be filled by increased productivity and an increase in the market penetration. The second is a **strategy gap** which can be filled by the three Ansoff boxes:

- new markets/existing products;
- new products/existing market;
- new product/new market.

If all else fails, the corporate objectives will have to be reduced. Finding a unique position or gap in the market is one of the hardest strategic decisions to be made. By representing the dimensions of the market and the positions of the competition diagrammatically, it is possible to spot a potential unsatisfied gap. If it was concluded that two important dimensions for the hotel industry were room size and room rate, then by charting these two dimensions for each of the major players in the industry, a diagram would be produced that might show a significant gap just waiting to be filled. For example, such a diagrammatic representation, with the right criteria, would have highlighted the gap between bed and breakfast and three-star hotels, now filled by budget hotels, or the gap left in the mid-market by the policy of upgrading to four-star.

## Porter's five forces

Porter's model describes five forces that determine the profitability of an industry:

- the bargaining power of the suppliers;
- the bargaining power of buyers;
- the threat of new entrants;
- the threat of substitutes; and
- the rivalry of existing competitors.

An understanding of these five forces allows the planner to systematically review the firm's competitive position in the industry, in respect of both the company and at individual properties. The threat of an impact on rate and profitability from new entrants to a marketplace is reasonably obvious, but the five forces model makes the planner consider the threat of substitutes. For example, improved transport is one of the biggest substitutes for hotel accommodation: the introduction of a shuttle airline service is potentially more damaging to a hotel's competitive position than the construction of an additional hotel. Equally, there may be competition from timeshare, a lower market-level hotel, visiting friends and relatives, or even caravans and camping.

Porter follows on this model with his matrix of **generic strategies**. In this model, Porter suggests that within any industry the planner must decide whether the firm is to be:

- a low-cost producer producing a comparable product at the lowest cost and therefore being able to sell at the lowest price, or
- a seller of a product with a high element of added value that makes the highest margin, or
- to be differentiated in some product attribute or attributes that are highly valued by the consumer, the reward for successful differentiation being a premium price.

A key dimension of the matrix is that of **scope**. The issue here is: does the firm intend to be the lowest-cost producer for the whole industry, or for only a very narrow segment with clearly recognizable needs? Similarly, will the firm differentiate for the whole market or just a niche? The natural extension of this theory is that differentiation costs money, and therefore by definition the firm cannot be low cost and differentiated. This may not hold true in practice, but the theory does seem to make sense; it does start to force strategic decisions to be made about the basis of the competition. The theory also suggests that the worst strategic course is to be stuck in the middle without any clear strategy. This approach by Porter to industry analysis is discussed in greater detail later on in this chapter, in the case study on computer reservation systems.

The use of strategic models has many shortcomings. In general, the models are too simplistic. Dangers may also arise when a firm follows the models too closely, and does not make allowances for the dynamics of the industry, or expects the models to provide the answers to questions. A good model in essence will only lead the firm to seek the right information and ask the right questions. This use of models can also be extended to the issue of industry competition.

## INDUSTRY COMPETITION

The issue of competition is complex, and can be studied from many different perspectives. In many cases it is regarded as the key to the success or failure of firms.

Competitive strategy can be defined as the search for a favourable competitive position in the industry. The fundamental arena in which competition occurs is in establishing a profitable and sustainable position against the forces that determine industry competition. Two central questions underlie the choice of competitive strategy.

- The first is the attractiveness of an industry's long-term profitability and the factors that determine it: not all industries offer equal opportunities for sustained profitability. It is the inherent profitability of an industry that is one essential ingredient in determining the profitability of a firm.
- The second question in competitive strategy is the determinants of relative competitive position within an industry. In most industries some firms are much more profitable than others, regardless of what the average profitability of the industry may be.

Competition can also be viewed from an economic perspective, and the usefulness of this approach will now be considered.

### Economic competition

There are several different concepts of economic competition. One view is that competition can be regarded as a **resource-based** phenomenon, and in this respect unique resources can be used to create lasting performance benefits. Firms in every industry have unique and sometimes overlapping resources. It is these resources that create three different types of market environment:

- monopolistic,
- oligopolistic, and
- perfect markets.

In a monopolistic market, a single firm dominates. In an oligopolistic industry, a few firms control the entire industry. Perfect competition refers to industries in which there are many firms, and no single firm dominates.

Since the 1930s, legislation in both the UK and North America has tried to eliminate monopolies, and government has enacted many laws designed to reduce the monopoly power of individual firms. The objective has been to encourage healthy competition among multiple firms. Over the years such legislation has made monopolies less viable and so more industries have had to become competitive. Consequently, the monopolistic way of viewing competition became less useful for understanding competitive industry structures.

The resource-centred view of competition focuses on the role of technological evolution and product market shift. These factors, it is argued, are at the heart of capitalistic competition and economic change. The argument here is that innovation in products, markets and technologies gives firms a distinctive long-term competitive advantage. These trends can completely displace all currently competitive firms. Other factors such as price, marketing strategies and financial resources are less important. Unfortunately, competition is a complex multifaceted phenomenon and neither of these two views of competition captures its complexity.

Another view of competition combines elements of what has been discussed so far and extends them to create an **industry organization** model of competition. This model argues that financial returns in an industry are a function of two variables:

- the competitive structure of the industry, and
- the conduct of firms within the industry.

Several economic variables determine the structure of an industry. They include the number and relative size of competitors, the barriers to entry into the industry, the degree of product differentiation, and the elasticity of demand. These variables jointly determine the average level of profits of an industry. Variances from average profitability are a result of an individual firm's actions. These actions affect product quality, advertising intensity, product efficiency, costs and profits. Over the past few years this view of competition has served as a basis for examining competitive structures in strategy formulation.

## COMPETITIVE FORCES THAT SHAPE STRATEGY

The essence of strategy formulation is coping with competition. The first fundamental determinant of a firm's profitability is industry attractiveness, and competitive strategy grows out of a sophisticated understanding of the rules of competition that determine an industry's attractiveness. The ultimate aim of competitive strategy is to cope with and ideally to change those rules in the firm's favour.

### Structural forces

The structure of an industry can be analysed by looking at the regulatory, technological, economic and commercial forces that shape the competition within it. Such a discussion draws on Porter's five competitive forces:

- the entry of new competitors;
- the threat of substitutes;
- the bargaining power of buyers;
- the marketing power of suppliers; and
- the rivalry amongst the existing competitors;

The collective strength of these five competitive forces determines the ability of a firm within an industry to earn, on average, a rate of return on investment in excess of the cost of capital. The strength of the five forces varies from industry to industry, and can change as an industry evolves.

Industry profitability is not a function of what the product looks like, or whether it embodies high or low technology, but of the industry's structure. The five forces determine industry profitability because they influence prices, costs and required investment. Buying power influences the prices that firms can charge, for example, as does the threat of substitution. The power of buyers can also influence costs and investment, because powerful buyers demand a costly service. The bargaining power of suppliers determines the costs of raw materials. The intensity of rivalry influences prices as well as the costs of competing in areas such as plant, product development, advertising and sales. The threat of entry places a limit on prices, and shapes the investment required to deter entrance. The strength of each of these five competitive forces is a function of industry structure or the underlying economic and technical characteristics of an industry. Industry profits may be thought of as a fixed pie in which individual firms' profits expand or shrink through the influence of these major structural forces. Changes in the size of the profit pie also change the profit share of individual firms in the industry.

## Threats to entry

New entrants to an industry bring new capacity, the desire to gain market share and often (with major firms) substantial resources. An important determinant of profitability is the number of competitors within an industry who compete for a share of industry profits. Entry barriers depend on technological and commercial relationships within the industry. The most important barriers to entry are:

- economies of scale,
- product differentiation,
- switching costs,
- access to distribution channels, and
- miscellaneous barriers.

**Economies of scale**

The scale of operation and production at the unit determines its economic efficiency, and as the scale of operation increases so does its economic efficiency. Economic advantages of scale occur because firms can buy raw materials in large quantities at discounts. They can also distribute overhead costs among the many units of the firm. These economies deter entry by forcing the new entrant to come in on a large scale or to accept a cost disadvantage. Economies of scale can also act as hurdles in distribution, utilization of sales force, financing etc. In every industry there is a minimum economic scale at which a production unit must operate for it to be efficient and competitive. If this minimum scale of operation is large, the firm requires a large amount of capital to become established. Such a large capital requirement will act as a barrier to entry. This large capital requirement also imposes higher risks, which prevent more competitors from entering the industry.

Units of multi-business firms may be able to reap economies similar to those of scale if they are able to share operations or functions that are part of other businesses in the company. Diversification within a multi-business firm will also reap economies within that particular industry. Thus related diversification around common operations or functions can remove volume constraints imposed by the size of a given industry. The prospective entrant is forced to be diversified or face a cost disadvantage. The benefits of sharing are particularly potent if there are joint costs. A common situation of joint costs occurs when business units can share intangible assets such as brand names and know-how; such a cost of creating an intangible asset need only be borne once. The asset may then be freely applied to other businesses, subject only to any costs of adapting or modifying it.

Another type of economies of scale entry barrier occurs when there are economies to vertical integration: that is, operating in successive stages of production or distribution. Here the entrant must enter in an integrated fashion or face a costly disadvantage.

**Product differentiation**

Product differentiation refers to how easy or difficult it is to distinguish products in an industry, and may be based on objective features of the product or on perceived features. Brand identification creates a barrier by forcing entrants to spend heavily to overcome customer loyalty. For example, to create high fences around their business, UK brewers couple brand identification with economies of scale in production, distribution and marketing. If creating product differentiation is technologically difficult and expensive, it limits the entry of new products into the industry. Creating differentiation requires creative product and package design, and may also require heavy investment in advertising and promotion to convince consumers that the product is really different and unique.

The need to invest large financial resources in order to compete creates a barrier to entry, particularly if the capital is required for unrecoverable expenditures and upfront advertising or research and development. Capital is required not only for fixed facilities but also for customer credit inventories and to cover start-up losses. Today's major corporations have the financial resources to enter almost any industry, which may in some cases limit the pool of likely small entrants. Even if finance is available on the capital markets, entry represents a risky use of that capital, which will be reflected in risk premiums charged to prospective entrants. These constitute advantages for the larger firms.

**Switching costs**  Switching cost is the cost that consumers must incur when they switch from one product to another. It determines how easy or difficult it is for consumers to switch, and if switching costs are high, consumers continue to use the same product. If switching costs are low, consumers tend to experiment with new and different products. They try several products and may even substitute products, from other industries to fill their needs: thus a high switching cost acts as a barrier to entry and discourages consumers from moving to new products offered by new entrants.

**Distribution channels**  The new firm entering an industry must of course secure distribution of its product or service. A new food product, for example, must displace others from the supermarket shelf via price breaks, promotions, intense selling efforts or some other means. The more limited the wholesale or retail channels are, and the more existing competitors have these tied up, obviously the tougher entry into the industry will be. Thus a barrier to entry can be created by the new entrant's need to secure distribution for its product. Existing competitors may have ties with channels based on long relationships, high-quality service, or even exclusive relationships in which the channel is solely identified with a particular manufacturer. Sometimes this barrier to entry is so high that to surmount it a new firm must create an entirely new distribution channel.

**Miscellaneous barriers**  Entrenched firms may have cost advantages not available to potential rivals no matter what their size and attainable economies of scale. These advantages can stem from the effects of the learning curve, proprietary technology, access to the best raw material sources, assets purchased at pre-inflation prices, government subsidies or favourable locations. Sometimes cost advantages are legally enforceable, for instance through patents. Monopolistic control over raw materials can also act as a barrier to entry. For example, De Beers controls more than 50 per cent of the worldwide supply of raw diamonds. This makes it very difficult for any new entrants to play an important role in the diamond industry.

Costs declining with experience, i.e. the learning curve, seem to be most significant in businesses involving a high labour content performing intricate tasks and or complex assembly operations. They are nearly always most significant in the early growth phase of a product's development, and later reach diminishing proportional improvements. If costs decline with experience in an industry, and if the experience can be kept proprietary by established firms, then this effect leads to an entry barrier. New firms with no experience usually have inherently higher costs than established firms and must bear heavy start-up losses. They usually adopt low or near-cost pricing in order to gain the experience and achieve cost parity with established firms. Established firms, particularly the market share leader, which is accumulating experience the fastest, will have a higher cash flow because of the lower costs needed to invest in new equipment and techniques. A number of firms have built successful strategies based on the experience curve through aggressive investment. This is in order to build cumulative volume early in the development of an industry, often by pricing in anticipation of future cost declines.

A final source of entry barrier is government policy. Barriers to entry change continually, owing to new regulations, new technologies and new competitive strategies. For example, at one time the US government controlled entry into the airline industry, by giving permission for airlines to operate particular routes. Airline deregulation in 1978 eliminated the requirement to obtain government permission to operate routes, and opened up the industry to free competition. Regulatory changes also create uncertainty for potential new entrants into the industry and thus may discourage new entrants. The government can limit or even foreclose on industries through which it controls licence requirements or limits on access to raw materials. The regulations on alcoholic liquor retailing in the UK provide one noticeable example. More subtle government restrictions operate in tourism, for instance in ski area development and the requirements of planning legislation.

The government can also play a major indirect role by affecting entry barriers through controls on air and water pollution standards, and through safety regulations. Increasingly, such controls are being determined at European Union level. Standards for product testing, common in industries like food and other health-related products, can impose substantial lead times on firms, which not only raise the capital cost of entry but also give established firms ample notice of impending entry into the market. Sometimes, full knowledge of a new competitor's product is gained, which allows the formulation of retaliatory strategies. Government policy in such areas certainly has direct social benefits, but often has secondary consequences for the entry of firms that go unrecognized.

## Rivalry among competitors

Competition and profitability within an industry also depend on the intensity of rivalry among existing competitors. This can take the familiar form of **jockeying for position** using tactics like price competition, advertising battles, product introductions, increased customer service or warranties. Every time one firm makes a strategic move it can expect retaliation from its competitors. However, price wars reduce total industry profits by reducing industry revenues: a point evidenced by heavy discounting in the London hotel market during the period 1991–93. Fierce rivalry within an industry can be detrimental to its profitability and can be dependent on several factors.

**The total number of competitors** is an important determinant in the nature of competitive rivalry, with the relative power balance among competitors moderating competitive rivalry. If competitors are nearly equal in size and power, they may tend to avoid direct confrontation. When firms are numerous, the likelihood of mavericks is great, and they may believe that they can make a strategic move without being noticed. When, however, the industry is highly concentrated or dominated by one or a few firms, the relative strengths of the leader or leaders can impose discipline as well as playing a coordinating role in the industry through devices such as price leadership.

The industry's **growth rate** determines the total size of the profit pie: hence the focus for many firms is on expansion through market share. Competition for market share is a great deal more volatile in industries where there is slow growth than where is rapid growth. Rapid growth ensures that firms can improve their results just by keeping up with the industry. If, however, the industry has matured, its growth rate is low and this limits the size of the total profit pie. For any one firm to do well or improve its performance it has to take market share from other competitors. This leads to retaliation and more rivalry amongst competitors. In short, pressures of rivalry are low in high-growth industries.

High **fixed costs** or **storage costs** can place significant debt burdens on firms because they generate pressure to liquidate inventories and maintain high capacity utilization. In such situations it is important for firms to turn over their working capital quickly and make the best use of their fixed assets. The significant characteristic of this cost issue is fixed costs relative to value added and not fixed costs as a proportion of total costs. Firms purchasing a high proportion of costs as outside inputs may feel enormous pressure to fill capacity in order to break even, despite the fact that the absolute proportion of fixed costs is low. Firms may be vulnerable to the temptation of changing price in order to ensure sales. This sort of pressure keeps profits low, particularly in some service businesses.

Industries with low **switching costs** have high competitive rivalry: consumers are free to choose and change their suppliers. Continuous switching between products by consumers creates high uncertainty for competitors and encourages them to engage in retaliatory moves. Product differentiation, in contrast, creates layers of insulation against competitive warfare, because buyers have preferences and loyalties to particular sellers. Equally, the lack of switching costs also makes it easier for consumers to shop around for the best price.

In some industries **production capacity** must be added in large units. These industries experience more intense competitive rivalry than industries in which capacity can be augmented in small increments, because large new plants are very expensive and require a great commitment of financial resources. Capacity additions can be chronically destructive to the industry supply–demand balance. Such an industry may face recurring periods of overcapacity and price cutting.

Competitors diverse in strategies, origins, personalities and relationships to their parent companies have different objectives and differing strategies on how to compete, and may continually run head on into each other in the process. The more diverse the competitors are in terms of their origins and operating styles the more diverse their competitive strategy will become. **Diverse strategies** elicit diverse responses and lead to higher competitive rivalry. Foreign competitors and competitors from other industries increase that diversity; they create new competitive moves and new forms of retaliation that increase the rivalry. Owner-operators of small service firms, on the other hand, because they attract a low rate of return on their invested capital, may find such a situation acceptable in order to maintain the independence of their self-ownership, whereas such returns are unacceptable and may appear irrational to a large publicly held competitor. In such an industry, the position of the smaller firms may limit the profitability of the larger concerns. For example, a business unit that is part of a vertical chain of businesses in its corporate organization may well adopt different and perhaps contradictory objectives from those of a free-standing firm competing in the same industry. A business that is cash-rich within the parent company's portfolio of businesses will behave differently from others within the same firm.

The willingness of individual competitors to retaliate against others also depends on their **stakes within the industry**. In today's environment most large corporations operate in multiple industries: this allows them to diversify their risks. Nevertheless, if a firm has an unusually large stake in any one industry it will pay more attention to strategic changes within that industry. If there is any threat to its performance within the industry it is likely to retaliate with much greater force. In such situations the objectives of firms may not only be diverse but even more destabilizing because they are expansionary and may involve a potential willingness to sacrifice profitability.

**Exit barriers** refer to costs that prevent or discourage a firm from getting out of an industry. These include high unrecovered fixed costs, labour commitments, unsold inventories and strategic interdependence among the businesses. Sometimes there are also emotional and psychological barriers to exit. In essence, exit barriers that are economic, strategic and emotional keep firms competing in businesses even though they may be earning low or even negative returns on investment. When exit barriers are high, excess capacity does not leave the industry and firms that lose the competitive battle do not give up. Rather, they grimly hang on and because of their weakness have to resort to extreme tactics, with the result that the profitability of the entire industry can be persistently low.

## Pressure from substitute products

One element that affects industry competition and profitability is the pressure from substitute products. All firms in an industry are competing in a broad sense with industries producing substitute products, thus creating revenue and profit pressures: the more attractive the price performance alternative offered by substitutes, the greater the effect on industry profits. Identifying such products is a matter of searching for other products that can perform the same function as the product of the industry. Substitute products that deserve the most attention are those that are:

- subject to the trend of improving their price–performance trade-off with the industry;
- produced by industries earning high profits.

In the latter case, substitutes often come rapidly into play if some development increases competition in their industry and causes price reduction or performance improvement. Analysis of such trends can be important in deciding whether to try to head off a substitute strategically or to plan strategy with it.

## Bargaining power of buyers

The power of buyers refers to their ability to get favourable terms of trade with sellers. Powerful buyers can attract price discounts, better credit terms, better product quality and more product support services from the industry. Because these concessions are costly they have the effect of reducing industry profits The power of buying depends on several factors.

If a large proportion of sales is purchased by a given buyer this raises the importance of the buyer's business. **Large-volume buyers** are particularly potent forces if heavy fixed costs characterize the industry and make it important to keep capacity filled. In contrast, with industries that have large numbers of buyers, each tends to be small and cannot exert much pressure on the industry. It has neither the power nor the inclination to elicit attractive terms of trade from sellers.

A high degree of **product differentiation** has the effect of limiting buyer power. In industries with highly differentiated products, most products have unique features. To obtain certain product features buyers may have no choice but to buy from a specific manufacturer or service provider. Another factor that determines the bargaining power of buyers is **switching costs**. Switching costs lock the buyers to particular sellers. Conversely, the buyer's power is enhanced if the seller faces switching costs. Flexibility in choosing between alternative buyers is a source of power. If switching costs are low, dissatisfied buyers can easily move from one supplier to another.

If buyers are either partially integrated or pose a credible threat of backward integration, they are in a position to demand bargaining concessions. (Backward integration by a company is the strategy of manufacturing raw materials or subassemblies that go to make products.) It is in this respect that backward integration can increase a firm's bargaining power. Buyer power can be partially neutralized when firms in the industry offer a threat of forward integration into the buyer's industry. However, the threat of backward integration is real only with powerful buyers, those that have the financial and technological capability to manufacture their supplies.

When a product serves as an input into other products it can severely affect the quality of the end product. In such cases, buyers have limited power over producers and are equally less price sensitive.

The power of buyers critically depends on the amount of information they have about product quality, cost structure and performance characteristics. When the buyer has full information about demand, actual market prices and even supplier costs, this usually gives the buyer greater bargaining leverage than when information is poor. With full information, buyers are in a better position to ensure that they receive the most favourable price, and can counter supplier claims that their profitability is threatened. In large companies, buying is now a specialized task handled by professional purchasing departments.

## Bargaining power of suppliers

Suppliers can exert bargaining power on participants in an industry by raising prices or reducing the quality of purchased goods and services. Powerful suppliers can therefore squeeze profitability out of an industry unable to recover cost increases in its own prices. The conditions making suppliers powerful tend to mirror those making buyers powerful. Just as the number of buyers is a determinant of buyer power, so the number of suppliers is a crucial determinant of supplier power. If an industry has many suppliers it has the option of buying from many different sources. In short, suppliers selling to more fragmented buyers will usually be able to exert considerable influence on prices, quality and terms. Another factor that determines the bargaining power of suppliers is how important the industry is to them as a customer. If the industry consumes a large part of a supplier's output it would be considered important and the supplier would be willing to meet the industry's demands for better terms of trade. If the industry is not an important buyer then it should have limited bargaining power. The supplier group poses a credible threat of forward integration, which provides a check against the industry's ability to improve the terms on which it purchases. While we usually think of suppliers as other firms, in labour-intensive industries labour supply can be an important bargaining chip. The key aspect in assessing the power of labour is its degree of organization, and whether the supply of scarce varieties of labour can expand. Where the labour force is tightly organized and the supply of scarce labour is constrained from growing, its power could be high. In some industries manufacturers have little flexibility in changing the cost of labour. They have to pay high wages, and this increases the cost of production and reduces profitability.

Porter's five forces will now be related to the strategic importance of computer reservation systems (CRS) within the airline industry.

## CASE STUDY: THE STRATEGIC IMPORTANCE OF CRS IN THE AIRLINE INDUSTRY

One strategic competitive issue confronting the international travel and tourism industry is the emergence of a few dominant airline computer reservations systems (CRS). Such systems control the sale and distribution of a wide array of travel-related services. Reservations systems were originally developed by the major carriers in the USA for their internal ticketing procedures. Today they have emerged to become one of the most powerful strategic tools of the travel, tourism and hospitality industries, with a wide range of sales and distribution applications. At the moment, a few giant computer reservations systems developed by major air carriers dominate the CRS industry, giving the airline owners a tremendous competitive advantage over their 'have not' competitors.

### Background

As worldwide growth in passenger aviation progressed over the past 30 years, ticket sales through travel agencies became an important component of the channel of distribution. By the 1960s, the airline industry had grown to the extent that computers were needed in order to keep track of the massive inventory of available seats. Originally CRS were developed to handle internal airline reservations systems; however, today these powerful tools can be regarded as a competitive weapon in the airlines' armoury.

It was in 1962 that American Airlines developed the first internal reservations system, which today has secured a dominant market position. From the early internal systems a natural progression was the expansion of the system to include on-line terminals with direct reservation capabilities located in travel agencies. American Airlines realized the potential of CRS technology and first began marketing it extensively in this way immediately following the deregulation of the US airline industry in 1982. American Airline's CRS, named Sabre, has assisted the company in capturing a large market share and has been central to its competitive strategy. Deregulation greatly influenced the development and globalization of CRS, and has led to the creation of other sophisticated systems: for example, Amadeus, Galileo, Apollo and Abacus. Meanwhile, CRS have also diversified into many other reservation functions, such as car rentals and hotel reservations.

## Current trends

Four main trends can be identified in multinational CRS development:

- commercial and regulatory pressures;
- globalization;
- point-of-sale distribution;
- the expansion of travel-related sales.

Commercial and regulatory pressures

Five aspects of CRS can be identified that have created commercial pressures and which will inevitably lead to regulation.

**Display bias** is the practice of programming the CRS to give the host airline's flights a superior position on the display screen, and in some respects can be described as anti-competitive. The display position of an airline's offering has considerable influence on the probability of its being chosen.

The **halo effect** is the tendency for travel agents to book flights on the CRS's parent rather than those of competing carriers, and is at the heart of the CRS debate.

**Code sharing** is another strategy that involves the integration of both the national airlines and regional airlines. These linkages are accomplished either through ownership or through the development of code-sharing agreements, whereby small airlines use the code letters of bigger partners and link up their flight schedules. While the ownership of a CRS is not a prerequisite for code-sharing agreements, its existence as a vehicle for implementing these arrangements generates advantages for both parties.

**Commission overrides** are extra commission paid to encourage travel agents to sell a particular airline's seats rather than those of another carrier. These incentives are over and above the base rate, and are rewarded to travel agents by airlines in return for an increase in volume or in market share.

**Market intelligence** provided by the CRS allows the tracking of travel patterns, market segments, and travel agent productivity. Not only can airlines use CRS to create new marketing programmes, they can also use the information to make critical strategic decisions, armed with statistical support. The success of these information-based strategies poses a serious threat to the competitive structure of the airline industry, particularly with respect to new entrants.

The primary concern for policy makers is the threat of monopoly abuses in both domestic and international travel markets.

Globalization

Because CRS revenue yields are declining even though booking volumes are increasing, the trend is towards mergers (Galileo International and Covia in 1992, for instance) largely for reasons of economies of scale, and to create a global operating base. In addition the operation of a one-site global data centre reduces its cost base significantly. The trend for mergers will continue, although it is expected that product availability will not improve.

Point-of-sale distribution

It has been estimated that the top ten travel agencies – most of whom specialize in corporate travel – account for 10 per cent of the total travel market. The attention of the CRS vendors is now fixed on working closely with their major customers, the multiple agencies. The trend is therefore clear: the CRS vendors' strategy is to secure loyalty through agreement with the major agencies. In addition, CRS policy towards product and service development favours their largest customers, and these technological advantages will slowly extend their dominance in both national and cross-border markets.

By the end of 1992, CRS vendors had achieved saturation in terms of penetrating business travel agents. The leisure travel market was the next development for the CRS vendors as they developed products aimed at increasing agency access and system usage. Currently in Europe non-business travel relies on Viewdata technology, thus generating enormous potential for penetration into the European leisure agencies. At present over half the total agency market – some 19,000 agencies – is equipped with Viewdata technology. Major equipment changes will have to be made in order to achieve the strategic move to CRS: CRS vendors will inevitably price competitively in the early years. Cross-selling strategies are becoming dominant in the European marketplace in order for the agencies to survive. This applies particularly to the sale of hotel accommodation and car rental.

Long-term developments are aimed at enhancing customer support and maximizing the agents' use of CRS as the primary travel booking tool. The trend is also towards contracting third-party systems developers to build the non-core CRS modules and specific user group requirements. For example, in the hotel sector, management companies will have the option to link into automated products tailored specifically for the European travel markets.

Market segmentation is another important development in the distribution network. The European vendors must develop their CRS technology to create a unique difference in the cost of servicing their agency customer base. This segmentation of the customer base will enable the European vendors to exploit their size fully and extend their share of the travel market. Clear product segmentation will enable more efficient targeting to the customer base and the squeezing of suppliers through better purchasing mechanisms. This will enable CRS vendors to put pressure on both the national chains and the less technologically advanced agents, thereby improving their margins while maintaining a competitive edge.

**The expansion of travel-related sales**

In developing hotel booking systems the basic theories of airline CRS have to be applied: the ability to deliver accurate, on-line information regarding availability, to ensure maximum yields and usage by agency staff. Paramount to the success of such systems is this ability to provide last-room and immediate guaranteed room availability as core functions. Reservation groups such as Utell International, with its Ultraswitch technology, are working closely with proprietary management systems companies to provide access to the hotels' booking database. The booking of hotels through a CRS at present represents 1 per cent of the total bookings. For business travel hotel bookings, this figure rises to 3 per cent. The pattern of technology usage in Europe and the USA is resulting in a mixture of hotel bookings that can be interfaced on all major CRS systems and national distribution systems. The major CRS vendors thus provide a communications network whereby other travel-related services can be interfaced and distributed on a global scale. The major problem, however, is the investment involved, which only attracts the international hotel chains. Equally, travel agents require the system to provide information on both domestic and international hotel chains, and to provide all aspects of the hotel tariff. For the development of sufficiently comprehensive databases, it is likely that the smaller companies will form alliances to provide travel agents with the appropriate products. As destination databases have been promoted as the appropriate information system to distribute and promote tourist information for both leisure and business markets, it is unlikely that the necessary funds will be raised to create the access required for these systems to be available on the core CRS, because of the necessary investment in more sophisticated systems and networking infrastructure.

## Future developments

The central issue for the CRS vendors in formulating their competitive strategy is in relating the individual system to the environment in which it operates. The state of competition in this particular industry can be related to Porter's five basic competitive forces. It is in focusing on this simple framework that the process of strategic planning can commence.

## The Environment

**Economic**

The declining business within Europe's airlines, linked to the desynchronization of economic growth between individual European countries, has had a significant impact on the CRS vendors' approach towards product development in the 1990s. On a wider basis, the world economies in 1994 were at different stages of the business cycle, with the USA, Canada and Australia well into the upturn, the UK, Italy and Japan experiencing gradual recovery, and much of continental Europe remaining in recession. By analysing key macroeconomic factors such as GDP, inflation rates, exchange rates and oil price movements, an indication of future demand for travel and hence for hotel accommodation can be determined, which will assist the CRS vendors in determining their competitive strategy.

Competitive/ regulatory

The general view within the travel trade is that CRS are not generating a satisfactory return on investment (perhaps moving into the mature stage of the product life cycle), and mergers and continued international alliances are therefore regarded by the vendors as the best option for cost containment. Worldwide, the advantages of CRS ownership are diminishing, largely as a result of government monitoring of costs and practices, which has resulted in the elimination of bias (both blatant and hidden). CRS ownership patterns in 1994 show that the systems are increasingly being regarded purely as distribution tools. Raising revenues from non-airline shareholders is now restricted by EU attention on competition policy in the CRS sector. This has brought about concern among the CRS vendors about achieving their long-term objectives, such as expanding their customer base through system enhancements, and improving their core services to increase the booking volumes on CRS. CRS vendors are expected to focus on their target markets by enhancing existing systems and providing more bespoke systems for specific markets, which in return will expand the customer base and increase booking volumes.

Financial

The change in European Union policy in the 1990s has affected the concept of a total travel booking management CRS in Europe. All development projects now have to be financially viable for the airline investors before agreements are made. Consequently, projects that are not beneficial to the majority of investors will not be funded by the CRS partner airlines, but may be funded by the national distribution companies. Airlines are therefore not in a position to fund system developments that are unlikely to cover costs. The core services will continue to be funded by the CRS vendors, but subsidiary services will not. However, the resources of the national distribution companies are unlikely to be adequate to develop the appropriate travel management products. This in turn is likely to diminish the appeal of CRS as a corporate booking tool. This **back-to-basics** approach conflicts with the initial objectives for the European CRS, based on providing travel agents with total travel management systems. The various market sectors will therefore probably develop distinctly different approaches towards CRS distribution.

Technological

Both Amadeus and Galileo introduced new back-office systems during 1993. Sabre's Travelbase back-office system was launched in Europe in January 1993, replacing its Agency Data System. Sabre is in a sense acting as a software developer for other systems such as Abacus. In the longer term, CRS vendors are modifying US systems for the European market. At present the major travel agencies are developing their own back-office systems, which meet their own specifications, and they are slow to take the back-office systems of the CRS vendors. Most corporate travel agencies with a sales turnover of over $9 million have some form of back-office system in place, but the majority are tailor made.

In-flight reservation services depend on a new generation of communication links involving the Inmarsat satellite. Most of the world's airlines are now committed to personal passenger communications systems in one way or another. The result will look rather like a PC screen in the aircraft seatback. Travellers of today and the future will be able to phone, fax and send data. For the future, passengers will have direct links into ground-based computer reservations systems, which will let them book or change tickets and hotel rooms from their seat.

In the near future, more CRS will begin to open up their information directly to customers, cutting the need for reservations to be made through travel agents. In the USA, Sabre has successfully introduced a PC-based on-line software package that gives travellers access to timetables and basic fare information. Galileo, too, is aiming to bring out a consumer application.

Each computerized CRS has a direct reference switch, which allows all providers to market their products to travel agencies and airlines. Now providers have to update each system individually. This is a very time-consuming process. With direct reference updating software, a hotel chain, for example, with a special offer for Easter, could enter all the information on one screen, and the updating software would automatically format it for each CRS and then transmit it. The use of the direct reference systems within a CRS is very important. A medium-sized German hotel chain recently had a connection to Sabre, and had been receiving approximately 500 reservations per month. They then started to use the direct reservations system daily to promote their hotel facilities and special offers. In the first month their reservations increased by over 80 per cent.

The evolution of CD-ROM technology has allowed the sale of travel-related products such as hotels by assisting the booking agent to sell the property more efficiently, because the property and its facilities can be shown to the customer. Two examples of this application can be seen at the hotel consortia Utell International and Best Western. Another example is the Reed-developed Jaguar system, now branded Sabrevision, which Sabre has now introduced in Europe. In its guise as a joint venture with Sabre, Jaguar seeks to function as a highly specific marketing tool, delivering pictures of hotels, cruise ships etc. and their facilities at the point of sale, at the same time as price and availability data are displayed. In the USA 5,000 of Sabre's 12,000 agencies are now linked to the product. Its potential application in the hotel industry is enormous, but until the cost of producing new discs drops dramatically, only the multiples and larger agency groups will be able to use this product as a strategic distribution and marketing tool.

The industry is also seeing the introduction of bar-coded directories connected to CRS, which will allow a travel agent to bar-code any hotel listed in such publications as the *ABTA World Guide*, and display on their computer screen all the details and booking conditions of that property. This approach will save time for the booking agent and does not require skilled staff in terms of knowledge.

## Concluding remarks

Apart from the CRS themselves, other service providers as well as third-party software suppliers are rushing to develop a range of applications. Pre-trip audit software, which continually checks already booked airline segments for cheaper fares available under the various airlines' yield management systems, is an interesting example. More significant is the development of integrated multi-media databases by major publishers or tour operators, in cooperation with the CRS companies.

Today, CRS is in a sense the tail wagging the dog because it has a tremendous effect on the travel industry's competitive structure, and will play an important role in the evolution of an increasingly international hospitality industry.

The future will revolve around the three R's of regulation, rationalization, and reorganization: **regulation** in that the power of today's CRS to control the international airline industry's sales and distribution process presents tremendous opportunities as well as serious problems for major airlines, travel tourism marketing intermediaries and government policy makers; **rationalization** so as to address the policies of fair competition, equal opportunities for small airlines, and the provision of services; and **reorganization** of the CRS industry and the airline industry in terms of international alliances. The battle to convert international agencies to a particular CRS is now at the forefront of the strategic development of the airline industry.

## OPERATING ENVIRONMENT

The operating environment, also called the **competitive** or **task environment**, comprises factors in the competitive situation that affect a firm's success in acquiring needed resources or in profitably marketing its goods and services. Among the most important of these factors are the firm's competitive position, the composition of its customers, its reputation among suppliers and creditors and its ability to attract capable employees. The operating environment is typically much more subject to a firm's influence or control than the general or industry environment. Thus firms can be much more proactive in dealing with the operating environment than with their general or industry environment.

### Competitive position

Assessing its competitive position improves a firm's chances of designing strategies that optimize its environmental opportunities. Development of competitor profiles enables a firm to forecast more accurately both short-term and long-term growth and its profit potential. Although the exact criteria used in constructing a competitor profile are largely determined by situational factors, a number of criteria can be identified, such as market share, brand or product line, effectiveness of sales, and distribution. Once appropriate criteria have been selected, there are ways to reflect their importance to a firm's success. Then the competitor being evaluated is rated on the criteria, and the ratings are multiplied by a weighting. The weighted scores are summed to yield a numerical profile of a competitor. This type of competitor profile is limited by the subjectivity of its criteria selection, weighting and evaluation approaches. Nevertheless, the process of developing such profiles is of considerable help to a firm in defining its perception of its competitive position. Moreover, comparing the firm's profile with those of its competitors can aid its managers in identifying factors that might make the competitors vulnerable to strategies that the firm might choose to implement.

## Customer profile

Perhaps the most valuable result of analysing the operating environment is the understanding of a firm's customers that this exercise provides. Developing a profile of a firm's present and prospective customers improves the ability of its managers to plan strategic operations, to anticipate changes in the size of markets and to reallocate resources so as to support forecast shifts in demand patterns. The principal types of information used in constructing customer profiles are geographic, demographic, psychographic and buyer behaviour. It is important to define the **geographic** area from which customers do or could come. Almost every product or service has some quality that makes it more or less attractive to customers from different locations. **Demographic** variables are most commonly used to differentiate groups of present or potential customers. Demographic information is comparatively easy to collect, quantify and use in strategic forecasting, and such information is the minimum basis for a customer profile. Personality and lifestyle variables are often better predictors of customer purchasing behaviour than geographic or demographic variables. In such situations, the **psychographic** study is an important component of the customer profile. **Buyer behaviour** data can also be a component. Such data are used to explain or predict some aspect of customer behaviour with regard to a product or service. Information on buyer behaviour can be a significant aid in the design of more accurate and profitable strategies.

## Suppliers

Dependable relationships between a firm and its suppliers and creditors are essential to the firm's long-term survival and growth. A firm regularly relies on its suppliers and creditors for financial support, services, materials and equipment. In addition, it is occasionally forced to make special requests for such favours as quick delivery, liberal credit terms or part orders. Particularly at such times, it is essential for a firm to have an ongoing relationship with its suppliers and creditors. In addressing this topic a firm will be able to forecast the availability of the resources that it will need to implement and sustain its competitive strategies. Assessment of suppliers and creditors is critical to an accurate evaluation of the firm's operating environment.

## Employees

A firm's ability to attract and hold capable employees is essential to its success. However a firm's personnel recruitment and selection alternatives are often influenced by the nature of its operating environment. A firm's access to the required personnel is affected primarily by three factors:

• the firm's reputation as an employer;
• local employment rates; and
• the ready availability of people with the required skills.

A firm is more likely to attract and retain valuable employees if it is seen as established in the community, competitive in its compensation package and concerned with the welfare of its employees. It is also important that it is respected for its product or service and appreciated for its overall contribution to the general welfare of the community. The skills of some people are so specialized that relocation may be necessary to secure the jobs and the compensation that those skills commonly command. A firm that seeks to hire such a person is said to have a broad labour market boundary: that is, the geographic area within which the firm might reasonably expect to attract qualified candidates is quite large. Conversely, people with more common skills are less likely to relocate from a considerable distance in order to achieve modest economic or career advancements. Thus the labour market boundaries are fairly limited for such occupational groups as unskilled labourers, clerical personnel or retail clerks.

## Organizational structure

Firms can make contacts with their environment at several points and at several organizational levels. At each of these contact points environmental interactions must be managed. It is through these interactions that the firm is able to get new information and resources, fulfil stakeholder demands and build a corporate image. Environmental contacts can serve as important sources of strategic information for the firm. This information can help in critical tasks by providing ideas for new products, marketing strategies, improvement in production techniques and efficient management of materials and inventories. Management of the organization–environment interaction begins at the top.

Having set the scene in terms of the environment in which the firm operates two key issues to be addressed are the organization's mission statement and the establishment of corporate objectives.

## MISSION STATEMENTS: AN INTRODUCTION

It is important to distinguish between the idea of a broad purpose and specific measurable milestones. The firm needs direction in terms of where a strategic leader wants it to go and how he or she would wish it to develop: hence the need for a mission for the firm – a visionary statement concerning the future. The mission is likely to be stated broadly and generally, and it is unlikely that it can ever be achieved completely. Thus the firm pursues the mission looking for new opportunities, dealing with problems and seeking to progress continually in its chosen direction. Improvements in the overall situation towards the stated mission are the appropriate measure of performance. Managers at all levels are likely to be set specific objectives, and to achieve them they should have quantifiable targets for sales, profit, productivity or output in performance. It is against these targets that managers are measured and evaluated. Objectives then become measurable points that indicate how the firm is making definite progress towards its broad purpose or mission. Strategies are developed from the mission and objectives, so a change of objectives is likely to result in changes of strategy.

Mission can be defined as the essential purpose of the firm concerning particularly why it is in existence, the nature of the businesses it is in, and the customers that it seeks to serve and satisfy. Following on from this, objectives can be defined as desired states or results linked to particular timescales and concerning such things as size or type of organization, the nature and variety of the areas of interest, and the levels of success. The expression **aims** is sometimes used as an alternative to mission. The term **goals** is usually regarded as synonymous with objectives, and it is important to distinguish between long-term and short-term objectives. The long-term objectives of a firm relate to the desired performance and results on an ongoing basis; short-term objectives are concerned with the near-term performance targets.

### Whose purpose does the firm serve?

A sense of mission is more than a definition of the business: it identifies the area that a firm is to operate in. A sense of mission can to some extent be distinguished from the ideas behind the words 'vision' or 'strategic' intent. The word 'vision' is usually taken to mean a picture of a future state of a firm: a mental image of a possible and desired future that is realistic, credible and attractive. A mission is a way of behaving, and is concerned with the way a firm is managed today, with its purpose or reason for being. Strategic intent is a desired leadership position, and therefore is a desired future state, a goal to do with winning. Mission is to do with here-and-now purpose, the culture and the business philosophy.

In determining corporate purpose the firm must answer the fundamental question as to whose purpose does the firm serve. Business corporations today serve many stakeholders and pursue a complex set of objectives. Complexity arises because firms have to fulfil the expectations of many stakeholders simultaneously. Some of these stakeholders have conflicting demands and yet none of the stakeholders has absolute power to impose their will. Firms are obliged to pursue purposes that at least minimally satisfy the diverse demands of these stakeholders. Organizational purpose should therefore reflect an acceptable balance between the conflicting objectives of these different stakeholders.

## Creating the mission

Corporate missions represent the broadest statements of the firm's vision and philosophy. They are general statements of what the firm stands for, its core values and responsibilities towards its stakeholders. Mission statements may also state the general domain of business operations. They describe the firm's relationship to its external environment, and establish the basic identity of the firm for its external stakeholders. Being broad and general statements, corporate missions are only direction-setting guidelines. They serve as the conscience of the corporation and a statement of values. They do not provide operational guidance for strategy formulation but they can still direct and focus corporate efforts. An example is given in Table 2.1.

**Table 2.1  A mission statement for one Forte hotel**

- To maintain our position as the most profitable provincial hotel in the company based on profit per room.
- To lead the Forte brand initiative by taking advantage of our opportunity to capitalize on a prime location.
- To improve our reputation as employers through improved living and working conditions and promotional opportunities.
- To respond to increased demands of clientele in terms of improved standards of accommodation, food and beverage and meeting facilities. To improve standards of service and hospitality.

Mission statements serve the important symbolic function of providing the firm's members with a vision for the future. Another symbolic function that they serve is to provide the cultural glue that holds the firm together as a unified entity, as dynamic visions of the direction in which the firm hopes to move. They provide a general sense of the path that the firm will take in the coming years to reach a desired state. A mission can be described as consisting of three components:

- An inspirational definition of what the firm exists for. For some firms the purpose is to make money for shareholders, and this is what clearly drives the behaviour of the firm. Other firms have the purpose of satisfying all their stakeholders: shareholders, employees, customers, suppliers and the community.
- The firm's strategy. This defines the area in which the firm is to operate, the rationale for its operation, the source of competitive advantage it is going to tap, the distinctive competence it is going to provide, and the special position it is going to occupy.
- The policies and behaviour standards defining how managers and employees should behave. These are part of the firm's way of doing business: the beliefs that constitute the firm's culture and underpin its management style.

People do things in organizations because there is a strategic logic and because there are moral and value-based reasons for doing so. A strong sense of mission comes about when personal and organizational values match, and when the three elements just identified are closely knitted together: that is, when they support and reinforce each other. A sense of mission is important because it generates trust and belief in the activities of the organization; it gives meaning to work, motivates people and brings about consensus and loyalty. It provides the basis for making quick judgemental decisions without having to review things from basics or exchange a great deal of information. Just as our own individual philosophy evolves over time, so do corporate missions. However, corporate missions are developed in a more explicit manner than an individual's philosophy and they are documented to simplify sharing among organizational members. Missions are a function of the firm's history and its vision of the future. To develop credible and meaningful missions that actually guide the firm and are not simply public relations statements it is critical to mould the firm's history within its mission. Corporate missions must show how historical values and business operations are to be transformed into future values and operations. Six steps can be identified in the development of mission statements:

1 Analyse historical missions, values and business operations and practices. Assess their adequacy and suitability in the light of environmental and industry trends.
2 Consult organizational stakeholders about directions the firm should take. Identify commonalities and differences among stakeholder demands.

3 Resolve conflicting demands through discussions with relevant stakeholders or by making judgements that balance competing demands. Rank demands to give them relative importance with respect to each other.

4 Describe the firm's values, guiding philosophy, business domains and its role in society in a way that key stakeholder demands are fulfilled. Describe what general business directions the firm intends to take.

5 Share the draft mission statement with key managers and stakeholders. Seek feedback and make modifications.

6 Discuss the mission statement with all members of the firm and explain how it should be used for strategy making and strategy guiding operations.

If produced correctly, a mission statement can last the organization many years. Occasionally, however, it may be necessary to revise a mission statement or to create a new one. When a mission statement loses its motivational value and becomes merely a rhetorical phrase, or when the mission encapsulated in a given statement is accomplished, it may be time to consider creating a new one. Revising an outdated mission can help a firm to regain its vitality. Reframing the mission can help it to rediscover its core values, its essential purpose and the rationale for its existence.

## The paradox of mission statements

People in an organization find themselves pulled in two opposing directions with respect to mission statements: one force pulls them to conformity and consensus and the other to individuality and difference.

The first pull leads people to develop a common set of beliefs or a mission for their organization. The second pull leads them to pay lip service to that common mission or to try to undermine it or to change it. The tension that this creates is the source of the dynamics of organizational behaviour, and can be one of the principal sources of both change and anxiety in organizations. There is in this respect a conflict between the needs of healthy individuals and the demands of a formal organization. Chains of command and task specialization require people to be passive; independent but psychologically mature individuals seek to be individual and different. This conflict can lead to frustration, hostility and rivalry, and to a focus on a part of the organization rather than the whole, as well as a focus on short-term objectives. To adapt, individuals develop defence routines, which then feed back into the organization and reinforce the adverse affects.

There will often be a difference between the espoused mission of a group of people and the mission in use. The espoused mission will be very general, so that it has more chance of commanding widespread support and not conflicting with individual desires. It will be general enough to encompass a great many of the more specific missions that will actually be driving behaviour. The more effective we are in creating a sense of mission, the more likely we are to arouse the individual to be different, to explore the new. Missions that are specific enough to drive behaviour are therefore inherently precarious. The more the mission articulates timelessness, the vague and the general, the more likely it is to last, but then the more it is likely to be espoused rather than be in use. The more a firm succeeds in perpetuating a given mission in use the more difficult it is for the firm to change.

There is no quick and easy way to change the culture, to foster a sense of mission within a firm. It is something that emerges slowly from the way people work together. Top managers may therefore be able to encourage specific thrusts around some clearly focused issues, such as those to do with customer care.

## FORMULATING OBJECTIVES

Following on from formulating the mission statement, corporate objectives provide the foundation for developing specific corporate and business strategic plans. While the company mission can be seen as encompassing the broad aims of the firm, objectives sum up the general sentiments of the mission statement and convert it into guidelines for decision making. Corporate objectives are also used to improve organizational performance and as a standard to measure that performance. The mission gives a general sense of direction but does not provide specific benchmarks for evaluating the firm's progress in achieving its aims; providing such benchmarks is the function of objectives. Corporate objectives describe what the firm wants to achieve in its various business areas. They describe the business portfolio of the firm in terms of specific products, markets and technologies, and explain what role different business units play in the total corporate portfolio. They show the direction in which the portfolio will change in the future, what product markets the firm hopes to enter and exit, what technologies it hopes to develop, and what levels of risk it will take. Corporate objectives describe the level of technological innovation, productivity and financial performance that the firm will seek over a five- to ten-year horizon in different areas of operation. This time horizon may vary from industry to industry depending on products and technologies. An acceptable level of corporate performance may be stated as profitability, return on investment, market penetration, market share, employee performance or social performance standards. Besides providing specific operational guidance, objectives are also useful for evaluating strategic performance. Effectiveness in this respect means how well a firm meets its own objectives. Judging the effectiveness of the firm and its strategy can be simplified if its objectives are stated in a clear and concise form.

## Developing corporate objectives

One approach to generating corporate objectives involves systematically assessing the potential of business units and divisions and setting feasible performance standards for them. This can proceed by refining the environmental assessments done for generating mission statements through identifying more specific trends, opportunities and threats. Assessment should be combined with an analysis of historical objectives to generate specific corporate objectives that reflect the core ideas of the organizational mission. Objectives should be stated in specific terms and provide directional guidance to planners and line managers. Objectives are normally set within the context of the planning process; they are an integral part of strategic planning and the decision-making process of the organization.

Business unit managers are the best starting point for generating objectives for their respective business areas. It is desirable to set objectives in terms of measures that are already in use in the firm's budgeting, strategic planning and accounting systems. Business managers' estimates of objectives must be reviewed and reconciled at the corporate level to ensure that they are mutually compatible and that they jointly meet the firm's complete objectives.

## Long-term objectives

To achieve long-term prosperity, strategic planners commonly establish long-term objectives in seven areas:

- **Profitability**. The ability of any firm to operate in the long run depends on its attaining an acceptable level of profits. Strategically managed firms characteristically have a profit objective, usually expressed in earnings per share or return on equity.
- **Productivity**. Strategic managers constantly try to improve the productivity of their systems. Firms that can improve their input/output relationship normally increase profitability; thus firms usually state an objective for productivity. Productivity objectives are sometimes stated in terms of desired cost decreases.
- **Competitive position**. One measure of corporate success is relative dominance in the marketplace. Larger firms often establish an objective in terms of competitive position, often using total sales or market share

as measures of their competitive position. An objective with regard to competitive position may indicate a firm's long-term priorities.

- **Employee development**. Employees value growth and career opportunities, and providing such opportunities often increases productivity and decreases staff turnover. Therefore strategic decision makers frequently include employee development objectives in their long-range plans.
- **Employee relations**. Whether or not they are bound by union contracts, firms actively seek good employee relations, and proactive steps in anticipating the needs and expectations of employees are a characteristic concern of strategic managers. Productivity is linked to employee loyalty and perceived management interest, which is in turn in the interests of workers' welfare. Managers therefore set objectives to improve employee relations.
- **Technological leadership**. Firms must decide whether to lead or follow in the marketplace, as either approach can be successful, but each requires a different strategic posture. Therefore firms may state an objective with regard to technological leadership.
- **Public responsibility**. Firms recognize their responsibilities to their customers and to society at large, and many firms seek to exceed the demands made by government. They work, not only to develop reputations for fairly priced products and services, but also to establish themselves as responsible corporate citizens within the wider community.

## Qualities of long-term objectives

What distinguishes a good objective from a bad one can be determined in relation to seven characteristics:

- **Acceptable**. Managers are most likely to pursue objectives that are consistent with their preferences. They may ignore or even obstruct the achievement of objectives that offend them, or which they believe to be inappropriate or unfair. In addition, long-term corporate objectives are frequently designed to be acceptable to groups external to the firm.
- **Flexible**. Objectives should be adaptable to unforeseen or extraordinary changes in the firm's competitive or environmental forecasts. However, such flexibility is usually increased at the expense of specificity. Moreover, employee confidence may be tempered because adjustment of flexible objectives may affect their jobs. One way of providing flexibility while minimizing its negative effects is to allow for adjustments in the level rather than in the nature of objectives.
- **Measurable**. Objectives must clearly and concisely state what will be achieved and when it will be achieved. Thus objectives should be measurable over time.

- **Motivating**. Studies have shown that people are most productive when objectives are set at a motivating level: one that is high enough to challenge but not so high as to frustrate or so low as to be easily attained. The problem is that individuals and groups differ in their perceptions of what is high enough. A broad objective that challenges one group, frustrates another and minimally interests a third can obviously create problems within the firm. One valuable aspect is that objectives should be tailored to specific groups.
- **Suitable**. Objectives must be suited to the broad aims of the firm, which are expressed in its mission statement. Each objective should be a step towards the attainment of overall objectives contained within the mission statement.
- **Understandable**. Strategic managers at all levels must understand what is to be achieved, and must also understand the major criteria by which their performance will be evaluated. Thus objectives must be stated so that they are as understandable to the recipient as they are to the giver. Objectives must be clear, meaningful and unambiguous.
- **Achievable**. Objectives must be possible to achieve, which is easier said than done. Turbulence in the remote and operating environments affects a firm's internal operations, creating uncertainty and limiting the accuracy of the objectives set by strategic management.

## Process

Mission and objectives commit the firm to pursue certain courses of action and limit it from pursuing others. The entire process of formulating the statements of organizational purpose should therefore be designed to make these choices realistic and participative.

Realism

In establishing organizational objectives there is a natural tendency to either overestimate or underestimate what is feasible. The tendency to overestimate comes through performance pressure from top managers. However, line managers who have at least as good an understanding as top management of what is feasible may be affected by this pressure tactic. They may react by subtly sabotaging the whole direction-setting process, making it a meaningless ritual for the organization. On the other hand, the tendency to underestimate objectives arises from lack of good information about what is feasible. In such a case, achievement of objectives will be completed each year and will fail to challenge either performance or improvements within the organization. Both these tendencies are counter-productive and should be avoided.

Formulation of objectives should aim to be realistic and fundamentally truthful, and managers must believe in the authenticity of the process.

While managers realize that guessing and estimating are an integral part of setting a direction, they should also be able to see the estimating element as an unavoidable part of the process because of the firm's inability to predict the future. Estimating should not be a reckless and arbitrary process. The marginal benefits to be gained by underestimating or overestimating objectives are not worth the risks they pose to the credibility of the entire direction-setting process.

Participation

The process of setting objectives that an organization adopts depends on the degree of centralization in decision making. The more centralized an organization is, the less participative this process is likely to be, and vice versa. Organizations that are too centralized need to make special efforts to open up the process to increased participation. In a top-down objective-setting approach, objectives are dictated by top management or even by the managing director. This type of process is quick and decisive, and confines organizational intentions to only a few people. However, such an autocratic top-down process has several drawbacks: it does not consider the cumulative learning and expertise of the entire organization, and it can be demotivating to the many managers who will eventually be involved in implementing the objectives. In the **bottom-up** process, lower-level managers are actively involved in setting objectives and in deciding what is feasible. However, this approach will skew the process towards a narrow departmental or divisional vision of units, and perhaps will ignore the wider company issues. A balanced process uses both the top-down and bottom-up approaches, although approval usually comes from top management, and final ratification is made by the board of directors.

Stakeholders

An important issue for the firm to consider is that stakeholders have a legitimate demand on the organization, and their views should be incorporated into the objective-setting approach. Some representative input from key shareholders and employees or unions is desirable. Another category is the more distant stakeholders such as the public, the media, communities or business associates, who also can make a valuable input. It is therefore important that a mechanism is implemented for eliciting the opinions of these stakeholders on the direction of the firm. Often different stakeholders will place conflicting demands on the firm. Resolving such conflicts while keeping the firm moving forward on some common ground represents a challenge for top management. In this sense, identifying the common ground between stakeholders is at the heart of resolving such conflicts. In most conflicts there is a common ground that can be identified as a basis for creating a compromise. Ultimate responsibility for setting acceptable objectives lies with top management. Even after making their best efforts at reaching a compromise there may still be instances of conflict, which may mean that some objectives cannot be pursued and others will receive low priority. By creating a priority scheme for objectives, managers can accommodate more objectives on the organizational agenda.

**SUMMARY**

This chapter provided the groundwork for the strategic planning process and set that process within the context of four questions: Where are we now? Where do we want to be? How are we going to get there? Where do we start? In discussing the usefulness of simple strategic frameworks this chapter identified the starting point to commence the strategic planning process.

After giving a definition of strategic planning, the discussion then progressed to an analysis of the environment within which the firm operates. Three aspects of the environment were identified: general, industry and operational. A range of techniques were also discussed in terms of this environmental analysis. Within this discussion, focus was placed on the industry environment, and on Porter's model of techniques for analysing industries and competitors. It was in this respect that it was shown how competitive forces shape strategy and have implications for the strategic planning process. Having discussed the issue of environmental analysis, the chapter laid a basis at the end for discussing mission statements and formulation of company objectives.

**FURTHER READING**

Abrahams, G 1990 EC airs its reservations over booking systems, *Financial Times*, 5 October

Archdale, G 1990 Computer reservation systems – the international scene, *Insights*, English Tourist Board, November, D18–D24

Bertelsen, J 1990 Asian Airlines fret over new treat: US computer reservation systems, *Wall Street Journal*, 22 January, B7A

Boberg, K B and F M Collision 1985 Computer reservations systems and airline competition, *Tourism Management*, **6**(3) 174–83

Copeland, D G 1990 So you want to build the next SABRE?, *Business Quarterly* **55**(3), 56–60

Feldman, J 1987 Regional airlines in the USA, *Travel and Tourism Analyst*, May, 15–18

Feltenstein, T 1992 Strategic planning for the 1990s, *The Cornell Hotel Restaurant Association Quarterly* **33**(3), 50–4

Fender, D J W 1990 Getting started: the use of simple strategic frameworks, *International Journal of Contemporary Hospitality Management* **2**(3), iv–vi

Forte, R 1990 Responding to the competitive challenge of the 1990s, *International Journal of Contemporary Hospitality Management* **3**(3), i–iv

Gamble, P R 1990 Developing an information technology strategy for hospitality organizations, *International Journal of Contemporary Hospitality Management*, Conference, Strategic developments for the 1990s, Vol 1, 3–4 May 1990, Dorset Institute, Poole, UK, pp. 29–41

Gilbert, D C and R Kapur 1990 Strategic marketing planning in the hotel industry, *International Journal of Hospitality Management* **9**(1) 27–43

Goodwin, N 1989 Global connections, *Travel Weekly's Focus on Automation*, 7 September, 7

Green, D 1992 Airline ticket shops bridge the Atlantic, *Financial Times*, 9 March

Hewson, D 1993 Galileo will get you there, *The Sunday Times Business Travel*, 21 November

Jordan, B 1989 Amadeus gains capacity, *Airline Executive*, October, 6

Lyle, C 1988 Computer-age in the international airline industry, *Journal of Air Law and Commerce* **54**(1), 162

Markillie, P 1993 Survey of airlines (6): By the seats of their pants – the handful of dollars will make or break the industry, *The Economist*, 12 June, 12

O'Brien, K 1993 *The Western European business travel market 1993–1997*, London: Financial Times Business Information, pp. 29–42

Odell, M 1993 Rules and reservations, *Airline Business*, August, 34–7

Porter, M E 1980 *Competitive strategy: Techniques for analysing industries and competitors*, New York: Free Press

Porter, M E 1985 *Competitive advantage: Creating and sustaining superior performance*, New York: Free Press

Prince of Wales Business Leaders Forum 1993 *Environmental management for hotels: the industry guide to best practice*, London: Butterworth-Heinemann

Proctor, P 1988 House members call for tighter regulations of reservations systems, *Aviation Week and Space Technology*, 19 September, 123

Truitt, J L, V B Teye and M T Farris 1991 The role of computer reservations systems, *Tourism Management*, March, 21–36

Tse, E C and C M Elwood 1990 Synthesis of the life cycle concept with strategy and management style: a case analysis in the hospitality industry, *International Journal of Hospitality Management*, **9**(3), 223–36

Wardell, D 1987 Airline reservations systems in the USA, *Travel and Tourism Analyst*, January, 45–56

West, J J 1990 Strategy environmental scanning and firm performance: an integration of content and process in the food service industry, *Hospitality Research Journal*, **14**(1), 87–100

# CHAPTER 3

# Strategic management in the hospitality industry

After reading this chapter you should be able to:
- Identify elements of the environment in which a hospitality firm operates and relate them to operational trends within the US hotel industry.
- Identify the determinants of global expansion in the hotel industry
- Apply the elements of the strategic management process to the wider leisure industry, including specifically the UK brewing and drinks industry, and European leisure theme parks.

## BACKGROUND

Strategy is often referred to the **art of the general**, as the term appeared first in military literature. This suggests that an organization will make decisions about resource allocation according to some predetermined plan of action. Strategy also implies that if an organization is to be successful, then there must be a match between the environment in which it functions day to day, the competitive methods that it employs to take advantage of the threats and opportunities in that environment, and the way it is organized internally. Without this match it is difficult to achieve long-term success. The important questions in relating these issues to hospitality firms are: Will they be able to achieve the necessary match? Will the environment support planned growth? Will the methods chosen to fuel growth and control quality be successful?

## THE GROWTH OF HOTEL GROUPS

### A theoretical analysis

The strategic implementation of a hospitality firm's expansion, particularly growth, is a complex process involving the understanding and utilization of many factors. For example, the growth of hotel groups can be explained by the potential advantages of size. These advantages, more accurately defined as **economies of scale**, take several different forms:

- **Financial economies** enable the group to raise finance internally and borrow on better terms.
- **Managerial economies** derive from the fact that administration costs do not necessarily increase in line with the volume of business, as in the use of centralized room bookings, for example.
- **Technical economies** are also associated with the benefits of centralization: for example, the provision of services such as laundry and maintenance from the centre to individual units.

Moreover, significant economies of scale can be derived from **risk spreading**, which enables groups to offset losses in one area against profits in another – a very important consideration in an industry characterized by uncertainty, seasonality, and multiple target markets. Additionally, there are **purchasing economies** to be achieved from the ability of groups to buy supplies in bulk and negotiate favourable terms. Finally, groups can benefit from **marketing economies** that offer the opportunity to create a recognizable group image in the market and promote it jointly, thereby increasing consumer awareness as well as reducing costs.

Economies of scale, coupled with the need to expand into key markets around the world, have been, in part, the cause of recent mergers and acquisitions of hotel companies. As a result of that trend, the international hospitality sector is evolving towards a new pattern of industrial concentration in which the global market is dominated by a small group of large hotel companies.

## Determinants of global expansion

The choice of region to expand into reflects the individual objectives of the firm, in either:

- locating to a region with an established demand; or
- locating in an area that will experience growth in demand in the future.

The next determinant of global expansion is the firm's ability either to raise the appropriate capital, which is difficult in recession, or to select an appropriate growth medium, such as acquisition, management contracts or franchising, topics that will be considered in later chapters of this book.

The major hotel corporations have been looking increasingly to Europe, North America (which between them receive three-quarters of all international tourist arrivals) and the Asia Pacific region (where the tourism market is growing rapidly) to expand their chains and maintain profit growth. Starting with the takeover of Inter-Continental by Grand Metropolitan in 1981 (subsequently sold to the Japanese company Siebu Saison), and Hilton International by Ladbroke plc in 1987, mergers have increased in frequency and magnitude. The international hotel industry, as far as chains and brands are concerned, has typically been dominated by the USA. However, in recent years two changes have occurred:

- European, and especially British and French, hotel interests have been playing an ever more important part, and now control some of the best-known chains and brands in the world.
- The emergent economic power of the Asia Pacific region is beginning to influence the international hotel scene.

The geographical distribution of the major corporate hotel chains is very concentrated. The USA, UK and France together account for 75.1 per cent of the total number of rooms controlled by the top 200 corporate chains around the world.

## Motivations for expansion

Hotel firms have traditionally been keen to expand overseas for a number of reasons. In addition to the obvious search for new markets as a prime route for growth, there is a need to expand profitability in areas that promise high revenue, and the perceived need to exploit differences in the business cycle in different areas of the world as an insurance policy against recession in the major markets. At present, the prevailing attitude among international companies is that in order to become successful, a hotel company has three basic options:

- to become global through greater market coverage, both geographically and by segment;
- to create a focused approach to a particular national or regional market; or
- to fill a well-defined niche in the marketplace.

These three approaches are not mutually exclusive. It is perfectly possible for a company such as Accor to seek to develop a global network of budget hotels: a strategy that simultaneously meets at least two of the above criteria. By contrast, the Canadian-based company Four Seasons Hotels aims for just one segment: the up-market business traveller. Primarily located in North America, Four Seasons Hotels limits its geographic dispersion to major cities, and specializes in the operation of medium-sized properties from 200 to 400 rooms. The premise of this strategy is to serve this particular target market better or more efficiently than its more broadly positioned competitors.

## Patterns of growth

For many hotel companies the key to prosperity in the current industry environment is growth. With the location-specific nature of the hotel industry, growth translates into greater market coverage, increased visibility, and greater opportunities for cross-destination marketing, in addition to the benefits of economies of scale and scope. Therefore hotel companies continue to seek new ways to increase their market share. The pattern of growth of hotel groups is a major determinant both of chain size and of prospects for further expansion. There are three basic forms through which a hotel company can develop:

• acquisition;
• management contracts;
• franchising.

But as groups expand, so the patterns of growth become more complex, causing the emergence of combinations of the above forms, as well as new ones such as sale and leaseback and joint ventures. A combination of affiliations increases organizational complexity but allows for more rapid expansion.

Global expansion, however, relies not just on the need to achieve international growth but on the examination of other criteria. Failure to understand these factors will result in expansion that will have risks that outweigh the possible rewards. Thus in order to assess the feasibility of expansion, the hotel chain has to find a receptive region in which to locate and then find a suitable growth medium that will achieve the growth objectives and maximize financial return.

The next part of this chapter will focus in depth on the hotel environment of the USA, as it is the most mature market and has the largest involvement in global expansion. This section will be an examination of the environment within which hospitality firms operate coupled with the trading patterns within the USA, which will give an insight into the pressures on hotel chains to go for global growth. It is these pressures that are the main determinants of global expansion.

## THE US HOTEL MARKET

### The events of the 1980s and early 1990s

The 1980s were truly a golden age for the US hotel industry. During this period approximately 7,000 hotels with 900,000 rooms were constructed. This growth was fuelled by favourable tax laws, which allowed investors to depreciate their investments rapidly. Development was also encouraged by the ease of access to capital. Savings and loans organizations, banks, institutional investors and brokers of junk bonds all succumbed to speculation, and invested or lent money for hotel properties. This boom in US hotel construction was fuelled by an inflation-driven real estate market, increased demand resulting from the maturing of the baby boom generation, intensified pressure for earnings by the capital market community, and a growing world economy. However, all this came to an abrupt end when the USA and global economies entered a period of significant economic recession in 1990–93, creating a situation of oversupply and high market saturation. Supply quickly began to outstrip demand.

Nethertheless, throughout this growth period, the guiding principle of most hotel developers was to find a market that was ripe for development and then build, and if the market began to look mature, then create a niche or brand. Unfortunately, senior management failed to give attention to several extremely important events developing in the US business environment.

- First, demographic trends, if realistically considered, could not support the additional supply coming on line.
- Second, the US Congress had been talking for some years about changes in the tax laws, and in 1986 this happened, taking away the favourable environment in which hotels had been considered as real estate investments and not as business ventures.
- Last, the savings and loans crisis, coupled with major restructuring of South American loans, caused the previously free-flowing funds to dry up.

No longer able to generate growth in attracting large amounts of capital, the hotel firms began to face the financial and business realities of the day. This reduced investment continued to drag down the industry's performance, and the Gulf War in 1991 brought the crisis to a head. This was exemplified by the fact that new hotel construction declined by 46 per cent in 1992. US occupancy rates in 1991 were at a low of 60.2 per cent, but in 1992 moved up slightly to 61.7 per cent, a trend that continued in 1993. This supply and demand disparity also resulted in deep price discounts for rooms, lowering overall average achieved room rates. It was only in 1993 that average room rates increased, rising by 1.3 per cent. This marginally positive performance was the first encouraging movement. However, despite this slightly positive sign it will be a while before the industry will reach occupancy levels of 65 per cent, generally believed to be necessary to generate viable earning levels. Faced with an increasingly hostile domestic environment, American hotel chains were faced with the choice of locating in progressively marginal domestic locations or expanding into the global market.

## Foreign investment in the US hotel industry

Because of the deteriorating conditions in the USA, several major US-based chains began to look to the global marketplace for capital and growth. Also, many foreign firms had began to acquire hotel assets in the USA. For example, in the late 1980s Westin was acquired by Aoki, Holiday Inn was acquired by Bass, Ramada was divided up by New World, and Four Seasons joined forces with Regent International. This foreign investment in the US hotel industry was possible because of favourable exchange rates, the lower cost of capital in the home country and, especially in the late 1980s, the lower average selling price per room, which had dropped from $20,713 in 1987 to $16,894 in 1992.

## Supply and market saturation

One method of classifying the hotel industry is into four general markets: luxury, quality, moderate and budget. For each segment, it can be argued, there are established US companies. For example:

- the luxury market is represented by Four Seasons,
- the quality segment by Marriott,
- the moderate by Holiday Inn core brand, and
- the budget by Motel 6.

Thus it is established that hotel chains operate within a submarket of the entire hotel demand. This situation makes each firm responsive to the circumstances of its own market rather than the total market. With this understanding, each firm has its own segment and can further specialize to maintain a competitive advantage. In the US hotel market of the 1980s finding an extra niche market was relatively easy; however, this is no longer possible in the 1990s because of the degree of market saturation and the imbalance of supply and demand.

The alternative is that instead of specializing, US companies have been diversifying into other segments. Evidence of diversification into more up-market segments can be seen in Holiday Inn's Crown Plaza, Ramada's Renaissance concept and Choice International's expansion of its Royale concept.

At the same time, established up-market companies are diversifying down-market, with Marriott introducing the Courtyard concept and Choice International establishing the Comfort Inns during the 1980s.

This situation certainly reflects saturation, but the move into different segments mainly in the mid-1980s was based on very uncertain growth rates. A poor understanding of the environment was inevitable with so many conflicting opinions. Unfortunately for Marriot and other operators, the future held excess capacity and the inevitable consequence of reduced room rate earnings. This misinterpretation of the environment was further compounded by two factors:

- First, there was a false belief that the hotel chains could weather recession, and even keep occupancy above 70 per cent, as they did in the mild depression of the early 1980s.
- The second mistake was to account only for the positive aspects of the baby boom. Marriott saw the potential of this segment and expanded accordingly. What they failed to account for was the huge decline in this segment in the 1990s and the inevitable consequence of increased market saturation.

With 3 million rooms in 1992, the US hotel industry is the biggest and most concentrated in the world. The US market also has the twin characteristics of explicit branding and segmentation around the hotel companies' brands. Because of the wide use of management contracts and franchising, US companies only consolidate a small proportion of their hotel receipts. In the case of management contracts the fee structure is typically based on 3 per cent of turnover and 10 per cent of gross operating profit. In franchising the fee is typically 4 per cent of rooms turnover. This means that hotel company profits are much smaller in the USA than in the UK.

## Demand

The important feature of the hotel market in the USA is that it is more dependent than in any other nation on its domestic demand and conversely is less dependent on foreign visitors. All this means that the USA is the most cyclically sensitive of all hotel markets to its home economy. Thus in order to reduce the risk of performance being related to one economy, US hotel firms have looked to international expansion in order to diversify into a portfolio of economies.

## AN ANALYSIS OF THE GLOBAL HOTEL INDUSTRY

An analysis of the hotel industry indicates that it is becoming more international in nature: a process started in the late 1940s by American groups such as Hilton and Inter-Continental. Both groups were, in those days, tied to airlines by equity holdings; the location of foreign-owned hotels was therefore associated with the growth of air traffic. This process of internationalization was in turn largely geared to the needs of the American business traveller. At the same time international investment within the hotel industry was also growing rapidly.

Hotel groups in Europe were more tourist-oriented and, for the most part, did not develop to any great extent until the late 1950s and the early 1960s, when economic prosperity in Europe encouraged the growth of mass international tourism.

Prior to the 1960s the international operations of hotel chains were more or less confined to Europe and North America, and during that decade domestic hotel agreements became common in the USA. Expansion by European concerns accelerated in 1987, when American operators began selling off their international divisions. This gave the large American operators experience of contractual arrangements. On the basis of this experience they turned their attention to the developing countries, where new business centres have emerged and where, as a whole, the tourist growth rate has been higher then in the industrialized countries. Key targets for the hotel groups have been the oil-exporting countries of the Middle East and North Africa and the newly industrialized countries in Latin America, South-East Asia and the Pacific basin. The expansion of multinational hotel companies into the Third World, where the risks of capital investment are regarded as high, has consolidated the importance of contractual methods of undertaking business, such as franchising, management contracts and licensing within the overall growth strategy of these companies. The international chain hotel companies were and still are expanding, at the expense of the small, mid-priced independent hotels.

## Expansion into Europe

Key indicators suggest that the US hospitality industry has reached the mature stage of its life cycle. This is evidenced by declining occupancy levels, growth in supply outpacing growth in demand, and increasing levels of price competition. In contrast, comparable indicators for Europe reveal that the industry has by no means progressed as far along its life cycle.

The European hospitality industry is still very fragmented with a great, yet unrealized, potential for significant economies of scale, and a high degree of product differentiation. As a result, from a supply point of view, Europe appears a favourable location for corporate expansion. Expansion has also been given a further boost by the completion of the Single European Market on 1 January 1993. The opening of frontiers and the removal of physical, technical and fiscal barriers is expected to promote further trade between Member States. This will require increased communication and arguably a greater number of actual contacts between business people around Europe. This growth in business travel will be accompanied by increased demand for hotel accommodation.

The same is true for non-business travel. At a practical level the easing of border controls and visa requirements will reduce the inconvenience usually associated with travelling abroad. These trends have been reinforced by the European Union's steps in the liberalization of transport and, above all, in its deregulatory approach to air transport. Growth in passenger numbers will also have a positive effect on the hospitality industry. In the context of a growth strategy , the approach of Accor has involved the establishment of a Europe-wide presence through the expansion of its segmented product line and the consolidation of its leading position in France and Europe, mainly through leasing/management contracts and franchises. Similarly, Ladbroke plc's growth strategy aims at achieving a major pan-European presence in capital and major cities, besides continuing to consolidate its UK portfolio. In addition to European hotel companies, firms from the rest of the world are also looking to expand into Europe. The growth strategy of New World/Ramada aims at an aggressive expansion into Europe's primary and secondary cities.

In summary, it can be suggested that the 1990s will see an increased degree of consolidation and globalization in the hospitality industry.

## The growing importance of hotel chains

**Ownership patterns**

Over the past ten years there has been a significant change in the ownership of hotels worldwide, with the tendency to construct and operate larger properties, which require larger investments. The hotel owner is usually a financial institution, insurance company or a number of joint-equity owning companies, which typically employ an industry expert to help control and monitor their hotel investment.

Independent hotels by their very nature tend to be smaller in size, and are increasingly surviving mainly in the higher market segments of the hotel industry. Although these may seem difficult times for independents, a select number will continue to have a privileged place in the market because they can make decisions on their own without recourse to institutional investors, they can be flexible, and can offer personalized services to a specific market segment. With this exception, however, the hotel industry is experiencing a gradual but steady switch from independently owned and operated hotels to hotel chain affiliation. Fifty years ago, less than one hotel in ten had any chain affiliation. Today, more than 60 per cent of all hotels in the USA belong to chains. This rapid growth of hotel chains can be attributed to three factors:

- the emergence of franchising systems;
- hotel management contracts;
- the need for corporate growth.

The expansion of hotel chain companies can also be explained by the desire for and availability of economies of scale. It is through this that the advantages provided by national and international reservation networks, staff training, and marketing programmes can be recognized. In the USA, Canada and Europe combined, there are an estimated 3,000 hotel groups with more than ten hotels each. The 200 largest companies account for the operation of at least 20 per cent of all bedrooms.

Regional trends A number of geographical trends can be identified among the world's hotel chains. In North America, hotel firms have a continuing interest in Mexico, the Caribbean and Europe, and in particular the growth of the budget hotel sector. Mexico continues to draw interest from international and domestic firms. US companies Days Inn and the HFS company have opened hotels in Monterrey, Mexico. Spain's Sol group has significant interests in the Caribbean, as does France's Accor. In South America, Hyatt International has opened hotels in Buenos Aires, Argentina and Santiago, Chile, and is looking at other suitable locations in South American cities.

In the UK, the recession in the hotel industry appears to have ended in 1994. According to London-based BDO Hospitality Consulting and Pannell Kerr Forster Associates, the up-market London hotels reported an increase in occupancy in 1994 compared with the previous year. However, on the European mainland, economic conditions worsened during 1994 in France and Germany, unaccustomed to a recessionary climate.

In Asia, Japan's corporate, economic and political problems have influenced not only the Japanese economy but the regional economy too. Hong Kong continues to be an economic focal point for the region. Mainland China has drawn interest because of its economic swing towards a free-market economy, the easing of political tensions, and the sheer size (and buying potential) of its population.

The strategy of being geographically diverse in terms of guest mix and location seems ever more beneficial. As economists worried about the mainland European recession in 1994, and analysts warned of an impending overbuilt Asian market, the USA was just starting to see its hotel supply and demand equation swing back into balance.

The evidence from this discussion is that the advice to keep a balanced portfolio and look beyond domestic markets holds true for hotel firms as well as for individual investors.

## The structure of economies

A theoretical basis These global trends can be set within the structure of economies, with such an analysis providing the basis for hotel company expansion strategies.

There are two forces that boost demand for quoted hotel chains: the structural changes in economies and the growth in concentration within the hotel industry. The structure of an economy can be divided into three phases, each of which exerts a different influence on hotel demand.

**Phase one** is an economy dominated by primary and secondary industries and single-site firms. The only business travellers are sales, marketing and distribution executives, and business demand for hotels is relatively low.

**Phase two** is an economy that has entered a period of transition, in which service industries dominate the economy. The growth in concentration within service industries creates national multiple chains such as retail and banking chains. These multiples employ a wide range of executives who have national or regional job roles and thus spend time travelling: this creates extra hotel demand. The main effects of this phase were felt in the USA between 1955 and 1980. The transition of an economy into phase two is represented by many developments that boost indigenous hotel demand, such as a greater proportion of white collar workers to blue collar workers and the increasing involvement of women executives. As a region moves through phase two it not only increases indigenous business demand, it also boosts personal spending in hotels as the emphasis of economic desires moves from the acquisition of leisure goods to participation in leisure activities. This participation in leisure activities boosts not only the number of people using hotels but the frequency with which they do so.

**Phase three** occurs when the service multiples' demand for hotel accommodation becomes embedded in the supply of hotel accommodation. Phase three is thus a period of sustained indigenous business demand for hotels, but exhibits slower growth than phase two. The slower growth in this period of demand means that supply of hotels must also be reduced if oversupply and its consequences are to be avoided.

Taking this analysis, continental Europe will be the next region to move through phase two. This transition will bring extra demand; corporate hotel companies from the USA and UK will be looking to expand internationally, and would look to this region for growth opportunities. However, not all countries will make the change simultaneously. The likely leaders of this transition will be France and Germany, because of the stage of development of those countries as well as their size. Countries sharing borders with these countries, such as Belgium, will also benefit from other countries' transitions.

Other areas of the world will take longer to reach phase two than continental Europe. The domestic infrastructure of hotels in these regions is very low. These countries supply a huge proportion of their hotels for foreign visitors, which means that the development of hotels away from central tourist locations is restricted. For example, in Russia there was an estimated room stock in 1991 of 75,000, 15 per cent of that in Britain and only 2.5 per cent of that in the USA. A huge majority of these rooms were located in Moscow and St Petersburg, where foreign visitors are targeted.

Britain and the USA have both realized the majority of structural growth available to them. Future growth domestically is dependent on the cyclical nature of the economy. Thus if these two regions wish to carry on expanding, as their shareholders may require, they will have to look towards global expansion to regions that have structural growth potential.

**Levels of concentration**

It is widely accepted that the greater the degree of fragmentation of the hotel industry in any country, the greater the opportunity for hotel chains to expand, to grow profits and restructure demand. Within the hotel industry, low levels of concentration mean high numbers of independently owned and operated hotels. Most of these are small hotels, located in secondary locations, poorly managed invariably by amateurs and providing inconsistent quality of products, facilities and services. The progress of industry relies heavily therefore on the corporate hotel companies, whose growth is faster, more substantial and more sustainable than the growth of privately owned hotel chains. The levels of concentration vary among countries, with the USA and UK exhibiting the most developed markets, as illustrated in Table 3.1.

**Table 3.1 Level of concentration in publicly quoted hotel companies**

| Country | Holding companies | Average room numbers per holding company | Room concentration (%) |
|---|---|---|---|
| USA | 19 | 44,198 | 30.0 |
| UK | 59 | 1,995 | 23.5 |
| Continental Europe | 28 | 4,712 | 10.0 |

*Source:* Slattery and Johnson (1991)

In general, the lower the level of concentration the greater the opportunities for publicly quoted hotel chains, owing to the reduced nature of competition. Thus an American hotel corporation looking to expand would be faced with two options: to locate in their domestic market, where they are increasingly forced into more marginal locations, or to locate in a region such as Europe, where concentration is lower and growth opportunities greater.

## STRATEGIES IN THE EXPANSION OF HOTEL BUSINESSES

The hotel industry has traditionally adhered to the true entrepreneurial spirit of profit making in a flexible, unrestricted business environment, seizing each opportunity as it comes, without considering its long-term impact. Today's fiercely competitive environment, due to a maturing industry and declining growth rate, has shifted competition towards a battle for market share.

The large number of competitors, difficulty in establishing differentiation, cost in new build, renovation of physical structures, plus high fixed costs, will continue to intensify competition within the industry. Adapting to the new rules of the global marketplace, hotel operators are developing new strategies for success. Some of these strategies include the following:

- **New product development**. Technology offers the means to construct new accommodation concepts, one of which comes close to resembling the automated hotel.
- **The diversification of products offered through multi-tier marketing**. Hotel chains began to diversify into markets below and above their usual focus some years ago as a response to intensifying competition. In the early 1980s, the US-based hotel company Choice International began a multi-tier strategy by introducing Comfort Inns and Quality Royale. This diversification trend has been followed by most leading chains, and should continue in the 1990s, as most companies wish to expand into secondary markets, which usually prelude the establishment of up-market hotels.
- **Conversion of older-service hotels into economy properties** that have the brand name of well-known chains, to adapt to shifting demand in markets where primary sites are hard to find. In Amsterdam operators of four- and five-star hotels have felt the effect of American visitors trading down in the early 1990s to two- or three-star hotels.
- **Embracing the product substitute**. Many of the larger hotel chains have linked resources with scheduled airlines, who offer frequent flyer programmes aimed at the regular business traveller.
- **Entry into related markets**. The Marriott Corporation and Accor have penetrated the market for continuing-care retirement communities (CCRC), offering housing, meals and health care for the elderly.
- **Creative marketing programmes to trigger latent hotel demand**. The greatest single challenge for the international hotel industry is to achieve greater market penetration by being more resourceful and expanding from the main industry into that of non-traditional competitors, such as the information and recreation industries.
- **The penetration of international travel and tourism markets that show potential for hotel growth**. For example, the Japanese government introduced a programme intended to double the number of Japanese overseas travellers from about 5 million in 1986 to 10 million in 1991. A similar increase is expected to the year 2000.

- **The delegation of authority and decision making down the line in order to keep close to the customer.** A growing number of firms in the hotel sector are committed to excellence and are paying more attention to the human resource elements in their operation.
- **Management contracting for non-traditional hotel owners.** For example, hotel development, particularly in Hong Kong and Singapore, has been characterized by multi-facility real estate developments. This trend is spreading to Western Europe, particularly to major city locations.
- **The increase of franchising as an option to expand** with the reduction or elimination of direct monetary investment by hotel chains as a major advantage. Franchising in the international hotel market is becoming more significant as large corporations move towards offering less capital-intensive, economy properties, which become fundable by proprietor operators.
- **Targeting the growing leisure market for business expansion** has become a practice for several airlines and hotel chains. For example, a study conducted for Marriott Hotels and Resorts in 1989 revealed that Americans are moving away from the two-weeks-pack-the-station-wagon trip. In 1993, 73 per cent of all US travel was for three days or less; 60 per cent was over the weekend.
- **Providing new self-service computer terminals in existing hotels** to enable hotel guests to check in and out. One of the most frequent complaints of travellers is waiting in long lines to check in and out of hotels. The front desk/reservations department can also be troublesome and inefficient for the hotel operator.
- **The development of expertise in the mainline industry.** A growing number of hotel management firms concentrate their efforts on opening and operating hotels, by providing a complete and totally integrated service package leading a property to growth and bottom-line profitability.

# THE OPERATING ENVIRONMENT OF THE 1990S

As the hospitality industry approaches the year 2000 the complexity of the environment in which businesses operate can be expected to increase, as will its variability and uncertainty. This means that the hospitality manager must be capable of knowing and understanding the events that occur in his or her business and within the general environment.

## Global trends in the 1990s affecting growth

A trend can best be defined as a series of events that, when grouped together or clustered together, point to a new or changing direction. In any given business environment there are several major and minor trends affecting the business at any given time, which must be watched and evaluated in order to assess their impact on the hospitality firm. In looking at the wider environment the corporate planner has to examine the relationships between changes in the environment and the effects that these changes will have on business demand. While expanding globally is an important strategic objective for hotel chains, the environment poses many challenges and obstacles for the hospitality industry as a whole.

## State of the economies

The state of the economy is the prime cyclical factor that determines the level of hotel demand, but because of the inherent complexity of the hotel business and its markets the effects are not uniform. Among its implications during economic recession has been a cutback in both business and leisure travel. The trend in the early 1990s has been for travellers to slice out the frills and excesses of accommodation and look for easily accessible hotel choices that represent value and dependability around the globe. This trend is not a short-term phenomenon, but rather a major structural change in the industry, which will continue to shape the types of products and services offered by multinational hotel firms for many years to come. Incentive travel, corporate entertainment and industry-wide conferences are three major aspects of hotel demand that are highly sensitive to the cyclical nature of the economy. Additionally, during recessionary periods there is tighter control on the prices paid by business travellers for hotel rooms: thus there are reductions in the average achieved room rates, substitution of hotel brands on a cost basis, reductions in the number of business trips, and reductions in the number of nights away from home.

The holiday market can be separated into short breaks, less than four nights long, and long holidays of more than four nights. The short-break holiday could account for 10 per cent of the demand for publicly owned US hotel companies. The long holiday market is deeply discounted through tour operators. Thus long holidays taken by independent travellers constitute only a minor market owing to the wide range of less expensive alternatives. In periods of recession one of the first reductions in spending is on leisure activities and foreign holidays, as interest rates, unemployment and earnings growth rates dictate the consumer's purchasing power. Substitution from foreign to domestic holidays does boost this sector of the market. However, because domestic companies are orientated towards the business market, they fail to realize the expectations of the holiday maker: as in the UK, where the domestic holiday started to show growth in 1989 and 1990, travellers opted for non-hotel accommodation. Demand for hotels by foreign visitors changes dramatically from one country to another, as illustrated in Table 3.2.

**Table 3.2 Foreign visitor demand**

| Country | Foreign visitor demand in quoted hotel chains (%) |
| --- | --- |
| USA | 20 |
| UK | 40 |
| France | 55 |
| Germany | 55 |
| Italy | 70 |
| Ireland | 75 |
| Spain | 75 |
| Netherlands | 80 |
| Belgium | 85 |
| Denmark | 90 |
| Portugal | 90 |
| Greece | 95 |
| Luxembourg | 100 |

*Source:* Slattery and Johnson (1991)

The situation in the European countries is different from that in the USA because they have inter-European travel, whereas the USA only has only long-haul visitors. This results in US hotels having a higher average stay than European hotels. The USA, UK and France differ from the other countries in that they have a lower proportion of foreign visitor demand and a higher indigenous demand. The other countries are more sensitive to movements in international traveller demand, as they have yet to develop strong indigenous demand. The collapse in travel during the Gulf War (1991) had a massive impact on the countries whose hotel demand was generated from international sources. Thus in evaluation, hotel chains upon locating internationally should look to economies with strong indigenous demand in order to achieve stable earnings. However, because of the high level of concentration of hotels already existing in these countries, hoteliers should locate in regions where they believe there is the most growth potential for indigenous demand.

Exchange rates   Exchange rates are an important cyclical indicator of movements in international demand. The relationship between hotel demand and exchange rates is complex. Minor fluctuations in a currency are absorbed by the travel agencies, airlines and hotel companies. It is only when there is a fluctuation of around 15 per cent that the consumer bears the impact. Changes in exchange rates for cash to spend at a destination will always be realized by the consumer at the destination.

For business travellers the tourism relationship with the cyclical nature of the economy can be inverted. As a currency weakens there is an effort for countries to export to that weak currency: this effort usually entails business trips and thus an increase in hotel demand to secure new orders.

Technology

Technology continues to surface as an important ingredient in the strategy of many hospitality firms. The term in this context refers to the development of communication, marketing and management support systems that allow firms to be more competitive in targeting and dealing with the customer. It is also recognized that there are product attributes that must be built into rooms to accommodate the changing communication needs of today's business traveller.

Sociocultural dimension

The sociocultural dimension within which hotels operate will have an impact upon growth, with the use of an increasingly diverse workforce; this is especially true in Europe, where workers from poorer Eastern Bloc countries have been migrating to the Western nations in search of employment. Management of an evolving workforce will provide new challenges for business leaders. Language, work ethics and cultural and social differences will be among the issues that human resource professionals will need to address. Health care and benefit packages will be more complicated and costly, and training and retraining will be necessary as new technologies present themselves. Meanwhile, the overall costs of business management will necessitate a reduction of the labour force.

Demographics and demand

The main thrust of demand for the short breaks and executive business travel market comes from people in the age range 35–50. This market is very lucrative to hotels, and profit margins can be increased through successful planning and marketing towards this group's needs. In the West, demographic trends indicate that this market is rapidly expanding towards a peak. The overall demand for the hotel industry is shaped by the baby boom generation. This group of individuals represents the largest proportion of the population in the economically developed nations of the Western world. So over the long term, as this group move into reduced income status through retirement, the industry can expect to experience no real growth in the decades ahead. This means that any new business for the hotel industry will result either from taking it away from someone else or from expanding into markets abroad where growth is expected to occur. The context of this trend is further shaped by the mature and sophisticated consumer, who today has many more choices of food and accommodation services and expects the highest level of service possible.

Many of these aspects of the operating environment can be applied to strategies adopted by the UK brewing industry, particularly with their diversification into the hospitality industry. This increasingly blurred distinction between two industries will now be considered.

# BREWING AND PUBS: THEIR LINK WITH THE HOSPITALITY INDUSTRY

## Background

The link between the brewing industry and public houses has long been established in terms of vertical integration, but over the past fifteen years there has been a wider move into the hospitality industry because of general environmental pressures. It is these pressures that will be considered in order to determine strategic trends within the UK brewing and pub retailing industry of the 1990s.

## Industry structure

Until recently the UK brewing industry was remarkably stable: only about 5,000 pubs had closed in the 30 years up to 1990. However, the industry is beginning to see the end of the traditional public house, with the closure of probably 10,000 of the UK's 70,000 pubs by the year 2000. Until the 1980s, the pub industry refused to move from its Victorian roots. It clung to an almost feudal system, peculiar to the brewing trade, of **wet rents** calculated on the number of barrels sold in the pub. This kept rents down – they did not change unless sales rose or fell – but also kept the publican captive, or **tied** to the brewer. Over the past few years, that system has largely gone, to be replaced by ordinary lease agreements that almost always involve steadily rising rents regardless of the amount of beer sold. Even if sales fall, the rent keeps rising: a system that has already put hundreds of publicans out of business.

This is one of the biggest factors forcing publicans to rethink their business and look for ways to improve financial returns. But, although this development is forcing change at a faster pace than ever before, the pub revolution has been developing for the past fifteen years.

One of the biggest changes in the British consumer catering market over the last 40 years has been the growing attention paid to the serving of food in pubs. With a total turnover of almost £10 billion, pubs constitute easily the biggest sector of catering businesses, and while alcoholic and non-alcoholic drinks account for approximately 75 per cent of this total, the proportion of food sales has been on the increase.

One key element influencing the industry's structure has been the regulatory environment in which it operates, and specifically the Monopolies and Mergers Commission Report published in 1989.

## Regulatory environment

Back in the mid-1980s the case for shaking up the beer industry looked persuasive. Six big brewers owned or controlled three-quarters of all the country's pubs. Control, through the tie, involved the publican paying a peppercorn rent and getting cheap loans from a brewer in return for selling its beer exclusively. This stranglehold on the retailing of beer helped brewers to reduce their risks in producing beer, and allowed them to wholesale it at higher prices than offered to the independent **free house** retail outlets. So the Government asked the Monopolies and Mergers Commission (MMC) to investigate. The MMC's recommendations were drastic. After a three-year inquiry the Commission decided that it was not in the best interest of beer drinkers for brewers to own pubs: a decision that contrasts oddly with a later ruling that said it was all right for oil companies to own petrol stations.

After a storm of protest from brewers, the UK government introduced a watered-down version of the MMC's proposals in 1989. The MMC's proposals gave brewers until November 1992 to sell – or at least release from any tied beer supplies – half of all the pubs they owned, above a limit of 2,000. Brewers with more than 2,000 pubs also had to allow their pubs to sell a **guest** beer from a rival brewer. Confronted with the traditional structure of Britain's brewing business, the MMC had a point. The breweries' exclusive control over their pubs stifled competition. The brewers predicted mayhem, but they succeeded only in getting the recommendations diluted.

These measures have certainly shaken up the industry – but not as the MMC intended. Instead, the outcome is remarkably similar to that predicted in a dissenting note to the MMC's 1989 report. One of the investigatory panel's members gave a warning against the proposals for cutting back the managed and tied estates, suggesting that the reforms would reduce competition and consumer choice, while producing public interest detriments. Events have confounded the MMC's expectations in four main ways:

- Big companies involved in both brewing and in running pubs have started to concentrate their operations on one or the other. This strategic shift was already under way in 1989, but the MMC accelerated that trend.
- Vertical integration has faded; brewing or pub-running cartels have not. Thus Grand Metropolitan quit brewing altogether and swapped its breweries for the surplus pubs of Courage (owned by the Fosters Brewing Group). Courage now supplies beer to many more pubs than it did before; there is now a supply agreement between Courage and Grand Metropolitan. Other big brewers have agreed similar supply deals: Allied-Lyons, for example, arranged to supply all Greenall

Whitley's pubs when Greenall quit brewing in 1990. The result: a swelling dominance of beer supply for the top four brewers. The big four controlled 58 per cent of the market in 1989; in 1993 they had 70 per cent.

- To deal with their 11,000 surplus pubs, as defined by the 1989 reforms, the leading brewer–retailers have sought to put commercial leases in place of direct ownership or the old, uncommercial tenancies: that is, those involving the cross-subsidy implicit in a tie. Faced with straight commercial contracts, many publicans have been severely affected by the cost of a twenty-year lease.
- In reviewing the management of their pub properties, several brewer–retailers have opted to pull the most profitable tied pubs into their directly managed chains. This will allow them to exploit the latest retailing trends and therefore reap the commercial benefits.

The MMC's guest beer rule, aimed at widening the choice of beers at the bar, has not worked well. Some independent brewers with renowned real ales have been successful. But a recent survey by the Campaign for Real Ale, a UK lobbying group, showed that only a third of eligible pubs have decided to stock a guest beer, and only half of those are from a true rival brewer.

There is not enough information in the early 1990s to be precise (partly because of the confusion created by the mass sell-off of 11,000 pubs under the Government's Beer Orders), but it seems that the MMC's objectives have not been fulfilled. Meanwhile, the Beer Orders have spawned a large crop of independent pub retailers such as Century Inns and Enterprise Inns. In the main, the pubs sold by the brewers were poorly profitable outlets. They have been picked up cheaply by the wave of budding pub operators, who have been able to transform the outlets by ploughing in a substantial amount of capital.

Already over the past three years the price of beer has risen in real terms. None of that is what Britain's MMC intended.

## Demand patterns

Another aspect that has influenced the industry's structure has been changes in demand patterns. The watershed year for the industry was 1979. Beer production peaked, and pubs have been on a downhill trend since then, with beer volumes in pubs falling by 25 per cent. On average, 50 per cent of what a pub sells is beer (25 per cent is other drinks), and as recently as the 1970s, 1 million males, predominantly in coalmining and steel towns, consumed 40 per cent of all the beer produced in the UK. Pubs today, however, are denied the luxury of such a rich seam of drinkers, and have had to refocus their strategic view on retailing and leisure. There has been more focus on improving financial returns, as the business was widely regarded as being paternalistic and overmanned.

From the Second World War onwards the UK has seen a rapidly changing consumer, with rapidly developing levels of affluence and sophistication. This degree of affluence was quite pronounced by the mid-1960s, and expressed itself in the 1970s and 1980s by a change in demand. There has been a big shift from ale to lager, which was a function of advertising and a change in social structures. By 1979 the incoming Conservative Government started de-industrializing Britain with its withdrawal of support for the large nationalized industries, a policy that affected demand from the big drinkers. The biggest change in demand had nothing to do with the Government's Beer Orders, but rather with the consumer. Brewers, with one or two exceptions, were slow to change and have been feeling the effects of this de-industrialization. The background to all these changes is the steady decline in the amount of beer drunk in Britain, whether it is bought in pubs or elsewhere.

## Supply

In 1990 the UK produced 38.6 million barrels, or 11.1 billion pints of beer. Of that total, 81 per cent was consumed in pubs, clubs and restaurants, and the rest at home. By the year 2000, it is expected that beer output will have fallen to 36.4 million barrels. With this reduction in supply and a change in industry structure the standalone publican is facing the full competitive might of the big brewers, with the latter's power becoming more concentrated. Allied-Lyons has merged its brewing interests with Carlsberg of Denmark, and Scottish & Newcastle recently bought the Chef & Brewer chain. It was on 22 October 1991 that Allied-Lyons, a food and drinks group, and Carlsberg, a Danish brewer, merged their British brewing businesses into a £510 million ($870 million) joint venture. In the same year Grand Metropolitan, the former owner of Watney Mann and Truman beers, quit brewing after a pubs-for-breweries swap with Courage, which is owned by Australia's Fosters. Three other brewers – Boddington, Greenall Whitley and Devenish – have given up making beer to concentrate on running pubs. The independents are also having to compete with pure pub retailers (those who do not own breweries) such as Greenalls, which recently expanded by purchasing another pub retailer, Devenish. Then there are specialist retailers like J D Wetherspoon, which is worrying competitors with the unusual idea of installing pubs in the buildings of, for instance, former high-street banks. Regent Inns is also making an art form out of rejuvenating badly managed outlets.

As a result there will be fewer breweries and pubs, and beer looks set to become more expensive. In fact, running a brewery and running a pub are becoming two very different sorts of business. There has, through pressures from the wider environment, been an inevitable restructuring. The industry is embarking upon a vigorous round of horizontal integration, with several companies consolidating their operations in either brewing or pub retailing. The Allied-Lyons and Carlsberg deal is the latest. Carlsberg-Tetley, as the joint venture is called, has about 18 per cent of the market. That will make it Britain's third biggest brewer after Courage (with 20 per cent) and Bass (23 per cent). The irony is that the trio will now have more than 60 per cent of the British market. Before the MMC intervened, they had less than 50 per cent.

## General environment

Altered employment patterns, demographics and drinking habits – as well as stiffer competition from the rest of the leisure industry – are forcing a complete reassessment of the traditional pub. The first old-style pubs to be affected, and ultimately to go out of business, have predominantly been in villages and on housing estates in areas of high unemployment.

By 1995, the demographic profile of the UK will show a 23 per cent decline in the number of 18- to 25-year-olds, traditionally big drinkers and big spenders on leisure. Although this age group accounts for only 14 per cent of the population, it consumes 35 per cent of the beer sold in pubs. The 35–55 age group, meanwhile, is forecast to grow by 15 per cent by 1997. Many in this group have large financial commitments and tend to socialize more at home. This means that off-licences and supermarkets will continue to enjoy growth in beer and wine sales, but the pubs will not.

Pubs are set to lose about 10 per cent of their drinks turnover by 1995: four out of every ten people who stop going to a pub will probably never return. But drinking habits were changing even before the brewers began to sell off their pubs. Most British pubs are being transformed from boozy institutions, and are now just as likely to be serving non-alcoholic drinks and meals for families.

One example is Whitbread, no longer just one of the big four brewers but the leader of a large pack of companies engaged in rethinking the role of the pub, its place in the wider context of the leisure industry, and the potential for squeezing more revenue out of these underperforming assets. Public houses are being transformed into operations with restaurants, family rooms, and ancillary leisure facilities such as skittle alleys.

## Competitive environment

It is clear that landlords of classic urban and rural public houses are having a tough time. A closer examination reveals that the traditional public house is up against strong local competition, and that a pub relying heavily on drink sales is unlikely to be viable. Rents are rising, rates are too high, overheads are rising and there is more competition in the marketplace: hence a lot of pubs are closing.

Demographics has provided much of the fuel for the recent price war among brewers in the wholesale trade. Big discounts, often as high as £80, on a 36 gallon barrel of beer have been the main weapon used by brewers to increase sales to pubs that they do not control. The consumer, though, has not benefited from this reduction in wholesale prices because publicans, aware of the decline in trade, pocket the extra profit. But for many publicans, this short–term windfall will not be enough to ensure their survival. For pubs to survive, they will have to offer by the turn of the century an operation that will have to appeal to families at four to five times the rate it was doing in 1994. The UK is also a car society, and pubs are not places that people walk to, so the industry is essentially trying to attract people to spend their leisure time and their leisure money. In the modern pubs of the 1990s, consumers are now a target once they walk through the doors. Before they reach the bar, they will pass tempting diversions such as food bars and video game machines. Pubs that are doing well are pubs that are famous for something, such as food. Each pub, to be successful, is managed like a brand, with the same marketing techniques and precision. Turning a pub into a place that will attract modern drinkers requires a great deal of investment, marketing flair and expertise. This may not be a problem for the big brewers, but for many small and independent pubs it may cause their demise. The great bulk of the 10,000 pubs expected to close are likely to be those run by individual publicans. The big managed house – one owned by a brewer or retailer – will be at a premium. Many of the marginal houses – smaller pubs, particularly tenancies – will cease to exist.

When the Government decided in 1989 to break up the brewers' pub empires, it pushed through reforms that, it said, would promote more competition, drive down beer prices, and give the pub-goer a wider choice of beers. The counter-argument was that the proposals would just turn a well-tested retailing structure upside down, to no useful purpose. The beer industry is now dominated by four big brewers instead of six. Analysts predict that the number might shrink to two or three; beer prices rose in real terms during the 1990s and the largest brewers are fixing agreements that will ensure that their brands remain dominant.

Having introduced the topic of the UK brewing industry in terms of structure, demand and supply, the focus of this chapter will now be placed on Bass, Whitbread and its links with the small brewers.

## CASE STUDY: BASS, WHITBREAD AND THE SMALLER BREWERS

During 1994, with little fuss, one of British brewing's historic institutions was abolished when Whitbread, one of the giants of the industry, sold £225 million of shares in eight smaller brewers. Thus ended the so-called **Whitbread umbrella**, whereby for 40 years Whitbread had held strategic stakes in local brewers to protect them from takeover by their bigger rivals. The obvious question now arises: Given that protection was necessary in the first place, are the regional brewers being thrown to the wolves?

In many industries, size means everything. However, in UK brewing there is evidence that middle-sized companies these days can not only hold their own against the giants, but can actually gain ground in terms of profitability. This can be simply illustrated by combining the results of a dozen regional brewers (Boddington, Devenish, Eldridge Pope, Fullers, Greenall, Greene King, Mansfield, Marston, Morland, Vaux, Wolverhampton & Dudley, Youngs) and comparing them with Britain's biggest brewer and publican, Bass. During 1993, the regional sample had combined sales of £1.8 billion and operating profits of £255 million, a margin of 14 per cent. Bass's brewing and pub divisions had combined sales of £2.3 billion and profits of £361 million, a margin of 16 per cent. Scale economies, it seems, are worth something in UK brewing: but not much, if one considers the best performers in the regional group, and the balance tilts the other way. Morland, the Oxfordshire brewer, had a margin in 1993 of 23 per cent. Over the past five years, its sales have grown by an average 19 per cent a year, while its earnings per share are up 11 per cent over the period. Greene King, based in East Anglia, has margins of 19 per cent and average sales growth of 7 per cent. Bass as a group raised its sales by 2.5 per cent a year over the period, while its earnings fell by nearly a third.

In one sense, Bass could argue that its poor performance is the result of Government action. Since 1989, when the Government took steps against the industry on competition grounds, there has been a ceiling on the number of licensed premises that the big brewers can own. Not only are groups like Bass and Whitbread barred from increasing their pub estates; in compliance with the Beer Orders (as the legislation is known) they had to get rid of pubs and take large restructuring charges against profits. In fact, the Beer Orders are less of a constraint than they appear. They limit only the number of pubs that the big brewers can own.

Bass, like many of its smaller competitors, has little desire to increase the number of its pubs. This is because the tied house system has left the brewers with a long tail of small, unprofitable tenanted pubs whose sole purpose is to use up the last of the brewery's output. The big or middle-sized brewers want to get rid of those pubs and acquire bigger, more profitable managed pubs instead. More fundamentally, the big brewers face the problem that, in some parts of their business, size can be a positive disadvantage. It is, of course, more economical to produce beer in huge, modern breweries, and to promote national brands through the national media, but distribution is another matter. Very often, the local brewer has all his pubs within a few miles of the brewery; and for a product consisting almost wholly of water, most of whose retail price goes to the Government, such a distribution pattern is an important advantage.

As for the pubs themselves, a crucial drawback for the big brewers is that they have failed to introduce branding into their outlets. Retail chains like Boots or Marks and Spencer can use a standard national format to drive smaller rivals out of business. For the big brewers, the reverse can be the case. Watneys, for instance, now jointly owned by Grand Metropolitan and Fosters, has in recent years expunged its name from many of its pub frontages, preferring modest anonymity. The result of this can be a reverse economy of scale. Run one pub, and you make a given profit. Run 50, and you have to hire an accountant, a buyer, a property expert and security staff. Quite possibly, none of those pubs will be more inherently profitable than the one you started with. If so, the extra overhead is a dead loss.

So what shape will the industry take, now that Whitbread has taken its umbrella away? Analysts argue for a degree of concentration, but they agree it will take a limited form. Rather than the big brewers snapping up the smaller, the medium-sized brewers will snap up the smallest. This may take time, as many of the smallest are protected by family holdings or restricted voting structures. The point is, however, that the middle-sized brewers from which Whitbread withdrew its protection are profitable enough to be able to take care of themselves.

Companies such as Morland, Greene King, Marston and Wolverhampton & Dudley have developed varied and successful strategies to cope with the changing world of UK brewing. In stock market terms, all stand on higher multiples and lower yields than the industry leaders. This analysis of the brewing industry can be further developed with the next case study, which looks at the growth strategy of Allied–Lyons, a UK-based brewing and drinks company.

## CASE STUDY: THE GROWTH STRATEGY OF ALLIED-LYONS

On the face of it, Allied-Lyons' £739 million purchase of Pedro Domecq (1993) makes the enlarged company the world's second biggest spirits producer after Grand Metropolitan, overtaking Guinness. In completing the purchase, Allied-Lyons gained some powerful brands with which to attack the fast-growing South American market, and also recruited some able managers, mostly members of the Domecq family, who thoroughly understand the Hispanic world of drinks. The overwhelming bulk of Domecq's profits – 97 per cent – comes from two countries, Mexico and Spain. Allied's products in those countries are already distributed by Domecq, and Domecq's own brands mostly have limited appeal outside those two countries, so there is little scope for Allied to push them through its own distribution system. Despite these negative issues the central strategic question is: What does Allied think it is getting from the purchase?

The answer, above all, is the prospect of growth. The enlarged company is getting faster growth in fast-growing parts of the world. Mexico, for instance, contributes half of Domecq's trading profits, and it is where Domecq has more than 40 per cent of the spirits market and an 80 per cent share in brandy. The Mexican business has to develop and probably change its focus from the domestic brandy business to imported products. That is a ten- or fifteen-year strategic development, and it will be much easier to do with the enlarged Allied-Lyons in control. Equally, there are a number of markets, especially in Europe, where Domecq still has its own distributors; in most of them Allied-Lyons will take over the distribution. In the long run, the company is hopeful that Domecq's brandies could be sold in China, where the distribution system is already in place. The deal has a further attraction: cash. Domecq was a very strong cash producer, and in the past, as a minority shareholder, Allied-Lyons had profits but not cash. Meanwhile, the deal carries Allied-Lyons further in its stated policy of concentrating on drinks and retailing, which includes pubs, Baskin-Robbins ice cream and Dunkin' Donuts. By implication, this leaves two unwanted divisions: food manufacture and the Carlsberg-Tetley joint venture in brewing.

The deal also confirms the UK's remarkable dominance of the world drinks industry. Allied-Lyons is now lodged at the top of the tree with two other British groups, Guinness and GrandMet. The only other company in the same league is Seagram of Canada. The chronological sequence of events leading up to this deal is listed below.

### Allied-Lyons
1961   Company created by merger of Ind Coope, Tetley Walker and Ansells.
1963   Name changed to Allied Breweries.
1968   Bought Showerings.
1976   Bought Teachers.
1978   Bought J Lyons for £60 million.
1981   Name changed to Allied-Lyons.
1985   Elders bids £1.68 billion for Allied-Lyons, which is finally rescinded in 1986.
1986   Bought 51 per cent of Hiram Walker, of Canada, acquiring balance in 1987 for C$1.3 billion.
1988   Equity link with Suntory, Japanese drinks group.
1989   Bought 69 per cent of Chateau Latour; bought Dunkin Donuts for £207 million; bought James Burrough.
1991   Bought 24 per cent of Champagne Lanson.
1992   Leased over 700 pubs to Brent Walker; Showerings sold to management for £140 million. Lyons Maid sold; breweries merged with UK arm of Carlsberg.

### Pedro Domecq Group
1730   Founded in Jerez, Spain.
1816   Acquired by Domecq family.
1941   Established Mexican operation. Further subsidiaries added to make it one of the largest drinks distributors in Latin America.
1994   The group, as the world's eighth largest spirits producer and distributor, is sold to Allied-Lyons for £739 million.
       Main activities: Production, distribution and marketing of brandy, whisky, wine and other drinks, mainly in Mexico and Spain.

The discussion so far has focused on industry structure, demand and supply, the influence of government legislation and, finally, corporate growth strategy. These areas have been related to the brewing and drinks industry with a link being established with the hospitality industry. The next area to be considered will be the twin issues of finance and culture, and these will be illustrated with an analysis of Euro Disney. The effect of government intervention is also obvious in this discussion.

## EURO DISNEY: THE TWIN ISSUES OF FINANCE AND CULTURE

### Background

In the mid-1980s, when the giant Walt Disney company first suggested the idea of building a European version of its famous theme parks, it became evident that the French authorities were keen to persuade the group to locate the resort and its 12,000 jobs in the depressed agricultural region of Marne la Vallée, 20 miles east of Paris. The 1980s were a time of rising unemployment in France: the socialists needed the jobs as well as the prestige that Euro Disney would bring, and Marne la Vallée, designated a new town in the 1970s, needed investment in order to assist in its anticipated expansion. Accordingly, attempts were made to persuade the Americans that Paris, despite its poor weather and high prices, was the place to locate the park.

Government assistance presented no problem. Around 5,000 acres of land was offered to the company at 1971 prices; road and rail links were promised; tax incentives and £420 million of loans at under 8 per cent for 20 years were also offered. Such were the incentives offered that as much as one in every nine francs spent on the development to date has come from the French public purse. With such an approach, France in 1987 duly defeated the 240 other European candidates in the race to host the fourth Disney theme park, joining the then existing trinity of California, Florida and Tokyo.

The project was supposed to take place in three stages spanning the years to 2017. By then, the Magic Kingdom and associated developments were to cover an area a fifth the size of Paris. Such was the dream.

### The project

The reality has foundered on the rocks of the European recession of the early 1990s. So far, less than a third of the land allocated to Euro Disney has been developed; and for more than three years the losses have risen alarmingly. It was in 1991 that the company admitted that it would have to shelve indefinitely plans for phase two of the park, the centrepiece of which was to have been an $85,000\,m^2$ theme park based on the MGM film studios. Euro Disney had seen the second phase as the solution to one of its key problems: pitifully low hotel occupancy levels at the resort. The company view was that expanding the park's attractions and making them last more than a day would mean that visitors would have to stay overnight, so boosting the resort's revenues. The problem was that the

Americans, who would have had to back the Ffr5 billion ($865 million) borrowings needed for the expansion, feared that the expansion might end up being part of a larger problem for the parent company.

## Demand

Having outlined the nature of the project and the level of government support, one aspect to consider is demand for the park's facilities and the factors influencing that demand.

During 1994, Euro Disney agreed terms with its banks for a FFr13 billion ($2.25 billion) rescue package, after it suffered a sharp fall in attendances during 1993.After the opening of the park in April 1992 attendances were initially disappointing. The number of British people visiting Euro Disney in the early years of the project halved as the value of the pound fell against the franc. About 9.5 million people visited the theme park during its second full year of operation, against 10.5 million visitors during the first year.

However, during 1993 Euro Disney secured a significant increase in attendance from the French through a successful campaign of aggressive advertising and price promotion. During that year Euro Disney was also hit by a fall in the number of German visitors. Both the Spanish and the Italians were also put off by high French prices, as their currencies had also weakened. It was these exchange rate fluctuations that affected overall attendances at the park .

Few wanted to pay the high entrance fees, or purchase expensive food and beverages. The specific marketing response was to cut entrance fees to the park after 5pm and promote it to the local French population, an approach that raised visitor levels to approximately 11 million a year. While more visitors were attracted by special deals, this increased the number of people going to the park but reduced margins. The central problem for Euro Disney was that such visitors did not want to make use of the hotels, which were at least as expensive as equivalent hotels in central Paris, barely 40 minutes away by the overland rail link. Ironically, the superb infrastructure installed by the French government has proved part of Euro Disney's undoing, making central Paris easily accessible. Occupancy rates during the first three years were running at only 68 per cent in peak season, and around 45 per cent for the year: a figure that compares dismally with the near 100 per cent achieved in the USA.

The assumptions within the strategic planning process (specifically pricing) for the theme park were all wrong. Disney looked at how much they were charging in the USA and compared that with similar leisure spends in Europe. They found that European leisure prices were higher, and multiplied up for Euro Disney. The US-based Disney Corporation, however, has proved reluctant to face this pricing issue. More recently it is understood that advance bookings for the spring and summer season of 1994 have been depressed by uncertainty over the progress of the financial restructuring. Now that the rescue has been agreed, the theme park should see an increase in bookings.

Despite the financial rescue, Euro Disney is expected to remain in the red during 1994. Analysts forecast a net loss of FFr1.5 billion for the year to 30 September 1994, with the company scheduled to break even only in the 1995–96 financial year.

## Finance

Conceived in the 1980s, the project originally envisaged early profits, and funds for expansion could come from the sale of the five hotels built on the site in the first phase. It also over-optimistically aimed to raise money through developing commercial and residential property in and around the resort: a grand design scuppered as the Paris property market crashed in the early 1990s. Such property profits were supposed to generate almost a third of the 1993 revenues originally projected at the time of the company's flotation. Such errors of stategic judgement were only part of the problem.

The real seeds of Euro Disney's difficulties lay in the structure of the financial agreement drawn up by the parent company in 1987 with the French authorities, which in effect forced the Americans to give up half their share in the project. French laws on inward investment stipulated that Euro Disney would have to be controlled from within the European Union. Disney was thus compelled to set up a public holding company, Euro Disney SCA, and to offer 51 per cent of the shares for sale to the public in a heavily promoted $1 billion (£670 million) flotation. The Americans were unhappy at the prospect of giving away half the resort's expected earnings in this fashion.

At the time, the parent company was under considerable pressure from shareholders to secure what they considered to be the group's rightful share of Euro Disney's anticipated profits. As the legislative rules meant that Disney could not achieve this by making Euro Disney a wholly owned subsidiary, the group sought instead to secure its position by loading costs onto the public company. The resort is managed by a wholly owned subsidiary of Disney, called Euro Disney SA. This company must pay management fees of at least 3 per cent of its revenues, as well as, in certain circumstances, management incentive fees, royalties, and a share of any capital gains to Disney US. The upshot of this was that the benefits of any improvement in trading went disproportionately to Disney US. Assuming things went well and the park managed 16 million visitors a year, the parent company would make profits of FFr2.3 billion. The lion's share of this would go to Disney, however; Euro Disney would secure barely FFr800 million, and in addition shareholders in Euro Disney have only limited voting rights. Dislodging Disney as manager of the park is virtually impossible, even if the American stake in the holding group fell to nothing. The situation is further complicated by the fact that a second company, Euro Disney SNC, was created with the aim of making the project as tax-efficient as possible. This is the operating company that technically owns the resort's assets – the Magic Kingdom theme park, the hotels and other elements of the development – which are leased back to the public company for 20 years. Most of Euro Disney's debts lie in this operating company, which in its turn is owned by a mixture of French institutions and the Walt Disney Corporation, which has a 17 per cent stake. Such an arrangement left little flexibility when Euro Disney's revenues began to fall short of target. There have been other restrictions too.

As the French authorities in effect bought the jobs that came with Euro Disney, the company operated with staffing levels that some considered to be more than 10 per cent higher than necessary. But the main problem has proved to be Disney's original reluctance to deal with the issue of prices charged. The hotels are a fact of life; they cannot be unbuilt and they have to be made to pay. However, the high fees have created a vicious circle. Payments to Disney mean that Euro Disney must in turn charge high prices. Yet high prices are one of the most off-putting aspects of the resort. Europeans have proved less eager to pay to queue for hours in the rain to ride the Euro Disney roller coaster, when lower US prices meant that they could fly to Florida or California for almost the same amount, and wait in the sunshine. Those that did go proved more careful with their finances than the Americans expected.

Despite a mounting chorus of complaints during 1993–94, the most that the parent company has so far agreed to has been the temporary deferral of its fees. Waiving them, or altering the structure to give Euro Disney a financial breathing space, had been out of the question, at least until the financial problems arose.

The Disney Corporation's attitude has historical roots. By 1989, when the project was finalized, Disney's three theme parks were contributing more than two-thirds of the company's annual revenues of $3.4 billion, yet Disney felt short-changed. In 1955, when Walt Disney himself had opened the first theme park at Anaheim in California, the success of the project was measured in thousands, not millions of dollars, so the company secured only a modest area for development: the park takes up about 75 acres in all. Surrounding landowners, who saw the value of their land soar, were thus able to cash in on the Disney magic. When Disney World's Florida resort opened in 1971, Disney made sure it had room to expand: the site then covered 11,000 acres. But, once more, others were quicker than Disney to anticipate what turned out to be a virtually insatiable demand for hotel space. Again, Disney felt that others were benefiting unfairly from its efforts.

However, it was the Tokyo theme park that really upset Disney shareholders. Disney has no equity in the Japanese version of Disneyland, which opened over a decade ago at a cost of $625 million. The only income that it receives is royalties, to the level of 10 per cent of gross earnings on rides and admissions and 5 per cent on food and merchandising. The land, finance and construction of the park were the responsibility of Oriental Land, a Japanese company. After an uncertain beginning, the Tokyo park has turned into a highly profitable operation. The last thing that Disney wanted with Euro Disney was a repeat of Tokyo. This time, the Americans wanted to be sure that they gained fully from what they confidently believed would be an equal success story. Euro Disney in this sense is paying for the successes of its forebears. None of this would have mattered if the resort had hit its ambitious revenue targets, but unfortunately it did not.

During 1994 the parent company and its bankers succeeded in piecing together a rescue deal for Euro Disney. But the critical issue was: what did the restructuring mean for the finances of Euro Disney and its US parent? When Disney first mapped out a European version of its hugely successful US theme parks, it calculated that it would make a profit from its opening year. This unfortunately was not the case.

However, the crux of Euro Disney's difficulties was its financial structure. Disney had financed Euro Disney's construction through the flotation of the remaining 51 per cent stake and through loans. Euro Disney had originally expected to reduce its debt by selling property around the park, but the recession forced it to abandon this. Meanwhile, the high level of French interest rates raised the cost of servicing its remaining debt. Early in 1993 the company hoped to restructure its finances by persuading its bankers to relax the terms of their loans. But when the recession deepened it realized that more drastic action was required.

In November 1993 Disney summoned the banks to tell them it would support Euro Disney until 31 March 1994 but that, unless a rescue was agreed, it would close. The two sides have since formulated an agreement. The main elements were a FFr6 billion rights issue and a FFr1.4 billion transaction whereby Disney would lease two of the theme park rides: the Temple of Doom and Discovery Mountain. The US group would also waive its rights to royalties and management fees for five years, while the banks accepted an 18 month interest holiday on their loans. This package halved Euro Disney's debt from FFr20.3 billion to FFr10 billion. The company should also save FFr800 million a year in interest charges and FFr450 million in payments to Disney US.

Analysts believe that the financial deal is positive for Disney. It is believed that the lease financing deal, together with the equity, will take Disney's total new financing commitment up to around $750 million, and over the long term Disney will more than recoup that. Disney's loss of royalties and management fees will not hurt much either, as they only amounted to $ 36.3 million in 1993, a small sum relative to Disney's $1.7 billion of operating income.

Another positive element is that the deal removes a large element of investor uncertainty over the fate of Euro Disney, and its financial implications for Disney. That uncertainty has been hanging over the US company's share price for a long period, undermining an otherwise strong earnings outlook, supported by its film business. Disney's US theme parks should also see renewed growth, helped by the opening of more attractions. Analysts say that these factors and a final solution to the Euro Disney problem should go a long way to restoring investor confidence.

## Culture

The issue in considering culture in relation to Disney is: can the corporate culture that operates successfully in California and Florida be effective in Paris? Unless managerial practices and organizational structures are congruent with corporate cultures, and in turn corporate cultures are compatible with national cultures, these practices, structures and cultures will not be productive. Euro Disney is simply a US cultural product that happens to be manufactured in France for European consumers. The result is that through this aspect, culture has contributed to Euro Disney's severe financial problems. This is in sharp contrast to Tokyo Disneyland, as the Japanese are very good at imitating others and have managed to make an excellent replica of the original. The central point is that both France and the USA have powerful domestic cultures which, for all their attractions, are not easily exportable to each other. The USA can export its culture to most places other than France, but France finds it difficult to export its culture across the language barrier to the Anglo-Saxon world. Tokyo Disneyland is objectively as good as the Anaheim version and is a welcomed counterpoint to Japan's powerful culture. Euro Disney is objectively not as good as the US version and sits badly within French culture. When it comes to people's behaviour in organizations, culture counts. Therefore, when trying to import managerial practices such as leadership styles, communication patterns and motivation techniques, from one country to another, problems arise. National and ethnic cultures are a major determinant of people's behaviour, and when the corporate culture of Disney is incongruent with the national or ethnic culture, the result is failure.

Some multinational hospitality corporations try to apply their Western developed corporate cultures uniformly to all their properties, regardless of their fit to the local culture. Other companies engage in the process of bridging **cultural gaps**. The real lesson of Euro Disney is not that the Americans and French between them have made a mess, but that it is very difficult to build international trade in cultural activities. It is clear that the corporate culture of Disney, which operates successfully in the USA, will not be effective in Paris without some major modifications.

**SUMMARY**

There are many differing factors that generate the global expansion of hospitality firms, all of which influence the firm's decision for international growth.

Analysing these factors is difficult, owing to the complexity of the hospitality industry and the unique aims, objectives and trading environments of each firm within the industry. However, by examining the trading environment of the past decade we can understand the pressures affecting a firm's future, and gain an insight into the options available to the strategist who is trying to progress the firm as far as possible.

When one considers the hotel industry, a majority of hotel companies are being forced into global expansion, through the exhaustion of growth opportunities in their domestic economies and the desire to reduce the cyclical influence of a single economy on the hotel chain's performance. These factors, considered as the wider environment, are the key motivation behind global expansion.

Hotel chains will only expand internationally if it is feasible to do so. Once a decision to expand has been taken the firm must locate in the best location available. There are a number of options available. Expansion can occur in places of existing demand, but relatively low hotel concentration. Alternatives are to expand in places of expected hotel demand growth, such as continental Europe, or to expand into key global gateway cities and face the challenge of achieving coordination of a dispersed hotel portfolio. Whichever choice is made, the hotel strategist must accurately forecast the potential of a region; if there is no mechanism for doing this, expansion is risky and not viable.

Another consideration is that expansion must be achieved through the most suitable growth medium. This could be franchising, management contracts or strategic alliances. Each of these has advantages but also disadvantages, which if not understood and avoided could make global expansion a less feasible strategy.

The factors generating global expansion of hotel chains can be summed up in three questions: why expand, where to expand to and how to expand. If hotel chains can formulate their strategies around these questions then they will have the opportunity to compete in the competitive and increasingly global market.

The regulatory environment, while important to hotels, was discussed in greater detail within the UK's brewing industry. In addition to changes in demand patterns, it is the MMC's report that has shaped the brewing industry of the 1990s.

The issues of finance and culture, while specifically related to Euro Disney in this chapter, span both hotels and the brewing industry. For instance, the human resource policies of a global hotel firm have to reflect the requirements of the countries in which that firm operates. Such requirements extend to the customers that the firm intends to attract.

**FURTHER READING**  Anguilar, F J 1967 *Scanning the business environment*, New York: Macmillan

Denoble, A and M D Olsen 1982 The relationship between the strategic planning process and the service delivery system. In Pizzam *et al.* (eds) *The practice of hospitality Management*, Westport, CT: AVI Publishing, pp. 229–36

Dev, C and M D Olsen 1989 Operating environment and strategy: the profitable connection, *Cornell HRA Quarterly* **30**(2), 9–13

Go, F and P Welch 1991 *Competitive strategies for the international hotel industry*, Special Report No 1180, London: Economist Intelligence Unit

Go, F, F P Sung, U Muzaffer and B J Mihalik 1990 Decision criteria for transnational hotel expansion, *Tourism Management* **11**(4) 297–304

Hotel and Motel Brokers Association Transactions 1993 *Travel and Tourism Analyst*, No 3, London: Economist Intelligence Unit, p. 53.

Kwansa, F, C Dev, N K Isak, M K Meyer, M D Olsen, N Saleem and J J West 1986 An analysis of major trends and their impact potential affecting the hospitality industry. In *Proceedings of the Annual Meeting of the Council on Hotel Restaurant and Institutional Education*, Boston MA. pp. 168–93

Miles, R E and C C Snow 1978 *Organization strategy structure and process*, New York: McGraw-Hill

Olsen, M D 1989 Issues facing multiunit hospitality organizations in a mature market, *Journal of Contemporary Hospitality Management* **1**(2), 3–6

Olsen, M D 1993 International growth strategies for major US hotel companies, *Travel and Tourism Analyst*, No. 3, London: Economist Intelligence Unit, p. 51

Pinto, E and M D Olsen 1987 The information needs of finance executives in the hospitality industry, *Hospitality Education and Research Journal* **II**(2), 181–90

Porter, M 1980 *Competitive strategy*, New York: Free Press, Ch. 2

Radisson Press Release 1993 Minneapolis, Minnesota, 22 May.

Slattery, P and D Littlejohn 1991 The structure of Europe's economies and demand for hotel accommodation, *Travel and Tourism Analyst*, No. 4, London: Economist Intelligence Unit, pp. 20–37.

Slattery, P and S M Johnson 1991 *Quoted hotel companies: the world markets*, London: Kleinwort Benson Securities

Slattery, P, G Freehely and M Savage 1995 *Quoted hotel companies: the world markets*, London: Kleinwort Benson Securities

West, J J and M D Olsen 1988 Environmental scanning and its effect on firm performance, *Hospitality Education and Research Journal* **12**(2), 127–36

# Strategic analysis of the environment, resources and capability of the hospitality industry

OBJECTIVES

After reading this chapter you should be able to:

- Undertake an environmental analysis and suggest a possible need for changes in strategy by identifying opportunities and threats within that environment.
- Show that resource capability is one important element that the strategic manager should consider, and illustrate how such resources can be analysed.
- Identify the extent to which the organization's culture and power structure influence strategy, and consider the relevance of stakeholder theory.

## INTRODUCTION

It is strategic analysis that provides an understanding of the strategic situation that an organization faces, and allows for future choices to be made. Analysis of an organization's situation is a complex task, and can include the environment, its resources and capabilities. The matching of the organization to the environment introduces the concept of the complex and diverse nature of the environment and the need to create an overall picture. In considering the environment a major problem is one of uncertainty, not only historically but also in terms of future influences.

The approach adopted by many strategic managers in analysing the environment in which a hospitality firm operates is to use a range of models to allow a more integrated understanding. Some of those models have already been discussed in the first three chapters, and they will now be considered in greater depth.

## ENVIRONMENTAL ANALYSIS

The nature of any environmental analysis involves the problem of uncertainty, which tends to increase with the rate and frequency of change. The situation can also have a high degree of complexity, which can be a function of three factors:

- the diversity of environmental influences faced by a hospitality firm;
- the amount of knowledge required to handle environmental influences;
- the interconnection of different environmental influences.

Different organizations face different situations with different levels of complexity. Highly dynamic conditions require management to undertake an analysis of the future as well as the past, and may involve identifying possible future changes. Complexity can include not only changing technology but a wide range of operating companies, perhaps in different countries with different parts of the organization responsible for different elements of the resources available and the authority to control those resources. In order to process what can be a wide range of information, the construction of a model is frequently regarded as a help to assist management in the strategic decision-making process.

## Auditing and the use of models

The first stage in analysing the environment is an audit of past and current influences. The importance of such influences is not static, and will change over time: for example, consider the changing economic cycle within which all firms operate. Aspects of the environment that can interact with the hospitality firm can include:

- economics,
- demographics,
- sociocultural factors,
- technology,
- capital markets,
- labour markets,
- ecology,
- government, and
- competition.

The issue here is that there will not be one definitive list of environmental factors that affect a hospitality firm; indeed, the relative importance of all these factors will change over time.

A first stage in this auditing process is sometimes referred to as a PEST analysis. It tries to identify the key forces at work in the wider environment by focusing on the **political, economic, social** and **technological** influences on the organization. Such an analysis is essentially trying to answer the following questions:

- What environmental factors are affecting the firm?
- Which of these are the most important at present?
- Which will be important in the next few years?

Taking this approach, a checklist of influences can be created that can be used in a range of models available to guide analysis. In this respect analysis can become part of a firm's long-term development. In identifying not only the key influences, but the drivers of change, it is possible to examine the differing impacts on the firm, both historically and in terms of future trends. The speed of change in technology may suggest a very short lifespan, and will therefore have implications for a firm's impact analysis of the key external influences.

A development in the use of this PEST analysis is that key trends can be built into the construction of scenarios, which again will aid analysis over the longer term. Once key factors have been identified, a view can be constructed of possible future situations. The benefit in this approach is that managers can test the sensitivity of various strategies by asking the inevitable questions: What is the response if . . .? or What will be the effect of . . .? Four elements can be identified in developing scenarios:

- Build a PEST analysis with a limited number of key assumptions restricted to the environmental forces rather than the response of the firm or its competitors.
- It is important to understand historically the trends with regard to assumptions being considered, their impact on market conditions and organizational strategies, and what these assumptions themselves depend upon.
- A number of scenarios can be built, ranging from optimistic to pessimistic.
- Scenarios can be built up from the factors and assumptions, particularly if they are few in number, or they can be built around a number of dominant themes if those factors are numerous.

## The competitive environment

The broader aspects of the environment have now been considered, although the specific competitive environment can also be subjected to analysis as an aid to developing a firm's strategy. Such an approach looks at the factors that directly influence the firm's capability to position itself more effectively against its rivals. The five forces approach proposed by Porter has already been considered in a previous chapter, and the discussion here will be on the key questions arising out of Porter's model.

Porter's framework allows the strategic manager to consider the competitive forces that need the attention of the firm. The forces at work will vary by industry, and indeed a PEST analysis may unearth underlying forces that drive the competitive environment. Porter's analysis should not be regarded as fixed in time, because the forces will change; this should be reflected in the manager's analysis. Not only can this analysis be applied to the firm in question, it can also be applied to competitors. To some extent the firm can influence the five forces and so diminish competitive rivalry and therefore refine the hospitality firm's strategy.

It is therefore key to a firm's success that it understands its positioning relative to its competitors and translates that knowledge into an effective strategy. The first stage in understanding a firm's position is to undertake a competitor analysis. Having identified the key environmental influences, the next stage is an analysis of the key competitive forces. An impact analysis of the competition can only be advanced if consideration is given to the strategies of each competitor, centred around the following areas:

- objectives,
- resource strengths,
- record of performance,
- current strategy,
- any assumptions underlying a competitor's approach to strategy formulation.

A careful look at recent historical trends within the competition may be an indication of how they will react in the future.

From considering each individual competitor a further stage in analysing the competitive environment is to attempt to answer the question: Who are the most direct competitors and on what basis is competition likely to take place?

Not all companies in the same industry can be regarded as competitors, and so the idea of **industry** can be misleading. One way of sharpening up the analysis is by focusing on strategic groups. **Strategic group analysis** aims to identify clearly defined groupings, so that each represents organizations with similar strategic characteristics, following similar strategies or competing on similar bases. Porter suggests that strategic group analysis can be undertaken by considering a number of key characteristics. In this respect the analyst is seeking to establish which characteristics best differentiate firms or groups of firms from one another. This analysis is useful, because it provides a better understanding of the basis of rivalry within strategic groups and the differences with other groups. There may be the possibility of mobility between groups, depending on the barriers to entry. Finally, this strategic group analysis may assist in predicting market changes and help to identify strategic opportunities for new strategies and new strategic groupings.

While strategic group analysis relates to organizations, consideration of market segments and market power looks at an analysis of customers and so seeks to determine market position *vis-à-vis* the competition. Just as one can establish strategic groups, so it is useful to identify market segments, each with different characteristics, needs and wants. In undertaking a market segmentation analysis it is important to remember that there are many bases for segmenting the market. These can be categorized under three headings:

- characteristics of the individual;
- purchase/use situation;
- users' needs and preferences for product characteristics.

Having identified the basis for segmentation the next stage is to assess the attractiveness of the different market segments. This can be achieved by applying the principles of Porter's structural analysis to the market segments being examined. In this respect, entry and substitution need to be considered. When linked to the principle of market power the value of market segmentation is enhanced, as relative market share can be considered a measure of market power. Analysis of market segments can therefore be related to market share and can be linked back to performance benefits of scale and the experience curve effect. Both a quantitative and a qualitative approach to such an analysis can be taken. The result of all this is that a view can be taken as to whether the firm should focus on one or more segments or take a broader approach to the market, and in doing so a strategic choice can be made.

This theme of identifying a firm's competitive position is to relate a strategic business unit (SBU) in relation to others, the market or segment and establish a **growth–share matrix**. The matrix allows an examination of the SBU in relation to market share, relative market power and the growth rate of that market. Depending on the position within the growth–share matrix, different competitive strategies will be appropriate: for example pricing low, or high amounts of advertising and selling when the market is mature, competition is fierce and market share is difficult to achieve. In basing this analysis on an SBU growth–share matrix it is therefore possible to achieve a balanced mix of SBUs. Such a matrix is useful in providing a visual display of the strengths of a portfolio, particularly the ones that have the potential to generate cash and those that are the cash users, and so a strategic direction can be determined. The problem in adopting this matrix approach is the lack of precise measures in the positioning on the matrix, and this might lead to management making decisions based on a less than objective viewpoint. There may be competitive problems in pulling out of a market and allowing a competitor to become even more dominant.

Another form of portfolio analysis, which maps SBUs according to attractiveness and competitive strength, is called the **directional policy matrix**. The SBU can be positioned in terms of both strength and market attractiveness along key indicators identified in the PEST or Porter's five forces analysis. Positioning can be judgemental, or some kind of scoring mechanism can be used. The whole purpose of this approach is that it allows management to focus on the key forces in the environment and determine an appropriate strategy for the portfolio as a whole. All these approaches depend on sufficient information being available to construct the matrix in the first place, and obtaining such information is not always easy.

This ability, just identified, to sense changes in the environment is important, because perceived changes in environmental influences signal the possible need for changes in strategy. The evidence is that firms that are good at sensing the environment perform better than those that are bad at it. However, it is important to stress that the techniques of analysis just discussed are no good in themselves unless the organization has the people with the ability to effect change. It is the sensitivity and flexibility of the people, the quality of management, organizational culture and its structure that will affect the success of this analysis.

## RESOURCES AND CAPABILITY

We have already pointed out the importance of matching the organization's strategies to the environment, but they must be sustainable, and this requires an understanding of the firm's capability and resources. Consideration of capability requires an assessment of core competences, and this analysis will reflect the old strategies, which inevitably are geared to the past. The problem therefore is that a focus on resources may not pay proper attention to the environment and the expectations of stakeholders. Capability is largely determined by the separate activities that the hospitality firm undertakes, such as production and marketing. It is an understanding of these various value activities, and the linkages between them, that assists in assessing capability. Five stages can be identified in assessing strategic capability:

- The resource audit looks at both the quantity and the quality of resources (inside and outside) that are available to the firm.
- A value chain analysis considers how resources are being utilized, controlled and linked together, and so relates resources to their strategic purpose.
- Capability is usually assessed by comparisons with industry norms or historical or best practice.
- Capability may be affected by the balance of resources, which may be inappropriate.
- An analysis of resources requires more than just the creation of lists, and so the identification of key issues will allow the organization to gain a strategic insight.

In order to undertake this analysis of resources and capabilities a first stage in this approach is a resource audit.

## Resource audit

This stage of analysing strategic capability looks at the resource base under a number of areas, such as physical resources, human resources, financial resources, and intangibles. In taking this perspective an audit should look not only at those owned but also those that the firm has access to. Strategically important resources can be outside the firm's ownership. At this stage it would also be useful to identify which resources are critical to the firm's capability. This auditing process can be developed further with a value chain analysis.

## Value chain analysis

Value chain analysis attempts to identify how a firm's activities underpin its competitive advantage, by linking resources to performance. This analysis involves identifying the building blocks within the organization and assessing the value added from each. It moves on from the profitability of each step to an identification of the value activities, and hence the firm's competitive advantage. The primary activities of the firm are grouped around five main areas:

- inbound logistics,
- operations,
- outbound logistics,
- marketing and sales,
- service.

Each primary activity is linked to support activities, which cover:

- procurement,
- technology development,
- human resource management,
- infrastructure.

Most industries do not undertake all these value activities, and therefore the firm is part of a wider value system in creating its hospitality products or services. Therefore it is not enough to look at the firm's internal position; value can be created within the supply and distribution chains.

Resources are of no value unless they are valued by the final consumer, and therefore a view must be taken as to how the resources have been utilized. It is both the value activities and the linkages between them that are a source of competitive advantage for the firm. The way to discriminate between activities and linkages is to focus on the few critical factors that sustain the competitive position. These are referred to as the **cost** or **value drivers,** and they determine the cost or value of each activity.

In assessing how resource utilization influences strategic capability, it is important to distinguish between efficiency and effectiveness. Efficiency is important when competing on a cost basis, whereas effectiveness can be related to sustaining a strategy of uniqueness for the product or service. It is these twin issues of efficiency and effectiveness that will now be considered.

## Efficiency and effectiveness

Cost

The distinction between efficiency and effectiveness can be investigated further by first analysing **cost efficiency**. This analysis can be achieved by firms in a number of ways, and it is possible to assess how such approaches relate to the cost drivers already mentioned. One such approach frequently mentioned is to consider the economies of scale that can be identified in distribution, marketing or capital investment costs. The input costs of supply that flow from intermediaries are another area that deserves attention, and such a supplier relationship needs to be controlled. The design of the production process is another area that can produce cost savings in terms of capacity, productivity and yield. The experience curve has already been mentioned: over time a firm may learn to undertake tasks better, and this may influence unit costs. Cost savings can also be a function of market share. If a firm grows more slowly than the competition, competitors will gain a cost advantage through experience. The weakness in considering experience is the collective experience gained across firms in the same industry. Equally, this factor should not be seen in isolation, as other factors affect cost, and as a final point some companies may gain experience in some key aspects such as technology.

Value added

Value added or effectiveness links the matching of products or services to the specific needs of the customer, or more usually the market segment. One aspect in judging value added is to determine the extent to which customers would be willing to pay more for a unique feature: that is, what value would clients place on this uniqueness? An analysis would, in addition to the product or service, extend to such features as distribution channels and credit available. Communication through the medium of brand image or marketing literature contributes to effectiveness, and so all these aspects allow an analysis of the value drivers of a business.

Resources

Resource measurement and control can create a conflict between efficiency, performance and control. High stock levels, while important for customer service, will affect the costs of inventory management. In focusing on inventory, one approach is to pay regard to the 'critical few rather than the trivial many': sometimes known as **ABC analysis** or **Pareto analysis**. The key factor in considering such control mechanisms is that they should aid the decision-making process, yet many provide historical data after the event. It has already been shown that the value system is not just contained within the firm itself. Control of resources can therefore extend in a number of ways. Vertical integration is one approach; another way is to insist that suppliers conform to detailed specifications.

A further approach in controlling resources is the philosophy of **total quality management** (TQM). TQM takes the view that it is better to involve all individuals and groups within the value system, both inside and outside the firm, and this attitude can extend to suppliers and distributors. Finally, merchandising through joint promotion or incentive can be another way in which one firm exercises control over another. Control of resources in a strategic sense focuses on the value system and the management of the linkages within it. Such an approach becomes more complex as the hospitality firm becomes international.

**Financial capability**

From a strategic perspective different stakeholder groups assess the financial standing of the firm from different viewpoints. The concept of stakeholders has already been introduced in Chapter 1, and will be extended further in this chapter. The expectations of stakeholders vary: from those of shareholders and bankers to those of managers, suppliers and employees. To use financial ratio analysis without noting these differences in expectations can distort the strategic perspective. Shareholders, for instance are interested in their investment, while bankers are concerned with the risk attached to their loans. Suppliers are obviously interested in being paid, a point that relates to the liquidity of the firm, and employees will want their wages (again the link here is back to the firm's liquidity). The performance of the firm is the concern of management, and allows them to succeed in satisfying the aspirations of the other stakeholders just mentioned.

A consideration of ratios within a financial analysis is important, although for it to be of benefit some form of comparison will need to be established. Equally, expenditure above the average is not in itself bad if such a policy brings with it added value. A hierarchy of importance can be attached to ratios, depending on the industry in question, and so the manager needs to be selective. Finally, this importance of particular ratios will change over time, depending on the stage in the life cycle that the hospitality firm has reached.

The importance of looking at financial analysis from a stakeholder analysis perspective is that ratios tend to exclude one key stakeholder: the community, and the social cost of the firm's activities. Exclusion of this particular stakeholder can be considered a weakness. It has also been shown that performance should be related to perceived value enjoyed by the customer, and the need to add maximum value at minimum cost. The focus in most financial analysis tends to ignore customer expectations.

## The need for comparisons

The discussion so far, particularly with regard to financial capabilities, has implied a need for comparisons in order to generate an effective choice and implementation of strategy. Value analysis and linkages are key elements of value chain analysis, and over time the value system changes. An insight into resources and capabilities can be gained by considering historical trends, industry norms and best practice.

**Historical trends** This form of analysis looks at previous years to identify any significant changes in the key financial ratios. By taking this approach, possible strategic drift can be identified, and so trends can be identified that are not otherwise apparent.

**Industry norms** In order to put a firm's resources and performance in perspective, a historical analysis can be built, comparing it with other firms, and so capability can be determined. The problem with this approach is that the industry as a whole may be performing badly. Equally, a significant difference in a particular ratio may be one firm's way of differentiating itself from the competition by offering a higher level of service.

**Best practice** There are obviously problems in using the first two forms of analysis, and so the basis of comparison could be with best practice and the use of benchmarks of performance related to best practice. One example of this approach is to create a detailed competitor profile, identifying key performance statistics that relate to critical value activities. Once those key value activities have been identified, key performance targets or benchmarks can be established.

Best practice may be found in a number of industries, and so benchmarking is best analysed for separate value activities.

In building on this analysis of best practice, a base budget review goes back to the fundamental questions: Why is a service offered? Why in that particular way? Are there examples of best practice elsewhere? Should the service be reshaped in the light of these comparisons?

## CASE STUDY: FORTE PLC, DIAGNOSING ORGANIZATIONAL PERFORMANCE

A major part of analysing a firm's current status is the appraisal of its present and past financial performance. The process can reveal a great deal of information about the firm, the industry and the effectiveness of management. The aim of this case study is to provide the theoretical background necessary to carry out a financial analysis of Forte plc. Objectives to be met are:

- to discuss how financial analysis is carried out;
- to describe the range of financial ratios for examining financial data, and to discuss the significance of each ratio in assessing the financial position and performance of a business;
- to illustrate the importance of comparing company financial data with the industry;
- to highlight and examine the limitations in comparing financial data with industry average.

## Financial analysis

Financial analysis is a comprehensive term that refers to any use of available financial data to evaluate the performance, condition, or future prospects of an organization. Many tools and techniques are available for examining an organization's performance. The most useful tools for managers are those that increase understanding of the cause-and-effect relationship in an organization, those that compare with industry trends, and those that allow comparisons with other organizations.

The primary source of financial data is the firm's annual report. The objective of financial analysis is to establish relationships between data items and to highlight changes and trends that may explain the firm's past performance and give clues to its future performance. In general, financial analysis involves:

- converting data into ratios and percentages that indicate relationships and trends;
- comparing the relationships and trends with the standard of performance.

## Financial ratios

A ratio expresses the relationship of one figure with another figure, and provided the information is available such ratios are relatively easy to calculate. They can sketch out the financial profile of a business, although interpreting them can become more complex. It is important to identify through skill and judgement whether changes in financial ratios are significant and what the underlying cause of any change might be. The ratios can be used to analyse the firm's performance over time to compare it with the industry average.

## Ratio classification

Although there are numerous ratios that may be computed from financial statements, there are certain ratios that are commonly used. According to the particular aspect of a business, ratio classifications may be identified as:

- profitability;
- liquidity;
- gearing (leverage);
- activity (efficiency).

Profitability ratios

Profitability ratios indicate the firm's operational efficiency and by relating this to other key figures a clearer view of performance can be gained. Profitability is the net result of a large number of policies and decisions chosen by management. The major ratios are as follows:

- **Net profit margin**. The ratio expresses the net profit as a percentage of sales. It can be used to show efficiency after all expenses and income taxes have been considered.
- **Return on equity (ROE)**. ROE reveals the rate of return on equity as a percentage of the equity shareholders' stake in the business.
- **Return on capital employed (ROCE)**. This ratio expresses the profit available to the suppliers of capital. Like ROE, it is a useful measure of performance, as it measures the input in the form of capital employed against output in the form of profit.
- **Return on investment (ROI)**. This ratio expresses the net profit (after tax) as a percentage of total assets. It is an essential ratio, as it measures the assets held by the business. Differences between businesses in the age and condition of their fixed assets will complicate the interpretation of this ratio.

Liquidity ratios

Liquidity ratios are used to judge how well a business is able to meet is short-term financial commitments. It is vital for a business to maintain good liquidity, as even a profitable business may be forced to cease trading if there are insufficient liquid resources. There are two common ratios used:

- **Current ratio**. The current ratio shows the relationship between current assets and current liabilities, and is an indicator of short-term cash solvency. It is a crude measure of liquidity because it does not consider the liquidity of individual components of current assets. For example, stock is not so easily converted into cash.
- **Quick or acid test**. This is a more stringent measure of liquidity than the above ratio, as it focuses on cash and excludes stock and prepayments, which are not easily converted into cash.

Gearing (leverage) ratios

Gearing ratios are used to assess the financial risk of a business. Gearing deals with the financial structure and financial capacity of the firm. It measures the magnitude of investors' and lenders' claims on the business, and indicates the firm's ability to meet long-term obligations. The ratios that can be used here are:

- **Debt to equity ratio**. This ratio shows the relative commitment of shareholders and creditors. A high ratio would indicate that the firm is committed to a high level of long-term debts, or that equity has declined.
- **Debt to total assets**. This indicates the percentage of total funds that has been provided by creditors. This is important, as creditors must be paid before any profits can be paid to shareholders.
- **Interest cover**. Interest cover examines the firm's ability to meet its regular financial commitment. It attempts to measure the amount of protection available to lenders: the higher the ratio, the greater the ability of the business to cover its interest payments.

Activity
(efficiency)
ratios

Activity ratios are used to measure how efficiently the company is utilizing its assets. They provide useful insights into management policies and operational efficiency. The ratios that may be used here are:

- **Stock turnover**. This ratio shows how fast a company moves its stock. It expresses the relationship between the average stock held and the cost of sales. The **stock days** can be calculated by inverting this ratio.
- **Debtor turnover**. This is used to show the number of days required to collect receivables. If debtor turnover is much lower than the industry average, this may suggest that the firm adopts a more liberal credit policy than its competitors, or that it has a weak credit policy.
- **Credit turnover**. The ratio is similar to that of debtor turnover, except that it looks at the number of days before paying the firm's creditors.
- **Total asset turnover**. Asset turnover is a rough measure of how well assets are being used to generate sales. It is particularly sensitive to the type of industry involved.

## Comparisons with standards of performance

Once the financial calculations have been made, they must be compared with certain standards of performance for interpretation. The most common of these standards are:

- the historical performance of the organization;
- the performance with industry average.

A thorough analysis would include an evaluation of performance against both sets of standards.

Comparison
with historical
performance

Here, the firm is evaluated in the light of its past performance in order to reveal underlying problems and trends that may affect future performance. Information, such as sales and profit growth, gross margin fluctuations, changes in working capital, and increases/decreases in funding of particular accounts, indicates the financial health of the firm and provides clues to management's philosophy and future performance.

In this case study of Forte plc, a period of five years (1990–94) has been analysed in order to make a substantial critique of the company.

Comparison
with industry
average

A comparison of the firm with the industry average in the same period also yields critical information. For example, in making a comparison of historical performance it may reveal that the firm's sales are deteriorating, but when these ratios are compared with the industry average it may reveal that sales have declined significantly for the industry as a whole. So comparison with the industry average can carry new implications in the light of new information because it serves as a benchmark of what is typical in a particular industry.

## Limitations of financial analysis

There is a very wide range of information available for the purposes of analysing company accounts. The following points identify certain assumptions and limitations in carrying out a financial analysis of a company.

- It is assumed that all economic, social and market fluctuations are to have the same effect on all companies.
- The limitation in comparing Forte plc with the industry is that the industry is made up of many small firms and only a few large firms. It is also made up of various markets, such as hotels, retail shops and restaurants. It could be that one segment of the market is not doing so well, thus bringing the total industry figure down.
- The annual reports from Forte provide the source information, but they are consolidated: that is, the separate subsidiary companies are put together in one report, giving only an overview.
- Published company reports can be biased, as the directors of the company will highlight and emphasize the positive points and try to cover up any negative impacts that the company may have suffered throughout the financial year.
- The annual reports are completed according to accounting principles that the company wants to follow, allowing them to present their accounts in favourable ways.
- A number of financial reporting agencies provide extensive information on Forte's accounts and the industry average for the period 1990–94, and it is these sources that this case study is based on.
- It was found that information obtained from different sources can conflict. For example, Forte's published accounts are different from information available on the financial reporting agencies Datastream or Extel. One explanation is that individual published company reports may use different accounting standards when drawing up their final accounts. The financial reporting agencies, however, formulate all accounts on the basis of the same accounting standard being used.

It is clear from the above comments that there is no ideal standard of comparison.

## Ratio analysis of Forte plc

While a number of ratios have been discussed, the areas that will now be considered in relation to Forte plc and the industry average are:

- profitability analysis;
- working capital analysis;
- activity analysis;
- gearing analysis.

**Profitability analysis**

From the figures in Table 4.1, Forte's **net profit margin** has fluctuated; it decreased in 1991–92 and subsequently has slowly started to grow again. In contrast, the industry average has seen net profit margins decreasing dramatically throughout the five-year period. The industry and Forte net profit decreases during this period could be due to certain economic conditions:

**Table 4.1 Profitability analysis (%)**

| Ratios | Forte | | | | | Industry average | | | | |
|---|---|---|---|---|---|---|---|---|---|---|
| | *1990* | *1991* | *1992* | *1993* | *1994* | *1990* | *1991* | *1992* | *1993* | *1994* |
| NP margin | 13 | 10.7 | 6.4 | 11 | 11.3 | 15.5 | 14.8 | 7.6 | (3.2) | 5.7 |
| ROCE | 14.2 | 9.4 | 5.8 | 11 | 10.1 | 13.5 | 13.9 | 7.1˙ | 4.1 | 7.7 |
| ROE | 8.3 | 5 | 1.2 | 4.4 | 3.7 | 8.3 | 7.6 | 1.6 | (15.7) | (1.2) |

1 The demand in continental Europe gateway cities was reduced.
2 US demand remains weak, although this is cushioned by a significant reduction in growth of national room supply.
3 The Gulf War broke out in 1991, which virtually stopped international travel between capital cities, where the majority of the hotels are located. The main brands affected were the high-market brands: Forte Crest, Grand and Exclusive.
4 The recessions in the UK and USA had a bitter and lasting impact, which started in September 1990, with slow recovery in 1994. Forte suffered again with its high-market brands, which are mainly located in London and primary provincial areas.

Other factors that could have affected Forte's net profit performance are:

• falls in productivity during the late 1980s;
• loss of market share to its major competitors;
• the hotel division's stifling corporate bureaucracy.

The general trend for Forte and the industry is that **ROCE** (Table 4.1) has been fluctuating in line with profit margins. This is because profits had been reduced during the period 1992–93, as deduced from analysis of the profit margin.

The company's long-term loans also increased significantly during the five-year period, and only during the last two years has the company been trying to reduce its long-term debt drastically. This is surprising, as over the past three years Forte has made several key disposals, which not only raised more cash than had been expected but also increased the significance of hotels to the group: the sale of airport catering services; the sale of Gardner Merchant to management for £402 million in 1992; the sale of Forte's 50% share in Kentucky Fried Chicken in the UK to Pepsico for around £40 million in 1994; and the sale of 16 restaurant properties, mainly trading under the Dome Café format, to the Pelican Group for £11.5 million in June 1994.

During the period 1990–94 Forte had also acquired and started many new projects in order to strengthen its portfolio. These included the acquisition of Crest Hotels for £300 million in 1990; in 1992, a joint venture with AgipPetroli to operate eighteen hotels in Italy; also in 1992, the acquisition of Sogerba, which operates 52 motorway restaurants in Europe and 43 motorway service facilities in France for £64 million; and the most recent acquisition, in 1994, the Meridien hotel chain from Air France.

Forte's strategy of restructuring and focusing on hotels as its core activity is reflected in 1993 where ROCE is increasing. In comparison with the industry, Forte is performing much better. The findings of the ROE ratio are very similar to the other profitability ratios (Table 4.1). Poor trading records have resulted in low ROE, with 1992 being the worst for both Forte and the industry.

**Working capital analysis**

From the figures identified in Table 4.2 and 4.3, it is clear that Forte is using creditors to finance its working capital. This is of course a riskier and more aggressive method, but its advantage is that it is cheaper than using long-term debts. The company has been able to maintain this by decreasing debtor days and increasing it creditor days. By comparing the current ratio with the acid test it is shown that Forte is managing its liquidity well by ensuring that minimum funds are tied up in stock. This can also be illustrated in the low stock days that the company maintains. These points are also illustrated to some extent in the activity analysis detailed in Table 4.3.

The acid test ratio shows that the industry is not as efficient as Forte. This is because Forte is primarily in the business of hotels and restaurants, where stock is perishable, whereas the industry is made up of many firms where high stock levels are maintained.

**Table 4.2 Working capital analysis**

| | Forte | | | | | Industry average | | | | |
|---|---|---|---|---|---|---|---|---|---|---|
| | 1990 | 1991 | 1992 | 1993 | 1994 | 1990 | 1991 | 1992 | 1993 | 1994 |
| Ratios | | | | | | | | | | |
| Current | 0.97 | 1.02 | 0.97 | 0.74 | 1.15 | 1.15 | 1.22 | 1.47 | 1.21 | 1.29 |
| Acid test | 0.82 | 0.85 | 0.82 | 0.59 | 1.03 | 0.79 | 0.83 | 1.03 | 0.81 | 0.89 |
| Working capital cycle (days) | 12 | 12 | 8 | (11) | (8) | 20 | 25 | 27 | 13 | 7 |

**Table 4.3 Activity analysis**

| | Forte | | | | | Industry average | | | | |
|---|---|---|---|---|---|---|---|---|---|---|
| | 1990 | 1991 | 1992 | 1993 | 1994 | 1990 | 1991 | 1992 | 1993 | 1994 |
| Stock turnover (per month) | 3.25× | 2.78× | 3.2× | 3.32× | 3.48× | 1× | 1.1× | 1.03× | 1.3× | 1.2× |
| Stock days | 8 | 10 | 9 | 8 | 8 | 26 | 25 | 27 | 24 | 24 |
| Debtor days | 40 | 43 | 42 | 27 | 29 | 41 | 41 | 40 | 32 | 27 |
| Creditor days | 36 | 41 | 43 | 46 | 45 | 47 | 41 | 40 | 43 | 44 |

Gearing analysis  Forte's gearing has been increasing over the past five years, with a slight decrease in 1994. The industry is also increasing its gearing, but this is greater than Forte, as illustrated in Table 4.4.

**Table 4.4 Gearing analysis**

|  | Forte | | | | | Industry average | | | | |
|---|---|---|---|---|---|---|---|---|---|---|
|  | *1990* | *1991* | *1992* | *1993* | *1994* | *1990* | *1991* | *1992* | *1993* | *1994* |
| Debt to equity ratio (%) | 35 | 35 | 43 | 46 | 43 | 39 | 38 | 46 | 54 | 51 |
| Interest cover | 2.9× | 2.6× | 1.5× | 1.3× | 1.5× | 3.6× | 2.8× | 1.4× | (0.6)× | 1.1× |

Not surprisingly, gearing rose in 1992, when the company was undergoing major acquisitions to fulfil its strategy to penetrate and increase exposure in the growing European market sector. In 1994, Forte's debt was still above the £1.2 billion level, but the company was able to maintain cash positive for the year ended January 1994 for several reasons:

- The disposal of the company's stake in KFC coupled with the sale of Alpha would have brought in around £217 million.
- Interest charges fell as debt was restructured.
- The enhanced scrip dividend has cut the cost of the dividend and reduced the tax charge for the year.

The increase in gearing can also be due to higher capital expenditure. Forte has also kept a longer-term view by continuing to maintain high capital expenditure, even during the recession. Its aim is that by investing materially in the refurbishment of its Exclusive and Grand hotels it will prepare the brands for economic recovery and so produce greater than expected room rates in the medium term for these brands.

Forte is intending to restructure its debt and thus its gearing level. It renegotiated its debt in 1993–94 so that only 48% was repayable within five years, a further 20% being repayable between five and ten years, and the remainder beyond ten years. At present Forte is extremely sensitive to the value of sterling. Weakness in sterling would increase gearing, as approximately half its debt is in sterling, one quarter is in US dollars, and the remainder is mostly in European currencies. The latest acquisition of the Meridien chain from Air France would have also increased its debt in the French franc.

**Interest cover** is very low for both Forte and the industry. Forte had been able to maintain an interest cover of four times during the latter half of the 1980s; judging from the figures it still has a fair way to go before it can reach this level again.

Interest cover fell to its lowest in 1993; this was reflected in the industry, where this fall was negative. Only through slightly better trading and the benefits of cost savings was Forte able to improve this in 1994. Only as we see more disposals of Forte's obsolete hotels, rising profits and income and lower interest charges will it be possible for it to reach acceptable levels of interest cover.

## Summary

This analysis of key financial ratios applied to both Forte plc and the industry has shown that indications of organizational performance can be deduced. Such an analysis, while having limitations, can be considered useful in the strategic management process.

## The balance of resources

One issue not addressed so far is the balance of resources within the firm as a whole, and in this respect three issues can be identified:

- the balance of activities and resources within the firm;
- the balance of people in terms of skills and personalities within the firm;
- the balance of flexibility within the firm with uncertainty in its environment, and the firm's attitude to risk.

Portfolio analysis

In order to explore these three issues an important element in assessing capability is to determine the extent to which activities within the firm's portfolio are complementary, and so a suitable mix needs to be achieved. Such a classification of business units can be related to both market share and growth, and so the position of the firm can be determined in relation to its competitors. Such an analysis should be applied to units dealing with particular market segments and not whole markets, and so time should be devoted to considering the overall mix of the firm's activities. This approach will result in different targets and expectations for different parts of the firm, and will therefore extend to the resource allocation process. The original approach to portfolio analysis was taken by the Boston Consulting Group, which looked at a business's need to plan its cash flow requirements across its portfolio; yet one weakness of this approach is the lack of attention paid to the behavioural aspects of this specific portfolio. In many organizations the critical resource is not cash but management time and energy. Some indeed may argue that if the activities are operated separately and the corporate centre is reduced the free market will allocate resources more effectively.

Skills and personalities

What some writers have described as **non-tradable assets** comprise the mix of skills and abilities required to run a business, and it is these that can be regarded as a source of competitive advantage. A range of skills can be seen as linked together within the value chain. Not only must there be a balance of skills, there must also be a balance of personalities in order for the business to operate effectively.

Flexibility

The firm's resources needs to be both flexible and adaptable, and such an issue cannot be divorced from the level of uncertainty faced by the firm. Flexibility has no strategic importance without an appreciation of the issue of uncertainty. Once the areas of uncertainty have been identified, a view can be taken as to whether they can be accommodated or whether they present a constraint on strategic development.

## Identifying the key issues

Having identified the elements of resource analysis, the key issues in terms of strengths and weaknesses need to be determined. It is from this **SWOT analysis** that a judgement can be made as to future courses of action.

SWOT stands for **strengths, weaknesses, opportunities** and **threats**, and applied in a structured way it can be a useful analytical device. Three steps can be identified:

1 The current strategy needs to be identified, and specifically the one being followed.
2 The changes in the firm's environment need to be determined.
3 The resource profile of the firm needs to be analysed in terms of both capabilities and limitations.

This analysis will give a view as to the extent that environmental changes and influences provide opportunities or threats within the current strategies and the firm's capabilities. In following this analysis systematically there is a requirement for an understanding both of the environment and of the resources within the firm.

This analysis can also be applied to a comparison with the firm's competitors. In identifying the core competences of the firm in relation to the competition, any weaknesses that need to be avoided can also be identified. This approach will need an analysis of the competition's resources as well.

Four questions are raised in this analysis:

- Who owns the core competences?
- How durable are the competences?
- How transferable are the competences?
- How replicable are the competences?

In answering these key questions the robustness of the core competences can be determined.

This analysis of the environment, resources and capabilities will now be applied in the following case study of the Holiday Inn Birmingham and its decision on a proposed refurbishment.

## CASE STUDY: HOLIDAY INN BIRMINGHAM, PROPOSED REFURBISHMENT

The central issue to be considered in this proposal is to refurbish the Holiday Inn

Birmingham, over a two-year period commencing November 1993, at a cost of £2,607,000 ($3.5 million) including day-to-day investment of £100,000 ($135,000).

## Background and description

The Holiday Inn Birmingham is a 288-room core brand hotel, which first opened in June 1973. The hotel has one restaurant, two bars, sixteen meeting rooms of varying sizes, leisure facilities and free guest car parking. The hotel was purchased by Bass from Holiday Inn Corporation in 1987 and was initially operated as a Holiday Inn franchise. The hotel has traded successfully under Bass stewardship but now requires refurbishment to current core brand standards to regain a competitive position in the market.

## Strategic fit

The UK is regarded by Bass as a key market for development and distribution in the five-year period to 1998. In support of this growth in distribution it is essential for the brand to gain and hold presence in major international cities (such as Birmingham) within the markets under development.

The Holiday Inn Birmingham is located in one of Europe's major international cities – the second city of England – and is well situated in a downtown location at the hub of the refocused city centre. The International Convention Centre and Birmingham International Airport are a 20 minute drive away.

The company's strategy is to develop distribution with the minimal investment and to maximize shareholder value. The investment of maintenance capital expenditures must be targeted to support the firm's strategic aims and maintain profitability.

## Market commentary

Economic environment

The sources of the city's hotel business are dominated by domestic visitors, who accounted for over 90 per cent of room-nights sold in 1992 (82 per cent in 1991).

During this period the Birmingham hotel market consisted primarily of corporate business (50 per cent) and full rate (15 per cent) in 1992. Conference and exhibition business was 8 per cent in 1991 but doubled to 16 per cent in 1992, reflecting the impact of the new International Conference Centre. Business at weekends and during the summer months is limited, with group tour and leisure segments together accounting for less than 15 per cent of rooms sold.

The upturn in the general economy during 1993 is now recognized in a number of key economic indicators. With a new convention centre fully opened and utilized, 1995 is expected to mark a base improvement in Birmingham's fortunes.

Competitive overview

The major city hotels in the market sector are identified in Table 4.5. The Copthorne, Hyatt and Novotel are regarded as the main competitors to the Holiday Inn.

Market segmentation

The 1992 key operating indicators of the competition were as indicated in Table 4.6. Holiday Inn's position in the market is depressed because of the poor physical

**Table 4.5 Competitive overview**

| | |
|---|---|
| Forte Crest | 254 rooms |
| Hyatt Regency | 319 rooms |
| Copthorne | 212 rooms |
| Holiday Inn | 288 rooms |
| Plough & Harrow | 44 rooms |
| Swallow | 98 rooms |
| Novotel | 148 rooms |

**Table 4.6 Operating indicators of competing hotels**

| | Rooms available, 1992 | Occupancy, 1992 (%) | ARR (£) |
|---|---|---|---|
| Holiday Inn | 105,408 | 55.8 | 47.44 |
| Copthorne | 78,690 | 63.8 | 47.02 |
| Hyatt Regency | 116,754 | 50.2 | 62.57 |
| Novotel | 54,168 | 56.5 | 40.68 |
| Total competition | 249,612 | 55.8 | 49.51 |

condition of the hotel. Sheraton are understood to be considering the development of a new 350-room city centre hotel.

## Supply and demand generators

The City of Birmingham is undergoing a gradual transformation towards a more service-based economy and away from its traditional manufacturing roots. This process is continuing, with several major regeneration and investment projects planned, notably the expansion of the National Exhibition Centre and the redevelopment of the Brindley Place and Heartlands areas, both close to the city centre.

The International Convention Centre (ICC) and the National Indoor Arena, both opened in 1991, are major new facilities that offer the prospect of attracting a variety of national and international events to Birmingham. These developments will continue to provide an increasingly important source of hotel demand. The ICC is a five minute walk away from the Holiday Inn Birmingham.

## Sources of business

The top ten accounts which generate approximately 27 per cent of all the hotel's business, are identified in Table 4.7. Holidex, Holiday Inn's computer reservation system, generates around 15 per cent of all bookings.

Table 4.7 Sources of business

| Company | Room volume, 1992–93 | Room volume forecast |
|---|---|---|
| NCR | 3,500 | 7,000 |
| BCVB | 3,000 | 2,200 |
| Bass plc | 2,250 | 2,250 |
| Carole Duffy | 2,000 | 1,500 |
| WGT | 1,500 | 1,000 |
| Trinifold Travel | 1,500 | 1,500 |
| Central TV | 750 | 1,500 |
| JBA | 800 | 800 |
| AIG Europe | 500 | 500 |
| Moulinex Swan | 500 | 500 |
| Learning Tree | – | 1,500 |
| Lombard | – | 1,500 |
| Total | 16,300 | 21,750 |

## Hotel property overview

The hotel, which first opened in 1973, currently (1993) has an uncompetitive bedroom product and a dated appearance, both internally and externally. The hotel is subject to a favourable ground lease, which expires in 2093. The site is leased from Central Television, who occupy the adjoining office block.

The hotel's lifts are in need of an overhaul, and there are no stairways from the reception. The boiler for the public areas was overhauled during 1991, and approximately 35 per cent of the individual air-conditioning units in the bedrooms have been replaced. The replacement of the remaining bedroom air-conditioning units was budgeted for 1992–93 but has been held pending this asset management review of the property.

Three alternatives can be identified in this review:

- to refurbish the hotel up to current core brand standards over the course of two years;
- to accelerate the refurbishment and complete in one year;
- to dispose of the hotel immediately to a franchisee.

## Projected results

The major assumptions incorporated in the projected results are:

- The UK has reached the bottom of its recession; business confidence will recover slowly during the remainder of 1993, and consumer demand will increase after Christmas 1993.
- Birmingham will strengthen its position as the second city of England and move away from its sole dependence upon manufacturing industries, providing a more stable trading base for the future.

If the hotel is not refurbished, operational staff foresee continuing downward pressure on the key drivers of occupancy and rate over the next three years (1993–1996). The key drivers under this assumption are identified in Table 4.8. If the hotel is refurbished over 1993–94 and 1994–95, the key drivers in current-day values are projected as those identified in Table 4.9.

## Description of improved business mix

The refurbishment will strengthen the hotel's position generally, but in particular in the locally negotiated commercial and seminar segments. These points are illustrated in Table 4.10. The refurbishment of rooms will have an effect on the

### Table 4.8 Effect if no refurbishment takes place

|  | Occupancy (%) | ARR (£) |
|---|---|---|
| 1992–93 | 58.7 | 48.06 |
| 1993–94 | 58.5 | 50.21 |
| 1994–95 | 55.2 | 48.01 |
| 1995–96 | 53.5 | 46.01 |

### Table 4.9 Effects on the hotel if refurbishment takes place

|  | Occupancy (%) | ARR (£) |
|---|---|---|
| 1992–93 | 58.7 | 48.06 |
| 1993–94 | 57.3 | 50.21 |
| 1994–95 | 61.0 | 51.51 |
| 1995–96 | 62.5 | 52.50 |

*Note:* Inflation is assumed at 4%

### Table 4.10 Improved business mix

| Number of rooms | Current projection, 1993–94 | Refurbishment increment, 1993–94 | Adjusted to give 1994–95 | Refurbishment increment, 1994–95 | Adjusted to give 1995–96 |
|---|---|---|---|---|---|
| Tours | 6,001 | −600 | 5,401 | −1,902 | 3,499 |
| Employee discount | 499 |  | 499 | 74 | 573 |
| Sports | 6,577 | −639 | 5,938 | −325 | 5,613 |
| Weekender | 2,264 |  | 2,264 | 110 | 2,374 |
| Leisure | 6,227 |  | 6,226 | −617 | 5,609 |
| Personal | 0 |  | 0 | 0 | 0 |
| Corporate | 9,351 | 1,501 | 10,852 | −52 | 10,800 |
| Commercial | 23,087 | 601 | 23,688 | 1,636 | 25,324 |
| Rack rate | 2,250 | 887 | 3,137 | 863 | 4,000 |
| Seminars | 4,752 | 556 | 5,308 | 874 | 6,182 |
| Airline crew | 1,521 |  | 1,521 | 73 | 1,594 |
| Airline delayed | 0 |  | 0 | 0 | 0 |
| Total sold | 62,528 | 2,306 | 64,834 | 734 | 65,568 |
| Average room rate | 50.21 |  | 51.51 |  | 52.50 |

leisure segments because of the close proximity of the exhibition halls. The improvement in rate is business-mix driven, not a real increase in tariff.

## Sale to franchisee

Since the property valuation review in October 1992, trading in Birmingham has continued to be depressed. The hotel was valued at 1 October 1992 at £11 million ($19.5 million) excluding tenant's fixtures and fittings. It had been valued in 1989 on a comparable basis at £22.8 million ($40.5 million). The prospects for the hotel and past valuations imply that a refurbished property, trading in better economic conditions, should command a much better market value than in its present state.

Risk factor

The potential for this location is good. A major risk surrounds Central TV's provisional plans to build a second office block on the site during the next five to ten years. While the end result should create additional demand for hotel rooms, the period of development may have negative impact on the hotel's trading. The refurbishment of the hotel does not require any additional management resources. The refurbishment would be project managed locally and supervised by the Holiday Inn's Architecture and Design Department based in Brussels.

## Financial analysis

Sensitivity

One of the key assumptions in the refurbishment proposal is that, without the refurbishment, there will be a decrease in both the hotel occupancy and the average room rate. If the occupancy and rate projected in the budget are maintained in the future, and do not decrease, the net present value of the refurbishment excluding terminal values is negative (£1,062,000), ($1.4 million) or including terminal values (£307,000) ($415,000).

The breakeven for shareholder value, based on the key drivers in the stabilized year, is:

|  | Excluding terminal value | Including terminal value |
|---|---|---|
| Occupancy | 61.0% | 51.5% |
| Average rate | £51.82 ($70) | £47.70 ($64) |

A change in occupancy of ±1 per cent or rate of ±£1 affects shareholder value by:

|  | Excluding terminal value | Including terminal value |
|---|---|---|
| Occupancy ±1% | ±£98,000 ($132,000) | ±£170,000 ($230,000) |
| Average rate ±£1 | ±£220,000 ($297,000) | ±£380,000) ($51,000) |

Depreciation

Some assets that are to be replaced in the refurbishment are not yet fully written down. The additional value of depreciation charged for these assets in 1993–94 is £219,000 ($295,000) and in 1994–95 is £80,000 ($108,000).

## Capital investment: scope of work

The planned work will address the major aspects of the hotel that give rise to quality and functional standards. Refurbishment will be focused on the bedrooms, bathrooms, lifts and bedroom air conditioners, and will be phased over a two-year period. The cost of this refurbishment is budgeted at £2,507,000. The annual amounts are £1,747,000 in 1993–94 and £760,000 in 1994–95. There are minor day-to-day capital plans, which would go ahead with or without the refurbishment. The value of these is £100,000. The total spend over the course of the two-year period is projected at £2,607,000 ($3.5 million).

This case study has illustrated some of the issues involved in analysing the environment, resources and capabilities. A further issue, directly relevant to an international company such as Holiday Inn, is cultural influences and stakeholder analysis, and this will now be discussed.

## CULTURAL INFLUENCES AND STAKEHOLDER ANALYSIS

### The wider environment

It has already been pointed out in Chapter 1 that one key aspect of the strategic management process is an analysis of the wider environment. The cultural context and the influence of stakeholders are aspects that affect strategic formulation and implementation, and an understanding of them is an important element of an environmental analysis.

The cultural context

There have been a number of research studies into how national culture influences organizational structure, with the central conclusion that individual countries are markedly different from each other. This research is a reminder that the way in which organizations analyse and respond to their environment is strongly tied up with national culture, which is a key frame of reference for managers. While it is perhaps dangerous to stereotype nations, two extremes can be identified:

- cultures where uncertainty is managed by attempting to reduce it; where organizations are seen as having control and being proactive; and where the hierarchy, the individual and the work tasks are stressed;
- cultures where uncertainty is accepted as given; where the organization has less control and is reactive; and where the orientation is towards group and social concerns.

The adaptive model of stategic management is more likely to be found in the second type of culture.

These **external influences** not only include the values of society just mentioned but also the issue of organized groups. Individuals often have allegiances to organized groups that are very influential on their beliefs, values and assumptions, and are regarded as a key frame of reference. These allegiances may be highly institutionalized and directly related to their work situation, or more informal and unrelated. The membership of professional bodies or institutions can be particularly important in organizations with a high proportion of professional staff.

**Internal influences** in respect of an organization's culture can be related to the three aspects of values, beliefs and assumptions. While values tend to be easy to identify because they are usually written down, they also tend to be vague. Beliefs are more specific, but again they are issues that people in the organization can discuss and talk about. Finally, assumptions are the real core of an organization's culture. They are the aspects of organizational life that are taken for granted, and which people find difficult to identify and explain.

**Stakeholder analysis**

The attitudes of individuals both inside and outside an organization will be strongly influenced by the cultural context. This influence is likely to occur because individuals share expectations with others by being part of a stakeholder group. In this respect, individuals will need to identify themselves with the aims and ideals of these stakeholder groups, and this may occur within departments, at different geographical locations, or at different levels in the hierarchy. Most individuals tend to belong to more than one stakeholder group.

Equally important are the external stakeholders of the organization. Often they may seek to influence company strategy through their links with internal stakeholders. Even if external stakeholders are passive, they may represent real constraints on the development of new strategies.

Understanding stakeholders, and how they are likely to influence the organization's strategy, is a very important part of any strategic analysis, and forms the core of an assessment of the cultural and political dimensions of strategy.

As the expectations of stakeholder groups are likely to differ, it is quite normal for conflict to exist within organizations regarding the importance and/or desirability of many aspects of strategy. In most situations a compromise will need to be reached between expectations that cannot be achieved simultaneously, and the problems of suboptimization, which will have to be tackled where the development of one part of an organization may be at the expense of another. What emerges is the need to understand the expectations of different stakeholder groups, and to weigh these in terms of the power they exercise. Mapping out the various expectations within an organization, and where they conflict, contributes significantly to an understanding of the core beliefs in the organization and .its strategic position. Together with an assessment of the power structure of the organization, this is necessary in order to assess future strategies in relation to their cultural fit and how easy or difficult change is likely to be.

When analysing stakeholders the formal structure of an organization is not the only basis for identification. It is also necessary to identify the informal stakeholder groups and assess their importance. Individuals tend to belong to more than one group, depending on the issue at hand. Assessing the importance of stakeholder expectations is an important part of any strategic analysis. It consists of making judgements on three issues:

- how likely each stakeholder group is to impress its expectations on the organization;
- whether they have the means to do so, i.e. power;
- the likely impact of stakeholder expectations.

Two approaches to this mapping process can be identified: the power–dynamism matrix and the power–interest matrix.

The **power–dynamism matrix** is a useful way of assessing where the political efforts should be channelled in order to develop new strategies. The attitudes of stakeholders, both external and internal, can be related to possible changes. The point of this approach is that new strategies can be tested before an irrevocable position is established. In taking this approach a relationship between predictability and power can be suggested.

An important development of the **power–interest matrix** is that stakeholders can be classified in relation to the power that they hold and the extent to which they show interest in a particular strategy. The central value of this type of stakeholder mapping is in assessing whether the political and cultural situation is likely to undermine a particular strategy. In this respect the approach taken is one of assessing cultural fit.

## Power

It has already been shown that, in most cases, power will be unequally shared between the various stakeholders, and one group or faction of a group may dominate. Power can be seen as the extent to which individuals and groups are able to persuade, induce or coerce others into following certain courses of action. This is the mechanism by which people who had one set of expectations will dominate or seek to compromise with others.

Power can be derived in a number of ways, one of which is hierarchy. Hierarchy provides people with formal power over others, and is one method of influencing strategy, although such formal power can be limited. Influence can be an important source of power, and may arise from personal qualities or because of a high level of consensus. Individuals associated with the core beliefs or frame of reference are likely to accrue power, although this can be influenced by a number of factors, including access to the channels of communication.

Control of strategic resources is a major source of power, although such importance can vary over time or according to circumstance. Individuals can also derive power from specialist knowledge and skills. Most people know that the wider environment affects performance, and so control of the environment can be a source of power. Some groups will have significantly more knowledge of or contact with and influence over the environment than others. Finally, exercising discretion is a significant source of power, particularly if individuals are involved in the decision-making process. Personnel discretion can influence interpretation and execution.

As with internal groups, people and organizations within the external environment can influence an organization. Dependence on resources, both buyers and suppliers, can be seen as an important source of power. Involvement in implementation through linkages within the value system can be an important source of power for suppliers, buyers and channels. Specifically, distribution companies can influence trends in consumer tastes, which in turn can influence manufacturers. Such a point can be enhanced if the appropriate knowledge and skills are critical to the success of the organization.

As there are many different sources of power, and each is dependent on circumstances, one way of approaching this complex situation is by identifying the indicators of power. The status of an individual or group can be related to both hierarchy and reputation. Another approach to assessing power is to measure a group's claim on resources: for instance, in terms of budget and number of employees. In particular, trends in the proportion of resources claimed by that group may be a useful indicator of the extent to which its power is waxing or waning. A useful comparison can be made with similar groups in comparable organizations. Representation in powerful positions, for instance on important committees, could be an important measure of power, although individual status should also be taken into consideration. Finally, the symbols of power, such as the location of offices, can provide pointers as to who is viewed as powerful within the organization.

No single indicator is likely to uncover the structure of power, although by taking all the indicators together it may be possible to identify which people or groups appear to have power. It can therefore be emphasized that alongside an internal assessment of power, a similar analysis of external stakeholders needs to be carried out.

## Business ethics

Managers have important obligations to a wide variety of stakeholders. This raises the question of how the activities of organizations affect the behaviour of individuals and the values of society, and concerns important ethical questions about the role of managers in the strategic management process. Such an issue has centred initially on social responsibility and has been extended towards business ethics. Ethical issues concerning business exist at three levels:

- At the macro level there are issues about the role of business in the national and international organization of society, and the relative virtues of different political/social systems.
- At the corporate level the issue is often referred to as corporate social responsibility, and is focused on the ethical issues facing individual corporate entities when formulating and implementing strategies.
- At the individual level the issue concerns the behaviour and actions of individuals within organizations.

The key issue for managers is to understand and influence the social stance that the firm is taking. A range of stereotypes can be identified with, at one end, the profit maximizers. It is these firms that believe that 'the business of business is business' and that it is the domain of government to prescribe through legislation the constraints that society wishes to impose on free enterprise. A second category believes that the long-term success of the firm is through a well-managed relationship with external stakeholders. In this respect proper operations in the short term will have longer-term effects in avoiding yet more legislation. A third, more progressive, group believes that the external stakeholder expectations should be explicitly incorporated into a firm's policies and strategies. Performance in this respect can be measured both in a pluralistic way and by considering profitability. Reductions in profitability may be considered in return for a social good. However, at some point there is a conflict between social responsibility and survival, or between social responsibility and the expectations of investors.

While one can consider the overall stance, a more detailed agenda of issues needs to be developed. The difficult issue for managers to assess is the extent to which their approach will be legitimate and sustainable, with a cost–benefit analysis being required.

On an individual basis, corporate social responsibility raises some ethical issues: to whom are managers responsible? Irrespective of any legal position there is a clear ethical and moral responsibility to other stakeholder groups.

The themes of environmental analysis, resources and capabilities, industry structure and stakeholder theory will now be illustrated with a case study on the British brewing company Whitbread.

## CASE STUDY: WHITBREAD

Modern brewing dates from the nineteenth century and the introduction of mechanization into what had traditionally been a manual process. In 1914 there were 3,647 breweries but by 1950 the number had fallen to 567. Today there are fewer than 100 breweries in the UK, and the five largest companies control over 80 per cent of production. This degree of concentration is probably no more than that experienced in most mature industries, and indeed the UK brewing industry remains more fragmented than almost any other in Europe.

## Tied system

Many pubs in Britain are tied to one particular brewer. This means that the two parties have struck an exclusive purchasing agreement whereby, in exchange for low rent or a 'soft' loan, the publican contracts to buy beer from no other brewer. In fact this system is common throughout Northern Europe, although it is illegal in the USA and Australia. The system came into being more or less by accident in Britain. During the late nineteenth century beer sales declined because of economic depression and the growth of the temperance movement, so that pubs came under severe financial pressure. Although brewers had no strategic wish to own pubs, they began to buy pubs that were in financial trouble in order to keep them open as outlets for their beer. The more ambitious brewers saw the acquisition of pubs as a way of expanding their output of beer. By 1979 over 73 per cent of pubs were owned by brewers, and their publicans were tied to one particular brewer. It is clear that the tied house system provides benefits. These arise because it enables would-be entrepreneurs to enter business without raising capital. This in turn ensures that a larger number and variety of pubs exist than would otherwise be the case. The output afforded to the brewer generates economies of scale, which mean that the price of a pint of beer is kept relatively low. Set against these benefits, some commentators see disadvantages to the tied house system. The largest is generally reckoned to be the way in which it can act as a barrier to entry by new or overseas brewers. Without pubs it could be very difficult to gain a distribution for new brands.

## Monopolies and Mergers Commission

Discussion of the pros and cons of the tied house system brings us on to the Monopolies and Mergers Commission (MMC) report on the industry, called *The Supply of Beer*, and published in 1989.

There is a long history of regulation and official investigation into the UK beer industry. Indeed, throughout much of the developed world there is control over who can buy alcohol, where they may buy it and when they may buy it. In 1969 there had been a wide-ranging MMC enquiry into beer and pubs. In 1986 the Director-General of the Office of Fair Trading (OFT) referred the industry to the Monopolies and Mergers Commission, who conducted a monopoly enquiry. This was against a background and flurry of takeover activity, much of it centred on the Australian group Fosters, and of course it was at this time that there was much Conservative Government deregulation. The enquiry was to take two and a half years and to prove very debilitating and destructive of industry resources.

The MMC report was eventually published in March 1989. The Commission said that it had found a complex monopoly to exist, and that this operated or might be expected to operate against the public interest. It made recommendations which, had they been adopted, would have imposed structural change on a scale hardly ever experienced in any industry in the UK. The six major integrated brewers would have to sell nearly 22,000 or 50 per cent of their stock of pubs, and desist from the practice of lending money to free pubs in exchange for a product tie.

In the end, the original recommendations were diluted by the time that they became law in the form of the tied estates orders. The principal requirement was that the six largest brewers sell 11,000 or approximately 25 per cent of their pubs. In addition, the pubs that they retained and tied would be entitled to buy one guest cask-conditioned beer from another brewery. The pubs owned by small and medium-sized brewers were unaffected by these changes. The Commission expected these changes to strengthen the position of regional brewers and reduce the price of beer: at least, that was the theory. The orders were draconian for the major brewers, costing them an estimated £500 million, but they were not the only victims, as many pubs were forced to close.

There is now almost universal condemnation of the orders and their impacts, and the hoped-for consumer benefits have not arisen. Some regional brewers have done well; some have suffered. According to the Policy Review Institute in Oxford, the price of beer rose because of the Beer Orders in the period 1990–92.

## Whitbread's structure

The outcome of the MMC report has had an impact on the way in which Whitbread is structured. In 1990 the company reorganized its trading operations to create four divisions, reflecting both the Beer Orders and changes in consumer tastes.

**The Pub Partnership Division** was set up to manage the task of selling off the 2,000 plus pubs required by the MMC. Now it handles the company's relationship with the 2,200 pubs that the company retained with tied tenants. A major change arising from the MMC report is that most of these tenants have moved from a short-term tenancy agreement to a long lease.

**Whitbread Inns** is responsible for the 1,600 pubs that the company manages directly. It is now the company's largest division in terms of operating profit.

**Restaurant and Leisure** manage a series of branded chain retailing businesses owned by Whitbread. The names of the three UK businesses and the three overseas are Churasco and Merado steakhouses in Germany, Keg Restaurants in Canada and Australia, Pizza Hut, Beefeater and TGI Friday.

The **Whitbread Beer Company** was established, as the company appreciated that it needed to separate its beer business from retailing and pubs. In the period post the MMC report, Whitbread's beers were going to be forced to compete in totally new markets, and it would do the company no good to rely on its traditional tied trade. Eleven thousand tied pubs were going to be freed, and all tied outlets would be able to buy one of their cask ales from whichever brewer they chose. While all these structural changes were going on, the consumer was also changing.

The fundamentals that anyone in the beer business needs to understand are brands, efficiency and service. These have been the core of the Whitbread Beer

Company strategy for the past five years, and it was the recognition of this at a very early stage that helped Whitbread to increase its share of the UK beer market from approximately 12 per cent in 1989, when the MMC reported, to nearly 14 per cent in 1994. This may not sound spectacular, but it equates to an increase in Whitbread's beer sales of around 18 per cent attributable totally to market share gains worth approximately £440 million pounds over five years. Put into perspective, it is around 645 million pints. Unfortunately, a lot of this market share gain has been eroded by a decline in the UK beer market of just over 1 per cent per year during the period 1989–94.

## Brands, efficiency and growth

The focus on brands, efficiency and service has been at the heart of this growth. Brands will be the focus of this particular case study. Efficiency has been vital in maintaining profitability in a sector that has been ravaged by price wars in the supermarkets. Dramatic improvements in manufacturing and distribution efficiencies have been required to sustain the company's price competitiveness. This has involved a big reduction in the number of employees. The issue of service is of vital importance to the success of any business, but the service requirements for the beer business are probably different from what other industries are used to. The key to service success is in understanding your first tier of customers: not drinkers, but supermarkets, pub owners, club owners, and beer wholesalers. The Beer Company has been working hard on its communications with customers, its accuracy and speed of deliveries, its responsiveness to customer complaints, its staff training programmes, and many other issues.

The Whitbread Beer Company has made great progress in improving its efficiency and service standards, but brands are also a key business driver. The advertisements that promote Whitbread's beer brands are the result of detailed studies of consumer interests and changing trends.

## Beer trends

Beer sales have been declining over the last few years. This means that people have been drinking less, in fact about 1–2 per cent less per year, and there are all sorts of reasons for this. One aspect has been health concerns, the other more important reason is that the number of 18–25 year olds in the population is decreasing, and they are also drinking more wine, so sales of Britain's traditional drinks – beer and spirits – have suffered. What Whitbread had needed to do was to anticipate and respond to these trends. As a result of this approach the company achieved market leadership in the fast-growing take-home market, where traditional brewery ties play less of a role. The company took over market leadership from Courage in the middle of 1992. Whitbread's brands have been winning out against intense competitive pressure from the other major brewers. Bass alone spent nearly £40 million in advertising its brands in 1993 and the total spend from all brewers was around £120 million. While the beer companies were making the TV companies and other media extremely wealthy they were also tearing each other's throats with price wars, which were particularly instigated by the Australian owners of Courage, Fosters.

## Boddingtons

To consider all these issues, one example to illustrate this trend is the brand Boddington beer. This brand was named Consumer Brand of the Year for 1993 by the Marketing Society.

Back in 1989 however, the need was for was for Whitbread to review and restructure the industry and consider trends in consumer tastes. All the indications were that real ale or cask ale was on the way back, yet Whitbread didn't have a really good cask ale. Boddingtons, one of the CAMRA (Campaign for Real Ale) favourites, was for sale, and the sale was completed on 27 November 1989. What Whitbread gained, in addition to the normal assets, was 200 years of brewing tradition and a part of Manchester's heritage. It is regarded as a landmark and part of the heart and soul of the region. The marketing function at Whitbread had to be careful about what the company said about the brewing of Boddingtons, and to not antagonize CAMRA. The company committed itself to not changing the ingredients of the beer. The advertising campaign at the time was saying what a good pint it was and focusing on the clear, good head and that it was not fizzy. However, at the time the research and development department at Luton were again considering the change in consumer tastes. There was more drinking at home and there was a demand for quality beers in cans. Draft-dispensed Boddingtons was unique: in some respects its characteristics were similar to those of stout.

What Whitbread had been working on was a method of producing a pub draught-quality stout for Murphy's. Murphy's was launched in 1988, and Guinness launched what it called the 'widget' in 1988, which gave pub draught quality in a can. By 1989 Whitbread had a solution for Murphy's and realized the potential for Boddington's beer. In 1991 the company launched a draught flow for Boddington's. In order to create a demand for Boddington's draught flow within the consumer's mind an awareness campaign was created in ten days by a unique advertising series. Such ads were shown at the beginning and end of commercial breaks between major feature films and sports events. At the same time, there was a print campaign for Boddington's. The task was simple: to explain the product's uniqueness and feature its creaminess; to appeal to mainly southern cask ale drinkers, but at the same time not alienate the drinkers in the North-West. The campaign had to be very focused in terms of being simple, impactful and branded by colour scheme. It appeared on the back covers of magazines only and therefore there was minimal spend but with high awareness. The results were that one year after the introduction of the Boddington's widget, the beer brand established take-home leadership. In 1989, Boddington's was not in the top ten, but since early 1992 Boddingtons has gone from strength to strength. TV advertising has been unique and very product focused. What this case history of Boddington's has shown is that, with some creativity, clarity about what you want your brand to stand up for, and understanding changes in consumer tastes, a strategic manager can master the art of marketing and live up to the Whitbread corporate mission statement.

Whitbread has a number of beer brands that, unlike Boddington's, the company does not own. The company has licences to brew and sell them in the UK only: Heineken, Stella Artois and Murphy's Irish Stout. In the case of Murphy's the question to ask is: why was it worth Whitbread taking a licence? Would it have been better to develop its own stout? After all, the company did not need a licence with Boddington. Why also did the company take licences for Heineken and Stella Artois? Alternatively, why didn't it develop its own lager as Bass did with Carling Black Label or Courage did with Hofmeister. Such questions lead us conveniently to the licensing of restaurant brands and the latest developments within Whitbread.

Whitbread has a licence for TGI Friday and Pizza Hut in the UK, although the company structure for Pizza Hut is in the form of a joint venture. The advantages of this approach are very much the same as they are for beer. Whitbread has moved very logically from beer to pubs, to pubs with restaurants and coaching inns, to restaurants and to hotels. Rarely does one see such a simple and clear corporate strategy. The company has slowly but surely transferred its skills and core competences from the business base to new but related industries. Whitbread's restaurant and leisure division (the others are beer and pubs divisions) has eight businesses within it. This also adds up to a division with sales of over £1 billion. These are a number of examples that one can give as to how the company is interpreting changes in consumer tastes within its restaurant and leisure businesses.

In summary, the history of Whitbread's businesses has always been about interpreting and responding to changes in consumer tastes and lifestyles. The job of a strategic manager is to interpret these changes and trends in order to give clear guidance to operators and other functions as to what will succeed in the future.

**SUMMARY**     The focus of this chapter showed that resource capability is only one element that the strategic manager should consider. A second element is the ability to sense changes in the environment that in turn suggest a possible need for changes in strategy by identifying opportunities and threats. Research suggests that the better a firm is at environmental analysis the better it is expected to perform. A third aspect considered in this chapter was the extent to which the firm's culture and power structure influences strategy. Within this context, stakeholder theory was discussed. It is the expectations of individuals and groups that influence a firm's purpose and hence its strategy.

**FURTHER READING**  Hofstede, G 1991 *Cultures and organization: software of the mind*, London: McGraw-Hill

Johnson, G and K Scholes 1993 *Exploring corporate strategy*, 3rd edn, Hemel Hempstead: Prentice-Hall

Kotler, P 1991 *Marketing management: analysis, planning, implementation and control*, 7th edn, Englewood Cliffs: Prentice-Hall

Porter, M E 1980 *Competitive strategy*, New York: Free Press

Porter, M E 1985 *Competitive advantage*, New York: Free Press

Stacey, R 1992 *Managing chaos*, London: Kogan Page

Wheelen, T L and J D Hunger 1995 *Strategic management and business policy*, 5th edn, Reading, MA Addison-Wesley

# CHAPTER 5

# Strategic options, evaluation and formulation

**OBJECTIVES**

After reading this chapter you should be able to:
- Identify the competitive strategies available within the hospitality industry.
- Relate the various strategic options available to a firm and the analytical methods available for their evaluation.
- Understand the problems and limitations of those analytical methods in contributing to the decision-making process.

## STRATEGY FORMULATION: AN INTRODUCTION

Strategy formulation has been written about extensively, with many models offered in the literature. The actual approach to formulation of a strategy is often dependent upon the type of firm and its leadership. Thus, for example, the strategy employed will not determine whether hotel expansion takes place, but rather where it takes place, the phasing of the expansion, the degree of market representation required, and the support services needed to maintain and develop the concept. For any firm to reach its full potential, formulation must be approached from the perspective that it will assist the firm in aligning itself with its environment, as noted by writers such as Hofer and Schendel (1978), Porter (1980) and Dev and Olsen (1989) (points developed within the first four chapters of this book). Thus it is important for a firm to find the optimal pattern or fit between the environment and the firm's strategy. Research evidence suggests that hospitality firms that are effective in environmental analysis do perform better.

The environment as described here can be divided into two areas: the general and the task. The **general environment** consists of the broad forces that affect an industry and society. They include trends in technology, politics, economics, and sociocultural activities. The **task environment** relates to the forces working within an industry environment, such as changes in the supply of resources, shifts in competitor behaviour, the impact of industry-specific legislation and regulation, and changes taking place in the customer market within which the firm competes. Environmental analysis is made difficult by the lack of reliable information, and the manager's ability to assess it. To be successful, the firm must build a network of sources about the environment that are reliable and provide valid assessments regarding its impact. However, despite the best of sources and probable estimates, it is still impossible to predict the exact effect of the environment on the firm.

## COMPETITIVE STRATEGIES IN THE HOSPITALITY INDUSTRY

Competitive strategy experts have argued that there are only a limited number of strategic positions that are likely to make a firm an effective competitor.

The nature of the hospitality industry seems to reflect characteristics that fit well into what Porter has described as a **fragmented industry**: that is, an industry in which no firm has a significant market share, or can strongly influence the industry's outcome, and which essentially involves undifferentiated products. Furthermore, the hospitality industry appears to represent what could be classified as a **hostile environment**: that is, an environment in which overall market growth is slow and erratic, there is an intense upward pressure on operating costs, and there is intense competition resulting in high market concentration. Clearly, the hospitality industry possesses many of the characteristics that would classify it as a fragmented, low market share, hostile environment. In the face of such conditions, strategic positioning is likely to be of particularly crucial significance.

Miles and Snow (1978) argue that organizations can be categorized according to their response patterns. They also emphasize that categories of competitive strategy are related to particular industry environments. Table 5.1 shows four different strategic orientations and their respective growth policies.

**Table 5.1: Strategic orientations and growth policies**

| Strategic orientations | Growth policy |
| --- | --- |
| Defenders | Growth focus is deeper penetration into current markets |
| Prospectors | Growth focus is through the location of new markets, products or services |
| Analysers | Growth focus is through both market penetration of existing markets and also through market development |
| Reactors | Management fails to articulate a viable strategy |

*Source:* Miles and Snow (1978). Reproduced with the permission of McGraw-Hill, Inc.

## Strategy implementation

Strategy formulation leads to a decision on the type of strategy to be implemented. The four-point framework for developing strategy developed by Thompson and Strickland illustrates the key elements necessary to ensure the proper implementation of the organization's chosen strategy.

- successful performance of the recurring administrative tasks associated with strategy implementation;
- creating a fit between the firm's internal processes and the requirements of strategy;
- making adjustments for the firm's overall situation in which implementation must take place;
- choosing how to lead the implementation task.

These four components reflect the fact that the firm must have in place systems that are designed to match its resources with its chosen strategy. This suggests that the structure of the firm – that is, its hierarchy, complexity, formalization, and allocation and control of resources – must be reflected in the type of strategy.

## Growth strategies

Many hotel firms' primary growth strategies are very similar (Table 5.2): growth and quality of products and services supported by technology appear to be the most favoured approaches. Growth appears to be mainly based around franchising and management service contracts, with some asset-acquiring activity by a number of firms. Conversions accomplished through the acquisition and 'cherrypicking' of small chains is also an increasingly popular growth strategy.

There is division amongst the large hotels as to whether or not segmentation is the way to implement their growth strategies. Companies such as Holiday Inn Worldwide, Choice Hotels International and Marriott believe strongly in the marketing of several brands, whereas remaining

**Table 5.2 Growth strategies and competitive methods**

| Growth strategies | Competitive methods |
| --- | --- |
| Joint ventures | Technology-based systems |
| Franchising | Brand development |
| Strategic alliances | Product quality |
| Management contracts | Sophisticated pricing |
| Conversions | Global marketing and advertising |
| Acquisition of small firms | |

*Source: Travel & Tourism Analyst*, No. 3, 1993, The Economist Intelligence Unit

chains focus on the quality and luxury markets. The factor in this respect in supporting the projected growth in the up-market luxury segments is increased business travel. While economies in the developing world are likely to generate increased business travel, it is questionable whether all the hotel capacity projected will necessarily be at the top end of the market. With more companies taking more care to control travel expenses, it seems possible that the hotel chains representing more **value for money** may be better positioned to reflect this trend in business travel expenditures.

Most hotel operators do not need to be told that they have faced a hostile environment for the past several years. In an environment where supply is expanding faster than demand, and regulatory and competitive pressures are increasing, hotel executives must ask whether there is a strategy that will give them a chance to outperform their competition. While reaction to the environment is better than no action at all, it is preferable to be proactive and stay ahead of important trends. If management is ahead of emerging trends then it is possible to develop strategies and organizational structures that will permit the firm to achieve maximum performance over the long run.

## Defensive strategies

The long-term trends in the environment of the hospitality industry have resulted in the emergence of defensive strategies by many corporations. The defensive strategy is described as the attempt by firms to prevent the erosion of their market share.

These strategies have been documented by continuing research at the centre for Hospitality Research and Service at the Virginia Polytechnic Institute and State University in Blacksburg, VA, USA. This research programme has produced key characteristics of such defensive strategies (Olsen et al., 1992):

- US firms expanding into foreign markets
- Increased expenditures across the industry for marketing
- Merger and acquisition activity
- Regionalization or second-tier chain development
- The buying back of franchises by franchisors
- Privatizing firms using such tactics as leveraged buyouts
- Shortening of concept life cycles
- Price discounting

Defensive strategies are implemented when a firm wishes to reduce the levels of risk that the environment exposes it to. It can be argued that single-economy-based businesses need to employ defensive strategies to lower risk. This means that firms have to expand internationally to reduce the effect of a single economy on their business. Companies such as Manchu Wok (part of Canadian-based Scotts Hospitality) are doing this, and expanding into the USA and UK. Manchu Wok's parent company, Scotts Hospitality, is also faced with the need to reduce the risk of trading with a narrow portfolio of products over a limited geographical area. Scotts Hospitality has decided to build fifteen international hotel properties by 1997. However, its defensive strategy goes further, as it has also diversified away from hotels by purchasing the 157-store Perfect Pizza chain in 1991, acquiring a 50 per cent joint venture stake in Home Rouxl Ltd, and a 50 per cent stake in Courtland Leisure Ltd, a food court operator.

## The orientation of corporate hotel chains to expansion

There are hotels in every country of the world. However, the poor quality of management, inconsistency of facilities, and underdeveloped markets, mean that the full economic significance of the industry is yet to emerge. Corporate hotel companies are represented in 140 countries of the world and are the dominant force in the restructuring of the worldwide hotel industry. If a hotel chain embarks upon a period of growth, the locations it decides to expand to will be determined by its growth orientation. Two categories can be identified.

**High-density home-market companies**

The most common pattern for the restructuring of the worldwide industry has been for hotel chains to evolve and expand towards national coverage within their home country before attempting international expansion. This pattern has predominated in the USA, UK and France: the three most developed hotel markets in the world. Around 83 per cent of the quoted hotel rooms in the world are controlled by chains from these countries. Marriott, Forte and Accor are three major examples of companies that have evolved in this way. This means that global expansion will only occur once there is saturation of the domestic market. For these companies, the global market is of secondary importance to the domestic market in which they have a majority of their interests. These high-density home-market companies have been pushed into the global market by the domestic environment failing to give growth opportunities as good as those in other world regions.

**Low-density home-market companies**

There has been increasing growth in international hotel demand since the end of the Second World War. To meet this demand, hotel chains have evolved that operate in many countries without necessarily having a mass of hotels in their home country. Hilton International, Inter-Continental and Sheraton are examples of companies that operate in 48, 46 and 66 countries respectively. For these companies global expansion is routine, and the global market is of higher priority than the domestic market from which they have their origins. These companies have not been pushed into the global market by the harsh domestic business environment, but were lured by the positive aspects of the international market.

## GLOBAL GROWTH BY HOTEL CHAINS

In the development of hotel chains worldwide there is only slight evidence that high-density home-market firms are able to capture demand in more than one country, to colonize foreign markets rather than having a token presence. Queens Moat Houses' penetration of the German and Dutch markets and Accor's acquisition purchase of Motel 6 in the USA are examples. The high-density home-market firms are being driven to international growth as opportunities in their domestic markets recede, while the low-density home-market firms see international growth as a way of life.

## Accommodation capacity

In considering the environment of the international hotel industry, it is evident that the recession of the early 1990s has affected the whole world and not just the USA and Europe. Hotel occupancy rates in Asia, Europe, Latin America, Africa and the Middle East would suggest that supply is outpacing demand, as illustrated in Table 5.3.

**Table 5.3 Occupancy decline 1990–93**

| Hotel chain | Occupancy rates | | | |
|---|---|---|---|---|
| | *1990* | *1991* | *1992* | *1993* |
| Asia/Australia | 70.2 | 67.7 | 69.7 | 70.2 |
| Latin America | 67.4 | 53.8 | 58.7 | 61.6 |
| Europe | 65.6 | 62.3 | 60.6 | 60.7 |
| Africa/Middle East | 63.0 | 60.0 | 60.8 | 61.6 |

*Source:* Horwath International (1991)

Thus in most regions demand is disappointing, with only South America and some areas of South-East Asia indicating some short-term improvement. If firms are going to succeed in this environment they must be concerned about the optimum level of capacity needed. As a global economy fights its way out of recession, some opportunity will exist, but it is important that the experiences of the US hotel chains in the 1980s, when supply outpaced demand, are not forgotten.

### Receptive expansion areas

Europe

As stated earlier, the corporations wishing to diversify into the international market need to locate in regions with the greatest potential, and it can be suggested that Europe holds the greatest opportunities. However, the US chains may find sweeping into Europe hard to achieve, for many reasons.

The cultural fabric of Europe makes it almost impossible to implement homogeneous brands. Indeed, there are so many definitions of a hotel across Europe, that it is hard to measure current hotel supply in the region.

The European hotel environment has suffered in the same way as that in the USA; however, trade depression was further compounded by the collapse of the Eastern Bloc and the unification of Germany.

Despite this there has been rapid expansion of room stock by 20.5 per cent between 1989 and 1992. Also, much of this room stock has been located in the UK and France, the two most structurally advanced nations in the region. However, the hotel corporations instigating this growth are European based and not American.

It is fair to say that American chains have been acquired by British companies and thus have a presence in the European market. For example, Ladbroke owns and operates Hilton International and Bass owns Holiday Inn. The global expansion of Holiday Inn is much in evidence in Europe. However, the dominant players in the region are Accor and Forte. Accor is experiencing difficulty rolling out Pan-European brands against the cultural disparities. An example is the Formule 1 growth in the budget hotel sector; the standards of communal bathrooms acceptable in France have not been accepted in other countries. It can be argued that it is difficult to build transnational budget brands, as Accor attempted, and this then prompted Accor to purchase established budget brands like Motel 6 in the USA.

This all proves how established companies in the market are having difficulty in regional expansion. This acts as a deterrent to potential firms wishing to expand into Europe.

Gateway cities

It has been established (by hotel and leisure analysts, such as Slattery at Kleinwort Benson, London) that location of hotels occurs initially within primary cities, and as concentration increases there is growing pressure to locate in peripheral areas. For example, in the USA in 1991 9.2 per cent of corporate hotel rooms were located in the four major hotel cities, but in Europe, where the market is less saturated and there is less pressure to locate in more marginal areas, the top four hotel cities had 23 per cent of all corporate room supply. Primary city locations are attractive because they have high concentrations of population, they are tourism nodal points, and are central business centres for the nation.

The increase of international trade through the development of the infrastructure of less developed nations, the growth of the global service industries, and the growth of long-haul tourism due to advances in technology, increases in leisure time and demographic changes, all mean that there is increased demand for hotels. However, the location of this demand is a series of **gateway cities**. These cities are intercontinental nodal points for business and tourism travel.

The hotel brands locating in these cities hope to be able to offer the international traveller familiar standards wherever they travel around the globe. For this to happen, the firms are rapidly having to create hotel brand portfolios in these cities, and then communicate their location to the traveller through marketing. Holiday Inn has located in gateway cities such as Bangkok, Beijing, Tokyo and Melbourne, and relies on its international brand advertising to attract its guests.

Location within these cities is also of strategic importance. To capture the business traveller, Holiday Inn has located in the central business districts, as in Melbourne, Australia, whilst for the international tourist it has located in the prime shorefront properties, such as Cairns in Australia. The principle of location in gateway cities is to place a hotel in the largest concentration of your existing target market.

## Opportunist growth

Some companies are looking to expand globally wherever there is opportunity to do so. Radisson Hotels International, which claims to be America's fastest-growing up-market hotel company, is also expanding into the international market. Radisson's expansion strategy locates hotels in countries where there is **high potential** for growth in hotel demand. It has located across Eastern Europe in countries that include Russia, Poland, Germany, Latvia and Hungary. However, it is the locations it has chosen in these countries that make Radisson an opportunist. For example, it located the Radisson Hotel Szczecin in only Poland's fourth largest city, before it was represented in Warsaw, the capital.

Opportunist growth can seriously compromise a hotel chain's branding and reputation. For example, London-based Edwardian Hotels entered a partnership with Radisson in December 1991. Edwardian is an established brand and will continue to serve its target market, which means that Radisson will have to compromise its brand and target market in order to work with Edwardian. This means that there will be huge disparities in standards between Radisson hotels, which will frequently leave guests alienated and disillusioned.

Opportunist growth has short-term advantages, but the constant realignment of the firm's structure to accommodate new properties may affect performance. In deciding upon a global strategy a company should prefer expansion into high-potential global regions rather than individual properties that can yield an adequate return in the short term.

## Factors determining the implementation of growth strategies

A hotel firm may decide to implement a strategy for global expansion for a variety of reasons, although most companies are being forced into this market. Once the decision has been made to go global there are still specific factors to consider. There are many determinants that will help to achieve growth objectives, operational performance and the general success of expansion. If a firm fails to recognize the importance of these factors the consequences could be disastrous; by understanding them the firm can assess the true feasibility of global expansion.

This section discusses the role of the most influential factors involved in a global expansion programme and their impact on the feasibility of international growth.

US global hotel chains

Through the discussed expansion methods and the inevitable strengthening of the US economy, it can be expected that US firms will continue in their aggressive overseas expansion. Table 5.4 shows the major chains that are likely to emerge as strong players worldwide.

**Table 5.4 Dominant global hotel firms**

| Hotel chain | Estimated rooms | Estimated hotels |
|---|---|---|
| Holiday Inn Worldwide | 327,059 | 1,654 |
| Best Western International | 266,123 | 3,310 |
| Choice Hotels International | 214,411 | 2,295 |
| Marriott | 167,000 | 746 |
| ITT Sheraton | 131,348 | 423 |
| Hilton Conrad International | 94,452 | 259 |
| Hyatt International | 74,801 | 159 |
| Radisson Hotels International | 35,613 | 67 |
| Four Seasons | 12,011 | 33 |

Source: *Travel & Tourism Analyst* No. 3, 1993, The Economist Intelligence Unit

Role of new technology

The need for control and support of hotels within a portfolio that is geographically dispersed can be met through the use of computer reservations systems (CRS). Indeed, this technological link can be essential for hotel survival; therefore a corporation looking to expand must be able to use and manipulate a computer system to its needs.

At present there is increasing use of CRS systems by hotel chains; however, 33 per cent of hospitality businesses believe there is a considerable gap between the computer systems available to their businesses and their specific needs. To utilize computer systems fully, hotel chains must innovate to achieve systems that meet their objectives. Internal CRS development was first conducted by Holiday Inn, and continual modification to its needs and trading environment has resulted in its latest Holiday Inn Revenue Optimization (HIRO) system. Holiday

Inn considers its reservations system to be a major competitive advantage, with 22 million reservations each year.

The role of CRS is more diverse than a pure sales function. The infrastructure needed for a competent CRS operation can also provide, almost as a by-product, collection, dissemination and presentation of financial information; sales promotion feedback; customer identification and history; and the means of optimizing rates, yield and/or occupancy across a group. All of these functions are true advantages when one considers that individual hotels are located huge distances apart and have very little specific regional data supplied to them, as would be the case in a domestic hotel chain.

Technology will become one of the most competitive methods that chains will employ to ensure growth. The large investment made in technology by Holiday Inn Worldwide, Radisson, and Choice Hotels International will have to prove successful if these chains are to compete successfully. Once the large investment has been made it will become part of the core technology of each firm and will require monitoring, updating and additional research and development investment in order to remain competitive. Technology will shape the future of marketing programmes, product design and corporate strategies.

## STRATEGIC OPTIONS, EVALUATION AND FORMULATION WITHIN THE HOSPITALITY INDUSTRY

At the heart of corporate strategy should be the issue of strategic choice. The first stage in this is to consider the strategic options available to the firm, which are dependent on that particular firm's circumstances. Three related topics should be discussed around this issue:

- the basis on which a firm may seek to achieve a lasting position in the environment, i.e. generic strategies;
- the alternative directions in which the firm may choose to develop within its generic strategy;
- the alternative methods by which any direction or strategic development might be achieved, e.g. joint ventures, alliances or acquisition.

These three elements of strategy are not independent of each other, and this should be borne in mind in the following discussion.

### Generic strategies

We have already suggested that specific strategic options can be set within the context of an overall generic strategy, and this pulls together many aspects discussed in the first four chapters of this book. One important approach in this context is Porter's generic strategies; however, although it is widely accepted, problems can be attached to Porter's approach. In order to gain sustainable competitive advantage, Porter suggests that there are three ways in which a firm can achieve that objective:

- A **cost leadership** strategy is one in which a firm sets out to become the lowest-cost producer in the industry.
- A **differentiation** strategy is one in which a firm seeks to be unique within the industry; with this uniqueness it is able to charge a higher than average price. In this sense it is seeking to differentiate itself from the competition.
- A **focus** strategy is one in which a firm targets a particular segment group and refines its strategy to serve that segment to the exclusion of others.

Long-term profitability requires the choice of one of these fundamental generic strategies; otherwise, in Porter's view, the firm will end up **stuck in the middle**.

Problems and constraints

Whilst the framework provided by Porter can be regarded as useful, the problem for the manager is in trying to translate this framework into practical strategies that provide success for the firm.

Sustainable cost leadership should be regarded as the lowest cost compared with that of competitors over time. Cost leadership can be achieved through economies of scale, market power and the experience curve effects. Dominant firms do not automatically have sustainable cost leadership. There are cases of such firms losing market share while others overtake them. Market share is not the central focus but rather the advantages that it can bestow on the firm. One important distinction is that cost leadership can be applied to the whole industry or to specific market segments. Porter uses the terms 'cost leadership' and 'low price' as interchangeable. However, cost should be regarded as an input measure for a firm, while price is an output measure; a cost-reduction strategy does not necessarily mean that the firm would choose to price lower than the competition. A cost-based strategy, by itself, does not give competitive advantage, as the opinions of the client or consumer have to be taken into account in order to gain competitive advantage; in particular, such a consumer view has to be taken in relation to the competition.

Porter's view of differentiation is one of a firm selling something so unique that it is in a position to charge a higher price. However, one alternative to this approach is that selling a differentiated product or service at a similar price may achieve market share and volume for the firm. It is therefore in this sense possible to differentiate on low prices: that is, a cost-based strategy that cuts across two of Porter's generic strategies and would have been viewed by Porter as being stuck in the middle and therefore dangerous. This differentiation strategy also prompts the question: Who are the competitors? Even in the same industry, firms may compete on a different basis. Equally, firms may be competing on a range of issues, such as ambience, location and levels of service, which suggests that differentiation involves more than just the physical product.

**Market-based generic strategies**

Porter's approach seems in many cases to be based on internal measures as a basis for competitive strategy, and what is perhaps more important is to relate an internal strategy to the market or client base. It is this market-based view that needs to be added as a new dimension to Porter's generic strategies.

**Price**

There is a market segment in many industries that is willing to accept substantially lower quality goods at very significantly lower prices, and such a segment can be regarded as price sensitive. Companies could be competing in the same industry but be attempting to appeal to a specific market segment with a low income, or to budget-conscious clients. Another approach could be to reduce price while still maintaining quality of the product or service, but this approach can lead to a price-based battle with the competition. Success with this approach can only be maintained if the firm has the lowest cost base compared with the competition. A problem leading on from this strategy is that the firm will have to operate with a reduced profit margin and will be unable to reinvest in its product or service. Success with this particular strategy can be achieved if the firm focuses on a specific product market segment and others do not or cannot match the firm's cost base.

**Differentiation strategies**

In essence, a differentiation strategy is one in which the firm:

- offers perceived added value over the competition at a similar or somewhat higher price; or
- offers what the customer believes is a better product at the same price; or
- gains enhanced margins by slightly higher pricing, so that it achieves higher market share and therefore higher volume.

Such approaches are likely to be successful if the firm can clearly identify who the customer is and what the customer's needs and values are. Also, the firm must understand what is valued by the customer; a major differentiating factor is the manager's ability to stay close enough to the market to sense and respond to customer tastes and values. However, over time, customer values change and therefore the basis for differentiation needs to change with them. A firm following a differentiation strategy may therefore have to review continually the basis for differentiation and keep changing its strategy.

The hybrid
strategy

It is possible to combine differentiation and price strategies. Here the success of the strategy depends on the ability both to understand and to deliver against customer needs while also having a cost base that permits lower prices that are difficult to imitate. Such an approach generates greater volumes and maintains profit margins because of a low cost base.

Focused
differentiation

Focused differentiation can be seen as competing in a particular market segment by offering a higher perceived value to the customer at a significantly higher price. In so doing the firm is trying to convince the customer that its product is differentiated from those of its competitors. However, the problem with industry globalization is that the firm may have to choose between taking a broad approach or a more selective focused strategy. Equally, the market segment that the firm wishes to compete in needs to be clearly defined, along with the values and needs of the customer. This may create problems as the firm is attempting to compete in different market segments. Also, focused strategies may conflict with the various stakeholder expectations inside and outside the firm, and so such a strategy may be at the expense of growth. Finally, the advantages of the focused approach may have to be monitored carefully, because the market situation may change not only from a customer point of view but from the responses of the competition.

Failure strategies

Increasing price without increasing perceived value, or maintaining price and reducing value, can in most cases lead to failure. However, if the firm is in a monopoly position, it may be that such a strategy can be sustained, particularly if the organization is protected by legislation, or there are high economic barriers to entry.

## Implementation of generic strategies

Having discussed generic strategies, the firm has to put them into operation and ensure that they can be sustained and so produce a profitable long-term advantage.

Cost leadership can be related to the different activities within the value chain and any experience curve benefits that can be derived from those activities: for instance, volume purchases and consequent reduced unit costs, a build-up of experience and knowledge, or greater internal efficiencies. An analysis can also be made as to where competitors are vulnerable in terms of costs within their value chain, and therefore it may be possible for the firm to drive down its costs in these areas as a further means of gaining competitive advantage.

Sometimes it is the intangible aspects of strategy that suggest that value should not just be related to the product and technology. Service, in terms of delivery or after-sales service, linked to an understanding of customer needs and values, can be one means of differentiation. Hence differentiation can be achieved not just by one element of the value chain but by multiple linkages with all elements of the value chain. If these linkages can be established, a sustainable basis for differentiation can be found. For instance, a quality image, staff training, information systems, and control of suppliers will all contribute to a strategy of differentiation and the linkages within the value chain.

Another approach to differentiation and improved competitive standing is to build in switching costs within the strategy (switching costs will be incurred if the customer believes there is an actual or perceived cost in switching from one product to another). If there are actual or perceived switching costs, the firm may achieve a differentiated position in the market. It is therefore important for managers to consider not only their own value chain but the value chain of others, such as buyers and suppliers, and they therefore need to consider the linkages between and within value chains in order to provide a competitive advantage for the firm.

There are a number of challenges for managers in putting these generic strategies into operation and then sustaining them. They first have to identify customer needs and values, either in broad terms or by specific market segments. They then have to decide on a specific generic strategy appropriate for the firm. The strategy must relate customer needs to a mix of activities, to achieve a coherent set of linkages and differentiate the firm from the competition. If cost efficiencies can be gained through the experience curve, the firm will gain an advantage over the competition.

## Strategic direction

A number of alternative strategic directions for the firm can be determined and set within the context of product and market choices, which in many cases will be related to the environmental opportunities for growth that are available to the firm. However, strategic direction can concern not only growth but also consolidation and efficiency. Four main alternative directions for development can be identified:

- withdrawal, consolidation and market penetration;
- product development;
- market development;
- diversification.

**Withdrawal, consolidation and market penetration**

**Withdrawal**, either completely or partially, may be the most sensible course for a firm to take. For instance, declining performance may be an opportunity for withdrawal from some activities within the firm as a whole in order to raise funds or cut losses and allow the firm to consolidate or grow in other areas. Alternatively, large diverse companies may view their subsidiary companies as assets to be bought and sold as part of an overall corporate portfolio.

**Consolidation** suggests changes in the way that a firm operates, although the range of products and markets may remain unchanged. The firm may choose to maintain market share by growing with the market and so maintain a competitive cost structure in relation to the competition. As a product moves into the mature stage of its life cycle the firm may choose to increase its marketing activity in order to highlight perhaps more intangible aspects of the product or service. Equally it may seek to improve its cost structure through productivity gains or higher capital intensity.

The strategy of **market penetration** may enable the firm to gain market share but will be dependent on the nature of the market and the position of the competition. The relevance of this approach will depend on whether the overall market is growing, is static or is in decline. For instance, in static markets the experience curve suggests that market penetration would be difficult, as the advantageous cost structure of market leaders would normally prevent the incursion of competitors with lower market share. However, this would not prevent firms from adopting the market penetration strategy in mature markets if they chose some form of collaboration with other firms.

**Product development**

A firm may decide on the search for alternatives that build upon the company's present knowledge and skills. This may be a viable choice, and such an approach can be described as product development. Firms need to follow the changing needs of their customers by a policy of continually introducing new product lines. Although such an approach may raise problems for the firm, new products may be vital to its future, but the process of creating a new product line is expensive, risky and potentially unprofitable. Most new products never reach the market, and of those that do, relatively few succeed. For this reason there has been a trend towards technology transfer and collaborative ventures.

**Market development**

This approach can be seen when firms, with their present products, venture into new market areas exploiting new uses for the product, or spread into new geographical areas. If the firm's distinctive competence lies with a particular product and not the market, a continued exploitation of the product by market development would normally be preferable. Exporting could also be seen as a method of market development. There may, for instance, be operational or logistical reasons that make the international option more favourable, such as changes in the relative cost of labour, transport or supplies. Firms might also need to take this approach for defensive reasons such as tariff barriers or import controls that might have been introduced in important overseas markets.

Diversification   The term 'diversification' can be used to identify directions of development that take the firm away from both its present products and its present market at the same time. A number of types of diversification can be identified.

**Related diversification** is development beyond the present product and market but still within the broad confines of the industry within which the firm operates. It may take the form of backward integration of the inputs to the firm's current business. Forward integration looks at the firm's outputs, such as transport or distribution, and horizontal integration refers to development into activities that are either competitive with or directly complementary to a firm's present activities.

**Unrelated diversification** is development beyond the present industry into products and markets that at face value may bear no clear relationship to the present product or market. However, increased ownership of more value activities within the value chain does not guarantee improved performance for the firm or better value for money for the customer or client.

Synergy is a commonly cited reason for both related and unrelated diversification. Potentially, synergy can occur in situations where two or more activities or processes complement each other to the extent that their combined effect is greater than the sum of the parts. While related diversification may build upon synergies rooted in products or markets, unrelated diversification is usually based on financial synergy or managerial skills. Other reasons for unrelated diversification may be the aspirations of corporate leaders, the opportunity to employ underutilized resources in a new field, or the desire to move into a different area of activity, perhaps because the present one is in decline.

## Method of strategic development

Growing out of the generic strategies just discussed and identified, there are different potential methods of development; while the structure of these choices is discussed here, they are further expanded in relation to the hospitality industry in Chapters 7, 8 and 9.

For many firms, internal development has been the primary method of strategy development. The final cost of developing new activities internally may be less than the acquisition of new companies. This is obviously a strong argument in favour of internal development for smaller firms, which may not have the resources available for major investment. Another issue is that of minimizing destruction of other activities. The slower rates of change that internal development brings may make it favourable in this respect. Internal development avoids the often traumatic behavioural and cultural problems arising from trying to integrate the two firms involved in an acquisition.

Development by **acquisition** tends to go in waves, and has been selective in terms of industry sector. One reason for developing by acquisition is the speed with which it allows a firm to enter a new product or market area; other reasons could be the lack of knowledge or resources of a particular element or strategy within that particular market area. If the market is static, for instance, it would be difficult for a new firm to enter that market, and so entrance by acquisition reduces the risk of competitive reaction. When an established supplier in an industry acquires a competitor it may be for the latter's order book in order to gain market share, or in some cases to shut down its capacity and help restore a situation where supply and demand are more balanced and trading conditions are more favourable. There are also financial motives for acquisitions, particularly with asset stripping, where the main motive for the acquisition is short-term gain from buying up undervalued assets and disposing of them piecemeal. Another reason may be that the firm is buying into another firm that is already a long way down the experience curve and may have achieved efficiencies that would be difficult to match, particularly by internal development.

The reasons for **mergers**, as opposed to acquisitions, may be similar, although what distinguishes them from acquisitions is that they tend to come about voluntarily.

**Joint development** and **strategic alliances** are approaches that have become increasingly popular over the past few years. There are a variety of arrangements, which may vary from formalized interorganizational relationships to loose arrangements of cooperation between organizations with no shareholding or ownership involved. The form of the alliance is likely therefore to be influenced by:

- **asset management** – the extent to which assets do or do not need to be managed jointly;
- **asset separability** – the extent to which it is possible to separate the assets involved between the parties involved;
- **asset appropriability** – the extent to which there is a risk of one or other of the parties involved appropriating the assets involved for themselves.

The reasons for these different forms of alliances are varied but usually concern the assets involved in the alliance, be they financial, physical, or simply management know-how.

Joint ventures are usually arrangements whereby firms remain independent but set up a new organization jointly owned by the parents. Consortia may well involve two or more organizations in a joint venture arrangement and would typically be focused on a particular venture or project. At the other extreme, networks are arrangements whereby two or more firms work in collaboration without formal relationships but through a mechanism of mutual advantage and trust. More opportunistic alliances might also arise, which are likely to be focused around particular ventures or projects, but again are not so highly formalized. Such arrangements are much nearer to market relationships than to contractual relationships, and may exist because the assets do not need joint management or cannot be separated easily from the firms involved. There are also intermediate arrangements that exist, such as franchising, licensing and subcontracting. All these intermediate arrangements are likely to be contractual in nature but are unlikely to involve ownership. They typically arise because:

- particular assets can be isolated for the purpose of management, or
- these assets can be separated from the parent firm to their advantage.

Licensing or franchising is likely to take place, however, where there is a low risk of assets involved being appropriated.

## SUITABILITY OF STRATEGIES

Having identified a variety of strategic options, the need now is to evaluate those options and to judge their merits. One way to do this is to make a judgement on the basis of suitability, feasibility and acceptability.

### Evaluation criteria

In evaluating **suitability**, the firm is attempting to assess the extent to which a proposed strategy fits the situation identified in the strategic analysis (as identified in a SWOT analysis) and how it would contribute to the competitive position of the firm. In this sense, suitability is a criterion for screening strategies before they are assessed for acceptability or feasibility. The strategic manager is asking a number of questions, such as:

- Does the strategy exploit the firm's strengths or environmental opportunities?
- Does it overcome the firm's weaknesses or threats?

All this should be set within the context of the firm's purposes, such as profit targets or growth expectations.

To evaluate in terms of **feasibility** is to be concerned with whether a strategy can be implemented successfully and whether it is achievable in terms of resources. Some issues to be addressed are:

- Can the strategy be funded?
- Is the firm capable of performing to the required level?
- Are the necessary marketing skills available?

The reactions of competitors need to be identified and discussed, along with whether the firm has the required skills at both management and operational level. It is also important to consider all these issues with respect to the timing of the required changes.

The criterion of **acceptability** suggests a relationship with people's expectations, and therefore prompts the question: Acceptable to whom? Such issues reintroduce the topic of stakeholder theory and in particular the mapping of stakeholders' expectations. The way in which stakeholders line up is dependent on the particular situation or the strategy under consideration, and so an analysis of stakeholders is an acceptable method of testing the acceptability of strategies. In this respect, the evaluation of stakeholder expectations is crucial.

## A framework for evaluation

In assessing suitability, a balance needs to be determined between detailed evaluation and following the intuition of management, because in many cases the judgement of management is important. Suitability has been shown as the means of screening options, with the three tests of suitability being:

- strategic logic,
- cultural fit,
- research evidence.

From this approach a shortlist can be created from which the more detailed use of criteria concerning feasibility and accessibility can be applied.

## Strategic logic

Many analytical methods are useful both for understanding the current situation and for evaluating strategic options for the future. They have evolved out of the rational and economic assessment of strategic logic, and are primarily concerned with matching specific strategic options with an organization's market situation and its relevant strategic capabilities. Three approaches can be identified:

- portfolio analysis;
- life-cycle analysis;
- value system analysis.

**Portfolio analysis** The prime concern of evaluation at the corporate level is that of achieving a balanced range of portfolio and strategic business units. Options for the future can be plotted onto a matrix, such as the Boston Consultancy Group matrix. The long-term rationale of business development can be highlighted by the matrix. Taking this approach, one question to ask is:

Will the strategy move the firm to a dominant position in the markets and will the funds for investment be available?

It is important to have a balance of activities that matches the range of skills within the firm, to avoid the situation where some groups are badly overstretched while others remain underemployed. The use of such a matrix can help the strategic manager to think about an acquisition strategy. This matrix approach can be used for assigning development priorities between the various strategic business units.

**Life-cycle analysis** One development of the product portfolio concept is life-cycle analysis or product–market evolution analysis. The two dimensions to this approach are the market situation, described in a number of stages ranging from embryonic to ageing, and a competitive position described in five categories ranging from weak to dominant. The purpose of this matrix is to establish the appropriateness of particular strategies in relation to these two dimensions. The first stage in this approach is to determine where the firm is currently positioned on the matrix. The position within the life cycle is determined in relation to eight external factors or descriptors of the evolutionary stage of the industry:

- market growth rate;
- growth potential;
- range of product lines;
- number of competitors;
- spread of market share between these competitors;
- customer loyalty;
- entry barriers;
- technology.

It is the balance of these factors that determines the position within the life cycle.

The competitive position of the firm within the industry can also be established by looking at its characteristics in relation to its industry life cycle. Given the wide variety of strategic options, the main value of this matrix is in establishing the suitability of particular strategies in relation to the stage of industry maturity and the organization's competitive position.

**Value system analysis** It has already been emphasized that an understanding of how costs are controlled and value is created within the value system is very important when assessing the strategic capability of a firm. It was also noted that the linkages between the value activities are just as important as the activities themselves. The logic of strategic development can be tested by the same measure, and in particular the extent to which the strategy will change the value system and therefore the competitive position and/or value for money that the firm is able to sustain.

The concept of synergy can be applied in this context. This is concerned with assessing how much extra benefit can be obtained from providing linkages within the value system between activities which have either been previously unconnected or for which the connection has been of a different type. Synergy can be sought in several circumstances, such as market development, product development, and backward integration. Synergy could also arise through many different types of link or interrelationships: for example in the market, by exploiting a brand name; in the firm's operations, by sharing purchasing facilities, maintenance and quality control; or in product and process development, by sharing information and know-how. Synergy is often used as a justification for diversification, particularly through acquisition or merger.

It has been argued that firms that diversify by building on their core businesses do better than those that diversify in an unrelated way. However, this can be a difficult argument in practice for a number of reasons. For instance, the notion of a core business is not at all clear, as it could be defined by product, market or technology, and is often defined in historical terms. Also, core competences are more culturally based within one firm, and are often difficult to transfer from one situation to another, so it is perhaps wrong to suggest that diversification may be more successful as it builds on core competences. This at least partly explains the difficulties that many firms have had with diversification: assumptions are made about the transferability of core competences when in fact they are not transferable. It has been argued that synergy should not be regarded as necessarily arising from horizontal linkages within the value system through the sharing of activities or skills; it can also arise from a shared strategic logic between businesses or business units.

Another area in which value system analysis can be useful to an assessment of the suitability of strategies is in the locational decisions of international companies. The logic of gaining competitive advantage through the management of individual value activities suggests that the separate activities of design and marketing may often be located in different countries. This needs to be balanced against the importance of well-managed linkages, which prove more difficult to achieve the more dispersed the separate activities become internationally. The most successful international companies are those that can develop organizational arrangements to exploit the advantages of specialization and dispersion while managing linkages successfully.

## Cultural fit

While strategic logic is important, it is also relevant to review the options within the political and cultural realities of the organization, and so cultural fit focuses on the extent to which particular types of strategy might be more or less simulated by an organization. Indeed, one of the key roles of the leadership of organizations is to shape and change culture to fit the preferred strategies better. This tension between strategic logic and cultural fit has sometimes been described as a **head versus heart** issue. However, the key judgement is whether or not such strategies are suitable for the firm's current situation, particularly if significant environmental change has occurred. The purpose of strategic logic analysis is to indicate whether or not the organization's paradigm requires some fundamental change. Whether paradigm changes are required or not the assessment of strategic options in terms of cultural fit is valuable. If the organization is developing within the current paradigm this analysis helps to identify those strategies that would most easily be assimilated. In contrast, if the paradigm needs to change, the analysis helps in establishing the way in which the culture will need to adapt to embrace the new types of strategy.

One of the key determinants of how culture might influence strategic choice is again the stage that an organization has reached in its life cycle. It is possible to discuss the relationship between life-cycle culture and strategy and so link it to life-cycle models. A combination of these perspectives and different stages in the life cycle can prove valuable in establishing options that fit both the strategic logic and the cultural situation.

In its **embryonic stage** the firm's culture is shaped by the founders. Once the organization survives, such personal beliefs become strongly embedded in the organization and shape the type of development that subsequently occurs. These core beliefs hold the organization together and become a key part of its core competence; an organization will typically seek out developments that fit its culture.

The **growth phase** of organizations involves a large variety of cultural changes in different circumstances, and in some cases cultural developments can dictate strategic choice. The cohesiveness of culture seen in the embryonic stage tends to dissipate into subcultures, each of which may favour different kinds of development. As a middle management emerges within the organization, in turn there is a diversity of expectations and the dilution of a single dominant culture and the preference for one type of strategy. There may also be uncomfortable dilemmas to face, as strategic logic may dictate one approach although the original beliefs of the organization may favour another approach.

By the time organizations reach **maturity** their culture tends to have been institutionalized to the extent that people are not aware of it, or even find it difficult to conceptualize culture in a meaningful way. Such organizations tend to favour developments that minimize change and are evolutionary from the current situation. However, whereas incremental developments may be easier from a cultural point of view, they may well prove wholly inadequate if environmental circumstances are changing rapidly.

In **decline** a cohesive culture may be seen as a key defence against a hostile environment. Organizations face difficult decisions concerning retrenchment, investment and withdrawal from products and markets that are engrained in the culture of the organization. In some situations the difficulties of adjustment can be so great that the organization's owners choose to sell out to another organization, which may then be able to instigate radical changes.

## Research evidence

So far this chapter has attempted to suggest the suitability of strategies either by establishing the logic behind the strategy or through assessing the cultural fit. As the major purpose of strategic change in most organizations relates to the need to sustain or improve performance, this part of the chapter will review the evidence that is available on the relationship between choice of strategy and the performance of an organization.

The strategic importance of market power has already been discussed; in understanding the likely impact of the environment on an organization, market power is a crucial factor in the analysis. Much analysis has used market share as a measure of market power, and there is considerable evidence that market share and profitability are linked. The link between performance and relative market share, which is emphasized by the experience curve, tends to show that return on investment rises steadily in line with relative market share. An explanation for this link is that they are both largely concerned with the cost benefits that market share brings. Firms with high market share seem to be able to buy more competitively or to produce components economically in house. Also, some economies of scale benefit firms with high market share: for example, marketing overhead costs tend to decline as the percentage of sales. The indications are that firms with high market share develop strategies of higher price and higher quality than lower-share competitors. High-share firms tend to be more profitable, generating the cash resources needed for research and development to improve and differentiate products, and thus enhancing their market position and also justifying higher prices, which in turn increase profits.

Another aspect to consider is consolidation strategies, with the upgrading of product or service quality. The evidence is that quality is of very real significance for the improvement of profit performance. The best situation appears to be a combination of high share and high product quality, but even firms with lower market shares demonstrate significantly higher profit performance if they have products or services of superior quality.

It can also be suggested that a reliance on increased marketing spending to consolidate a firm's position in its market is not in itself a satisfactory way of improving performance. Heavy marketing expenditure may actually damage a return on investment for firms with low market share. This does of course pose problems for a firm that is trying to maintain or improve its standing in its existing product market. Trying to do so by increasing marketing expenditure is likely to result in reduced profitability. In other words, attempting to buy market share is unlikely to be successful. Equally, high marketing expenditure is not a substitute for quality: indeed it appears that high marketing expenditure damages return on investment when quality is low. It must be concluded that simply gearing up marketing expenditure as a means of consolidating a firm's position is not sufficient.

Finally, improved productivity through capital investment can be regarded as another consolidation strategy, but in isolation, and at a high level can damage a return on investment. This is particularly true for firms with weak market positions. Also, as high capital investment is a barrier to exit, those suffering from low margins are reluctant to get out, so they continue to battle on and make the situation worse. Indeed, raising capital intensity in an attempt to improve profit returns is most likely to be successful for firms that already have a strong position in the market, are unlikely to meet fierce price competition, and are able to make real reductions in production costs. It is for some of these reasons that many firms prefer subcontracting as a means of improving productivity.

It has so far been argued in this chapter that higher relative market share is very often of strategic advantage to firms. However, the process of building market share, market penetration, is not without its costs. Short-term profits are likely to be sacrificed, particularly when trying to build share from a low base. Similarly, product development can bring uncomfortable dilemmas to many firms as it may prove expensive and unprofitable, particularly in the short run. Product development may require a commitment to high levels of spending on research and development. It is evidence of this type that has convinced many firms to look seriously at technology transfer or acquisition of similar firms as alternatives to their own research and development efforts.

Diversification is probably one of the most frequently researched areas of business, with specialists looking at the relationship between the choice of diversification as a strategy and the performance of the firm in financial terms. The link of diversification to financial performance is unclear, apart from the important message that successful diversification is difficult to achieve in practice. The success of diversification is contingent on the circumstances of a firm, such as the level of industry growth, market structures and the firm's size. The relationship between performance and diversity will also vary with the period of time studied: that is, at the point in the business cycle. A key contingent factor is the resource situation of the firm, particularly the existence of underutilized resources. It could perhaps be suggested that successful firms choose diversification if opportunities in their current product–market domain are limited. Finally, the concept of diversity should not be interpreted too narrowly in product terms: diversity has other dimensions, such as market spread. There is some evidence that profitability does increase with diversity, but only up to the limit of complexity within the organizational structure, beyond which the relationship reverses. This raises the issue of whether managers can cope with large diverse organizations.

## SCREENING OPTIONS

One of the benefits that should emerge from the assessment of suitability is an understanding of the underlying rationale behind particular types of strategy. However, within these broad types there are likely to be a range of specific strategies that a firm could follow, and the process of evaluation normally requires a narrowing down of these various options before a detailed assessment can be undertaken. This is not to suggest that options eliminated at this stage will not be given further consideration later. The basis for comparison in assessing strategic capability should not only be expressed in absolute terms or against industry norms, but should also identify the incentive to change from the present strategy to the new strategy. One particular relevant comparison would be to evaluate what would happen if the firm chose to do nothing; this would provide a valuable baseline against which to assess the incentive to change.

A useful technique that incorporates this approach is **gap analysis**, which can be used to identify the extent to which existing strategies will fail to meet the performance objective in the future. Gap analysis should also apply to measures other than profitability, but some of these may be easily quantifiable, such as productivity or volume sales, whereas others may be more subjective but none the less very important, such as levels of quality or service. Three contrasting approaches to screening options can be identified:

- ranking options;
- decision trees;
- scenarios.

### Ranking options

Ranking is a systematic way of analysing specific options for their suitability or fit with the picture gained from the strategic analysis. Each option is assessed against a number of key factors that the strategic analysis has identified in the firm's environment, resources and culture. One of the major benefits of ranking is that it helps the analyst to think through mismatches between a firm's present position and the implications of the various strategic options. More sophisticated approaches to ranking assign a weighting to each factor, in recognition that some will be of more importance in the evaluation than others.

## Decision trees

Whereas ranking assumes that all options have equal merits in the first instance, the decision tree approach ranks options by progressively eliminating them. This is achieved by identifying a few key elements or criteria that future developments are intended to incorporate, such as growth, investment and diversification. Decision trees combine the identification of options with a simultaneous ranking of those options, although a limitation of this approach is that it tends to be simplistic, as it very much takes a 'yes or no' approach.

## Scenarios

Ranking evaluates options against a specific list of items or criteria derived from the strategic analysis; decision trees achieve the same outcome by eliminating options through progressively introduced additional criteria to be satisfied. A third approach to screening is that of scenario planning. Scenarios can therefore be produced to screen strategic options by matching them to possible future scenarios. The outcome of this approach is not a single prioritized list of options but a series of contingency plans that identify the preferred option for each possible scenario. Equally important in taking this approach is the firm's ability to monitor the onset or otherwise of a particular scenario in time to implement the appropriate strategy.

## THE STRATEGIC EVALUATION OF CHOICES

An assessment of the returns likely to accrue from specific options is a key measure of the acceptability of an option. However there are a number of different approaches to the analysis of return:

- profitability analysis;
- cost–benefit analysis;
- shareholder value analysis.

## Profitability analysis

Three common approaches to this traditional financial analysis of profitability can be identified:

- The firm can forecast the **return on capital employed** a specific time after the new strategy is implemented.
- **Payback period** can be used where a significant capital injection is needed to support a new venture. The payback period is calculated by finding the time at which the cumulative net cash flow becomes zero. The judgement is then whether this is regarded as an adequate outcome and whether the firm is prepared to wait that long for a return. Managers seek very different rates of return depending on the industry, so such behaviour is better understood if payback is being used as a targeting device.
- **Discounted cash flow** (DCF) analysis is perhaps the most widely prescribed investment appraisal technique. It is essentially an extension of the payback period analysis. Once the net cash flows have been assessed for each of the preceding years, they are discounted progressively to reflect the fact that the funds generated early are of more real value than those in later years. The net present value of the venture is then calculated by adding all the discounted annual cash flows after taxation over the anticipated life of the project. DCF analysis is particularly useful in comparing the financial merits of strategies that employ very different patterns of expenditure and return.

While these three forms of profitability analysis are widely used, they do have certain limitations. Financial appraisals tend to focus on the tangible costs and benefits, and do not set a strategy in its widest context. For example, a new product launch may look profitable as an isolated project but may not make real strategic sense in terms of the market acceptability for the product within the firm's portfolio. In reverse, the intangible costs of losing strategic focus through new ventures is often overlooked. Also, the use of return on capital in evaluating strategic options can be criticized because it is backward rather than forward looking. It does not concentrate on assessing the business's capability of generating future cash flows or value.

This discussion has focused so far on the evaluation of strategic options pursued through internal development. However, another common situation in which evaluation is required is strategic development through acquisition. The value of the firm being acquired needs to be assessed, as do the likely cost savings, along with the likely proceeds from disinvestments or sale of assets and the anticipated impact on the value of the merged firms. There are three key ways in which a company can be valued:

- The balance sheet value of the net assets of the firm can be used, although there is a danger with this that some key assets may not appear, and others may be undervalued.
- If the intention is to continue the business as a going concern, earnings

potential may be a key strategic issue, and the costs of the business may be rationalized on merger, particularly those of overheads and the relevant synergy gained. Forecasting such cost savings may be difficult.

- A third approach is market evaluation, which would apply to a publicly quoted company. However, during the bidding period the cost is likely to rise beyond the starting share price.

## Cost–benefit analysis

In many situations the analysis of profit gives too narrow an interpretation of return, particularly where intangible benefits are an important consideration. Cost–benefit analysis attempts to put a money value on all the costs and benefits of a strategic option, including both tangible and intangible returns. The basis of quantification used needs to be justified carefully, and is likely to be the subject of disagreement from different interested parties. One of the greatest difficulties in such an approach is deciding on the boundaries of the analysis. Despite such difficulties, cost–benefit analysis is an approach that is valuable if its limitations are understood. Its major benefit is in forcing people to be explicit about the various factors that should influence strategic choice. A detailed cost–benefit analysis would assign weightings to the various items in order to reflect their relative importance to the decision about whether or not to proceed with a particular strategy. This would also normally be combined with a sensitivity analysis of the key net present value and internal rate of return outcomes in relation to the main assumptions.

## Shareholder value analysis

Shareholder value analysis developed during the 1980s, placing emphasis on the value creation process and the responsibility of directors to create values and benefits for shareholders. Such an approach concentrates on strategies and not just investment projects. The financial analysis must be driven by an understanding of the value creation process and the competitive advantage that the firm derives from the process. In particular, it is crucial to identify the key cash generators of the business: the value and cost drivers. Assessment of the acceptability of a strategy through net present value is likely to be critically dependent on a relatively small number of these value and cost drivers. These become the key factors that link the analysis of the key competitive strategy to the likely acceptability of that strategy in terms of improvements in shareholder value. The value and cost drivers often act in conjunction with each other, so managers need to make judgements on how these interdependencies may work, rather than expecting simplistic answers from precise financial measures.

## ANALYSING RISK

One measure of acceptability against the strategic options being assessed is the risk that the firm faces in pursuing that strategy. A useful analysis is the projection of key financial ratios, which give a measure of the risk that the firm would be taking by pursuing various strategies. For instance, the capital structure of the firm may change in pursuing different options.

One measure of risk is the extension of long-term loans, which will increase the gearing of the firm and increase the financial risk. In order to take this approach there needs to be an examination of the likelihood that the firm will reach breakeven, and the consequences of falling short of the volume of business while interest on loans continues to be paid. Another consideration is the likely impact on the firm's liquidity: reduced liquidity increases the financial risk of the business.

An increasingly important element in this assessment of risk is firms that intend to trade internationally. The nature of the debtors they would have to take on would have to be considered, and whether or not they would be able or willing to take export guarantee insurance to mitigate this risk.

**Sensitivity analysis** is a useful technique incorporating the assessment of risk. During a strategic evaluation this technique allows each of the important assumptions underlying a particular option to be questioned and changed. In particular, it seeks to test how sensitive the predicted performance or outcome is to each of these assumptions. Sensitivity analysis asks what would be the effect on performance if, for example, market demand grew by only 1 per cent or by as much as 10 per cent: would either of these extremes alter the decision to pursue that particular strategy? This process helps management to develop a clear picture of the risks of making particular strategic decisions and the degree of confidence they might have in a given decision. In theory, the uncertainty factors surrounding key variables in the evaluation could be assigned probability distributions, and statistical analysis could be used to assess how these uncertainties combine in an overall risk analysis strategy. However, it is difficult to assign a probability distribution to so many variables. Sensitivity analysis has proved to be a good way of communicating to decision makers the areas of uncertainty underlying the evaluation, and of allowing them to use their judgement in the choice process.

**Decision matrices** can be applied when there are many circumstances where specific aspects of strategic choice can be reduced to simple choices between a number of clearly defined courses of action. This is often the case when choosing between different development methods for a particular strategy. In deciding which option to choose it is necessary, before any detailed analysis, to be clear about which type of decision rule will be used to weight the various options against each other. The

**optimistic** decision rule would choose the best outcomes for each option. The pessimistic decision favours the best of the worst outcomes. The **regret** decision rule would favour options that minimize the lost opportunity that might occur by choosing any particular option. The **expected value** rule introduces an important new dimension: the probability that each outcome would occur. Although decision matrices are helpful in analysing some aspects of the strategic choice, they need to be tempered by other considerations, which would not be directly included in such a simplified analysis.

The principle of **simulation modelling** is useful in strategy evaluation in those aspects that lend themselves to a quantitative view. Financial models are often used to assess strategic options. Risk analysis is a technique that seeks to assess the overall degree of uncertainty in a particular option by mathematically combining the uncertainties within each of the elements in the option. However, one of the limitations of the use of strategic modelling is the need for large amounts of high-quality data concerning the relationship between environmental factors and company performance. The danger in all this is that the model will become a gross oversimplification of the reality and fail to encompass the most important uncertainties and risks, particularly as competitor reactions are difficult to assess and/or incorporate into the model.

**Heuristic models** are a means of identifying solutions in a systematic way, and are most valuable in complex situations where there are many options available to an organization and many different requirements or criteria to be met. Many strategic decisions are concerned with finding a satisfactory option rather than the best option, and so the criteria listed are compared against the various options until one is found that satisfies most or all of the criteria.

## ANALYSING STAKEHOLDER REACTIONS

The importance and relevance of stakeholder analysis has already been referred to, and so the focus here is on their reactions to new or proposed strategies.

Stakeholder mapping is a very valuable tool in assessing the likely reactions of stakeholders to new strategies, the ability to manage these reactions, and hence the acceptability of a strategy. This is important, as a new strategy might require a substantial issue of new shares, and this could be unacceptable to powerful groups of shareholders as it dilutes their voting power. Plans to merge with other firms or to trade with new countries could also be unacceptable: for instance to the unions, the government or some customers.

Very often the initial evaluation of a strategy using stakeholder analysis will identify critical mismatches with the expectations of some stakeholders. The evaluations might then proceed to the next stage of the analysis, where a number of issues can be addressed. For instance, a strategy could or should be amended to fit the expectations of the stakeholders better without unduly sacrificing acceptability as assessed by the other measures of risk and return. It is unlikely that an optimum strategy exists, so successful strategies are those that seek an acceptable compromise between the conflicting interests of the various stakeholders. Analysis of stakeholder expectations also helps in determining how likely the strategy is to be successful when implemented. Also, there may be a need to try and persuade or encourage existing stakeholders to shift their position in order to give the strategy a chance. The accurate assessment of those political activities that the firm needs to undertake to support a new strategy is an important aspect of evaluation, and is often neglected in favour of the more numerical and rational analyses already discussed. Both can be seen as necessary.

## ANALYSING FEASIBILITY

Having considered the acceptability of strategic options and discussed stakeholder analysis, it is now important to assess the feasibility of those strategic options, and whether they are achievable in resource terms.

A valuable piece of analysis in assessing financial feasibility is **funds flow forecasting**, which seeks to identify the funds that would be required for any strategy and the likely source of those funds. This approach starts with an assessment of the capital investment needed and a forecast of the cumulative profits earned during the period. The working capital required by the strategy can be assessed by separate consideration of each element of the working capital using a simple pro rata adjustment related to the forecast level of increases in sales revenue. Tax liability and expected dividend payments are identified, along with any shortfall in funds, which can be funded by a variety of methods. Such funding will incur interest payments, which need to be built into the funds flow analysis. This approach would normally be programmed onto a computer spreadsheet, which would assist in identifying the timing of any new funding requirements.

Another approach is **breakeven** analysis, which is a simple and widely used technique, helpful in exploring some key aspects of feasibility. It is often used to assess the feasibility of meeting targets of return, and as such combines a parallel assessment of acceptability. It also provides an assessment of the risk in various strategies, particularly where different strategic options require markedly different cost structures.

It is often helpful to make a wider assessment of the resource capability of the firm in relation to specific strategies. This can be done through a **resource deployment analysis**, which is a way of comparing options with each other. The resource requirements of alternative future strategies should be laid out, indicating the key resources for each strategy. A resource analysis of the company should then be matched with the resource requirements for possible strategic options. This analysis can be closely linked to the competitive strategy by focusing the analysis on those value activities that must strongly underpin the cost advantage or value creation process, and in this way could be part of a shareholder value analysis. The real benefit of such an analysis should be the identification of those necessary changes in resources that are implied by any strategy and an analysis of whether those changes are feasible in terms of scale, quality or timescale.

## SELECTION OF STRATEGIES

It is a widely accepted view that a rational choice of future strategies should occur against objectives. When quantified, the firm's objectives are used as a yardstick by which options are assessed. Evaluation methods are therefore central to the decision-making process, and are expected to provide quantified answers regarding the relative merits of various options, to indicate the right course of action.

A common way in which the selection of strategies occurs is also by referring the matter to a higher authority. Those managers responsible for evaluation may not have the authority to give the go-ahead to the solution. Equally, those senior managers who must decide on a strategy may not have participated in the evaluation of the options: thus the evaluation process can be seen as a means of raising the level of debate that occurs among senior managers when they are using judgement on a selection of strategy. In large, diversified organizations there will be different types of evaluation occurring at the centre from those in the divisions and in the subsidiary companies.

There are many circumstances in which the uncertainties that a firm faces are such that evaluation processes leave the choice of directions for the future very finely balanced. Nevertheless, some firms will need to come off the fence and commit their resources and efforts to a particular strategy. An overall final decision on a strategy may be deferred, while some resources are committed to partial implementation. This allows the firm to gain more experience and understanding of the suitability of each strategy. This testing and learning approach becomes an important precursor to the bid for resources to higher authorities which might follow. However, the weakness of this approach is that the firm may only ever develop by tinkering around the edges in a very minimalist way, and may never really make a fundamental reassessment of its present situation and future opportunities. This would be incrementalism at its worst.

There is often disagreement on strategy between stakeholders who have similar power within the firm. This may be between management and unions or between two different groups of managers. In these circumstances it is not unusual for an outside agency, such as a consultant, to evaluate the situation for the firm. Often this process of evaluation is described as objective and rational by virtue of the consultant's detachment from the situation. In practice, consultants are aware of the political reasons for their involvement.

**SUMMARY**

Strategy evaluation has often been presented as an exact science with a range of analytical methods, being really only useful as a source of information to strategic decision makers. It has been seen that the contributions that these various analytical methods make to improving the quality of strategic decision making will differ considerably. However, even the most thorough strategic evaluation cannot possibly anticipate all the detailed problems and pitfalls that might be encountered in the implementation of a strategic change. So it is necessary to recognize that strategic decisions will be refined or even reversed as part of their implementation.

**FURTHER READING**

Christopher, M 1988 Logistics and competitve strategy, Logistics World, December, pp. 8–12

Christopher, M 1986 *Effective logistics management*, Aldershot: Gower

Das, T K 1991 Time: the hidden dimension in strategic planning, *Long Range Planning* **24**(3), 49–57

Eildon, S 1981 Zero-based budgeting: promise or illusion?, *Omega* **9**(2), 107–12

Fombrun, C, N Tichy and M Devanna 1990 *Strategic human resource management*, New York: Wiley

Glautier, M W E and B Underdown 1991 *Accounting theory and practice*, 4th edn, London: Pitman

Hardaker, M and B Ward 1987 Getting things done, *Harvard Business Review*, **65**(6), 112–20

Horwath International 1991 *Worldwide hotel industry*, New York: Horwath International

Kotler, P 1991 *Marketing management: analysis, planning, implementation and control*, 7th edn, Englewood Cliffs: Prentice-Hall

Lumby, S 1991 *Investment appraisal and financing decisions: a first course in financial management*, 4th edn, London: Chapman & Hall

Miles, R E and C C Snow 1978 *Organizational strategy: structure and process*, New York: McGraw-Hill

Olsen, M D 1993 *Travel and Tourism Analyst*, No. 3, London: The Economist Intelligence Unit

Peters R and R Waterman 1982 *In search of excellence*, New York: Harper & Row

Phyrr, P A 1973 *Zero-based budgeting: a practical management tool for evaluating expenses*, New York: Wiley

Scholes, K 1991 *Learning to live with devolution*, Sheffield Business School

Scholes, K and M Klemm 1987 *An introduction to business planning*, London: Macmillan, Ch 5

Steiner, G A 1979 *Strategic plannning*, New York: Free Press

Torrington, D and L Hall 1986 *Personnel management: a new approach*, Englewood Cliffs: Prentice-Hall

Vesey, J T 1991 The new competitors: they think in terms of speed to the market, *Academy of Management Executive*, **5**(2), 23–33

# CHAPTER 6

# Strategic implementation, planning and control

OBJECTIVES    After reading this chapter you should be able to:
- Discuss issues concerning strategy implementation with respect to resource planning at both the corporate and the operational level.
- Identify critical success factors and the key tasks to be listed, along with the planning tools available in achieving this implementation exercise.
- Consider that the implementation of strategy and resource planning is achieved through the people within the firm, its organizational structure and design.
- Discuss the strategic role of information systems and the use of technology.
- Identify the way in which strategic change is managed.

## RESOURCE PLANNING

The successful implementation of strategies will invariably require some degree of change within the firm's resource profile, and it is important to plan these resource changes carefully. Resource planning usually entails two levels of consideration:

1 the broader issues of how resources should be allocated between the various functions, departments, divisions or separate businesses;
2 the more detailed issue of how resources should be deployed within any one part of the organization.

Support for the strategies in this context is concerned with the operational aspects of resource planning, and is supported by a detailed assessment of strategic capability, in particular value chain analysis. The planning of resources is also a part of the evaluation of strategy and can be considered at two levels: the corporate level and the business level.

### The corporate level

At the corporate level in an organization, resource planning is mainly concerned with the allocation of resources between the various parts of the firm, whether those be business functions, operating divisions, geographical areas or service departments. Two important factors determine the overall approach to the allocation of resources:

- There is the perception of the degree of change required in the resource base if strategic change is to be achieved successfully. This could be the extent to which the aggregate level of resources might need to change, or the need for significant shifts between resource areas within an unchanged overall resource.
- Another aspect is the extent of central direction of the allocation process: whether detailed allocations are dictated from the corporate level or are in response to the detailed plans and aspirations of the various units of the firm. This relates to how the firm is structured, or where strategic decisions are made within the structure.

In order to illustrate these twin approaches to resource allocation, three situations can be discussed:

- when there are few changes in overall resources;
- when there is a growth in the overall resource base;
- when there is a decline in the overall resource base.

**When there are few changes in overall resources** If the managers in a firm perceive strategic development as requiring few changes in the level or deployment of resources they are likely to manage resource allocation in ways that reflect this perception and are characterized by formula-driven allocations or bargaining. Many firms will use a formula as a starting point in establishing allocations. There will then be some room for bargaining or fine tuning around this historical position. However, such a formula-driven process may lead to disagreements about the validity or fairness of the formula. Inevitably some degree of arbitrariness in this type of formula will be introduced into the discussion.

In **zero-based budgeting**, previous budgets are ignored, and the budgeting process is based on the firm's current objectives. In this way, funds are allocated according to client needs or demands. Another approach is through bargaining between the centre and departments or divisions, but this is rarely seen in its pure form. Perhaps what is really required is some degree of discretion about how resources are allocated by a department or division itself within its global sum. The issue of how the centre of an organization can retain control over the overall strategies while providing more freedom for departments or divisions is a key point to consider. It is also important to remember that it is the perception of the degree of change that will determine appropriate resource allocation.

**When there is a growth in the overall resource base** When firms are implementing strategic changes that require significant changes in resources, different approaches to resource allocation may be necessary. For example, during growth, resources can often be reallocated in relative terms without any particular area of the firm suffering a reduction in resources. One approach is that priority areas could be established centrally and the resource allocation could be imposed from the centre. Another approach is that the centre could allocate resources through a process of open competition. This could be done through operating an internal investment policy, under which divisions or departments can bid for additional resources. This could be described as **constrained bidding**. It gives departments or divisions of the firm the opportunity to bid for additional resources, but within defined criteria and constraints.

**When there is a decline in the overall resource base**

Many of the issues faced by firms experiencing growth also apply in static or declining situations, but there are important differences. In particular, resource allocation will require some areas to reduce in absolute terms to maintain other areas and/or to support new developments. In some firms the reallocation is simply imposed centrally. In other circumstances the reallocation may be achieved in an openly competitive way: for example, a freeze may be imposed on replacement of staff; or, as vacancies arise, they are made subject to open competition and go to those units with the most pressing case. Again, there is a middle road: constrained bidding for resources. In this case resources will be diverted from one area to another. This is often achieved by earmarking a proportion of the total organizational resources for a reallocation to new ventures; this is sometimes described as **top-slicing**. Reductions could, for instance, be achieved by amalgamating related areas or activities. There are, however, some circumstances where resource allocation is achieved by more overt and less subtle processes: for instance, by simply closing down one part of the firm. Such extreme forms of central direction are tolerated in firms facing crisis as a necessary evil to ensure survival.

One of the particularly difficult aspects of resource allocation at the corporate level in large organizations is the extent to which overlap, sharing or duplication of resources should be allowed to occur between the various parts of the organization. This arises in many different ways, from the extent to which services should be shared between departments to bigger issues, such as whether two divisions should have a common sales force. Issues of this type are very closely tied to the structure of the organization. It is therefore obvious that strategies that are dependent on a high degree of coordination or cooperation between departments or divisions will need to have more central direction over detailed resource allocations in order to underpin those strategies. In contrast, where divisions or subsidiaries are largely independent, such detailed direction from the centre is less important. Where sharing or overlap does exist, there are choices of the process by which these shared resources can be allocated. Three main ways can be identified:

- indirectly by an overhead recovery charge to the centre of the division;
- directly by charging out for services taken;

- directly by passing managerial responsibility to a designated division, which then cross-charges other users.

Direct measures keep accountability and responsibility for resource management in the same hands, but run the risk of creating a new bureaucracy to administer the charging-out system. Many organizations therefore combine charging out in two main areas: internal services, which can be delivered in the genuine supply–customer relationship, and major items of overheads when an incentive is needed to encourage divisions to think more strategically.

## The business level

A firm needs to understand which particular value activities most contribute to the success of its strategies. Moreover, strategic capabilities are often determined by the way in which linkages between these value activities are managed. In planning the implementation of new strategies, these same issues of central importance in resource planning can be identified. In this respect, planning must establish which value activities are of greatest importance to the successful implementation of the selected strategy. Equally, planning must address resource requirements through the value chain, including linkages between the value activities and the value chain to suppliers, channels or customers. It is important to understand how the detailed operational resource plans depend on the strategies of the firm. It is therefore helpful to put the detailed plans in a strategic framework by ensuring that a number of questions are addressed. There is a requirement to identify exactly what resources the strategy will require and to what extent those resources build on or are changed from existing resources. There is also a need to fit the present resources with the required resources.

## Resource identification

Effective planning of resources depends on the extent to which the planner is clear about the detailed resource needs. The danger in this approach is that new strategies will be considered in the context of old expectations or the existing basis of operating, rather than in terms of what is required in the future. Although the resource requirements of specific strategies will inevitably vary, useful observations can be taken from looking at two separate examples of strategy:

- **A low-price strategy** will require an emphasis on cost-efficient processes, with an ability to renew investment to maintain advantages in these areas. Attention will need to be paid to achieving simplicity of operating processes and low-cost distribution systems.

- **A strategy of differentiation** will require strength in marketing, research and creativity, with an emphasis on product development. It is therefore obvious that there is a need to identify those value activities that are critical to the success of particular types of strategy.

The competitive position of a firm also depends on how well matched its management systems and approaches are to support the strategies being used. Therefore a cost-efficient strategy is underpinned by ensuring that these plans are supported by management systems that will ensure that cost efficiency is actually delivered. This is likely to involve such things as tight cost control and detailed reporting. In contrast, strategies of differentiation are likely to require looser systems of reporting and control. There is a stronger emphasis on coordinating separate value activities to ensure that they are genuinely adding value in the process of creating and delivering the product or service.

The difficulty in taking this planning approach is that new strategies may require firms to shift their approach, particularly as the planning and control of resources is geared to support old strategies and not new ones. Equally, generic strategies are not absolute choices in the sense that, for example, pursuing a differentiation strategy absolves management from any need to plan cost efficiency or vice versa. In reality both would be important in underpinning a successful strategy. Diverse organizations are likely to position different products and businesses in different ways. This requires specific configurations of resources for each market or client group, and may prove difficult for resource aspects held in common across products and services.

**Resource fit**

The central question in resource planning is how the required resources fit the existing resource configuration of the firm. The key task therefore is how to change. Assessment of this fit with existing resources begins to establish the extent to which implementation is likely to require major changes within the firm and is achievable by an adjustment of the current resource base and organizational arrangements.

**Required resources**

There must be consistency in the way in which the various value activities are planned in order to support the strategy. This identifies one critical ingredient of successful strategies: the way in which the linkages between these important value activities work, including those with suppliers, channels and customers. The problems of establishing any workable plan for the launch of a product or service are not only created by the inherent complexity of these linkages but are often made worse by the political dimension. This arises because the responsibility for managing the separate activities is divided within the firm and probably between different departments. The different perceptions and objectives of these departments need to be reconciled in the planning process.

## Preparing resource plans

Having identified the principles behind the planning of resources at both corporate and business level, we can now move on to the process of preparing resource plans.

**Critical success factors and key tasks**

One of the major shortcomings of strategic implementation in many firms is the failure to translate statements of strategic purpose into a practical statement of those factors that are critical to achieving targets, and the key tasks that will ensure success. It is therefore important that these issues are addressed systematically, and this can be done by using the value chain as a framework.

First, it is important to agree the critical success factors for the specific strategy, while attempting to keep these to a manageable list. In creating this list it is important to ensure that all factors are genuinely necessary and that the list is in fact sufficient to underpin success. Key tasks can be attached to each critical success factor. These may relate to individual value activities, to improvements in support activities, or to changes in linkages within the value system. Once these key tasks have been identified, management responsibility can be allocated. Some of these key tasks may be symbolic.

**Planning priorities**

A resource plan is the output of a series of questions, and sets out what resources need to be obtained and which can be disposed of. This plan may well be in the form of a budget; it may also be usefully expressed as a sequence of actions or timetabled priorities in a written plan. The circular nature of the planning problem is quite usual in developing such a plan of action, and raises the question of where to start. Should it be the market forecast, the available level of funds, or production level constraints?

A useful guideline is to enter the problem through what appears to be the major change area. A firm planning new strategies of growth may well start with an assessment of market opportunity. Someone starting a new business may well begin with an assessment of how much capital is available. Planning priorities will require consideration of how activities need to be sequenced and scheduled. There can be conflict between these two planning tasks, as the schedule of activities that need to be completed may not be consistent with the best sequence of activities to put the plan into effect. Some activities may be prerequisites for later activities. Sometimes, the sequence of activities is dictated by the ease with which tasks can be done. Because some value activities are more important than others, the planning of the other activities is regarded as subsidiary to these major tasks. In contrast, the scheduling of completion times for activities may be determined by other factors such as efficiency, to avoid periods of overuse followed by low utilization: this is particularly relevant in firms operating in a highly seasonal market. Other activities may occur frequently, but need to be scheduled at precisely the right time, such as major television advertising; and of course customer service is strongly affected by the scheduling of tasks such as orders within the company.

**Key assumptions** All plans are based on assumptions. They may be assumptions about resource availability, or about the capacity of the firm to adapt existing resources or coordinate the resource requirements of a new strategy. Assumptions may also concern the environment: that a market will grow, that funds can be raised or that suppliers will deliver on time. If these assumptions are made explicit, the plan can be used as a model to help both in the evaluation of strategy and in the investigation of alternative means of implementing that strategy. Different assumptions can therefore be tested; two methods already discussed that are applicable to testing assumptions are sensitivity analysis and breakeven analysis.

**Financial planning and budgeting** Financial planning is concerned with translating the resource implications and decisions into financial statements of one sort or another. At both an organizational and a departmental level the budget is in effect a model of required resources. A number of types of budget or financial plans can be identified.

**Capital budgeting** is concerned with generating a statement of flow of funds related to a particular project or decision. A capital budgeting exercise may well seek to determine what the outflow and inflow of funds associated with the project will be, and what the implications of different means of financing the project would be. It would probably make an assessment of how worthwhile the project will be through some measure of return on investment. Unfortunately, capital budgeting often relates to specific strategies but neglects the impact on overall organizational performance.

Annual **revenue budgets** are commonly used to express the detailed resource plan in financial terms; they are also used as a means of measuring or controlling performance against the plan. Financial plans and projected profit and loss accounts may well be useful in projecting – perhaps over a period of years – implications of decisions for a firm's overall performance. They are particularly useful in highlighting potential shortfalls in resources or the impact of a changing mix of resources in terms of overall performance.

The budgeting process is usually tied into the power structure within the firm, and this can be a very real difficulty in the budgeting process. In order to address this, some firms have taken a **zero-based budgeting** approach, in which the historical size of the various budgets is given no weight in establishing the future deployment of resources.

## Staffing plans

Strategic change invariably has a significant impact on the people within the firm, and so staffing plans attempt to anticipate these changes in a number of respects. An important part of resource planning is to work through in detail the staffing requirements of particular strategies: this will include the number of people required and the types and levels of skills required. Some staff may need to be redeployed or transferred, and there may be some redundancies, which will require consultation with the unions. There are the issues of job grades and rewards, which are important factors in the resource plan. There is also the need for the plan to be linked to the strategic direction of the firm and the type of change being experienced. While incremental change may be possible by working largely with existing staff and developing them, the greater the need for global change, the more likely it is that new staff will be required. This is not just a matter of planning for senior executive changes: it may be addressing blockages in promotion lower in the hierarchy.

The recruitment and training policies within a firm are run by people comfortable with the dominant paragdim: to change this it may be necessary to bring in people with different experiences. Methods of selection may also need to change, even in quite simple ways. The greater the degree of change, the more likely it is that training will need to provide a basis for understanding and internalizing change.

## Network analysis

Network analysis, also known as **critical path analysis**, is a technique for planning projects by breaking them down into their component activities and showing these activities and their interrelationships in the form of a network. By considering the times and resources required to complete each of the activities it is possible to locate the critical path of activities that determines the minimum time of the project. The network can also be used for scheduling materials and other resources, and for examining the impact of changes in one sub-area of the project on others. This type of analysis breaks down the programme of implementation into its constituent parts by activity. It is therefore easy to build on the value chain analysis already discussed. The approach also establishes priorities, by identifying those activities upon which others depend.

A network enables the analyst to examine the implications of changes in the plan, or deviations from the plan. Network analysis can be very valuable in establishing the sequence in which tasks need to be planned. A good network should also assist in drawing up a time schedule. There are a number of elements of network analysis, such as **programme evaluation review technique** (PERT), which allows uncertainty about the times of each activity in the network to be taken into account.

## ORGANIZATIONAL STRUCTURE

One of the most important resources of any firm is its people and its structure.

### Structural types

The simplest structure is **no formal structure** at all. This is the type of organization found in many very small businesses. There is little division of management responsibility, and probably little clear definition of who is responsible for what. The main problem here is that the organization can only operate effectively up to a certain size, beyond which it becomes too cumbersome for one person alone to control.

A **functional structure** is based on the primary tasks that have to be carried out, such as production, finance and accounting. However, within a multidivisional structure the divisions themselves are likely to be split up into functional management areas. This functional structure allows greater operational control at a senior level in an organization, and linked to this is a clear definition of roles and tasks. However, as organizations become larger or more diverse, senior management may become burdened with everyday operational issues rather than taking a strategic perspective. Such organizations are also likely to require greater cooperation between different functions, as they cannot rely on lengthy vertical chains of decision making.

The main characteristic of a **multidivisional structure** is that it is subdivided into units, and these divisions may be formed on the basis of products and services, geographical areas or the processes of the enterprise. Divisionalization often comes about as an attempt to overcome the problems that functional structures have in dealing with diversity. Its main advantage is that each division is able to concentrate on the problems and opportunities of its particular business environment. The result can of course be a complex organization. At some level in the organization, a division will then have to be split into functionally based departments dealing with specialist tasks of that business. This raises the problem as to which functions are to be included in a division (and at what level), and which functions are properly placed within the corporate head office rather than within any one of the divisions.

In its most extreme form a firm may really be little more than an **investment company**: for instance, Hanson plc. It may simply consist of shareholdings in a variety of individual unconnected business operations over which it exercises little or no control. The role that the parent company takes may be limited to decisions about the buying and selling of such companies, with little involvement in a product or market strategy. Central corporate staff and services may be very limited. One benefit from such an approach is that the organization does not have to carry the burden of high central overheads, as the head office staff or parent company is likely to be small. Equally, profits from one company may be set against losses from another, and all companies may be able to obtain cheaper finance for investment from the parent company. The greatest weakness of this structure, however, is the risk of a lack of internal strategic cohesion, and duplication of effort between business units.

A **matrix structure** is a combination of structures: it often takes the form of product and geographical divisions or functional and division structures operating in tandem. Matrix structures are often adopted because there is more than one factor around which a structure could be built, so that pure divisional structures would be inappropriate. The firm may regard geographically defined divisions as the operating units for the purpose of local marketing, while product divisions are responsible for the central worldwide coordination of product development, manufacturing and distribution to the geographical divisions. The matrix structure can improve the quality of decision making in situations where there is a risk of one vital interest of the enterprise dominating strategy at the expense of others. Formal bureaucracy is replaced by direct contact between individuals. The structure is also supposed to increase managerial motivation and development, because of the wider involvement in strategies. However, this approach may run the risk of a dilution of priorities, and it may take longer to make decisions than in the more conventional structures. Also, responsibilities may be unclear, and so organizations with matrix structures may have to cope with a good deal of conflict because of the lack of clarity of role definition and responsibility. Senior managers must be capable of collaborating across the matrix. The structure does not suit managers who are fiercely competitive internally and who do not like ambiguity.

Few organizations adopt just one of the structural types just discussed. The skill is in blending the structures to the organization's circumstances. It is common to adopt a mixed structure to address problems such as functional structure within subsidiaries. The main business that employs the majority of employees might have a functional structure, with more peripheral business interests organised as divisions or subsidiaries. The converse of this is the company that is divisionalized except for certain key functions, which remain at the centre and which may have responsibility across all the divisions. Another way of coping with the need for organizational change without fundamentally affecting what already exists is to externalize change by moving the responsibility for it outside the enterprise or into a joint venture.

The growth in size and importance of **multinational businesses** brings further structural implications. The basic form of structure for a multinational is the retention of the home structure and the management of whatever overseas subsidiaries exist through direct contact between the manager of the subsidiary and the chief executive of the parent company. This is most common in single-product companies, or companies whose overseas interests are relatively minor. Beyond this simple structure the critical issue is the extent to which local independent responsiveness should take precedence over global coordination. A common form of multinational structure is the **international division**. Here the home-based structure may be retained first, whether functional or divisional, but the overseas interests are managed through a special international division. The logical extension of this structure is geographically based international subsidiaries, which evolve and are part of a multinational whole, but operate independently by country. In such circumstances, control by the parent companies is likely to be dependent on some form of planning reporting system and perhaps an ultimate veto over national strategies.

Some companies have moved to what is known as a **global product** or **integrated** structure. Here the multinational is split into product divisions, which are then managed on an international basis, so monitoring cost efficiency and enhancing the transfer of resources, particularly technology between the geographical regions. Difficulties experienced by management in this global division approach are mainly concerned with central coordination: management lose their sensitivity to local needs, particularly in terms of marketing and competitive activity.

Some structures have moved to combine the local responsiveness of an international subsidiary with the advantages of coordination found in global product companies. These have been called **transnational corporations**. With this approach, each national unit operates independently, but is a source of ideas and capabilities for the whole operation. National units achieve a global scale through specialization on behalf of the whole corporation, and the centre manages a global network, first by establishing the role of each subsidiary and then by sustaining the culture and systems to make the network operate efficiently.

In summary, the global role of subsidiaries is largely determined by their capabilities and the nature of their national markets, and this discussion of multinational organizations is illustrated by the basic structure of organizations.

## ORGANIZATIONAL DESIGN

Structure in itself will not ensure the success of the strategy, although an inappropriate choice of structure could impede success. Developing the flesh on the skeleton of this structure is the province of organizational design, which consists of a number of elements:

- centralization and devolution;
- organizational configurations;
- management systems.

## Centralization versus devolution

This is the extent to which the centre of an organization releases its control of decision making to units and managers lower down the hierarchy. In looking at the possible relationships between the centre and the parts of the organization, and how responsibilities for decision making can be divided, we can identify three stereotypes.

Strategic planning

Here the centre operates as the master planner, developing a detailed central plan and prescribing detailed roles for divisions and departments. They are seen as agencies, which deliver parts of the plan, and their role is confined to operational delivery of the plan. The main benefit of operating in this way is the high levels of control and coordination that the centre is able to exert over strategy. McDonald's, the fast-food chain, uses such an approach, which allowed it to internationalize while maintaining consistent product quality and company image. However the danger of such an approach is that the centre may become out of touch with divisions, and management may take a purely tactical approach in their relationship with the centre. The quality therefore of strategic thinking may therefore suffer.

Financial control

This is almost the opposite extreme from strategic planning: the centre sees itself as a shareholder or banker for the divisions. With this approach, there is little concern for defining the product market strategy for divisions. The main roles of the centre are setting financial targets, appraising the performance of divisions, and assessing capital bids from divisions. Such an approach questions whether the centre is needed at all, and it could be argued that the company could be dismembered into its constituent parts, with the stock market taking over the role of shareholder. However, the way in which the centre can add value is through its bargaining power and management skills, particularly in financing and control.

Strategic control

In the past few years, changes in the centre–division relationship of companies have been mainly concerned with a move from the tightly prescribed relationships of strategic planning to those of **strategic control**. Here the centre is a strategic shaper: it goes beyond mere financial control to a concern with the overall strategy of the organization, and the balance of activities and the role of each division. It also considers organizational policies such as employment and market coverage etc. The centre's role is not fulfilled through a master plan imposed from the top: rather it is built through the process of agreeing business plans produced by the divisions. This is a bottom-up process within central guidelines. The centre remains responsible for assessing the performance of divisions against their business plan, within which the annual budget has an important part. Strategic control requires the organizations to establish a clear understanding of how responsibility for strategy is divided between the centre and the divisions. The centre must have the capability to do its job, which is defining key policies, allocating resources to divisions and assessing the performance of divisions. All other tasks are candidates for devolution to divisions. This devolution, however, can create too much internal competition and rivalry.

## Organizational configurations

Structure is in practice more complex than a mere hierarchy: it consists of a number of building blocks and coordinating mechanisms, which together make up the detailed configuration of an organization. It has been suggested that there are essentially six pure configurations, or basic building blocks of organizational design, that can be adopted to fit the context that different types of organization face:

- the operating core, where basic work is produced;
- the strategic apex where the general management of the organization occurs;
- the middle line – all those managers who stand between the apex and the core;
- the techno-structure staff analysts who design the systems whereby the work processes of others are delivered and controlled;
- support staff – those who support the work of the operating core;
- the ideology, which consists of the organization's values and core belief.

The relative size and importance of the building blocks will vary, as will the methods by which the work is coordinated within the organization. Coordination can exist by a number of methods, such as:

- mutual adjustment through informal contact between people in the operating core;
- direct supervision through the hierarchy;
- standardization of work processes through systems that specify how work should be undertaken;
- standardization of outputs;
- standardization of skills and knowledge;
- standardization of norms, by which employees share the same core beliefs.

## Choosing a configuration

The choice of configuration revolves around the two issues of the building blocks and the coordinating mechanisms. Out of this approach, one or more of these six configurations, in terms of both circumstances and situations, will develop, which is best suited in terms of the shape and *modus operandi* of the organization. This brings us to the relationship between organizational design and the situation in which the organization is operating. Although few organizations will fit neatly into just one stereotype, this framework can be used to think through some important issues concerning structure and strategy fit in an organization. Remember that the strategy–structure relationship operates both ways: the configuration will influence how an organization perceives its circumstances, both internal and external, and how it positions itself in terms of seeking out or avoiding particular types of strategic development.

## Management systems and control

A key ingredient of this organizational design process is the management systems, and particularly those relating to information control and rewards. It is useful to think of control systems in two broad categories. The first is systems of **information and measurement**. This category would include financial systems such as budgets and variance analysis. There are also systems that regulate the behaviour of people rather than simply measure the end result of their efforts. **Reward systems** are the most important example of this type of system.

Control through information and measurement

The successful implementation of strategy will require managers to find ways of measuring how implementation is proceeding, and the extent of the variance from what is expected. If people are clear as to what is expected of them, and are provided with information that shows the extent to which these expectations are or are not being met, they will change their behaviour or redirect their energies or attention to remedy the situation. Some issues need to be considered in the overall design of such controls.

We need to distinguish between various levels of control: for example, strategic, management and operational. The complexity of strategic change usually requires a subdivision of control within a firm: hence the creation of responsibility centres, which should be in line with the degree of devolution within the firm. It is crucial to identify factors critical to the success or failure of the strategy and to develop performance indicators for these factors: a value chain analysis should assist with this process. There may be a temptation, as in many firms, to simplify control systems to the extent where they do not adequately reflect the degree of diversity in the firm's activities; so there is a need to allow diversity and control. Many aspects of strategy are difficult to measure quantitatively, so there is a need to avoid misleading measurements. There is, finally, a danger that systems will be concerned with purely negative monitoring of performance. The result can be that departments and individuals become over-concerned with minimizing the risk of such negative variances.

**Control through reward systems**  The design of reward systems is also a key element in creating a climate for strategic change. The need is to decide what the most important issues are for the reward system to deal with in order to influence the behaviour of people within the firm. Reward systems are also important for their symbolic impact, as they are visible signal types of behaviour that is to be encouraged within the firm. They can include both monetary and non-monetary reward systems. Remember that reward systems have both positive and negative impacts. In addition, the nature of the reward needs to be considered in terms of the objectives to be achieved. A number of issues can be raised in considering the reward system approach of a firm.

The nature of rewards needs to be varied according to time horizons: one can take a short-term or a long-term perspective. Firms wishing to encourage greater risk-taking are likely to find that it is helpful to develop quantitative measures of performance upon which to base bonus awards or share options. How can or should reward systems reflect individuals' capabilities, efforts and job satisfaction? Rewarding individuals for effort and performance can prove difficult unless the organizational structure and systems of control allow an individual's performance to be isolated from the efforts of others. Should the reward system seek to influence the behaviour of individuals or of groups? Care also has to be taken to balance the corporate interest with the business unit interests. The greater the independence of the units from the centre or from each other, the more likely it is that unit-based reward systems will be sensible.

## Influences on organizational design

The elements of organizational design have now been discussed. These elements need to work together to support the firm's strategy. Typical styles of organization develop to support particular strategies.

It is important to match organizational design to the types of strategy that the firm is pursuing, but this is a two-way process. Organization configuration also influences preferences for particular types of strategy, so different generic strategies will often require different forms of organizational design. A firm following a low-price strategy will need to find a way of ensuring cost-efficient operation with an emphasis on cost control, whereas a firm following a differentiation strategy may need higher degrees of creativity and probably a rapid response to problems and opportunities. A firm that seeks to follow differentiation and low-price strategies for different parts of its business is likely to experience conflict in terms of organizational design.

The nature of the tasks undertaken by the operating core of a firm has an important influence on the various aspects of organizational design. There are likely to be links between the types of production process and the approach to management. The more sophisticated and complex the technology of a firm, the more elaborate the structure becomes, for a number of reasons.

First, it is likely that a good deal of responsibility and power will devolve to those specialists concerned with the technology itself. The firm therefore tends to operate on an ad hoc basis. In turn this may create the need for liaison between such specialists: more sophisticated technology can give rise to increases in centralization or devolution. More sophisticated information technology may facilitate tighter central decision making on merchandising, planning and layout. Conversely, the same technology might allow evolution by providing systems which can be used locally.

Other influences on organizational design stem from the size, accountability and culture of firms: the larger the corporation, the more likelihood there is of divisionalization. Large corporations are also likely to move towards some form of devolution. The nature of a firm's accountability will also affect organizational design. In commercial enterprises where there is a pronounced dependence on some external body such as a parent company or shareholder group, the firm may be accountable to these external bodies. Owner control may also be an important influence on structure.

It is important to consider the nature of the environment in choosing a firm's configuration; it is also influential on the other design factors, such as centralization and control systems. In an environment that is simple and static, firms gear themselves to operational efficiency: they standardize their operations and their management. Management styles tend to be mechanistic and centralized; increasing complexity tends to be handled by devolving decision responsibility to specialists. In dynamic conditions the need is to increase the extent to which managers are capable of sensing what is going on around them, identifying change and responding to it. It is unlikely that the bureaucratic style of management will encourage such behaviour.

## STRATEGY, INFORMATION AND TECHNOLOGY

The lifeblood of any organization is information. It can be regarded as the glue that holds successful planning together. In order to secure a competitive advantage the firm's information system will need to incorporate speed and control. Thus it is imperative that the right information is available at the right time and in the right place. To achieve this, information needs and sources must be identified in order to design an information-processing system. The central rationale for an information system is to support managerial decision making. The key to all this is to blend the critical aspects of both strategic and operational decision making in allowing it to be supported by the information system. Given that the firm's objectives have been set, information needs are seen as a measure of performance in order to assist decision making and in many cases the need for management action. A number of stages can be identified in developing such a system.

The firm's central focus should be on identifying the critical success factors within its strategies and objectives, and it follows that by taking this approach information needs can be determined. These information requirements provide the fundamental performance data from which to assess the success of the firm's strategy.

One element of the information system is environmental scanning, and there is a need to identify the critical sources useful to management. These must be reliable, accurate, valid and valuable sources of information, both qualitative and quantitative. Monitoring of the sources will depend on the scale, complexity and instability of the environment faced by the firm. These sources can include individuals, institutions and organizations who are leading generators and promoters of change within the environment. Any change in the behaviour or relationships of these sources could indicate trends, which could have an impact on the firm's strategy.

Having identified the sources of change, critical indicators should be regarded as those aspects that have implications for the success of the firm's strategy and which should therefore be monitored. Such monitoring should enable management to identify any potential threats and opportunities. Though environmental trends are frequently viewed as a starting point for environmental scanning activities, this may be inappropriate, as trends are essentially the cumulative effects of prior actions and events. To identify causal factors underlying environmental change the scanning process should concentrate on the initiating, not the confirming, factors. A further element in considering the environmental scanning process is the relationship between the information generated and the internal management information system. It is at this point that the strategic planning process is supported by the external and internal components of the firm's information system.

Identification of the firm's critical information factors facilitates a more accurate focusing of information needs for strategic purposes. Within the various functions of the firm, information providers should be identified in order to assist management to determine whether the success factors have been achieved. Through analysis of the information, management decision making will be supported in the strategic planning process.

Unfortunately, systems with a primary emphasis on internal information frequently give attention to subsystem integration and the use of software capable of utilizing information already available within the firm's database, hence tending to look internally rather than considering information available externally. This introduces the problem of redevelopment and design. Four problems can be identified around this design issue:

- organizational size, and the issues that this raises for the transfer and communication of information and the active involvement of relevant parties;
- managerial decision making, which is not always conducted through rational procedures, as personal perceptions and relationships will affect the operation of the information system;
- lack of communication between the designer and the user, which may result in failure of the information system;
- a lack of awareness of and commitment to the use of information technology in the planning process by senior management.

The creation of a strategic business information system can contribute to long-term competitive success. The secret of this success is in the system's design and its support for managerial decision making. At the heart of this process are the firm's strategic objectives and plans, and it is here that the link is established with the information system.

## Technology

While many people would assume that there is a link between strategic management and information technology (IT), the influence lies not so much in the hardware and software but in the way that it is used. It is possible to separate technology into three broad categories:

- technology as apparatus;
- technology as technique;
- technology as organization.

The effect of technology on various aspects of organizational behaviour can be considered from two perspectives:

- Quantitative approaches can consider the relationship between technology and the size or structure of the organization.
- Systems approaches take a more descriptive and holistic overview.

Hence the link in all this is to establish the impact of materials technology on social technology. Materials technology can be seen, touched and heard, while social technology seeks to order behaviour and relationships.

The role of IT in strategic management is still evolving, both theoretically and practically. Over the years there has been a change from formal analytical approaches to strategic planning, through competitor analysis to the recognition that IT is an enabling mechanism that facilitates organizational change. There has been in this sense a move away from regarding IT as merely hardware and software to using it in terms of expertise (management know-how) and politics (networks of decision makers).

The rate at which innovations are adopted, and the way in which they affect the behaviour of a firm, depends on a number of factors. Two approaches are sometimes identified: **technology push** refers to the way technology affects the nature of goods and services, while **knowledge pull** sees the collection of relevant data as offering a significant competitive advantage. The need to change must come from within the prevailing organizational culture, and therefore the rate of change will be governed by this constraint, and by the attitude of key managers. There may in this respect be a difference between attitudes and adoption, and this will relate back to management style and the firm's decision-making structure. Favourable attitudes are needed before there is a move towards adoption, because an element of risk is attached to those who support new initiatives in IT. In taking a strategic perspective it is important in considering IT to examine the wider environment.

Information has already been referred to as the lifeblood of the strategic management process. The need for an understanding of IT requires the manager to have not only functional competence but also computer literacy and the ability to deploy IT effectively.

Another aspect to consider is the changing demographic structure of the European Union, which will have implications for the use of IT, particularly in its implications for staffing levels. Simply absorbing additional labour without the use of productivity-enhancing working methods or the use of IT will lead to a decline in productivity. Changing demographics, with the workforce getting older, will see increasing competition for the traditional (young) labour market of the hospitality industry. If this traditional labour market looks for employment in other service industries, reliance may be placed on an ageing workforce, with less knowledge and abilities in IT. If the hospitality industry were to lean towards an older workforce, issues of training and capital investment in IT would assume greater strategic importance.

The discussion so far has shown a move towards the strategic use of IT systems, and in this respect five levels of progression can be identified:

- **Localized exploitation** sees IT used to improve isolated operations, but not benefiting related areas of operation.
- **Internal integration** sees the adoption of both hardware and software to assist in achieving solutions in the firm's information needs. Both technical and organizational factors are combined, but the roles and responsibilities of management need to be defined.
- **Business process redesign** sees a move away from the business process constraining IT development to the business process redesigned around the available IT capabilities. In this respect there is a switch in emphasis.
- **Business network redesign** occurs when vertical integration takes place; shared networks of information are created, and so there is a requirement for coordination.
- **Business scope redefinition** comes about when the information network extends to a level where it is possible to redefine the mission and objectives of the firm.

The basis of the strategic role of information technology systems is that they support managerial decision making, and it is in this respect that they can be of assistance to management.

It is clear in this discussion that for IT to be strategically useful the perceptions of management are important in its implementation. The hospitality industry will need to value managers trained in IT; the main obstacle to the implementation of an effective strategic role is largely managerial.

## Problems and opportunities

While temporary advantages may be gained from IT systems, they do not represent a long-term competitive advantage, as they can be easily copied. The real benefit comes from IT supporting new and more flexible forms of organization structure. Equally, the nature of work is changing, and so the rate at which managers can learn new skills will determine the rate at which a firm can respond to change. This all requires a new approach to leadership that is proactive rather than reactive, and is innovative in nature. What leaders need to do is, in a sense, to make the workers uncomfortable with an unworkable present and prepare them to act quickly to influence the future. The move within the hospitality industry from a strategic perspective must be away from an obsession with technology delivering data and towards relevant management information. There is a need to move from an essentially clerical perspective to a higher level of decision making.

From a strategic perspective there are two key issues in the implementation of new forms of service delivery managed through new technological processes:

- Solutions can be found not only in materials technology but in developing the managers that must work them.
- Problems of development lie in the organization's culture and the synergy that may exist between different parts of a large company.

It is clear from this discussion that for IT assume a strategic role in the hospitality industry, it must be *perceived* as possessing a strategic capability. Such recognition must come from management. While technological innovations are relatively easy to manage, it is the implications for social processes that present the problem for the hospitality industry. In the final analysis it is only when both these two aspects are addressed that progression up the five levels of IT implementation can be achieved.

## Facilities management and outsourcing

An alternative approach to IT is **facilities management**: an agreement between two firms to outsource not only the IT department and the software it uses, but the actual function and staff as well.

The driving force towards facilities management is the need to cut down all expenses brought about by the pressures of the economic and competitive environment in which the hospitality industry operates. It can therefore be seen as a radical alteration in the way that a firm does business, in order to remain competitive.

For example, the core skill for a hotel company is its business of providing accommodation, and a hard look at the accounting services reveals that a line could be drawn between what accounting information is truly necessary in house, and what is not. It may be vital that the firm has information for making policy and interpreting business information, but not that it provides it in house.

Increasingly, outsourcing is the way financial management is going. The IT component is of less interest to the customer: it is not the important element. It is the way a specialist firm develops the people that is important, and so it takes an organization – a process – and completely redefines the way the service operates and the way it interacts with its customers. The value-added service that the specialist firm provides is its skills in service definition and management.

## MANAGING CHANGE

The discussion so far on the strategic management process has essentially focused on the management of change. There are a number of problems associated with the management of change, particularly because in terms of direction the firm builds up a momentum reinforced by success, and the management process can get out of control. Equally, the culture of the firm is likely to support this momentum. Finally, there may be political resistance within and around the firm to change.

## Management: the obstacles to change

The top management of any hospitality firm frequently want to make their managers less bureaucratic, more entrepreneurial, more empowered and empowering. The fallacy that new beliefs – or **culture change** – lead automatically to new behaviour is just one of many basic mistakes that hospitality firms make when trying to change, renew or transform themselves. Other mistakes include lack of sustained leadership of the change process, and too frequent modification of the emphasis and content of the process. Another common mistake is to underestimate the extent of the innate barriers against change that exist in most firms. With few exceptions, big companies suffer a litany of barriers: internal distrust, poor communications, disenfranchised middle management, a low level of employee motivation, stifling of entrepreneurial spirit, slow decision-making, lack of collaboration across internal boundaries, and inhibited learning. For change processes to succeed against such odds, three complementary steps must be taken:

- Managers need to identify the main **external challenge** to the firm's strategy.
- The **organizational context** within which decisions are taken, and the rules governing people's tasks, roles and relationships, must be altered.
- The **world view**, or **mind-set**, of managers needs changing by linking it to the firm's new strategic thrust.

In spite of the modernization of corporate structures and systems, the mindset of most managers appears to have remained remarkably similar to the 'Taylorist' model developed at the beginning of this century by Frederick Taylor, the 'father' of so-called **scientific management**. Few modern managers would advocate the exercising of authority in the blatantly coercive ways that Taylor espoused in order to control 'dumb and lazy workmen', as he put it. However, even in knowledge-intensive companies, managers are still influenced by Taylor's principles of hierarchical order, narrow specialization and **command and control systems**, all of which were designed to achieve the compliance of an uneducated workforce. Modern bureaucracies may use subtle means for achieving compliance, but their highly educated managers and knowledge workers are nevertheless stifled rather than mobilized to contribute all their intelligence and energy. This latent energy should be unleashed in almost revolutionary fashion in the change process itself. Faced with the all-too-frequent barrier of conservatism among senior executives, it can be argued that organizational renewal (often) benefits from the shared expectations, collectively held change agenda, and peer pressure that middle managers can bring. This is not to say that change processes can only be successful if they start in the middle or near the bottom of an organization. Unlike many other writers, we would argue that top-down change can also succeed in certain circumstances.

Two approaches to change can be identified:

- incremental change;
- transformational change.

While organizations can change in different ways, in most cases the process is **incremental**. Such an approach builds on the skills and knowledge already present, and so change is likely to be efficient. The weakness in this approach is that because change takes place within the paradigm of the firm it may ignore the need for more fundamental change to avoid strategic drift. More **transformational** change may be required if the firm is faced with major events within either the general or the competitive environment.

One view is that the organization is a social system built on influence paths and loops. This view therefore suggests that change occurs by mutually reinforcing and amplifying the stimuli within the system. The change agent seeks to manage change incrementally within the current system. However, in situations of more transformational change this systems approach may not be adequate.

Other explanations for change are that it takes place by shifts in the paradigm through challenge, information or experimentation. A deteriorating market position may contribute to this shift, which may create a crisis within the organization. This could create a need for change and debate within senior management, and the search for information. Conflicts and new information may lead to the process of experimentation and the emergence of a new paradigm, which will require consolidation.

## Determining change needs

An important element in managing change is to assess the type and magnitude of change required. First, it is important to assess the extent to which incremental or transformational change is required and then to identify any barriers to change.

It has already been pointed out that incremental change, while typical within organizations, may give rise to strategic drift, and so it is important to determine when more fundamental change is required. Determining such conditions is frequently a matter of judgement as there is no absolute set of conditions to identify strategic drift. However, a firm with little focus on its external environment may face the problem of drift, particularly if there is a lack of market information. Also, deteriorating performance relative to the firm's competitors may also be an example of drift. Finally, a highly homogeneous culture or major power blockages may also present problems.

In identifying the barriers to strategic change it is possible to decide the mechanisms that would be useful in order to resolve these problems. While routines, control systems, structures, symbols and power or dependence relationships may represent blockages, they can provide the focus for deciding how to implement change. Organizational structure and design has already been discussed, and so here the focus is on the style and role of the strategic manager: the management of change.

## Managing the process

The management of change considers not only the style of management but also the tactics of change.

Five styles can be identified in managing change:

- If there is misinformation or a lack of information, **education and communication** might be appropriate. Such an approach requires mutual respect and trust between managers and employees.
- **Participation** helps to strengthen ownership of and commitment to a decision. The risk in taking a participative approach is that the setting up of project teams, for instance, may lead to solutions being found within the existing paradigm.
- In **intervention**, the senior manager coordinates the process but delegates certain aspects to various groups, while maintaining overall control and ensuring progress.
- In **manipulation**, a clear crisis or opportunity is identified, and circumstances are dramatized in order to establish the conditions for change.
- **Coercion** is an explicit use of power, and may only be successful when time is short or the organization faces a crisis.

## Education and training

Leading management educationalists spend a lot of time these days telling firms how to cope with change. Ironically, the turmoil and uncertainty in their own business provides ample material for a good case study. Like other sectors, business schools in Europe and North America have been hard hit by the recession of the early 1990s. The problem, though, has not merely been adjusting to a cyclical pattern of demand. Teaching content and styles, traditional delivery methods, and even the very basis for schools' existence have all been thrown under the spotlight by the quickening pace of economic and technological change. Among trends on both sides of the Atlantic several stand out: a sharper focus on immediate corporate concerns (as manifested in the growth of short executive courses tailor-made for individual companies); increasing emphasis on the so-called multidisciplinary – as opposed to functional – teaching approach; and growing interest in international issues. In striving to find the right formula for survival in the twenty-first century – which in Europe means finding an appropriate model for training the new breed of Euro-manager – business schools are locked in an urgent struggle for students, staff, money and other scarce resources.

Management education only became a respectable and established academic discipline in the USA in the late 1950s, but its expansion over the last three decades is a remarkable success story. The US method has been widely exported, and in the process has influenced the development of regional systems such as that in Europe. The contribution of business school research has been acknowledged in the award of at least four Nobel prizes for economics to business school professors. Suddenly, however, a discipline renowned for its interpretation of relatively predictable long-term business trends is being asked to provide instant solutions for firms in a much faster and less certain economic environment. The good news is that even if its nature is changing, demand for management education is probably as great (if not greater) than ever. Annual company spending on executive education in the USA, for instance, is estimated to have doubled from $2 billion to $4 billion between 1987 and 1992. Intensifying competitive pressures, organizational restructuring, integrating strategy and development, and recognition of the value of management education as a competitive weapon are among reasons frequently cited by companies for this increased spending. But if the cake is not necessarily shrinking, getting a slice of it has become much tougher. The corporate sector's concern with immediate problems has blurred the boundaries between management education and consultancy, creating new competition from (among others) big management consultancies, trade associations and redundant executives. Business schools have had to rethink their strategies radically. The soul-searching takes slightly different forms in Europe and in the USA, but can be summarized in the four Is: internationalization, integration, implementation and innovation.

- **Internationalization** is reflected, for example, in the increasing number of overseas students on MBA courses in the UK, and in attempts to broaden faculty recruitment, diversify teaching materials, and promote a greater number of exchange programmes.
- **Integration** is seen in the way that schools have been trying to move away from the vertical curriculum 'silos' – accounting, marketing, finance and the like – and to replace, or at least supplement, them with

course structures that encourage a more holistic approach to problem solving, thereby better reflecting the real world.

- **Implementation** is a reaction to old jibes that MBA really stands for 'management by analysis' or 'management by academics'. Thus skills courses, team building, business ethics, negotiation and, above all, leadership have become features of the modern management education curriculum.
- **Innovation** implies that the static model of the 'golden age' is nowadays in constant need of revision and fine tuning. The encouraging thing from a European point of view is that Europe's management education suppliers may be better placed to make the necessary adaptations than their US counterparts.

The USA's strong research tradition is thought by many to have hampered the development of a true interdisciplinary approach, while the rich endowments often provided by alumni have encouraged some business schools, unwisely, to remain detached from employers. The immediate strains on business schools in the UK and continental Europe, nevertheless, are real enough. The proportion of funds that they can obtain from the public sector in the UK and France is falling, while the trend away from open executive programmes, attended by managers from many companies, towards shorter company-specific courses has financial implications. Single-sourcing, moreover, or at least reducing the number of suppliers, is happening as much in the management education sector as it is in others. Lower salary expectations and the uncertain jobs market have combined to cut demand for full-time MBA courses by roughly 15 per cent over the last two to three years, though the latest figures from the Association of MBAs (Amba) suggest that 1993–94 has seen a recovery in the UK.

The management challenge for business schools is well beyond merely balancing the budget. The test is in finding faculties able to respond to the growing demand for teaching across disciplines, sufficiently versed in international issues, and with the right skills to address companies' immediate problem-solving needs. The trick is to do this without sacrificing schools' research capability, and without losing the leading-edge knowledge that distinguishes management education from management consultancy. To use a piece of jargon from the latter's lexicon, the successful schools of the next century will have 'rightsized' rather than 'downsized'. Cutting human capital is a last resort for many businesses at the moment, but business schools are especially reluctant, not just because their brains are their biggest asset but because a well-rounded faculty is not easily reassembled. This in part explains the intense interest in training managers in emerging markets like those of Eastern Europe, India and even the Far East.

A business school's most precious – but at the same time most costly – resource is the brains of its faculty. The élite schools of management education in the USA are rapidly retooling their MBA programmes, adjusting to the changing climate for business in the USA and elsewhere. Successful for decades at turning out highly skilled specialists to staff corporate bureaucracies, universities are now striving to mould leaders who can manage change. With most of the giants of corporate industry downsizing, re-engineering, and revamping their market focus, businesses need a different product from that which traditional MBA programmes have been turning out. Research has been undertaken in key industries to determine their views on how changes in technology, environment, demographics, and international politics are changing their jobs: in essence, the basic objective is to define the characteristics of twenty-first century enterprise.

What the market needs is managers who can operate across functions, in flat hierarchies, in teams, and who can handle globalization. Most programmes are domestic and do not deal at all with technology. The new-look MBA strives to incorporate new disciplines, such as information management, leadership, innovation, people skills, and crisis management into curricula heavy with coursework in traditional fields such as marketing, finance, accounting, human resources, and management strategy. Along with the new topics comes a new teaching approach, integrating diverse material so that students learn to operate effectively across functions. This innovation is more difficult for faculty than students, since it requires the often balkanized departments of academe to cooperate.

Companies and universities are beginning to value verbal and analytical skills as highly as mathematical aptitude. There is also an internationalization push, particularly with extensive commercial experience working at corporations. The case method of teaching is moving towards a more integrated curriculum, a diversification away from case study, and an explicit emphasis on creating business leaders rather than general managers. The criticism of the case method is that in a case study the parameters are well defined; in the real world, the problem is that the problem is not obvious at all. A course in leadership has become part of the required curriculum. With schools sensitive to criticisms that 'egghead MBAs' with financial or accounting acumen but few social skills fit poorly in most corporate cultures, people skills are now seen as important.

## Routines, symbols and the political process

Changing organizational routines may represent a blockage to the management of change when some form of new strategy needs to be introduced. Such a blockage may lead to strategic drift. It is important that managers trying to effect strategic changes take personal responsibility not only for identifying such changes in routines but also for ensuring that they actually occur. It is therefore important to identify critical success factors and key tasks, and therefore drive planning and implementation of a strategy down to the operational level.

Change processes are not always formal and can in some cases be symbolic. The issue here is how such symbolic acts can be managed to signal change. For change to be meaningful it has to be relevant to individuals in the day-to-day reality of their jobs. Many mundane aspects of organizational life take on a symbolic significance, such as cars or the size of an office. The most powerful aspect of change is the behaviour of senior management, and it is they whose behaviour should be in line with the change required. This behaviour should be evidenced by deeds and words. One example could be the replacement of senior members of the board by more younger members.

It is likely that change will require management to consider the power structures of the organization. It needs to be understood that analysis and planning may take on a political perspective. Managers need to be sensitive to the political dimensions of their activities, not just because they may be blockages to apparently rational behaviour, but also because political activity might itself help to effect change. The problem of building a power base is that the manager becomes identified with existing groupings, thus losing support among potential supporters in other groups. In implementing change the main problem will be carrying the body of the organization with that change, and senior management may have to cope with the tactical political manouevring of other managers resistant to change.

Managing strategic change also requires an analysis of the characteristics of an effective change agent, a point that focuses on the issue of leadership. The leader should have a clarity of direction and should be sensitive to the context in which the change takes place. The leader's style should be appropriate to the context in which change takes place, and there should be an ability to use the political and symbolic processes within the organization. A range of personal traits can be seen in such leaders: visionary perspective, a detailed analytical approach, the ability to communicate strategic intent, a readiness to challenge the status quo, the ability to achieve focus and clarity, and the ability to maintain performance and make it happen. Such personality traits are, not surprisingly, very rare.

**SUMMARY**  This chapter showed that one aspect of strategy implementation is resource planning, at both the corporate and operational levels. The former refers to the allocation of resources within the various parts of the firm to support the overall strategy. The latter notes that the firm's value chain presents a useful framework in identifying its resource requirements. In considering the operational level, critical success factors need to be identified, and the key tasks required need to be listed. Planning tools available in achieving this exercise include budgets, financial plans and network analysis. The implementation of strategy and resource planning is achieved through the people within the firm, its organizational structure and design. The strategic role of information systems and the use of technology is important in the implementation stage. Finally, the way in which strategic change is managed is also important, as organizational design in itself will not ensure successful implementation.

**FURTHER READING** Abrahams, P 1991 Eastern Europe, *Financial Times*, 17 September, 11

AHMA 1989 *Looking forward: a management perspective of technology in the lodging industry*, Washington DC: American Hotel Motel Association

Anthony, R N and J Deardon 1976 *Management control systems: text and cases*, 3rd edn, Boston, MA: Irwin

Barlett, C and S Ghoshal 1989 *Managing across borders: the transnational corporation*, Harvard Business School Press

Barlett, C and S Ghoshal 1986 Tap tour subsidiaries for global reach, *Harvard Business Review* **64**(6), 87–94

Boshoff, H 1989 Testing plans against alternative futures, *Long Range Planning* **22**, 69–75

Bowey, A 1982 *Handbook of salary and wage systems*, 2nd edn, Aldershot: Gower

Bungay, S and M Gould Creating a strategic control system, *Long Range Planning* **24**(3), 32–9

Burn, J and M O'Neil 1987 *Information analysis*, London: Paradigm

Burns, T and G Stalker 1968 *The management of innovation*, London: Tavistock

Castan, A *et al* 1990 *1993 and beyond: the impact of EC legislation on the hotel, catering and tourism industries*, Paris: Cornell–ESSEC

Chandler, A D 1962 *Strategy and structure*, Cambridge, MA: MIT Press

Channon D 1973 *The strategy and structure of British enterprise*, London: Macmillan

Child, J 1972 Organizational structure, environment and performance: the role of strategic choice, *Sociology* **6**, 2–21

Cohn, S F 1980 Industrial product adoption in a technology push industry, *Industrial Marketing Management* **9**, 89–95

Collins, T 1991 Finance managers attack IT record on cost cutting, *Computer Weekly*, 14 November, 4

Craver, D 1990 Training the hybrids in their own image, *Computer Weekly*, 5 April, 16

Davids, M 1988 Labour shortage woes, *Public Relations Journal* **44**, 24–9, 59

deMicco, F and R Reid 1988 Older workers: a hiring resource for the hospitality industry, *Cornell Hotel and Restaurant Administration* **28**, 56–61

Doz, Y 1986 *Strategic management in multinational companies*, London: Pergamon

Flood, G 1991 Brewers tap into a winning system, *Computer Weekly*, 26 September, 4

Fox, A 1974 *Man mismanagement*, London: Hutchinson

Galbraith, J R and R K Kazanjian 1986 *Strategy implementation, structure, systems and process*, New York: West

Gamble, P R and G Smith Expert front office management by computer, *International Journal of Hospitality Management* **5**(3), 109–14

Gamble, P R 1986 Computers and innovation in the hospitality industry: a study of some factors affecting management behaviour, PhD thesis, University of Surrey

Geller, A N 1985 How to improve your information system, *Cornell HRA Quarterly* **26**(2), 19–27

Geller, A N 1985 Tracking the critical success factors for hotel companies, *Cornell HRA Quarterly* **25**(4), 76–82

Gilad, B and T Gilad 1988 *The business intelligence system*, New York: Amacom

Glueck, W F and R Fauch 1984 *Business policy and strategic management*, 4th edn, Singapore: McGraw-Hill

Gould, M and A Campbell 1987 *Strategies and styles*, Oxford: Basil Blackwell

Gupta, A and V Godvindarajan 1991 Knowledge flows and the structure of control within multinational corporations, *Academy of Management Review* **16**(4), 768–92

Harvey D 1991 Ups and downs of executive information systems, *Computer Weekly*, 16 May, 32–3

Hudson Institute 1987 *Workforce 2000*, New York: Hudson Institute

Kiechal, W 1984 To compute or not to compute, *Cornell HRA Quarterly* **24**(4), 9

Knight, K 1976 Matrix organisation: a review, *Journal of Management Studies* **13**, May, 111–30

Lawrence, P and J Lorsch 1969 *Organization and environment*, Boston, MA: Irwin

Leslei, McDowell D A and H Gummer The application and implications of microprocessors in the control function, *Journal of Contemporary Hospitality Management* **1**(1), 21–49

Levitt, T 1960 Marketing myopia, *Harvard Business Review*, July/August, 45–60

Linnerman, R E and F D Kennell 1977 Shirt sleeves approach to long range plans, *Harvard Business Review*, March/April, 141–50

McRae, S (ed) 1990 *Keeping women in*, London: PSI

Medlik, R 1989 Profit from productivity in tourism, *Tourism* **61**, 14

Miles, R E and C Snow 1986 Organizations: new concepts for new forms, *California Management Review* **28**(3), 62–73

Miles, R E and C Snow 1984 Fit, failure and the hall of fame, *California Management Review* **26**(3), 42–51

Mintzberg, H and J Quinn 1991 *The strategy process*, 2nd edn, Englewood Cliffs: Prentice-Hall, p. 672

Mintzberg, H 1979 *The structuring of organizations*, Englewood Cliffs: Prentice-Hall

Mumford, E and A M Pettigrew A M 1975 *Implementing strategic decisions*, London: Longman

Naisbitt, J 1984 *Megatrends*, London: Futura

Newquist, H P 1991 Where you least expect AI, *AI Expert* **6**(9), 59–61

Newquist, H P 1991 In unexpected places, *AI Expert* **6**(8), 59–61

Nystrom, H 1979 *Creativity and innovation*, Chichester: John Wiley

OECD 1988 *Statistiques des recettes publiques des pays membres de l'OECD*, Paris: OECD

Perrow, C 1973 A framework for the comparative analysis of organizations, *American Sociological Review*, **32**(2), 194

Peters, T and R Waterman 1982 *In search of excellence*, New York: Harper & Row

Porter, M and V E Miller 1985 How information gives you competitive advantage, *Harvard Business Review*, July/August, 149–60

Porter, M E 1985 *Competitive advantage: creating and sustaining superior performance*, New York: The Free Press

Pugh, D S and D J Hickson 1976 *Organization structure in its context: the Aston programme* **1**, Aldershot: Saxon House

Pugh, D 1984 *Organization theory*, Harmondsworth: Penguin

Rajan, A 1990 *1992: a zero sum game*, London: The Industrial Society

Roethlisberger, F J and W J Dickson 1964, *Management and the worker*, New York: Wiley, p. 517

Rumelt, R P 1979 Evaluation of strategy: theory and models In D E Schendel and C W Hofer (eds) *Strategic management: a new view of business policy and planning*, Boston, MA: Little Brown

Rumelt, R 1974 *Strategy, structure and economic performance*, Harvard University Press

Scholes, K 1991 *Learning to live with devolution*, Sheffield Business School

Scott-Morton, M S 1991 *The corporation of the 1990s*, Oxford: Oxford University Press

Shamir, B 1978 Between bureacracy and hospitality, some organizational characteristics of hotels, *Journal of Management Studies*, October, 285–307

Taylor, F W 1911 *Principles of scientific management*, New York: Harper

Thompson, D 1991 Imaging meets expert systems, *AI Expert* **6**(11), 24–32

Tyrell, R 1988 *Planning for social changes*, The Henley Centre

Venkatraman, N 1991 IT induced business reconfiguration. In MS Scott-Morton (ed) *The corporation of the 1990s*, Oxford: Oxford University Press

Verziji, J J 1981 *Planning and information systems for jobs allocation*, London: Macmillan

Wack, P 1985 Scenarios: uncharted waters ahead, *Harvard Business Review*, September/October, 73–89

Ward, J 1993 Information, management and organizational strategy. In D Faulkner and G Johnson (eds) *The challenge of strategic management*, London: Kogan Page

Webster, J 1991 *Revolution in the office? Information technology and work organization*, PICT Policy Research papers No 14, London: ESRC

West, J J and M D Olson 1989 Environmental scanning, industry structure and strategy making: concepts and research in the hospitality industry, *International Journal of Hospitality Management* **8**(4), 282–98

Winner, L 1977 *Autonomous technology: technics out of control as a theme in political thought*, Cambridge, MA: MIT Press

Woodward, J 1965 *Industrial organization: theory and practice*, Oxford: Oxford University Press

Yavitz, B and W Newman 1982 *Strategy in action*, New York: The Free Press

Zannetos, Z S 1968 Towards intelligent management information systems, *Industrial Management Review* **9**(3) 21–8

Zentner, R D 1981 How to evaluate the present and the future corporate environment, *Journal of Business Strategy*, Spring, 42–51

# Growth strategies: management contracts, strategic alliances and joint ventures

**OBJECTIVES**    After reading this chapter you should be able to:

- Identify key issues concerning the globalization of the hospitality industry and determine a number of developmental growth strategies.
- Understand the nature, development and history of management contracts in the hotel industry.
- Identify the elements of the relationship between the hotel owner and the operator.

## GROWTH STRATEGIES

### Introduction

The management contract has become a popular approach to growth in the hospitality industry because, as for franchising (discussed in Chapter 8), little capital is required compared with an asset acquisition strategy. Usually the management contracting firm will be expected to provide some equity, and will have to share some of the decision making with the owners of the property: an aspect that distiguishes it from franchising. Equally, performance expectations will be greater in a management contract than in franchising.

In order to realize these expectations, this type of strategy (management contracting) will require a strong list of competitive capabilities if a firm is to be able to sustain growth. Specifically, management firms will have to demonstrate that they can generate a specific number of room nights as a result of their competitive strengths. This drive for growth will require the management contracting firms to develop more sophisticated global pricing and marketing efforts.

For this strategy to work there have to be a large number of clients wishing to obtain managers for their hotels. In recessionary times this is common, as there are a large number of hotels in receivership. However, these properties may not conform to the firm's normal portfolio standards: thus there is a danger that the concept will be compromised. Success through expansion by management contracts will be largely determined by the firm's ability to attract properties that conform to its portfolio requirements.

## The nature of growth strategies

As the hospitality industry in many countries approaches the mature stage of the life cycle it has become increasingly involved in exporting products and services beyond national boundaries. A number of different development methods can be adopted by hospitality firms when they consider expansion. One such approach, franchising, will be discussed in Chapter 8. The focus of this chapter is on other methods: specifically management contracts and, to a lesser extent, strategic alliances and joint ventures.

The basic distinction in implementing growth strategies is between those with a global geographic scope and those limited to a particular national environment. The move in recent years has been away from a hospitality firm's domestic base to competition on a worldwide basis. In essence, hospitality firms seem to be moving from a multi-domestic orientation to a global perspective.

## Globalization

The move to globalization in the hospitality industry relies on the fact that consumers' needs for products and services have continued to converge between countries, as business practices and marketing systems have become more similar. Brand reputation and consistency have become important competitive weapons worldwide. Many of the strategic issues confronting a firm competing internationally are similar to those faced by domestic firms, although others are unique to international firms. Global expansion requires a global view on the industry, and this requires an analysis of the firm's environmental threats and opportunities.

The first stage in this global view is to collect and interpret market and competitor information. This should relate to the country in which the firm wishes to operate.

Strategy formulation involves assessing the firm's capabilities and how they can be effectively employed. However, a global strategy may encounter problems in the transmission of managerial skills, and capital requirements may use a number of alternatives including management contracts, joint ventures, strategic alliances or franchising. The advantage of marketing on a global scale is that it brings with it many strengths, such as the economies of scale in investing in global distribution systems.

Management's response to external pressures such as customer demand creates a need for internationally uniform standards of quality and pricing in an attempt to generate customer loyalty. The strategic choice in expanding globally requires the resources to respond locally to competitive threats. Such a response is aided by the formation of joint ventures, acquisitions, mergers and collaborative agreements.

Economies on a global scale are achieved when the hospitality firm is able to service its global customers. In identifying such economies, there has to be a balance between the costs of expansion and the resulting profits gained.

A firm expanding globally needs to consider the degree of ownership by the parent company: a point that will be influenced by the host government, and will include decisions on investments, repatriation of funds and employment of expatriates.

The primary organizational structural issue facing the global firm is the necessity of determining the combination of coordinating mechanisms necessary to achieve the desired multinational integration with the minimum of interference. The two structural issues that are likely to have the greatest effect on the process of strategic formulation are as follows:

- Should management activities be performed locally, or can some activities be standardized over a number of nations?
- How should activities be coordinated? The issues here include strategic planning systems, international policies, management incentive schemes and information systems. One cost within a global system is friction and antagonism within the organization, and so a balance needs to be struck between the various management hierarchical levels and their geographic location.

A multinational hospitality firm can identify three approaches in developing and retaining its competitive advantage:

- It can exploit differences in the input and output markets among the many countries in which it operates.
- It can benefit from scale economies in its various activities.
- It can exploit the synergies and economies of scope that may be available due to the diversity of its activities and organization.

It is these three areas of competitive advantage that should be used to optimize efficiency and minimize risk, and so there is a requirement to manage both the objectives of the firm and the means of achieving those objectives.

## Opportunities for globalization

In 1994 over 500 million people travelled worldwide, both for leisure and for business purposes, thus creating opportunities for global hotel chains. Global marketing has become critical to a firm's success, particularly within economic and politically stable countries. Over the next ten years competitive presures and economies of scale will both encourage the trend towards internationalization in the hospitality industry. Four issues can be identified as reasons why the major chains are taking this global view:

- As a number of Western industrialized countries have seen their hospitality industries move into the mature stage of the life cycle, so growth in those countries has been limited. In an effort to increase levels of growth and profitability there has been a need for hospitality firms to grow internationally.
- Hotel growth in the international markets can be linked to growth in tourism arrivals on a worldwide basis. Regions such as the Far East have experienced tourism growth above the average, with consequent hotel expansion.
- As travel increases, hotel clients are more likely to stay at hotels that they are familiar with and that can provide consistent service and an international reservation system. To this end, companies are trying to develop brand loyalty: awareness of a firm's global presence improves its market position.
- The final motivation for international expansion is one of protecting the firm from fluctuating economies. Different countries are at different points of the economic cycle: some may be in recession and others in the growth stage, and so an international approach can provide a hedge against a sudden drop in the firm's profitability.

These are some of the reasons for international expansion; but other factors can impinge on hospitality firms that take this global approach.

The pattern of capital investment in hotel projects is changing: in particular, developing countries and their governments are recognizing the economic value of tourism. Governments can sometimes serve either as intermediaries or as investors; at the same time they are liberalizing their trade and foreign investment policies. The globalization of the capital markets has affected the way properties are financed. There has been a move away from local financial institutions to the internationalization of capital flows. Regulatory restrictions are slowly being lifted, and so foreign investment in domestic financial markets is being encouraged. This globalization of funding sources will separate the finance from the location of the property.

As many countries in the 1990s move towards a free-market economy the need for hotel accommodation will grow. Growth will depend on both economic and political stability in those countries, in addition to the available sources of capital. One trend in the search for new sources of capital is the move towards the adoption of developmental strategies such as franchising, management contracts and joint ventures. It is these approaches that will dominate expansion plans as it becomes more difficult for large firms to finance ambitious growth plans.

Demographic trends in the industralized countries, where essentially the population is getting older, mean that problems of labour shortage will affect the hospitality industry. However, hospitality and tourism in the emerging countries of South-East Asia do not have a problem of labour supply, but there are problems in education and training, which may make it difficult for hospitality firms to maintain levels of service and standards.

Another influence on the move towards globalization is information technology, and the use of computerized reservations systems. Linked with developments in branding, computer reservations systems will allow for the evolution of a worldwide standard for the provision of hospitality services, which will allow companies to gain a competitive advantage. Brand loyalty will only be maintained, however, if the standards of that brand are delivered to the customer on a worldwide basis.

A limitation to hotel expansion in developing countries is the infrastructure designed to service it. Capacity in terms of the transport industry – that is, airlines and airports – affects the hospitality industry.

## Routes to global expansion

Many hospitality firms are taking a number of popular routes towards a global strategy. In general, this can be described as a *concentrated approach*, in which the firm directs its resources to the profitable growth of a single product in a single market with a single dominant technology. In the purest form of this approach, the firm must continually seek new product improvements, increasing promotional activity and an expansion of the distribution channels along with a price penetration strategy. A number of growth strategies can be identified within the hospitality industry: management contracts, joint ventures, strategic alliances and franchising, which will be discussed in this and following chapters. Other approaches, such as market segmentation and aquisition, have been discussed in earlier chapters of this book.

# MANAGEMENT CONTRACTS

## Definition

A management contract can be defined as a written agreement between the owner and the operator of a hotel or motor inn, by which the owner employs the operator as an agent to assume full responsibility for operating and managing the property. As an agent the operator pays in the name of the owner all operating expenses from the cash flow generated from the property, retains management fees, and remits the remaining cash flow, if any, to the owner. The owner supplies the hotel property, including any land, building, furniture, fixtures, equipment and working capital, and assumes full legal and financial responsibility for the project.

## History and development of management contracts

The first hotel property that was operated under a type of management contract was the 300-room Hilton in San Juan, Puerto Rico. It opened on 9 December 1949, and was run through a profit-sharing lease arrangement, which can be seen as a combination of a lease and a management contract. The Puerto Rican government built, furnished and equipped the hotel, providing all needed capital. The government then leased the hotel to Hilton in return for two-thirds of the gross operating profit. Hilton had only to provide expenses and working capital. A similar arrangement was adapted for Hiltons in Istanbul, Mexico and Cuba. With the Cuban revolution and the loss of the Hilton in Havana it became clear to Hilton that political developments outside the control of hotel management companies could cause the firm to lose a considerable amount of money. They therefore developed future arrangements in what has now become known as a *management contract*.

Under this arrangement, the property owners take the full risk of operating losses and have the ongoing responsibility of supplying working capital. Before the Second World War it was the norm for hotel operators to also own hotel properties. Within developed countries, and in the colonies of the major European powers, the economic and political situation was generally stable and suitable for real estate investments. The economic depression of the 1930s, however, caused a change in the willingness of banks and investors to invest in hotels, as many hotel owners defaulted on their mortgages. As a result, emerging hotel chains like Hilton had to invest their own equity in their developments. Rather than building expensive new hotels, Hilton mostly acquired and rebuilt older hotels, such as Stephens in Chicago or the Plaza in New York.

After the Second World War, world trade started to develop. Hilton International and Inter-Continental competed to provide hotel accommodation of American standard for US travellers abroad. Both hotel chains had close links to the dominating airlines, TWA and Pan-American Airlines, which encouraged them to provide accommodation in foreign locations. Overseas expansion, however, was not very attractive for hotel firms, as political and financial instability made capital investment a risky venture. In addition, the big chains were not able to provide enough capital themselves to cope with the fast growth of the travel market.

Leasing arrangements were difficult to establish, as English law did not apply in most locations, and many leasing arrangements were complicated and a costly process. In addition, overseas owners and developers were reluctant to commit themselves to long-term leases with untested operators. Management contracts as they were applied by Hilton accounted for these difficulties: they provided owner and operator with adequate returns for a suitable duration. However, other US chains did not follow the example of Hilton, and very few management contracts were signed during the 1950s and 1960s. Companies in the US and European markets relied on ownership, leasing and franchising.

In 1970 the ten major US chains had 22 management contracts; by 1975 they numbered 182. The economic recession at the beginning of the 1970s forced many hotels to revert to institutional lenders, and real estate investment trusts were keen to sell properties that had proved to offer little or no appropriate return on investments. US companies either formed their own management divisions, or looked out for hotel management firms that could turn their operations round before they were sold. Apart from their expertise in operating and marketing, big chains could provide the sophisticated reservation networks: a key factor for success. As a result, lenders would only invest in a hotel project if it was managed by a well-known company. During this time a number of US hotel firms diversified into management contracting. Simultaneously, new independent management contracting companies were formed to participate in new developments. By 1975, some 60 independent contractors held more than 500 management contracts.

The expansion continued until the beginning of the 1980s, when the recession forced smaller, less prudent, contractors out of the market. Until then the management contracts of these independent contractors were found almost solely within domestic US markets.

Outside the USA the development of management contracts during the 1950s and 1960s was a slow process, with European companies operating only a few of them. European contracts had more of an ad hoc nature, rather than being a systematic policy of diversification and expansion. Hallway Hotels Overseas, established in 1966, was the first big British company to develop and manage a number of hotels under management contracts in African countries. In 1969 the hotel development incentive scheme launched by the UK government supported investments in hotel projects by giving financial incentives. As a result, an overcapacity of hotel rooms emerged in certain parts of Britain in the early 1970s; at the same time, the economy went into recession. Short-term management contracts with experienced hotel contractors allowed some hotel owners to turn their initially weak investments into profitable ones. After the end of the incentive scheme in 1974, suitable hotel sites at a feasible cost were rare, and the money market was tight. In order to expand, some UK hotel companies turned to management contracts as a fast and profitable method of enlarging.

The worldwide travel market continued to expand during the 1970s, creating a need for hotel developments in many parts of the world. Demand in Africa and the Far East grew steadily, and the oil boom in the Middle East required a substantial amount of new hotel development to cover the fast-growing demand. The economic and political situations in these countries were unstable, and legal restrictions prevented the free movement of capital. The management contract was perceived as a sound way for hotel companies to gain market share within these countries. The need for development also grew as competition between hotel companies got tougher. Apart from Hilton International and Inter-Continental, Sheraton, Hyatt and Marriott have also been competing in the five-star market. Holiday Inn and Ramada have been competing in the four-star market. Forte and Grand Metropolitan both entered the management contract market successfully from the UK together with Meridien, a French company and subsidiary of Air France until 1994.

In the USA the Economic Recovery Tax Act 1981 provided financial incentives for real estate investors in hotels. Many new products were designed for specific market needs, and many new brands were launched on the market. Despite this development, competition for management contract arrangements was getting tougher, as many investing firms had gained valuable experience of the hospitality industry and could use their knowledge to negotiate contracts in their favour. Because of the rising negotiating power of hotel owners, hotel operating firms were forced into arrangements that included a partial equity stake of the operator.

As domestic markets became more and more saturated, hotel corporations increased their activities abroad. Major international hotel chains sought to expand to gateway cities of Europe, the Far East and Australia. In addition, the changes in Eastern Europe, the former Soviet Union and China are likely to open the doors to foreign investors and entrepreneurs. Such countries offer sound possibilities for expanding hospitality firms, and the use of management contracts will generate the appropriate business affiliation.

However, the terms of expansion are becoming more difficult for hospitality firms as international investors are becoming more knowledgeable and tougher negotiators. The market conditions in the 1990s are in their favour. The worldwide recession at the beginning of the 1990s left most of the hotel industry in a poor condition. Most independent chains, as well as many major hotel chains, suffered a lack of capital for necessary expansion plans. Banks and lenders hesitated to invest in hotel projects that were seen as offering a less than attractive return on investment. Investors can now choose their operating partners out of a wide range of reputable names, which are competing for profitable and strategically well placed locations. This forces them to invest part of their capital and share some of the risk involved in decreasing amounts of remuneration.

## The owners

Hotel owners or owning companies have a varied background and, unlike operators, they are involved in various activities. However, they all have one common interest: the securing of adequate returns on their substantial investment. Owners can be categorized into several groups. The first group includes institutional owners, insurance companies, investment trusts, banks and pension funds. They might see hotel financing as a potentially safe and asset-backed investment. Hotels might offer them regular dividends in the form of trading profits, and in addition a soundly located hotel property offers the potential of capital growth, as its value might increase over time. One example of trends in this hotel investment category can be seen in Japan. In 1986 the Japanese Ministry of Trade allowed the country's financial institutions to increase their foreign holdings from 10 per cent to 30 per cent, and as a result Japanese investment in major cities in Europe and the USA increased dramatically. In addition to office buildings, hotels were targeted by these investors.

A second trend in ownership is that real estate investment trusts, during the worldwide economic recession of the 1970s and late 1980s, suddenly found themselves hotel owners and hotel developers as the original hotel owners could not cover the interest on their loans. The owners went into receivership and the former lenders became owners of these distressed and badly managed hotels. The investment trusts either formed their own management divisions or looked for management contractors to generate quick improvements in the properties' performance in order to re-sell them as soon as possible.

A third category of hotel owner comprises construction firms, property developers and landowners. Unlike the first two groups, they have a continuing interest in hotel properties because of their business involvement. Constructors, developers and landowners see hotels as valuable attractions for the projects they get involved in. A hotel property in the right location might be able to attract other businesses, such as offices, or might serve as an additional attraction to a resort. A hotel is therefore seen as part of a developer's package rather than as a pure equity investment.

Another group of owners consists of industry-related companies, including shipping companies, tour operators, travel agencies, theme park owners and airline companies. Alternatively, food companies might be interested in integrating a hotel property into their portfolio. These so-called *vertical integrations* are either backward integrations (a tour operator investing in a hotel, for example) or forward integrations, such as the acquisitions of Holiday Inn by Bass plc, a brewing company. However, these industry-related companies have a tendency to integrate hotels completely, and operate them themselves through acquired companies rather than through management contracts.

Hotel investors can also be found in governments of developing countries: they might seek an international class hotel in their country for reasons of prestige or image. A prestige hotel might help these countries to attract further investments and/or to develop their tourist industry. Although this type of owner is eager to attract major chain operators, the governments of developing countries often have interests that collide with those of the operators. Often these investors seek to develop their own labour market, and put restrictions on the operator's employment plans. To benefit fully from their investment these governments try to force the operator to give priority to local employees rather than allowing the operator to recruit and/or transfer its chain's internal employees.

Finally, wealthy individuals are sometimes hotel owners: they often seek to be associated with the prestige and glamour of an international hotel. In addition, they seek to invest their money relatively safely, without the need to be continuously involved in day-to-day operational decisions, which they willingly leave to an experienced operator. However, the past has shown that their propensity to interfere is high.

Advantages for the owner

The owning companies of hotel properties have been able to benefit from recent market trends, because they now hold more negotiating power. This is partially due to their growing experience with hotel operators and partially to the increase in competition from hotel companies to obtain management contracts. Generally they are able to profit from a hotel operation without the need for involvement in the operational day-to-day business. However, more and more owners are able to negotiate for increasing responsibilities and rights. They are now in a position to approve or disapprove financial forecasts and budgets, and are able to observe and supervise the operation much more closely than before. By choosing a reputable operator, owners benefit from a range of services.

First, the possibility for financing the property is increased by a well-known operator with a strong brand image and a sound reputation. Second, the operator provides them with technical services such as building and design during the development stage, pre-opening services such as staff recruitment, and operational services such as the entire administration during operation. Apart from the management contract fee the owner has to pay for these technical services.

Owners usually carry the main share of capital bound up in the property, and this entitles them to negotiate for rights to terminate the contract in the event of sale or in the event of a shortfall of performance in terms of quality or profitability. Even though they usually negotiate contracts for a considerable period of time, say five to ten years, they obtain major freedom over their property and negotiate considerable flexibility. Because of their equity investments they are also able to profit from potential gains occurring from a value increase in the property.

**Disadvantages for the owner**    The first difficulty that owners face is the selection of an adequate operator. It is hard to assess potential operators because it is unlikely that owners will be able to gain a full insight into the operator's financial and operational status. They will therefore have to rely on the image of the operator's brand, and the impression they get from the operator's representatives and the operator's current business partners. In addition, owners can only estimate the impact that a potential operator might have on a business's profitability. Even though owners require a return on their investment, they have only a little input into operational decisions, and therefore have to rely largely on the capabilities of the operator to run the operation profitably. For a less experienced owner, in particular, it might prove difficult to assess and interpret the operation's financial results. Furthermore, inexperienced owners might have difficulties in interpreting quality standards, and are therefore bound to trust the operator in this regard.

Another disadvantage for owners might arise out of their relationship with the operator. The managers operating the unit might be more loyal to their head office than to their employer. The owner of a property may conflict with a general manager's long-term objectives, one of which, for instance, might be career opportunities within the chain. Therefore key managers might focus on short-term growth for a particular property, which might not be to the best advantage of the business's long-term future: for example, improving sales through discounting. An operator that also runs his own operations might give priority to these units as they tend to be more profitable. These units might benefit from more experienced staff and managing teams as well as a priority status within the hotel chain's reservation system. Again, the owner has to some extent to rely on the operator, as these situations (if they are occurring) would be difficult to prove.

In addition, owners usually carry the major share of equity contribution and the corresponding downside risk. Regardless of the profitability of the operation, owners are obliged to pay the agreed remuneration to the operator, at least for a certain amount of time, after which they might be able to terminate the contract. A financially strong operator that makes an equity contribution into the venture is even more difficult to remove, particularly if the owner decides to sell the property. As the main investor in the property, the owner also carries the depreciation cost of the operation. As long as the property's capital value increases and this is not offset by the cost of refurbishments, the owner's investment will remain sound. If these two elements get out of equilibrium the owner could be continuously losing money. In fact this expenditure on the property might be to the benefit of the operator's image rather than to the benefit of the operation's profitability.

## The operators

Advantages for the operator

The advantages for a corporation that chooses to grow by operating management contracts are twofold: first the advantages that result from a growth strategy, and second those that result directly from the management contract affiliation. An expanding corporation is able to increase its revenues, profits and relative market share, as well as its market power. The resulting financial strength can be used to finance technical changes such as reservations networks and management information systems. As major chains within the industry develop these systems, they secure and strengthen a hotel company's future.

Operational benefits for corporate operations are also possible: cost savings such as bulk purchasing for a hotel group can offer significant advantages. Apart from potentially lower prices, products could be supplied according to the purchaser's specification standards. In addition, better credit conditions might be a result of a stronger purchasing power, which benefits the operational cash flow.

In corporate organizations, there are advantages in the field of human resources. Better career and job prospects within a bigger hotel chain might attract more and possibly better educated candidates. Job rotations within the organization can help to increase job satisfaction and reduce the job turnover rate: therefore less money might be spent on the costly process of employee selection and training.

Another advantage for a corporate firm is the reduced cost of marketing. A corporate firm consisting of many single business units can organize marketing centrally, and so the expenses for cost-intensive surveys and research work can be split between the units. Sales campaigns and costs for national or worldwide advertising campaigns, as well as the operating costs for a computerized distribution network, can also be shared among a wide number of business units. Because of the increased size of the organization and its market presence, a strong brand image offering the potential for brand loyalty is built up more easily.

Following a strategy of management contracting enables the corporation to benefit from all the above advantages; in addition management contracts enable the operators to expand without large capital involvement. By contributing only a small amount into the operation, operators under a management contract carry a small risk compared with that of owner-operated properties. The management contract offers them the possibility of achieving higher returns with considerably little input, as most or all of the risk is carried by the owner. By contributing only a little or even none of the capital within the property, operators are free to invest their money in alternative markets, which might offer higher or more stable returns. They therefore do not carry any substantial costs attached to real estate investments, such as depreciation.

The reduced financial risk also enables hotel corporations to expand into markets that are economically or politically unstable or little known, especially in markets that are little known by the operator. A relationship with a local property owner can offer a range of advantages. It can give guidance to the expatriate operator in understanding local laws, religious customs and ethics. Particularly in countries like Saudi Arabia, a local partner can speed up bureaucracy thanks to the essential personal contacts. The ease of growth is enhanced and supported by a wider market coverage.

The possibility of penetrating new markets can show the firm's flag on a wide number of properties, thus increasing potential brand recognition and loyalty. The power of product quality and consistency for a major hotel brand is potentially secured. Unlike other business affiliations, contractors are at the forefront in trying to represent and influence their firm's image and quality. Major chains can rely on a well-trained workforce supported by formally tested managers who have served the company for a considerable amount of time. It is the day-to-day control offered through a management contract affiliation that is an essential factor in preserving first-class hotelkeeping.

**Disadvantages for the operator**
Within today's competitive market, operators have lost a number of privileges that they had before; market conditions now favour the owner.

In order to strengthen their position and get an owner to sign a contract, operators need to contribute capital and a powerful brand name. This is a limitation for independent and financially weak organizations, as they cannot provide the needed capital and/or strong brand image that enhances the negotiating position. They might not be able to get certain contracts; or the negotiated conditions might be to the advantage of the owner or developer of the property. In these cases, owners usually have a much stronger impact on operational decisions, which can hinder operators in achieving their managerial objectives.

The biggest weakness for the operator is the absence of a substantial capital involvement, which beside the limitations of operational freedom also carries the lack of potential gains through real estate investments. The increased competition for profitable sites or properties also has an impact on big and financially strong operators. They have to bid ever lower for contracts in order to be able to increase their chain's size and obtain the rights of a profitable project. The operator is always dependent on the owner's or developer's capital and opinions of a hotel. Should there be doubts about a new building development in a new market, the operator cannot expand, even if the market looks promising. An operator that takes over an existing property could sometimes be forced to make compromises regarding the property's building standards, as any changes have to be discussed and agreed with the owner of the building, who would finance such changes.

The operator's remuneration is limited to the management fee received from the owner, and is therefore dependent on the financial well-being of this party. The operator is bound to perform well in order to obtain the incentive fee. Should a shortfall of performance occur over a specified period, the owner can terminate the contract, and most of the effort for the development of the hotel operation and its image would be lost. Owners today are also able to terminate a contract should the quality of the operation diverge from an agreed and detailed quality assurance programme.

The owner has in many instances the right to approve or disapprove the capital expenditure budget of the operator.

## The contractual and financial terms of a management contract

The management contract is the basis for the relationship between the two separate legal identities, operator and owner. It is a lengthy and comprehensive statement, which regulates the rights of both parties. It specifies the timing and size of financial awards and reimbursement of the operator's expenses, the initial length of the contract and renewal clauses, the loan and equity contributions of both parties, and the performance criteria for the operator. The major areas of agreement covered in the management contract will now be explained, with details of the obligations and rights of each party.

Loan and equity contributions

The stronger negotiating position of owners increases competition among operators for hotel properties. It is therefore becoming more common within the industry that operators are obliged to invest some of their own capital in order to obtain a contract for an operation. Contributions can be made in the form of loans or equity. **Loans** are usually made at the beginning of a contract as a reserve, used only under certain circumstances. They are interest bearing. In 1992, provision of loans was found in 42 per cent of all management contracts made with operators in the USA.

Because of the increasing competition among operators, and a tight money market, more and more owners are also seeking to ensure the long-term interests of the operator through the provision of **equity** by the latter.

Through an equity contribution the operator is in a stronger position, benefiting from an increased influence on the property itself. In addition it becomes more difficult for the owner to terminate the contract. However, equity contributions are only made by well-capitalized operators: most independent operators are financially unable to make any contribution. Equity contributions by chain operators were found in 34 per cent of all US contracts in 1992 and in 19 per cent of all contracts with independent operators.

**Initial terms and renewal periods**

For the initial duration of the contract, the two parties follow different objectives. The owner's view is that a short-term contract may increase the operator's need to perform well. In addition they gain more flexibility by opting for a short-term contract. Operators, conversely, try to obtain long-term contracts: they argue that it takes considerable time to offset their initial investment and effort. They also like to ensure their quality objectives for a long time period, so as not to confuse customers with changing property management. The agreed initial contract period depends on the operator's capital strength. Chain operators that contribute equity are able to negotiate longer initial terms and more frequent renewal periods. Independent operators are usually not in a position to contribute any equity: therefore their initial and renewal periods tend to be shorter and renewals less frequent.

Caretaker operators, usually for owners in foreclosure, never contribute any equity to the operation. They are usually managing hotels for a short period of time to increase the sales value of the operation. The main aim of an owner who hires such an operator is to sell the business in the short term. The profit should be generated through the sale of the operation rather than through the potentially time-consuming process of operating the business.

Generally, as owners are gaining bargaining power, a shorter initial contract period is becoming more common within the industry. The renewal periods due to the increase in power of the owner are usually tied on an agreed performance level. Unless this performance level is met by the operator, the contract might not be renewed.

**Fee structures and operator-reimbursable expenses**

The contractor usually receives remuneration in the form of a **management fee** and a reimbursement of managerial and operational services offered to the owner by the operator's corporation. The operator collects all revenue from the hotel and auxiliary operations and pays all occurring operational expenses. The remaining profit, if any, is given to the owner. The owner agrees to pay the operator at agreed intervals a certain amount for providing services: the management fee. This usually consists of two payments: a fixed and an incentive fee. The **fixed fee** is about 2–3 per cent of gross revenue for chain operators and 1.5–2.5 per cent for independent operators. It tends to be smaller for larger properties and slightly larger for smaller properties. On top of the fixed fee, an **incentive fee** is paid as a percentage of gross operating profits. Recently however, it has become more common to pay the incentive out of the cash flow after debt service or a negotiated net profit line, to stimulate the performance of the operator.

The actual percentages and conditions negotiated depend on a wide range of factors. The fee structure is affected by the sales mix of the hotel, its current pricing policies, the hotel's cost structure (especially the level of debt service to be covered), and the general stability and growth pattern of the operation. In addition, the size and type of hotel, its complexity and its location affect the fee structure. These factors are determined by the property itself. In addition, the size of the remuneration is determined by the relative negotiating strength of the two parties, which depends on the capital contributed by each party, the parties' status, potential future business interests, and the prestige value of the contract. Because of the increasing competition for management contracts by operators and the rising negotiation power of the owners, the remuneration for the operator has decreased significantly over the last few years: operators have had to bid ever lower to obtain additional contracts. As well as the management fee, the operator usually receives a **reimbursement for services** offered by the head office of the chain. These services are usually only offered in a comprehensive way by big chains, and mostly include the following:

- **Technical services:** these might include development services during project development, such as architecture, building and design, plant and equipment specification, installation and the management of the project during that period.
- **Pre-opening services:** these set up the policies and systems that are necessary for the operation. The negotiation of concessions and supplier contracts and staff training are part of the services, as well as marketing activities prior to opening.
- **Centralized services:** these occur both prior to operating and during operation. The key elements are corporate marketing and sales activities, as well as the provision of a central reservations system. Other charges could be made by the operator for accounting services and management information systems as well as training staff and central purchasing.

In some cases these services are charged as they occur, such as costs for the reservations network, or on a per-room basis or a fixed percentage, such as marketing and sales services; in other cases the whole service is sold as a package. The amount of reimbursement is usually linked to the extent to which these services are offered. The amount charged is also dependent on the size of the management fee that the operator receives.

Both costs – management fee and operator expenses – are usually negotiated and related to the total charge that occurs for the owner. The total amount charged therefore depends on the strength and negotiating positions of both parties. In general these charges constitute a substantial amount for the owner, who will therefore try to reduce them by firm negotiations, and by trying to maximize returns by raising the potential revenue basis. In general, hotels operated under management contracts tend to be medium- to large-scale and sometimes prestigious units, although the portfolio of one operating company might consist of a mixture of very small units (30 rooms, for example) and larger units (up to 1,300 rooms).

## Operator performance provision and operating standards

There has been great increase in contracts that contain an operator performance provision. This is due to the stronger negotiating position of owners, who were, for example, able to negotiate and operate a performance provision in 37 per cent of all US management contracts with chain operators in 1992. For these provisions, a basic 3–5 year projection of gross operating profit is usually taken as a basis. However, the operator is usually able to negotiate certain clauses connected to this provision. A so-called **start-up exclusion period** is usually negotiated: this frees the operator from achieving a particular performance level at the beginning of the operation (between six months and two years). A **shortfall allowance** of 3–8 per cent on the projected period as well as a shortfall timeframe (commonly 2–3 consecutive years) is usually negotiated by the operator. Sometimes operators negotiate the ability to pay the difference out of their own pocket in order to keep the contract for the hotel operation. In the event of a shortfall a third party is usually consulted to determine whether the shortfall occurred in circumstances that are common to the whole of the industry or only apply to a particular operator. Finally, a **contract renewal hurdle** is sometimes agreed on: the operator is assessed against a predetermined performance level over the whole initial contract period. If he fails to achieve the projected results, he may not be able to renew his contract.

Owner input in operational decisions

Operators usually preserve their right of sovereignty over the operational management of the hotel property. At the end of the 1980s, however, operational results of hotel operations decreased significantly. As a result, most owners have become more cautious about the managerial process, and are trying to play a more active role in managing their hotels. Owners now try to negotiate a formal input into operational decisions that were formerly left to the operator.

First, operating policies, especially in the area of operating standards, were for a long time a nebulous area. It was up to the operator to interpret what was defined as an internationally accepted standard. Today a detailed document is produced to define these operating standards, together with a separate quality assurance programme. In general the operator still determines the operating standards; however, the owner has an input in developing and monitoring the corresponding operating policies. Any shortcomings of the operator are then reported by the owner to the head office of the operator.

Second, the owner demands the right of input into budgetary decisions. In the US in 1992, 85 per cent of all management contracts contained a clause whereby the owner had right of approval of financial budgets. Some operators argue that the owner's impact on capital expenditure may delay necessary replacement of furniture and fittings, and might negatively influence a product's quality. However, it can be argued that it is in both parties' interests to maintain a continuous product quality.

Alongside the input of owners' views on budgetary control, the thoroughness of financial and operating reporting increased. Owners as well as lenders became more cautious regarding their investment and demanded more insight into the financial and operational side of their property. The owner as well as the contractor usually negotiates to schedule regular meetings to discuss short- and long-term objectives on both sides, and to come to a better and more harmonious relationship.

Owners are also seeking more influence in personnel decisions, particularly the selection process for key staff members, such as departmental managers, including the general manager of the operation. Usually they can negotiate the right to influence this selection process, but operators insist on the right to make the final decision about key staff, including the general manager; and they still insist on the right to transfer any managerial personnel from the owner's property to another unit under their management.

Finally, owners are trying to negotiate a non-competition covenant, which would prevent the operator from placing any competitive operation within a specified geographical area around their property. However, chain operators in particular want to preserve their operational flexibility. Usually they are able to place another hotel product within the area as long as it is not in the same market and is therefore not a direct competitor.

## Contract termination

In general, any contract can be terminated while it is in force when one of the parties involved does not follow one or more elements of the contract, as long as these are seen as essential parts of the agreement. Operators are usually keen to hold their contracts as long as the hotel product is in line with the chain's business portfolio. Therefore this section focuses on the possibilities for the owner to terminate the agreement. Three cases can be identified.

First, **termination without cause** is found in every contract between operators and owners in foreclosure. Within the USA in 1992, the owner's right to terminate without cause was found in 22 per cent of all contracts held with chain operators and in 31 per cent of all contracts held with independent operators. As we have already seen, the independent operator is in a weaker position: owners have more bargaining power and can therefore insist on arrangements that provide them with more flexibility. Owners in foreclosure are generally focused on a quick sale of the property; in order to do so they need to be able to terminate the management agreement of their property at short notice. The owner must give advance notice of contract termination, depending on the operator's status (independent or chain operator); the usual notice period is between 30 and 180 days. The owner is also obliged to pay the operator an agreed termination fee for ending the contract before the agreed settlement date.

Second, **termination in event of sale** is becoming increasingly common in management contracts. Hotel sellers and buyers want to be able to terminate the contract in the event of sale to gain more flexibility in deciding about the operation's future. Chain operators are usually able to negotiate the right of first refusal or the right of first offer. These rights enable them to buy the property themselves with the right of priority. Independent operators are in a considerably weaker position without priority rights. If the contract is terminated on sale, the operator receives a termination fee from the owner.

The third case is **termination in the event of foreclosure**. In this case the original owners are not able to cover their debt arrangements with their lenders. The lenders obtain the right or the ownership of the property. Historically, management contracts survived foreclosure due to bad experiences in the past when lenders all of a sudden became owners of hotel properties. Lenders became more cautious regarding their rights on the property in the case of foreclosure. They now insist on a clause in the contract that gives them the freedom to terminate the contract and resell the property to any other party should this event occur.

## Developments in contracting

Operators or contractors can broadly be divided into two main groups: independent and major chain contractors. **Independent operators** focus mainly or exclusively on management contracts: they usually do not own any properties and are commonly smaller in terms of turnover and operating smaller properties. Many independent contracting firms originated during the 1980s, mainly in the USA, where until recently 500 such firms existed. Often set up to operate franchised hotels on a regional basis, many of these independent operators had to merge or were forced out of the market as big US and European chains went overseas to expand and compete internationally. Independent chains are generally financially weaker than major hotel chains. They are less often able to contribute loan or equity to any hotel project. In addition they do not have their own national or international brand and do not have their own reservations systems. As a result they are in a weaker negotiating position. This is reflected in shorter initial and renewal terms, termination conditions for the owners and smaller remuneration fees for their services.

The second main group of operators are **major hotel chains**. They tend to own and operate hotels under their own brand name. Their involvement is usually on a long-term basis and part of a strategic concept. Thanks to their capital, marketing and negotiating strengths, they usually benefit from better contract conditions (higher remuneration for more extensive services, longer contract terms, and better termination conditions) than their independent competitors. Hotels operated under major chains tend to be larger than those managed by independent chains.

However, owing to recent mergers in the industry the distinction between major hotel chains and independent operators is becoming blurred. In general, all operators are eager to find viable hotels that fit their portfolio in terms of location, market sector, chain image and branding. Both types of operator have to convince the property owner of their particular benefits: for example, the cheaper management fees of the independent operators versus the higher fees for more advanced services and a branded image of the major chain operators.

The issues surrounding a management contract are many and varied, and these are explored in the following case study of a Holiday Inn project in Egypt.

## CASE STUDY: MANAGEMENT CONTRACT WITHOUT INVESTMENT OR GUARANTEE IN ALEXANDRIA, EGYPT

### Background and description

Sheikh Abdul Majeed Abu Jadayel acquired a shell property on the sea front in Alexandria, Egypt, and his intention is to fit out the building as a Holiday Inn core brand hotel with approximately 160 bedrooms. The hotel would have full facilities, including rooftop pool and banqueting rooms.

While the cost of the property to the owner is unknown, the cost of completing the shell to Holiday Inn standards is estimated at E£30 million ($9.1 million). The anticipated timescale for completion is 21 months, with opening planned in the autumn of 1994.

Holiday Inn has negotiated a standard 20-year management contract with Sheik Abdul Majeed Abu Jadayel; the anticipated fees of E£6.8 million ($2.1 million) would be payable without any investment or guarantee required by the Sheikh.

Strategic value

Egypt is a prime Middle Eastern country in which Holiday Inn has (in 1994) no distribution at present. This proposal offers an excellent opportunity to regain distribution in Egypt without affecting key negotiations currently in progress for two potential management contracts in Cairo itself. The deal requires no investment nor guarantees of any kind and creates potential shareholder value of $2.1 million. Having considered this, Holiday Inn proposes to enter into a 20-year standard management agreement with Sheikh Abdul Majeed Abu Jadayel to operate the hotel without any investment or guarantee of any kind.

Strategic fit: impact on strategic goals

The HIW strategic plan includes the addition of 22 new management contracts by the end of 1997–98 in the Middle East region. The plan identifies Egypt as a prime country for development, with Cairo the priority target city and Alexandria heading the four secondary cities in which Holiday Inn ideally wishes to be represented.

Egypt offers enormous profit and growth potential. Holiday Inn needs to regain and expand distribution in Egypt if the brand is to achieve its full worth in the Middle East region. Holiday Inn was last represented in the country through two hotels that left the system back in 1984. The addition of this hotel in Alexandria will allow re-entry and act as a springboard for future development in the country.

Alexandria is a major international city and with a population of 3.4 million is the second largest city in Egypt. The city fronts onto the Mediterranean Sea, 100 miles from Cairo, is a major tourist centre for the Middle East with some 900,000 visitors during the summer, and has a thriving commercial port dealing mainly with Eastern Mediterranean shipping. The company considers the hotel's location in the city to be excellent.

The proposals are for a standard management contract without any investment or commitment to guarantees of any kind, thus supporting the aim to grow the business based on brand strength rather than capital outlay.

Negotiations, during 1994, are at an advanced stage with owners of two sites in Cairo. The achievement of a clean, no investment contract in Alexandria is likely to aid attempts to close these negotiations on terms favourable to Holiday Inn.

The owner is believed to be a long-term property holder with no financial need to achieve exit from the property or management contract other than under the normal terms and conditions of such contracts.

Branding

The appropriate brand for this property is considered to be the Holiday Inn core brand. In comparison with other Middle Eastern properties this building bears closest similarity to the Holiday Inn Abu Dhabi. The hotel has been considered as a Crowne Plaza but it was felt that to flag Alexandria as Crowne Plaza would devalue the Crowne Plazas at Kuwait and Dubai, and also high-quality core brand hotels such as Al Jubail and Jeddah.

## The market

Economic environment

The current market consists of a mix of commercial and tourist business. The Egyptian domestic tourist market is a major source of revenue during the summer months from June to September. It is anticipated that the hotel will cater for the business sector throughout the year, as well as serving the local market for functions, weddings, etc.

**Competitive overview**

The major hotels at present are the Sheraton, Pullman, Palestine and Ramada (Table 7.1).

**Table 7.1 Major competitor hotels**

|  | Total rooms available 1992 | Occupancy (%) 1992 | Average rate (£E) 1992 | Average rate (US$) 1992 |
|---|---|---|---|---|
| Montazah Sheraton | 91,887 | 55.55 | 141.67 | 42.93 |
| Palestine Hotel | 76,128 | 68.40 | 134.95 | 40.89 |
| Ramada Renaissance | 62,586 | 64.08 | 134.71 | 40.82 |

The Ramada is located on a secondary street and not on the sea front. The Sheraton and Palestine hotels are located at the extreme end of the sea front corniche. The Holiday Inn will benefit from its location at the heart of the business/leisure district, and will also enjoy a higher than average room rate due to the room mix, which will consist of 25 per cent suites.

**Supply and demand generators**

Business will be generated predominantly by the Egyptian, Arab and European sectors. During the summer months it is anticipated that considerable business will be generated from Saudi Arabia and the Gulf States. There is no present indication that the situation will change in the near future. It is emphasized that the business mix being predominantly Egyptian/Middle Eastern significantly limits the hotel's exposure to any fall-off in Western-related business resulting from any increase in Islamic fundamentalism in the region.

There are no other Holiday Inn properties that will be adversely affected by this addition to the chain. No alternative options have been considered, for the following reasons:

● The hotel's location is excellent: right on the sea front in the middle of Alexandria, close to the city centre.
● The management agreement terms and projected revenue figures are very favourable.
● The owner has an excellent reputation and is fully committed to the project.
● It is highly improbable that a better location exists anywhere in the city.

## Structure of the management contract

**Description of agreement**

The initial term of the agreement will be for 20 years, with options to renew in favour of Holday Inn for a further five year period. Advice received from the Bass tax and treasury department is that the best legal structure for tax purposes will be to operate the hotel through an Egyptian branch of a Hong Kong based company. There are no financial covenants or liabilities required by Holiday Inn. Subsequent investment required throughout the hotel's operation will be supplied from reserves or, failing adequacy of funds, from the owner direct. At present the property is 100 per cent owned, without debts or incumbents.

**Fee structure**

- **Basic management fee:** 2 per cent of adjusted gross revenue for years 1, 2 and 3, increasing to 3 per cent thereafter.
- **Incentive management fee:** 10 per cent of gross operating profit before deduction of fixed charges. Assessment fees: 2 per cent of gross room revenue
- **Technical service/commitment fee:** $145,000, payable 50 per cent upon signature of agreement and 50 per cent upon hotel opening

**Owner**

Sheikh Abdul Majeed Abu Jadayel is the sole owner of the property. The Sheikh is of Saudi Arabian nationality, and is well known and respected throughout the Middle East. His principal business is catering to airlines, schools and hospitals.

**Risk factors**

There are no particular foreseen economic, political or financial risks associated with this project. There are no restrictions to earnings repatriation. The Middle East region of HIW currently has sufficient resources to handle this project, and no additional organizational costs are anticipated.

## Property review

**Site plan and layout**

Plan proposals have been reviewed for the property, and will require amendment in order to satisfy Holiday Inn standards; the owner has agreed to carry out the necessary alterations as directed by Holiday Inn. This will be a condition of the contract, to ensure that quality and standards are achieved. In addition, the owner will enter in negotiations to obtain a beach club property opposite the hotel and, it is understood, has already acquired adjacent sites at the rear of the hotel to assist in back-of-house servicing. Development of plans will commence upon signature of the agreement with Holiday Inn.

**Quality issues**

In general, building standards and quality in Egypt are poor; however, this was openly discussed with the owner, who agreed to appoint one of the country's leading architects to design and supervise the works to international standards. This design will be developed in coordination with the Holiday Inn architect under the terms of the agreement.

**Property condition**

At present the property consists of an unfinished concrete shell, with basement, ground floor and seventeen floors. When complete, the property will consist of approximately 160 guest rooms and suites (all with a sea view), rooftop fitness area and pool, meeting room, banquet room, coffee shop, restaurant and limited car parking.

The owner is negotiating with the local government body to lease a large beach club with private beach opposite the hotel. If successful, the owner intends to connect the hotel by a pedestrian bridge over the existing road that separates the two properties, thereby providing a valuable addition to the property.

## Hotel operations overview

The key aspects of the projected operating performance of the hotel, with 160 bedrooms, are shown in Table 7.2. These figures are based on projections by the Holiday Inn Middle East management team, supplemented by the projection given in a local study commissioned by the owners.

**Table 7.2 Key projected operating results for the property**

|  | 1994–95 | 1995–96 | 1996–97 | 1997–98 |
|---|---|---|---|---|
| Occupancy (%) | 64.5 | 65.0 | 67.0 | 67.0 |
| ARR ($) | 54.12 | 60.34 | 67.04 | 74.26 |
| ARR in real terms | 49.09 | 52.12 | 55.15 | 58.18 |

**Operational assumptions**

Alexandria has an international airport; it is well connected by road and rail to Cairo; and it is the first major port in Egypt. The region is a large manufacturing centre and year-round tourist destination, being a historical city with many cultural attractions, as well as museums, old souks etc. During the summer season the population increases by an additional 900,000. A number of administrative (local) authorities relocate from Cairo to Alexandria during the summer.

In addition to Egypt Air, Olympic Airways, Lufthansa and Cyprus Airways have direct flights to Alexandria.

**Cash flow analysis**

The net present value of management fees assumes inflation at 5 per cent and a discount rate of 15.1 per cent. The net present value can be summarized as:

- initial 10 year contract: NPV 10 year fees $1.4 million (£E4,597);
- for 20 year contract: NPV 20 year fees $2.1 million (£E6,826).

Sensitivity to occupancy and rate is noted in Table 7.3.

**Table 7.3 Sensitivity to occupancy and rate**

|  | NPV ten years ($m) | NPV 20 years ($m) | GOP average margin (%) |
|---|---|---|---|
| Paper as submitted | 1.4 | 2.1 | 38 |
| Occupancy falls 5% throughout | 1.3 | 1.9 | 36.6 |
| ARR lower $8 throughout | 1.1 | 1.7 | 33.5 |

Neither the gross operating profit margin nor the company's shareholder value appear to be at significant risk based on these sensitivities.

# STRATEGIC ALLIANCES AND JOINT VENTURES

## Strategic alliances

Having considered the management contract as a development strategy, two other forms will now be discussed: strategic alliances and joint ventures. Franchising will be discussed in Chapter 8 and consortia in Chapter 9.

**Strategic alliances** give hotel chains the chance to expand rapidly by joining forces with another hotel chain. This particular strategy takes many forms, from joint marketing to a common reservations system. By using a common name, or one of the partners' existing names, it is possible to double a hospitality firm's portfolio overnight. Through carefully selecting a partner with similar properties, standards and expectations, the use of strategic alliances is an effective means of global expansion. While the focus of discussion here is on major hospitality firms, strategic alliances can also encompass independent hotels and consortia: an issue that will be considered later on in this book.

Although direct revenue does not increase, because the hotel chain still owns the original number of hotels that existed before the partnership, there are advantages that make strategic alliances a real alternative to franchising and management contracts. Economies of scale in terms of marketing are an obvious advantage, but the largest gain is that of frequent business travellers, who now use the portfolio as it is larger and represented in more locations. By gaining this segment of demand, the chain's turnover can increase dramatically, and while economies of scale reduce bottom-line costs, the operational profitability increases. Equally, if this strategy for growth is adopted, the firm can take advantage of international brand recognition and reduce the problems of management expertise when expanding in a multicultural environment.

Four Seasons embarked upon achieving global presence through strategic alliances. After opening in Tokyo in 1992, Four Seasons signed a strategic alliance deal with the ten units of Regent International Hotels Ltd, one of Asia's highest-regarded operators of luxury hotels. Under the agreement Four Seasons owns 20 per cent of the venture, which will comprise eleven hotels, six contributed by Four Seasons and five by EIE International Corporation, Regent's parent company. Four Seasons assumes management of Regent Properties in gateway cities such as Bangkok, Hong Kong, Kuala Lumpur, Melbourne and Sydney. This alliance instantly propelled Four Seasons into a coveted market. If the company had not gone down this route it would have taken ten years to achieve the same presence. The issue of strategic alliances will now be illustrated with a case study of the Radisson Edwardian Hotel Company.

## CASE STUDY: RADISSON EDWARDIAN HOTELS

Radisson International, one of the world's top ten hotel companies and part of the $9.9 billion portfolio of US-based Carlson Companies Inc., during 1993 expanded into the UK. Its focus for its hotel company is on international expansion, and the tie-up with UK-based Edwardian Hotels gives it strategic strength in London, Europe's major capital city. The central aim in all this is that, through establishing a new corporate identity (Radisson Edwardian Hotels) and joint marketing efforts, the global market penetration of both companies will be greatly strengthened.

The Edwardian company comprises nine four-star and five-star hotels, and the 1993 strategic alliance extends a joint marketing initiative announced in 1991. The 1993 agreement comprises four elements:

- the renaming of Edwardian to Radisson Edwardian Hotels and the marketing of a joint corporate identity;
- development, in partnership, of management contracts in the UK and Ireland;
- installation of the computerized reservation system Pierre 2000 in the Edwardian central reservation office;
- joint funding of personnel and offices in parts of the world targeted as major sources of business, including the Far East and Eastern Europe.

Neither company has an equity interest in the other, although the joint investment in the project from 1992 to 1994 was $2 million. The benefit for Radisson in this approach is that it gains a strategic presence in the UK with a company that will now grow more quickly and positively. Edwardian gains a strong partner of international dimensions. Central to this alliance is the computerized reservation system Pierre 2000.

A major proportion of hotel bookings these days come through travel agents. By setting up easy booking and commission procedures through the Pierre system, both parties can achieve an increased share of the market. The Pierre system interfaces with over 50 different airline systems to create a global distribution network that reaches over 125 countries worldwide. The system was developed to give travel agents more access to the hotel company's rooms inventory, along with information on packages and special promotions. Prior to the introduction of the Pierre system most other computerized reservation systems used a system of codes to describe rooms inventory. Radisson's approach is to introduce a description of the rooms inventory available. In addition to the provision of information, Pierre allows for loyalty bonuses to be paid for bookings made, along with a fast centralized payment of commission.

Radisson Edwardian has invested heavily in the latest bookings technology. All this investment allows the company to both communicate and work with airline carriers and travel agents, to the profitable advantage of all parties.

This case study example has shown that the ability of a company to attract a partner for a strategic alliance can greatly determine whether global expansion occurs, the rate of expansion and the success of any expansion.

## Joint ventures

Another approach to growth is the joint venture strategy. This is usually adopted by a large real estate developer or holder and a hospitality firm. The institutional investor in this equation is principally interested in longer-term capital appreciation, which entails a high level of risk. This trend can be seen in the German hotel industry.

The willingness in recent years of operators in Germany to agree to give all or a considerable part of the hotel owner's income in the form of a fixed rent has greatly contributed to hotels' becoming an accepted form of property investment. Since German reunification in the late 1980s, real estate firms have become more involved in the hotel market in Germany, in comparison with most other European countries. This has led to more funds being available for hotel investment and consequently to greater development activity. The best-known hotel investor in Germany is the Klingbeil group, with its purchase of the InterHotel GDR.

The former InterHotel GDR (now known as InterHotel AG) was sold by the Treuhand (a government organization) mostly to the Klingbeil Group, i.e. 28 out of 33 hotels, in November 1991. With around 10,000 rooms and a revenue of over DM 700 million the InterHotel AG is the largest hotel operation in Germany. The five remaining hotels have been sold separately, including the Grand Hotel Berlin and the Bellevue Hotel Dresden. These were the flagships, recently built or renovated, and could not be compared with the lower standards of the other InterHotels.

The Klingbeil Group, founded in 1968, consists of five main companies, and as at 1992 had raised DM 692 million mainly from private investors in order to finance over 120 project companies. The Group, which is mainly in the private property sector, started to build hotels only recently: at the beginning of the 1980s. These have been built primarily in cooperation with international partners: for example, the Sheraton Hotel Frankfurt, the Inter-Continental Hotel Berlin and the Steigenberger Hotel Hamburg.

The Klingbeil Group bought InterHotel GDR at the end of 1991 for DM 2.1 billion and divided it into a property company and a management company. The property company is in control of the possessions, and therefore has the ability to gain loans. The management company leases the hotels.

It could be argued that the sale of the main parts of the InterHotels group to the Klingbeil Group has not been beneficial to the development of the hotel industry, as it immediately led to a more or less monopolistic situation. Thus future investors had to negotiate merely with one counterpart, resulting often in overpriced premises or leasing contracts. The German-based Maritim hotels now run the Grand Hotel in East Berlin, which had been refurbished prior to reunification, and pay a high price for the lease. The Ritz-Carlton group announced interest in the property, but refused the agreement because of the high lease rate.

This particular growth strategy will now be illustrated with an analysis of the Forte–Agip joint venture in Italy.

## CASE STUDY: THE FORTE–AGIP JOINT VENTURE

After the Second World War, Italy embarked on a complete reconstruction programme. The creation of the state-owned group ENI (Ente Nazionale Idrocarburi) was one of the pillars of the country's energy policy. At the begining of the 1950s Enrico Mattei, president of the group, assigned Agip (ENI's subsidiary petrol company) the task of setting up a network of petrol stations along the main roads, with some support facilities. Towards the end of the 1950s catering facilities were introduced. The building of the first MotelAgip in Rome in 1959 stands as a turning point: away from the idea of service stations provided with a few rooms and some support services towards that of proper hotels provided with petrol stations. The 1960s saw more of these hotels built. At the end of 1961 the first motorway hotel was opened in Milan, San Donato. With 275 rooms, the motel gained a leading position in the Agip chain. Its success led to a second hotel being opened in Florence in 1962. Enrico Mattei understood that in order to create a suitable hotel structure, development projects in the future as well as the management of the new motels should be assigned to experts from the hospitality industry. For this purpose a new subsidiary company of Agip was created in 1960 under the name of Semi.

On the eve of the joint venture with Forte in 1992, most Agip motels had been renovated, equipped with the full range of specifications necessary for them to be rated as three- or four-star hotels. The change of their name in the early 1990s from MotelAgip to AgipHotel was further evidence of the chain's shift towards a new and more sophisticated hospitality concept.

Agip's agreement with Forte was ratified on 9 December 1992. According to the terms of the joint venture Forte has taken over the management of eighteen out of the forty Agip Hotels in Italy, while Agip has assumed strategic responsibility with respect to future development plans. To enter into the agreement Forte paid L17 billion (approximately £7.7 million). In addition, the agreement provides for the aquisition by the National Westminster Bank group of the real estate of fifteen out of the eighteen Agip hotels. The remaining three hotels are still owned by ENI: the San Donato Milanese hotel in Milan, owned by Snam (another company of the ENI group), and the Turin and Florence hotels.

The joint venture brought into existence a new company, Agip Forte International (AFI). Exactly 50 per cent of its capital is controlled by Forte, 40 per cent by Agip and 10 per cent by Snam. The new company has a 25-year contract for the lease of the eighteen hotels.

Forte's choice of the joint venture as a vehicle for the company's penetration into the Italian market was partly dictated by circumstances. It is true that the joint venture was Agip's only offer in line with the Italian government's policy of partial privatization. It is also true that where Forte had the opportunity to aquire, as in the case of Sogerba in France, it did not hesitate. However, the joint venture allowed Forte to grow at a time of recession without requiring the outlay of high levels of capital investment. Of the eighteen hotels included in the joint venture, seventeen are three-star hotels. They are managed under the brand Forte Agip and modelled according to the specifications of the UK Forte Posthouse brand. The Milan San Donato hotel operates under the more prestigious ForteCrest Agip brand, equivalent to the UK Forte Crest brand. The Agip name was kept because of its importance and high recognition in the Italian travel market. As a result of the joint venture all eighteen hotels will benefit from their inclusion in the Forte reservation system and its international network.

The longer-term trend in the European hotel market is towards the US and Asian situation, where the asset and its management are frequently separated. While many hotels in Europe began as private concerns, and most still directly manage the asset, matters have been changing, as illustrated by the trends in Germany. An increasing number of firms are using a variety of investment vehicles to delete their direct ownership of the hotel asset.

**SUMMARY**     This chapter has shown that with the globalization and expansion of the hospitality industry, stimulated by improvements to air travel, many of the original family-established hotel firms have sought to manage properties on behalf of other owners through the vehicle of management contracts. Such management contract structures are most in evidence where recent hotel development has taken place. While the ownership pattern and structure of the European hospitality industry is changing, in reflection of the major chains' desire for growth, historically most hotels are still owner managed. Direct hotel investment continues to be a specialist investment medium, undertaken by some hotel operating firms, favoured by wealthy individuals and only to a limited extent considered by institutional investors.

Other forms of developmental growth strategies were also identified in this chapter, such as joint ventures and strategic alliances. It was shown that if a hospitality firm chooses to take a global view and adopt any of these strategies, the strategic management process in those firms would have to consider a range of environmental factors and organizational issues.

**FURTHER READING** Bandella, V 1987 *Comparative analysis of hotel management contracts in Nigeria*, MSc dissertation, University of Surrey

Eyster, J 1993 The revolution in domestic hotel management contracts, *Cornell HRA Quarterly*, February, 16–26

Eyster, J 1988 Management contracts, *Cornell HRA Quarterly*, May, 42–55

Eyster, J 1988 Terms and termination, *Cornell HRA Quarterly*, August, 81–90

Eyster, J 1980 How to negotiate a contract, Part I and II, *Cornell HRA Quarterly*, February, 75–82; May, 49–60

Go, F and J Christiansen 1989 Going global, *Cornell HRA Quarterly*, November, 73–9

Kildokum, H 1990 *An analysis of hotel management contracts in Turkey*, MSc dissertation, University of Surrey

McClellam, R 1989 *The advance of the management contract*, MSc dissertation, University of Surrey

Olsen, M 1993 International growth strategies of major US hotel companies, *Travel and Tourism Analyst*, (3) 51–64

Slattery, P and S Johnson 1993 Hotel chains in Europe, *Travel and Tourism Analyst*, (1) 65–80

Stoner, C 1988 Own or manage? European Asia US chains disagree, *Hotels and Restaurant International*, January, 24–30

Warnick, R 1987 Management companies: a new perspective, *Lodging*, February, 36–54

# CHAPTER 8

# Growth strategies: franchising

**OBJECTIVES**    After reading this chapter you shoul be able to:

- Discuss the history, development, nature and types of franchising within the hospitality industry.
- Identify the competitive methods used to promote franchising in the USA, Europe and the UK.
- Identify the problems and opportunities of franchising and set them within the context of the firm's corporate growth strategy.

## BACKGROUND

With tourism in Europe expected to grow rapidly over the next ten years, there is an increasing need to raise customer awareness of the hotel brand through increased presence and marketing activity. Recent surveys of the European hospitality industry show that the top ten chains operating in Europe provide as much capacity as the next 40 chains combined. This means that the pressure for increased size in order to gain marketing economies, both from unaffiliated hotels and from chains, has never been greater.

Over the past twenty years, franchising has increased enormously within the hospitality industry, spreading the market and giving a new vision of business. In the USA it has been continuously growing, and in Europe it is also starting to be important, particularly within fast-food restaurants such as Pizza Hut, Pizza Express, McDonald's and Burger King. It is in these kinds of restaurant that franchising started to be applicable; since then this type of business has been expanded towards other areas of the hospitality industry, such as hotels.

### Franchising: a corporate growth strategy

Franchising can be considered within the wider context of a corporate growth strategy: specifically as a way to expand the market easily, and as a way to reach the market quickly. This approach reduces risks and as a consequence strengthens the product's positioning as well as the brand name: both so important to increased sales.

Franchising has many implications within corporate strategy: finance, the franchisor and franchisee relationship, marketing strategies, consumers, branding etc. All these points will be expanded in this chapter.

Global expansion of hotels through franchising is very popular, especially with established franchisors in the USA. However, any firm wishing to expand globally through franchising should be aware that the system has many disadvantages as well as advantages. Expansion into a dispersed global market will be challenging, and the costs of a poor strategy could quickly outweigh the benefits of success. Thus it is essential to understand franchising fully before deciding whether to expand globally through this method.

Franchising is one means of providing the capital needed for global expansion of hotel chains when the domestic economy is in recession and loan capital is scarce. It can be regarded as the primary engine for driving business growth for firms that do not have, or cannot obtain, the large amounts of capital needed to acquire assets in the context of an aggressive growth strategy. The high risk associated with expansion by aquisition in recession is the central reason why franchising has become so popular in the USA, where franchising as a whole grew by 114 per cent during the 1980s. This is simply because it diversifies risk away from the franchisor and onto the franchisee. Growth within the hospitality industry of the 1990s appears to be based mostly on two approaches: franchising and management contracts. The second category was considered in in Chapter 8. The elements of franchising will now be identified.

## Introduction to the term 'franchising'

The franchising system of distribution is a significant part of the US economy, creating annually more and more new business, new entrepreneurs, and new services as well as new export opportunities.

Franchising literally means *making free*. In its basic form, it is a method of doing business in which the parent company (the **franchisor**) sells to another party (the **franchisee**) the right to distribute its products or services. Generally there are three types of franchise system:

- product or trade name franchising;
- business format franchising;
- conversion franchising.

In **product or trade name franchising**, a manufacturer grants another party a licence to sell goods produced by the manufacturer.

Under **business format franchising** a well-known product or service owner allows another party to market its products or services using the parent company's name, trade mark and business format, i.e. production and marketing techniques. In return the franchisee pays the franchisor a front-end franchise fee and an ongoing royalty, usually 2–8 per cent of gross sales. In the hotel industry the franchisee pays an average fee of around 5 per cent of the room turnover for the right to brand the hotel. Within the hospitality industry, McDonald's and Holiday Inns are examples of business format franchising.

**Conversion franchising** is defined as an affiliation of formerly independent businesses, creating an economy of scale. This is in order to benefit from the collective power of a brand name and its national or international marketing promotion activities, purchasing and training. Best Western Hotels are an example of conversion franchising, but in Europe they are usually categorized as a consortium. Consortia will be considered in Chapter 9.

The affiliation between a hotel group and individual hotels can be of several types, ranging from ownership to consortia, depending on the group's degree of control over its hotels and whether it regards its business as asset based or cash based. **Brand name franchising** (which can be considered under conversion franchising) involves the conversion of otherwise independently owned and operated businesses into a group sharing an umbrella brand name. This typically requires the group members to pay a fee for using the brand name, its marketing and purchasing power. In this way brand name franchising is a form of mutual self-help organization. Although brand name franchises were originally established in the hotel sector to facilitate more effective competition against the corporate groups during the 1980s, an increasing number of company hotels became consortium members. However, this feature is becoming less pronounced, owing to the recession and the reorientation of many consortium organizations.

As in the fast-food industry, franchising in the hotel sector takes two forms:

- business format franchising, and
- brand name franchising (consortia).

Whereas consortia in the fast-food industry are in their infancy, they are well developed in the hotel sector. Franchising has been called the last and the best hope for independent businesses in an era of growing vertical integration within the hospitality industry. It helps small businesses to compete with the big ones; it also offers a unique opportunity to people with limited capital and experience.

## Reasons for the growth of franchising

Four general reasons can be identified for the growth in franchising over the past 20 years:

- the role of service activities;
- the value placed on self-employment;

- unemployment;
- the availability of finance.

**Role of service activities**

This is possibly the most important environmental factor responsible for the rapid growth of the franchising industry in recent years. Many service industries are personnel intensive, and they often rely on a distribution network consisting of a large number of outlets dispersed over a relatively large geographical area. The franchising technique is particularly suitable for this type of operation, as it offers considerable advantages in terms of staff motivation, and may also reduce some of the problems associated with controlling local management from a remote head office. Changing lifestyles, such as the increasing number of women going out to work, and the greater leisure time and affluence enjoyed in the West, have resulted in a growing demand for services. In short, the social and economic environment has become increasingly conducive to the emergence of a great variety of franchises.

**Value placed on self-employment**

The increased value that society currently places on self-employment has also encouraged the growth of franchising. Entrepreneurialism is viewed in a very favourable light, and a high level of self-esteem and social acknowledgement can be gained through self-employment. As a result, an increasing number of people are experiencing the desire to escape the bureaucratic environment of the large organization and go it alone by starting their own small business.

Many studies have shown that there is indeed a widespread desire amongst ordinary workers to run their own business. Unfortunately, most of these would-be entrepreneurs lack either the necessary skills or the confidence to set up a totally independent business. However, the franchising system overcomes many of the problems commonly associated with starting a business, and thereby provides a much easier route to self-employment and the social esteem that goes with it. The extent of the social value that is placed on entrepreneurialism can be seen in many of the advertisements that are often used to sell franchises. These advertisements tend to emphasize the social and psychological benefits of being your own boss, just as much as the potential financial rewards. So long as society continues to place a value on being self-employed, then franchising can be expected to grow.

**Unemployment**

While many people are attracted to self-employment as a means of escaping the frustrations of employee status, other less fortunate individuals are forced to consider starting their own business because there seems to be little prospect of securing any other form of employment. During the economic recession of the early 1990s many people turned to self-employment, possibly using their redundancy payments as capital. Franchising may be an alternative for many of these people as they may lack the necessary human capital (that is, the skills and knowledge) to start a totally independent venture, although there are also doubts as to whether or not they make the best franchisees.

**Availability of finance**

The growth of franchising has also been helped by the increase in recent years in the availability of finance on more attractive terms than are usually offered to independent small businesses. Banks have developed special arrangements specifically designed to provide suitable funding for franchisees. Furthermore, the financial institutions have warmed to franchising, and a number of franchisor companies have been successfully floated on the stock market. The growing involvement of the banks and financial institutions has proved to be the key element in the expansion of franchising, and has generally helped to increase the profile and respectability of the industry as a whole.

## THE SCOPE OF FRANCHISING

Many definitions of franchising have been offered over the years by different authors. This diversity is due in part to the fact that franchising covers a very broad range of business. Some definitions are very general, and try to include all possible types of franchise, while others are more specific and give much more precise definition of a particular type of franchise, but will not necessarily be broad enough to cover all aspects of the franchise industry.

All agree that franchising is a method of distribution, and it is perhaps easiest to view the great variety of distribution arrangements as a continuum with, at one end, a simple agreement between two parties for the distribution of a product or services, and at the other end, a complicated and comprehensively defined two-party relationship.

The British Franchise Association (BFA) – the UK franchise industry's trade organization – has proposed the following definition of franchising:

A franchise is a contractual licence granted by one person (the franchisor) to another (the franchisee) which:

- permits or requires the franchisee to carry on, during the period of the franchise, a particular business under or using a specific name belonging to or associated with the franchisor, and
- entitles the franchisor to exercise continuing control during the period of the franchise over the manner in which the franchisee carriers on the business which is the subject of the franchise, and
- obliges the franchisor to provide the franchisee with assistance in carrying on the business which is the subject of the franchise (in relation

to the organization of the franchisee's business, the training of staff, merchandising, management or otherwise), and

- requires the franchisee to pay to the franchisor sums of money in consideration for the franchise, or for goods or services provided by the franchisor to the franchisee, and
- which is not a transaction between subsidiaries of the same holding company, or between an individual and company controlled by him.

This definition does not mention any requirement for a franchisee to invest in his or her franchised outlet. Another example of a franchising definition is the one that appears in the by-laws of the International Franchise Association (IFA), which is the trade association of American franchisors:

A franchise operation is a contractual relationship between the franchisor and the franchisee in which the franchisor offers or is obligated to maintain a continuing interest in the business of the franchisee in such areas as know-how and training; wherein the franchisee operates under a common trade name, format and/or procedure owned or controlled by the franchisor, and in which the franchisee has or will make a substantial capital investment in his business from his own resources.

This definition is concise and quite comprehensive, but it raises a number of questions in addition to providing answers. This definition will be far better understood by those who already have a working knowledge of franchising and the type of transaction.

These two definitions have basic features that must be present in every **business format** franchise:

- There must be a contract containing all the terms agreed.
- The franchisor must initiate and train the franchisee in all aspects of the business prior to the opening of the business, and must assist in the opening.
- After the business is opened the franchisor must maintain a continuing interest in providing the franchisee with support in all aspects of the operation of the business.
- The franchisee is permitted, under the control of the franchisor, to operate under a trade name, format and/or procedure, and with the benefit of goodwill owned by the franchisor.
- The franchisee must make a substantial capital investment from his or her own resources.
- The franchisee must own his or her business.
- The franchisee will pay the franchisor for the rights which he or she acquires in one way or other and for the continuing services with which he or she will provided.
- The franchisee will be given some territory within which to operate.

## AN ANALYSIS OF BUSINESS FORMAT FRANCHISING

We have already pointed out that one main approach to franchising in the hospitality industry is through business format franchising. This is characterized by an ongoing business relationship between franchisor and franchisee that includes not only the product, service, and trade mark, but the entire business format itself; a marketing strategy and plan, operating manuals and standards, quality control, and continuing two-way communications. Franchising as both a legal and a marketing concept is not new. There has been a surge of interest within the last fifteen years, resulting in the rapidly expanding use of this marketing method. First-generation franchises are undoubtedly an important means of product distribution. Nevertheless, when writers use the term 'franchise' they are more often referring to what has become known as **business format** or **second-generation** franchises.

Business format franchises fall into three broad categories, mainly distinguished by the level of investment needed from the franchisee:

- the job franchise;
- the business franchise;
- the investment franchise.

**Job franchises** require a minimal financial investment by the franchisee, and can usually be operated from the franchisee's home. The largest part of the total investment may be, say, the purchase price of a van. The term 'job franchise' derives from the fact that the franchisee is in effect buying himself a job. One-man operations that do not require business premises, such as domestic maintenance services and mobile vehicle servicing, are ideal for job franchising

**Business franchises** require a much larger investment in stocks, equipment and business premises. Because the scale of operation is much larger than that of a job franchise, the franchisee will normally be unable to run the business alone, and will usually have to employ additional staff in order to operate effectively. The range of business franchises is vast, and includes photocopying and printing services, picture framing, business services (such as accounting), dry-cleaning and take-away fast-food operations.

**Investment franchises** require a relatively large investment by the franchisee, often in excess of £200,000. Franchisees who undertake investment franchises are concerned primarily with earning a return on their capital investment rather than with providing themselves with employment. One example of an investment franchise is a franchised hotel.

## The relationship between the two parties: franchisor and franchisee

Franchising can best be described as a system of distribution whereby one party (the franchisor) grants to a second party (the franchisee) the right to distribute products, or perform services, and to operate a business in accordance with an established marketing system. The franchisor provides the franchisee with expertise, trade marks, the corporate image, and both initial and ongoing support, in return for which the franchisee pays to the franchisor certain fees. The objective is that both parties benefit from each other.

The relationship between the two parties could, by virtue of the controls exercised by the franchisor over the franchisees, be held to be that of master and servant. A successful franchise relationship relies heavily on mutual trust between the two parties. The franchisor has to trust the franchisee to make appropriate operating decisions concerning the daily operation of the outlet, and similarly the franchisee has to feel confident that assistance is available from the franchisor should it be needed. The relationship will turn sour as soon as either party begins to mistrust the other. This is one of the reasons why the operating manual and the franchise contract should be as comprehensive as possible so that both parties know from the outset exactly what their rights and obligations are.

## METHODS OF GLOBAL FRANCHISING

Many of the established global franchisors originate in the USA, and their expansion is accounted for by the relative hostility and saturation of their US competitive environment compared with other world regions.

In the USA, franchise growth takes place through the sale of single or multiple franchises, most often with territorial and time restrictions. A common method is through the installation of a master franchisee, who may be an individual or a business. The master franchisee assumes virtually all roles of the franchisor by selling and administering subfranchises. While the use of hotel franchising through the master franchise arrangement approach has advantages of greater regional integration and even less risk to the original franchisor, there can also be some serious problems. If a franchisor is in conflict with a single-site franchisee their problems are less serious than a conflict with a master franchisee; a disagreement with the master franchisee can totally disrupt a firm's expansion strategy. In 1992 Scotts Hotels (UK) Ltd resigned its master franchisee arrangement with Holiday Inn in the UK and switched to an arrangement with Marriott. The result was that Holiday Inn's representation in Britain was dramatically reduced, and its flagship hotel at Marble Arch, London had also gone. The dispute originated from contractual differences but inevitably resulted in the redesign and rescheduling of the expansion strategy of Holiday Inn. This example of Scotts emphasizes that it is essential for there to be a good relationship between the partners in a franchise relationship. If this relationship fails, the consequences are greater than if there was conflict between manager and head office relating to an internally funded expansion strategy.

Joint ventures are a second method of franchise expansion. In this instance the franchisor joins with the local populace to determine franchise sites. Either joint ownership is established or management contracting is used. However, the performance of a hotel could be compromised through operation under a joint venture. The hotel will not be as responsive to the local environment in terms of customer traits and competitive behaviour as a hotel with just one local franchisee.

## Coordination in a dispersed market

The franchisor is faced with a problem when expanding globally to destinations thousands of miles apart. There has to be control over the franchisees to ensure brand uniformity, but the franchisor also has to promote innovation to keep the business proactive and ahead of the competition.

The franchisor therefore has to select a control system suitable to the objectives, which should include flexibility for new product development, a symbiotic relationship with the franchisees, and the extension of brand uniformity to geographically dispersed hotels. There are two methods of control that the franchisor can apply:

- The first is an economic–legalistic approach, with a strict set of monitoring mechanisms that ensure standardization, resulting in firm control and stability.
- The second method of control complements the needs of the franchisee and pulls the hotelier to the wishes of the franchisor rather than pushing, as the economic–legalistic approach would tend to do. This second approach emphasizes the partnership between the two parties in running a successful business. An example of control through this means is corporate advertising.

The franchisee needs advertising to encourage international business travellers and generally heighten public awareness of the hotel. The franchisor needs to provide advertising because it is part of the contractual agreement, but more importantly because they need to exercise control. To combine all the objectives the franchisor advertises the brand standards, which generates demand and also motivates the franchisee to reach and maintain those standards. Success in expansion through franchising is primarily dependent on maintaining a good franchisor–franchisee relationship and exerting control to ensure that the brand is standardized. The results of not achieving this could be portfolio quality disparities, which diminish regular customer demand, or the strategic problems associated with losing a master franchisee.

## COMPETITIVE METHODS USED BY FRANCHISORS

New technologies, selling strategies and marketing concepts are also presenting a competitive advantage to hotel franchisors. These new methods are being implemented not only to attract new customers but also to gain more franchisees within the right market segment. The implementation of new competitive methods is essential to keep a clear and privileged position for the franchisor, and only the most innovative methods could help to keep that position in the future.

The purpose of this section of the chapter is to introduce several of the methods that are being implemented in the hotel industry by franchisors. These can include:

- technology;
- branding;
- marketing, and in particular advertising and promotion.

### Technology-based systems

Technology is used to gain an advantage over slower-moving competition by providing better service, improved decision making and increased revenue.

Technological development has made a big impact on front office activities over the years, and is likely to continue to do so. Software packages cover virtually every front office function, from reservations, room allocation, guest history, billing and accounting to the production of management information.

Hotel operators now realize that a brand in itself it is not enough. Owners and management firms are demanding that franchisors also provide powerful reservation networks. The way that hospitality firms sell to consumers has changed dramatically over the past few years. Many US hotel chains have implemented or are in the process of implementing new reservations systems that utilize yield management to allow better control of their rooms inventory. They are using the latest technology to provide hotels with a wealth of information that can help to forecast demand and increase occupancy and revenue. The systems are also linked to airline computer reservations systems (CRS) in order to allow travel agents to make direct bookings. The link to a CRS is considered one of the most important benefits of joining any hotel franchise. With a sophisticated CRS, a hotel chain provides individual property owners and managers with a tool to increase reservations, maximize sales, implement yield management, enhance market capabilities and improve guest services. In the face of unprecedented operational and guest service challenges, a CRS may be essential to survival.

Even though the introduction of technology within the hotel industry has been a relatively recent event compared with experience in the airline industry, big international hotel chains have created their own systems; others are pooling their resources in powerful consortia, and a third group are buying or renting the technology.

The largest hotel reservations network in the world is owned by Holiday Inn. Its Holidex reservation system services Residence Inns, Embassy Suites and Hampton Inns, in addition to Holiday Inns. Future expansion is planned: to implement its continued growth plans, Holiday Inn Worldwide has spent over $60 million to enhance the Holidex system. The company sees this investment in technology as one of its key competitive methods in its approach to franchising. It includes:

- incorporating the ENCOR property management system worldwide;
- developing the Holiday Inn reservation optimization (HIRO) software system.

These systems should be in place during the mid-1990s. HIW will probably have to spend an additional $20 million on the necessary training and to make the system fully operational. Holiday Inn believes that the Holidex partitioning and hosted processing abilities (allowing other firms to subscribe to the system) are superior to those of any existing system, based upon its current ability to support several competing chains, and regards its system position as secure over the long term.

Best Western International has STAR, a global reservation system that allows property-to-property and worldwide reservations in 30 seconds. This on-line system has real-time inventory, so that when a room is sold, it is immediately depleted from the inventory. Choice Hotel International has launched its new reservation system, Sunburst 2001. This will give travel agents easier access to the firm's inventory, and comprehensive information on each of its hotels. It is also making use of additional technology, such as automated self-check-in/out machines in public areas, together with in-room video systems.

Like the other hotel firms examined, Sheraton has expended funds to develop an improved on-line reservations system. This has real-time inventories, and provides complete information on room rates and packages as well as a guest history. It maintains a freephone number that is linked to its seventeen reservations centres around the world, offering services to 44 countries.

Hilton jointly owns its computer reservations centre, Compass Computer, with Budget Car Rental, with both vendors operating in separate parts of the same system. Although this was among the first hotel central reservations projects, Hilton's system has been enhanced consistently over the years, and is today among the most functionally rich and successful of systems.

Marriott's Marsha system employs several advanced reservation techniques, such as on-line property access to the central database, that are not found elsewhere. Marriott is planning to expand the capabilities of the system further, particularly in such areas as management information systems (MIS) and statistical reporting.

Although considerable investment will be required to upgrade existing in-house reservation systems and link them with several selected mega CRS, the major hotel groups stand to benefit above all others in the short term and to gain a competitive edge. They will be the first hotels to forge on-line links, and this will enable them to extend the traditional Hilton and Holiday Inn philosophy by marketing a widely recognized branded hotel product. They have also recognized that the firms controlling the technology are likely to gain the greatest benefit. Their marketing strength will enable them to exploit the customer profile data that will progressively become available and direct their sales accordingly. They will also be able to afford yield management systems, which will further advance their knowledge of purchasing patterns and the effectiveness of pricing policies. The more sophisticated, complete and accurate the data become, the greater the competitive edge.

## Hotel product branding: segmenting the marketplace

Explicit within this discussion of hotel franchising and the companies involved is the topic of hotel product branding and segmentation of the marketplace.

Product branding is generating increased interest in hotel groups throughout the world. As competition increases and operating costs escalate, the multipurpose hotel offering a variety of costly facilities is finding it harder to operate profitably and serve such diverse groups as convention delegates, leisure travellers and aircrews.

The branding of hotels to identify particular properties with specific market segments is not a new concept, but the idea is generating increased interest among hotel chains with franchise outlets throughout the world.

Many hotels also acknowledge that product branding is a necessary step in a highly competitive international market environment in which the products on offer had become almost indistinguishable from one chain to another.

The principal market sectors that the international hotel chains seek to attract are varied, according to the location of individual hotels and the type and standard of hotel. Thus, branding has come about for three principal reasons:

- There is a need to tailor the hotel product to the specific needs of the customer.
- As hotel groups sought expansion through acquisition during the 1970s and 1980s, many chains found themselves purchasing a disparate group of properties, often of widely different star ratings. In this case it was a logical step to categorize the resultant hotel portfolio into different hotel types or brands: this was a more cost-effective and timely approach than seeking to bring all the hotels up to a common standard.
- The hotel classification and star-rating systems adopted in many countries lack consistency, and do not provide the customer with sufficiently clear indication of the style of hotel or level of service available. Branding within hotel chains can provide a more accurate indication to the customer as to the standard of hotel product and level of service expected.

Holiday Inn, like many other hotel chains, is developing a portfolio of hotel brands. Although hotel chains have different ways of approaching branding, they have a common aim: to attract a wide range of market sectors and to develop brand loyalty. This is being achieved not through the development of multi-role and multi-market hotels but through carefully planned hotel brands and sub-brands designed, developed, operated and marketed to satisfy the needs, expectations and budgets of clearly defined market sectors.

The USA is the home of hotel brands. Branding is more developed there than in most other hotel markets and, if branding theory is correct, harder brand hotel chains should have exhibited distinct success. During the 1980s the USA saw the emergence of a proliferation of hotel brands, and this has resulted in deteriorating performance and changes in ownership of many of the major hotel chains. It is too early to judge the success of all these acquisitions, although the case of Ladbroke's purchase of Hilton International is generally regarded as one of the best hotel transactions of the 1980s. Ladbroke has almost tripled its profits since the acquisition, and has enhanced the status and value of the Hilton International brand in the process. From this example it is also clear that the quality of hotel brand management is important to the success of the brand.

A specific feature of the US hotel chains is that most are involved in franchising hotels rather than in ownership and management. Franchising is responsible for the major expansion of branded hotels in the USA. It has been less popular internationally and rare in the UK. Among the reasons for the popularity of franchised hotels is that most chain expansion in the past four decades has been by new builds, and franchisors have been able to provide a formula for hotel owners and operators to ease and reduce the development costs. One of the reasons why hotel franchising is rare in the UK is that expansion has been by acquisition, and most older hotels cannot conform to the brand specifications of many franchisors.

## The use of marketing and advertising

The operating environment of today's hospitality industry is becoming increasingly volatile, uncertain and complex, and the assistance that franchisors can bring to franchisees is beyond doubt. The level of competitive intensity in the hospitality industry of the 1990s is rising to heights never before experienced by industry owners and operators.

In the hospitality industry, for instance, hotel marketers no longer rely on broadly defined market segments (such as corporate travellers, tourists, or convention business). Marketing experts are pinpointing select groups of potential customers and learning everything about their location, habits, attitudes, friends, travel companions, priorities, and pleasure points. In this decade hoteliers are looking at the customer instead of the type of product they can offer, and this is why market segmentation is considered one of the most important factors for hotel marketers.

The role

The role of marketing in the commercial hotel sector is to increase room occupancy by devising improved products that appeal to customers. It is notable that the role of marketing in business varies between types of economy. Marketing, as applied to capitalist businesses, aims to produce satisfied customers for a satisfactory returns to the business proprietors.

The growing strength of hotel groups within the hotel industry, internationally, has given rise to common standards, operations and marketing communications among their individual units.

The use of marketing in franchising

A major advantage for a franchisee upon joining a franchise system is the immediate access to a marketing concept, which has normally been tried and proved successful in a specific environment. Thus the franchisee achieves very substantial benefits from saving the time and expenditure that would be required to plan and implement a marketing system. Through this direct link to a marketing concept, the franchisee can gain easy market penetration and greater market exposure. Another major advantage is the acquisition of considerable expertise and experience in marketing, advertising and promotional activities organized by the franchisor prior to, during or after the unit's opening. For these reasons franchisors are continously developing new marketing concepts to attract new franchisees and also to be able to compete in the marketplace.

Advertising and promotion

Marketing includes a whole collection of activities that the company performs in relating to its market. Many of these activities are combined in the marketing mix, which is made up of the four Ps: product, price, promotion and place. Each component of the marketing mix can be manipulated in order to influence demand in the marketplace.

Promotion is communication by the firm with its various audiences with a view to informing them and influencing their attitudes and behaviour in a way favourable to the firm. It is aimed at enhancing the image and position of the company and its products. The promotion mix includes advertising, selling, sales promotion, public relations, sponsorship and direct mail. Therefore, it must be stressed that advertising is simply one element in the promotion component of the marketing mix: a point illustrated in Figure 8.1.

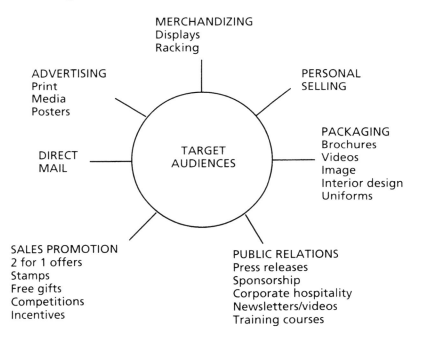

**Fig. 8.1 Marketing communication mix**

For hotels, advertising is used to enhance the brand name; it is a way of communication between the customers and the hotel owners. A proper marketing campaign can help to increase the number of customers and therefore hotel profits.

# THE US AND EUROPEAN EXPERIENCE OF FRANCHISING

## The history of franchising

Contrary to popular belief, franchising is not an American invention; it first emerged in Britain during the Middle Ages, when certain powerful nobles would pay a lump sum to the Government and would agree to provide continuing personal support and services in return for the right to collect local taxes.

Franchising resurfaced in the eighteenth and nineteenth centuries, when the long-term right to a monopoly in some form of trade or commerce would be granted to a franchisee either by a legislative body or by royalty. As consideration for the granting of this right, the franchisee would make an initial cash payment and would also have certain continuing obligations to the franchisor. The next major step in the history of franchising came with the **tied house** agreements between UK breweries and landlords, which developed during the eighteenth century and which still exists today. During the 1700s there was a period of growing concern over the increasing social problems resulting from the widespread availability of alcohol. Legislation was therefore introduced in order to regulate the sale of beer and spirits. Public houses were required to hold a liquor licence in order to be allowed to sell alcohol. As only a restricted number of licences were granted, the value of those inns that were successful in obtaining these licences rose rapidly. Consequently many prospective landlords found they simply could not afford to purchase hostelries. The breweries therefore stepped in and started buying the licensed premises themselves and leasing them to the publicans. As part of the agreement the publican would undertake to sell exclusively beer made by the brewery. The legislation also required that the standard of many existing inns be improved, so the breweries offered to finance the required improvements in many hostelries, in return for which the landlords would agree to a tie arrangement.

## Early development in the USA

The development of franchising in the USA can perhaps serve as a useful indicator for industries in Europe of how business can grow using franchising. Franchising first emerged in the USA when automobile manufacturers realized that franchised rather than company-owned dealerships made economic sense for several reasons:

- The amount of capital needed to set up a national distribution network would be immense. By using a franchised network the manufacturers did not have to provide this capital themselves.
- Franchisees would initially absorb any strong fluctuations in retail prices. The manufacturers would have to absorb all these costs themselves if they sold through company-owned outlets.
- Franchisees would also absorb a proportion of the costs of overproduction and styling errors made by the manufacturers.
- The manufacturers would be freed from the problems of disposing of second-hand cars traded in against new purchases.

The franchised form of car dealership was fully established by 1910 and is still predominant today. It is estimated that 95 per cent of new car sales in the USA are made through franchised outlets.

The second major industry to employ the franchise method of distribution was the soft drinks bottling industry, which developed around the turn of the twentieth century. The franchisee would be granted the right to use the packaging and brand name of the franchisor, from whom he would buy the concentrated syrup from which the final product was made.

The third major industry to employ the franchise method of distribution was the petrol industry. The majority of petrol stations were initially owned by the oil companies themselves. However, during the petrol price wars of the 1930s, the independent stations were found to have an advantage over the company-owned outlets because they had greater flexibility in setting prices at the appropriate competitive level on a local basis. This resulted in declining profitability for the oil companies, who therefore decided to franchise their stations in order to obtain the benefits of flexibility enjoyed by the independents while still maintaining a standardized corporate image right across the country. As a result, not only did the sale of petrol significantly increase, but the oil companies also started to receive large amounts of rental income from the franchisees, as they retained control of the premises used in the nationwide franchise network.

The fourth major development in franchising in the USA was the emergence of franchised wholesaler–retailer chains in the 1920s and 1930s. These were formed in response to the ever-increasing expansion of corporate chains, which began to squeeze out the independent retailers. The franchised chains allowed small retailers to enjoy the benefits of discounts obtained through bulk purchasing by the wholesaler, plus the benefit of the image of a large chain, while at the same time retaining the flexibility of an independent.

## Franchising in the 1950s and 1960s

In the USA the franchising boom (which was fuelled by sales of business format franchises) only lasted as long as the bull market of the 1960s. When the stock market went into decline in 1969 the expansion of franchising temporarily levelled out.

## Franchising from the 1970s to the present day

A second period of rapid expansion in the franchising industry emerged in the UK in the early 1980s. This process was aided in the UK when eight of the reputable franchise companies formed the British Franchise

Association in December 1977. The main objective behind the formation of the BFA was to impose a code of ethical conduct upon franchisors who were admitted to membership. The BFA represents a group of franchisors that the public can trust as being reputable, and also serves as a source of information for anybody interested in franchising and as a promotional body for the industry as a whole.

## Franchising and the hospitality industry

In the USA there are over 12,000 franchised hotel and motel establishments and chains, and they account for over 25 per cent of room stock. They have been seen in the USA as an essential ingredient for ultimate profit and brand dissemination, a point that is being expanded to the European hotel industry of the 1990s.

Unlike the USA, the affiliation practice of most European chains is independent ownership, but this has been forced to change. Owing to changes in the attitude of many stock exchanges to asset-based businesses, the weak property market and stagnating occupancy levels, the propensity for hotel companies to expand through ownership or aquisition is low. Instead, growth in the hospitality industry of the 1990s will derive from the use of other more cash flow orientated forms of affiliation such as franchising. So the issue to address here is: what role does franchising have in the hotel industry, and what are its prospects for growth? This role can be investigated from the point of view of developments in both the USA and Europe.

## HOTEL FRANCHISING IN THE USA

Rising sales, new products and the consumer's growing confidence in brand names has strengthened hotel franchising's popularity in the USA.

Hotel franchising started in the USA, in parallel with the development of the management contract. Holiday Inn properties were among the first new hotels built in the 1950s in the USA, and were less expensive to build than large centre-city hotels. Outlying land was relatively inexpensive, and the construction was basically a two-storey frame or concrete-block low-rise with simple foundations. Holiday Inns were located along the roadsides and at the key road junctions, regional shopping centres and office park developments and, as cities spread, other regional centres of business. Many of the properties, especially the earliest ones, were not built to last even twenty years. They cost a fraction of a large conventional hotel, and US banks were far less reluctant to finance them.

Despite the low construction costs, the Holiday Inn concept was to get others involved in financing and development: this was central to the company's aim to expand rapidly. The hotels were designed to be run by people who could be quickly trained and who could follow the simple operating manual and accounting systems that the franchisor provided. The food-service operation was also simple to operate, and although the menu prices were low, the franchisee could usually make a good profit, given the low investment cost and low payroll cost. The franchisor, in principle, even let the franchisee participate in volume discounts for purchasing furnishings, fixtures, equipment, and other items. Initially, if the franchisee could get by with limited decor and basic operating equipment, they could realize some savings. As time passed, however, it seems franchisors became more interested in making profits and less interested in passing savings on to the franchisees.

The franchisee got a baseline plan and specifications from which to build, plus the all-important brand name, along with national advertising, a reservation service, and a listing in the franchisor's directory. For all that, franchisees paid a relatively low initial fee and a percentage of their room revenue. It was an equitable arrangement. Using room revenue as a base was reasonable, and early fees were set at 3–4 per cent of room sales.

Before long, having seen the success experienced by the highway-hotel franchise companies, major chains like Hilton and Sheraton began to offer franchises. In addition to motels, they franchised medium and large full-service hotels at airports, in the suburbs, and even in city centre locations. They were more complex operations, which needed well-trained managers and department heads along with the required marketing skills. The company did not supply much real management back-up, with trained staff to come in and help, or the kind of marketing support that it provided to its own managed or partially owned hotels. Instead, franchisees had to put together a management team or hire an independent management company. These up-market hotels were complex to operate and market, and they began to face considerable competition, often from well-managed company hotels. So as up-market hotels' franchise fees began to go up, the cost–value ratio of the agreement declined.

A franchise firm gets most of its fees up front and has little interest in the franchisee's profit, provided the hotel is maintained in good condition. With a management contract, on the other hand, the management firm has real motivation to generate profits and thus maximize the incentive fee.

## American hotel chains

A specific feature of US hotel chains is that most are involved in franchising hotels rather than in ownership and management. A prerequisite for franchising is that a hotel brand acts as the blueprint for franchisees.

Franchising has been responsible for the major expansion of branded hotels in the USA. It has been less popular internationally and rare in the UK. One of the reasons for the popularity of franchised hotels in the USA is that most chain expansion in the past four decades has been by new build, and franchisors have been able to provide a formula for hotel owners and operators to ease and reduce the development costs.

A feature common to all franchise companies is a central reservations system, which comes second in importance to the brand itself, which initially attracts franchisees. The reservations system acts as a halfway house between individual customers booking their own hotel rooms and the hotel wholesaler.

The power of hotel brands has undoubtedly contributed to oversupply in the USA, with franchisors seeking to affiliate increasing numbers of hotels as a low-risk expansion activity bearing little direct investment cost. Equally, the power of the brands has been insufficient to prevent poor US hotel performance, liquidation and bankruptcy. In this situation the irony is that the franchise firms have been able to survive more easily than individual hotels, which prompts the thought that the larger the franchise chain, the greater its chances of survival.

## New strategies in American hotel chains

Hotel franchising in the 1990s is becoming more sophisticated and competitive than in the early days of franchising in the 1950s and 1960s. Hotel firms now offer as many as three or four franchised brands; franchise agreements frequently cover more than one property; and, increasingly, deals are signed with franchisees around the world. But one aspect of franchising has and, undoubtedly, will remain constant through the years, and that is the importance of a brand name. In the USA, in particular, independent hotels are converting to franchise brands in increasing numbers, in order to compete with the marketing muscle and national presence of the chains.

Firms that once offered just one franchise product – typically, a mid-priced hotel – are now developing economy, up-market and all-suite properties, ensuring that they have the right hotel no matter what the market.

## Market segmentation

Implicit in this discussion of franchising in the 1990s is the importance of market segmentation. The objective is to capture as much as possible of the complete area under a given market demand curve. This is accomplished by subdividing a market into components that satisfy individual customers more precisely than a mass market approach could. Three conditions must be present for successful market segmentation:

- Sellers must be able to raise prices more than is commensurate with cost increases: that is, the segments must have different price elasticities of demand to make the procedure worthwhile.
- The segments must be capable of separating targeted customers.
- Profits from various segments must exceed the costs of differentiating the segments. Market segmentation normally is costly, and therefore it will only pay to segment if sufficiently different demand elasticities exist.

Many US hotel companies are creating new markets for themselves and their franchisees with new brands. Many of the new products introduced in the late 1980s are in the economy segment, but several are all-suites properties.

More than a dozen new brands in the USA alone (still, by far, the dominant franchise arena) became available to franchisees in 1989 and have now become established in the 1990s. In many cases, the new brands were an extension of an existing, well-known brand and took full advantage of name recognition. Two examples are identified below.

**Choice International** is a US company that has taken full advantage of the name recognition of one of its existing brands while introducing a new product. The first Clarion Carriage House Inn, a subset of the company's Clarion line, was created by the 1987 merger of the Quality's Royal chain and Aircoa's Clarion collection. By affiliating with a chain such as Clarion, franchisees can not only market an established, respected brand name, but can also take advantage of the parent company's programmes, training and other services.

**Hilton Corporation** has also created a new product known as CrestHil. It is a smaller, two-storey hotel geared towards the business traveller and is located primarily in secondary cities where large meeting spaces and banquet facilities are unnecessary. The first CrestHil by Hilton opened in November 1989 in Buffalo Grove, Illinois, USA. Hilton Inns, which is franchising CrestHil, says it will give Hilton alternatives when considering a new market or replacing franchises that are not profitable.

## International growth strategies of major US hotel companies

Growth in the hotel industry appears to be based mostly on franchising and management contracts, with some asset-acquiring activity. Conversion, accomplished through the acquisition of small chains, is also an increasingly popular growth strategy.

Franchising is considered one of the most important growth strategies for many of the major US hotel companies because North American-based firms do not have, or cannot obtain, the large amounts of capital required to acquire assets in the context of an aggressive growth strategy. Therefore the main competitive methods included within the business format franchise will be services such as reservations systems, advanced technology and sophisticated sales, marketing and advertising programmes. The international growth strategies of a number of hotel companies will now be discussed.

**Holiday Inn Worldwide**

Since the sell-off of the Holiday Inn core brand to Bass plc, UK, in 1990 for over $2.3 billion, the chain has been trying to position itself for the long term. While its international properties enjoy a respectable position in the marketplace, Holiday Inn Worldwide (HIW) is threatened by its ageing core brand in the USA.

HIW's stated strategy for the future will be based upon continued product differentiation and growth in new markets, value for money, utilization of economies of scale, and a superior distribution process to bring in customers. Implementation of this approach to strategy relies on a matrix organization, which will consolidate finance, marketing and human resources at the head office level. Organizational units overseeing franchising and company-operated units will keep operational decision making close to the marketplace. Franchising will continue to be the main growth vehicle, supported by conversions arising out of acquisitions of smaller and weaker chains.

**Choice Hotels International**

Choice Hotels International, a unit of Manor Care Inc., continues to be the most aggressive of all chains. It is a franchise organization only, with brands ranging from budget to quality. They include Clarion, Quality, Comfort, Sleep Inn, Rodeway, Econo Lodge and Friendship Inns. The chain currently operates in 26 countries.

Choice's growth plans are aggressive. It has set a goal of 10,000 properties by the year 2000, with 8,000 outside the USA. To accomplish this, it is working hard to sign master franchise agreements throughout the world.

Choice International's future strategy will rely on franchising as its only growth vehicle, and it will count on its services to franchisees to make this happen. Like Holiday Inn Worldwide and several other chains, it continues to invest in technology to achieve this objective. Product segmentation will anchor Choice's global strategy. By focusing upon master franchises, Choice feels it will be better able to control the quality of its product while allowing franchisees to respond to local market conditions.

**ITT Sheraton**

ITT Sheraton is a network of approximately 450 hotels, inns, resorts and all-suites properties in over 70 countries. This network includes company-owned and managed properties, units under management contract and independent owners operating under licensing/franchise agreements. Approximately 94 per cent of the hotels and 89 per cent of the rooms inventory are either managed or franchised (of this total, approximately 62 per cent are franchised). With declining occupancy rates hitting Sheraton like the rest of the industry, the company has focused on upgrading properties and enhancing its image. It has also laid off over 400 management employees throughout its system for the purposes of simplifying its corporate structure. This move is expected to save Sheraton $50 million annually. The company is considering a public offering to raise cash to support expansion efforts.

Sheraton avoided the building boom in the 1980s and is now in the 1990s ready to take advantage of good values on distressed properties and investment in the upgrading of its current hotels. This strategy has resulted in the spending of $1 billion over the last four years, with the push focusing on the quality of facilities.

The company plans an aggressive growth programme, and now expects to expand the number of hotels in South-East Asia. It is closely watching developments in Vietnam and the Philippines, and also aims to double its presence in Latin America.

As the company continues to try to improve its North American properties, it can also be expected to seek growth in the international marketplace. Like its competitors, it will look for joint ventures, franchising and management contracts to fuel its expansion plans in the future.

**Radisson Hotels International**   Radisson is part of the privately owned Carlson Companies of Minneapolis, Minnesota. Radisson has been growing rapidly despite the industry's problems because it focused on management contracts and franchising instead of real estate investment. The company has concentrated on its strength in management, sales and marketing. It has 269 hotels, with 60,905 rooms, in 30 countries. Radisson owns only two and manages 31, while the rest are franchised.

Radisson's aim is to be the fastest-growing quality hotel chain, seeking to operate in the up-market business travel and leisure destination markets. Its plans for future development call for targeting Europe (especially Eastern Europe), the Asia Pacific region, the Caribbean, South America and Canada. Radisson's international strategy is based on strategic alliances, franchising and management contracts. In 1993 it developed marketing alliances with Edwardian Hotels in the UK and Movenpick in Switzerland. It concluded franchise agreements in Australia, Mexico and Canada, and is pursuing alliances with airlines such as JAL, British Airways and Lufthansa.

Marriott
Corporation

The Marriott name became one of the USA's great success stories throughout the 1980s. This hotel and service company was founded on the best of American traditions, hard work and reinvestment, and resulted in the Marriott name's being displayed on over 746 hotels in 1992. The company offers a wide variety of accommodation products, including Marriott Hotels, Resorts and Suites (full service), Courtyard Hotels (mid-priced), Residence Inn (extended stay), Fairfield Inn (economy segment), and Marriott Ownership Resorts (vacation timesharing). The company operates in 21 countries and has over 195,000 employees.

Unlike Holiday Inn, Radisson or Choice, Marriott built its strategy on owning and managing hotels as opposed to franchising. Marriott's most recent international venture has been the signing of a franchise agreement for at least 18 new hotels, most of them full-service, with Scotts Hotels Ltd (UK), the UK subsidiary of Canadian-based Scotts Hospitality. Twelve of these hotels are conversions from Holiday Inns. It would seem that Marriott has moved away from its traditional development policy internationally, with joint ventures, franchising and management contracts now appearing to be the preferred methods of growth. While the emphasis has been on up-market hotels, the introduction of the Courtyard concept in the UK suggests that the company will rely on product branding to facilitate growth strategies. As Marriott struggles to grow internationally, it will have to pursue the development of an improved global reservations system, following the failure of the Confirm reservations project (an integrated reservations system being developed jointly by American Airlines, Marriott, Hilton and others). It will also need to develop more clearly its international growth strategies and organizational structure.

Pricing has been very elastic in Marriott's business hotels segment, so the company has suffered from severe discounting by its competitors. It has attempted to meet this problem head on by trying to market its hotels to corporate clients on a purpose-of-visit programme, suggesting that hotels be booked according to the needs of the traveller; all bookings would be with one or more of Marriott's brands. This approach uses a computer system to improve its rate structuring effectiveness and to incorporate rate structures that allow non-refundable advance reservations.

## GOING INTERNATIONAL: THE EUROPEAN MARKET

The original franchise concept as applied by, say, Holiday Inn and Choice International, was a good idea, but when it was extended to sophisticated properties it made much less sense. In addition it often made even less sense outside the USA, where brands are less well known and central reservations services are less beneficial.

US hotel chains looking to franchise in Europe have to face many difficulties, because franchising is not appropriate in Europe: the vast majority of hotels are owner managed. There are some differences that must be taken into account for American hotel chains before they start using franchising in Europe.

## The European hotel industry: overview

Europe is now the major region for hotel chain development in the world, and will remain so in the years ahead. Within the region, account has to be taken of the capital famine that is constraining expansion by acquisition, and the limitations of the US domestic hotel brands in Europe. The trend of most European chains is to extend forms of affiliation such as franchising. Considerable corporate activity is to be expected in the coming years as the major chains seek to ensure that they have adequate room capacity to underpin longer-term market growth. Mergers and acquisitions are to be expected, as well as the construction of new capacity and expansion of the full range of affiliations, from joint ventures to franchising.

## Franchising in Europe

If the major American hotel franchisors are to expand in Europe with any force, they will need to redefine their brand specifications to accommodate the realities of European hotel supply; otherwise they will restrict themselves to newly built hotels, which will entail slow growth. There are several European chains – Accor's Mercure, Forte Heritage Hotels, Queen's Moat Houses-owned brands and Mount Charlotte Thistle – that have been created from the diversity of European mid-market supply, and which could expand rapidly through franchising. However, none of these companies has yet shown much interest in pursuing this possibility.

A second approach to franchising in Europe is seen in the few instances in which an existing European hotel chain has franchised a tranche of its hotels to one of the major brands. This is the case in continental Europe with the UK's Queen's Moat Houses, which has franchised most of its gateway city hotels to Holiday Inn in order to capture the international markets.

An extension of this approach is the master franchise of the kind that Scott's Hotels, a subsidiary of the Canadian company Scott's Hospitality, negotiated with Marriott in the UK. Under this arrangement all the Scott's Hotel properties in the UK are franchised as Marriott. Scott's will manage any future franchising of Marriott hotels in the UK which seek to operate as Marriott. Multiple franchising arrangements are attractive for the franchisors, as they facilitate the fast build-up of coverage in Europe with practically no capital cost. There have been some notable successes. Queen Moat Houses, for instance, regularly reports that in Germany its Holiday Inns achieve higher room occupancy and room rates than its domestically orientated Queens Moat hotels. The main characteristic feature of multiple franchising, however, is that it is concerned with the conversion of existing hotels to a different brand rather than adding new stock to the chain hotel company.

## European constraints on franchising

Franchising operations in the European market involve a number of problems:

- Many of the European hotels are old properties; also, they are already well established and do not need chain affiliation to attract business.
- Generally, in Europe, people prefer an older hotel with character as opposed to a new hotel.
- There are different ways to regard the hotel industry according to nationalities: for instance, French and German travellers are more inclined towards utilitarian, budget properties, while the British favour up-market facilities.
- Cross-cultural differences are one of the issues that franchisors need to contend with when branching out into new parts of the world.

Clearly, travellers in Europe are not as homogeneous as Americans. America is a big country, while Europe comprises different countries with different cultures. Within Europe it is necessary for hospitality firms to have different strategies depending on the country. As in the USA, operators in Europe face labour problems, which vary widely from market to market. Labour in Europe's hospitality industry has a high level of turnover. In addition to local problems with recruitment and retention, many European countries support significant labour costs with government-mandated benefit packages.

One of the most important barriers facing operators in Europe today is the lack of affordable sites. This shortage is especially severe in the hotel markets of the UK, France, Germany and The Netherlands. Sites are scarcer and more expensive, both to obtain and then, once obtained, to obtain planning permission and build on.

Government regulations are another significant factor in developing outside the USA. Costs of building also are raised by strict and complex building regulations that increase the cost of the construction and lengthen the time it takes to open a hotel.

While one advantage of doing business in Western Europe is the availability of products, equipment and distribution channels, unfortunately the lack of brand awareness serves to increase start-up costs for chain hotels in Europe.

## The principal European hotel companies

The top twenty quoted hotel companies in the EU together account for over 300,000 rooms, one-third of which are in the UK. The brands and broad market positions of the leading companies, which account for 238,000 rooms (77 per cent of the total), are described below.

Accor

The biggest of the European companies, the French Accor group, acquired Wagons-Lits in 1992, which raised its dominance of the European hotel market to a point where it is difficult to see how any of its competitors can catch up. Its hotel brands are Sofitel, Pullman, Novotel, Mercure, Altea, PLM Azure, Ibis, Urbis, Formule 1 and Motel 6. Motel 6 is based in the USA and currently has about 85,000 rooms. During 1992, all Accor's expansion took place within the burgeoning budget brands sector. Accor has the largest franchising share, with about 19 per cent of its 85,000 rooms franchised, primarily in its Ibis chain.

Forte

Forte is the largest UK hospitality company, and its UK hotel portfolio dominates its operations. Forte has approximately 900 hotels worldwide, representing 72,340 rooms and making it the UK's largest hotel and catering operator. Its hotel stock includes 35,066 rooms in the TraveLodge group in North America, the majority of which are franchised. The 1991 branding initiative by Forte produced the following structure: Exclusive Hotels, Forte Grand, Forte Crest, Forte Heritage, Forte Posthouse and Forte TraveLodge. The most recent development of the company in continental Europe has been in the budget brands market in Spain, France and Southern Ireland, and most notably in the joint venture with Agip, the Italian state oil company, under which Forte has taken on the management of eighteen of the Agip hotels in Italy. In 1994 it also purchased the Meridien Hotel chain from Air France.

Société du Louvre

Société du Louvre is a French company whose main shareholder is the Taittinger family. It has three main hotel chains: Concorde Hotels, which is predominantly a French top-of-the-range chain; Campanile, the main budget chain spread throughout continental Europe but still predominantly in France; and Première Classe, a low-priced hotel brand also in France.

Queens Moat Houses

Queens Moat Houses is a UK-quoted company (suspended in 1993, relisted 1995) with extensive coverage of the mid-market sector in continental Europe. It is distinctive in that it has built up hotel chains in the UK, Germany, The Netherlands and Austria, which operate in those domestic markets and which have a style reflecting in each case the cultures of the host countries rather than the imposition of a homogeneous brand from the centre.

In recent years, Queen's Moat Houses has expanded significantly in

Europe. The group now operates 102 hotels in six countries and is the largest franchisee in Europe, as well as controlling more hotel bedrooms in France than any other non-French hotel chain.

However, expansion has resulted in a significant increase in group debt; the level of debt was further affected by the acquisition of the Norfolk Capital chain in 1991 and heavy capital spending in the last seven years, and led to their suspension from the Stock Exchange in 1993. The Queens chains include Queens Moat Houses in the UK, Bilderberg in The Netherlands, Queens in Germany and Austrotel in Austria. In addition, a tranche of its properties is in city centre locations and areas aimed at international markets. The company franchises these hotels to other major global brands, such as Holiday Inn.

Ladbroke
The UK-based Ladbroke company is the world leader in horse racing (gambling), owns a major DIY (home improvement) chain in the UK and Spain, and operates as a property company, as well as owning Hilton International, one of the most powerful of the up-market hotel brands around the world. Throughout the world, Hilton focuses on international gateway cities and on the international travel (especially business) market. In the UK, Hilton also operates in the provinces, and targets domestic as well as international travellers.

Bass
Bass is the largest brewer in the UK and is the owner of Holiday Inn, the largest hotel brand in the world. The Holiday Inn exposure in Europe is inadequate for a brand of its size, and the company was shaken in 1992 by the transfer of Scott's Hotels in the UK from the Holiday Inn franchise to Marriott. However, it is to be expected that Holiday Inn will recover this loss by attracting new franchisees, although there remains much to be done for the brand to achieve the penetration in Europe that its size demands.

## ROLE OF FRANCHISING

Other than the definitions already identified, there are three main differences between brand name and business format franchising in the hotel industry.

The main operational difference is that business format franchises do not have the discretion to reject reservations offered from the central reservations system. As the business format hotel franchise companies are often little more than owners of a hotel brand, a central reservations system and other corporate services, the franchisee must use the corporate services such as central reservations, marketing, advertising, purchasing or training provided.

When a hotel business is franchised, it is marketed to two distinct groups. The outlet will need to continue to market to the end consumer of the services; it is also marketed to potential franchisees. A clear identity and a distinctive name and image that differentiate the hotel from the competition must therefore exist in order to sell not only the franchise, but also the end service. A prerequisite for business format franchising is therefore that there is a hotel brand such as Holiday Inn, TraveLodge and Ramada, which acts as a blueprint for franchisees.

A further difference lies in the comparison of franchise fees within the hotel industry. Some of the lowest total cost percentages of the proportion of rooms revenue belong to the brand name franchises (consortia), such as Best Western with 1 per cent and Preferred hotels with 1.3 per cent. This would suggest that as such organizations are more cost orientated than profit orientated, the average margin of profit realized by the business format franchise chains is in the range 4–4.6 per cent. The lower initial costs would also suggest that the brand name franchise would be preferable for many independent operators, who do not necessarily have access to the required capital that would permit them to become a business format franchisee. The initial fee required in such franchises within the hospitality industry varies with market level, with some of the cheapest being within the budget economy sector. The main strategic difference is that business format franchises rely on a standard set of specifications, each being of a consistent standard and management consistency in order to appeal to clearly defined target markets.

In the fast food industry, McDonald's agreements for example require each unit to have a set standard of specifications: quality of furnishings, external specifications, architecture and design, the same service offerings and products and all sharing the same brand name. Much of Europe's hotel stock is not of a consistent standard, with varying types of architecture and consistency being inherent to many hotel portfolios, and thus business format franchising has not proved feasible. There are only 38 franchised hotels in the UK, for example. In contrast to the requirements of business format franchises, brand name franchises require that the independent hotel be of a certain standard and offer certain specified amenities. Thus many consortia gained growth by specializing in certain niche markets.

## Opportunities

Unlike Europe, the USA is the home place of the hotel brand: it is more developed there than in any other market. This is because the main method of hotel stock expansion in the US has been through new build, thereby permitting cloning, whereas in Europe, especially the UK, the primary method of growth has been acquisition, which has led many of the acquired properties to show various design styles. Moreover, the EU internal market is stimulating hotel expansion but not in new-build investments. One area of possible expansion is budget economy service, owing to their location in peripheral sites and utilitarian nature. For example, budget hotel group Climat de France, part of the Elitair Group, has expanded to over 140 hotels, which are located in France, Germany, Spain and the UK, by using business format franchising. Another opportunity is the formation of alliances with branded food service companies to offer joint franchise packages. One example is Choice International Hotels and Pizza Hut. This helps the hotel to compete more effectively against stand-alone restaurants, as well as using specialist food and beverage skills to improve efficiency. Other hotel companies with branded food service include Radisson with TGI Fridays and TraveLodge with Little Chef.

## HOTEL FRANCHISING: THE US BED AND BREAKFAST INDUSTRY

One particular area of interest for franchising opportunities is the bed and breakfast industry, particularly in the USA.

The changing lifestyle of travellers has contributed to tremendous growth in the US bed and breakfast industry within the past ten years. The number of US B&Bs listed in guidebooks has increased from 1,200 to 9,500 in the past decade; another 15,000 US bed and breakfast establishments are not listed in the guidebooks. This growth has brought many changes to the US industry, some of which make B&Bs an attractive industry for franchising. Indeed, to get a foothold in the industry, Choice Hotels International is the first US national hotel chain to offer its franchising services to country inns and bed and breakfasts under the umbrella of the Carriage House Inns. This emergence of B&B franchising, which is an untested and new concept, has created some concerns with respect to its success and applicability.

### Definition

There are several definitions for bed and breakfasts. The American Bed and Breakfast Association classifies B&Bs in three categories as follows:

- **B&B Homestay:** a private owner-occupied residence, in which the frequency and volume of B&B visitors are incidental to the primary use of the building as a private residence. One to three guestrooms are made available to visitors for the purpose of meeting people or supplemental income. Breakfast is the only meal served and is included in the charge for the room.

- **B&B Inn:** a professional business operated in a building which is used primarily for providing overnight accommodation to the public even though the owner may live on the premises. Room size for a B&B inn normally ranges from four guestrooms to twenty. Breakfast is the only meal served and is included in the charge for the room.
- **Country inn:** is similar to a B&B inn, with the difference that country inns offer full service restaurants, which provide meals other than breakfast to overnight guests and the public.

This classification reflects the size and services, but does not take into account the diversity within each category. B&Bs vary widely: each one expresses the unique and personal style of its host. Generally speaking, the main concern of the innkeepers is to provide a unique guest experience and personal touch.

## Bed and breakfast and inn franchising

Bed and breakfast and inn franchising would fall under a business format or conversion system. A brief discussion of hotel and restaurant franchising, which commonly operates under these franchising systems, serves as a paradigm for bed and breakfast in franchising. Furthermore, given the differences among innkeepers with respect to individuality, taste and uniqueness, the bed and breakfast industry more naturally tends itself to conversion franchising (consortia) to accommodate some specific needs of its members.

## Choice Hotels International

As mentioned above, Choice Hotels International is currently the only national or global US company that offers its franchise services to the B&B industry as part of its market segmentation strategy. In late 1989 Choice Hotels International (formerly Quality International) became the first national chain to offer franchises to small up-market boutique inns and hotels under the brand of the Clarion Carriage House Inns. According to a summary of the licence agreement, Choice Hotels International will provide member inns with advantages such as marketing power, reservations power, sale support and directory exposure, as well as marketing resource professionals and other benefits. The licence agreement grants the franchisee the rights to a non-exclusive licence to use the system in the operation of one property at a specific location for a period of 20 years. Expanding on these benefits the following can be pointed out:

- **Marketing power:** Choice is considered to have the world's third largest accommodation system.

- **Reservation power:** access to the 2001 System, a technologically advanced telemarketing network that taps into Sabre, Apollo, Pars and Daras 2 as well as most travel agent consortia.
- **Sales support:** representation by meeting group tour and travel professionals within a worldwide network of 21 sales offices located in key business organization areas.
- **Directory exposure** in the 3 million Choice's travel and vacation directories distributed biannually, plus listing in other directories to targeted travel segments, such as senior citizens, group tours, and government and military organizations.

Other benefits of affiliation include: credit card discounts; furniture, fixture and equipment purchasing power; international public relations exposure; training programmes; personal travel discounts; and advertising discounts.

## Trends

Bed and breakfast franchising is untested; its history is only five years old, while the restaurant and hotel industries both possess proven success records. Hotel franchising can be described as a truly American phenomenon, which allows entrepreneurs to go into business themselves while receiving the benefits of national branding. In contrast, bed and breakfast franchising is in its inception. As of September 1993 Clarion Carriage House Inns had about 61 inn franchises in the USA and 15 franchises abroad, with 25 potential contracts in the pipeline. Although the success rate of these establishments was characterized as 'very satisfactory', there is no aggregate information to substantiate the extent of the franchisor's contribution to the revenues of the inn franchisees. Generally the inn franchisees have limited budgets to acquire the electronic data processing systems that will connect their activities to the franchisor's network. Although it is not possible to forecast the rate of growth in B&B franchising, an examination of the hotel, motel and restaurant industries reveals that broad acceptance of franchising occurred gradually over several decades.

The entry of franchising to the B&B industry has raised many questions and concerns. In restaurant and hotel franchising the franchisees are required to adhere to certain standards of service, decor or equipment in order to achieve a level of standardization that eventually would benefit the franchisees. Innkeepers believe that B&Bs are popular because of their individuality and the uniqueness of their facilities, services and hospitality. Consequently, standardization, which typifies hotel and restaurant franchising appears contradictory to their main purpose. The decade-long growth of the B&Bs in the USA has slowed down considerably in the 1990s owing to recession, competitive pressures from the hospitality industry, and competition between the operators. This is particularly the case in regions such as the US state of New England, where the market is already saturated. This trend has resulted in increasing numbers of B&Bs looking for innovative ways to market their properties in order to stay viable. Currently too few B&Bs and inns are affiliated with any franchise organization to derive any valid statistical data regarding the benefits of franchising for a B&B establishment. On the other hand, the prosperous history of franchising in general, and hotel and restaurant franchising in particular, suggests that brand recognition and franchisee-related benefits will contribute to its success.

**SUMMARY**

It has been shown within this chapter that franchising (in all its forms) can be regarded as the primary engine driving global growth within the hospitality industry. This is so because both US- and European-based firms do not have, or cannot obtain, the large amounts of capital needed to acquire assets in the context of an aggressive growth strategy. Thus the main competitive methods will be business format franchising, with services such as reservations systems, advanced technology and sophisticated sales, marketing and advertising programmes. Franchise companies are already spending large amounts of money on advertising programmes, and this can be expected to increase. In this increasingly competitive environment it will be incumbent upon franchisors to differentiate their services sufficiently to protect their market position and that of their franchisees.

**FURTHER READING**  Abell, M 1990 *The international franchise option*, Waterloo, London

Adams, J and K V Prichard Jones *Franchising practice and precedents in business format franchising*, 3rd edn, Butterworths, London

Allentuck, A 1993 Who is in charge? *Canada Hotel Restaurant*, April, 36–8

Acheson, D 1990 Crisis management, *Restaurateur*, October, 24–5

Archom, E 1993 Capture the flag USA, *Lodging* **18**(5), 13–14

Arnold, D E 1987 Study market's actual needs, *Lodging*, January, 34–5

Baum, C 1992 Forecast '92: economic outlook, nations' outlook, *Hotels* **26**(1), 48–55

Baum, C 1992 Franchisees speak: give us more than a reservation system, *Hotels* **26**(2), 44–6, 48

Baum, C 1993 Franchising evolves worldwide as technology and competition grow, *Hotels* **27**(2), 48–50, 52

Bell, CA 1993 Agreements with chain-hotel companies, *Cornell HRA Quarterly* **34**(1), 27–33.

Brooke, M Z 1985 *Selling management services contracts in international business*, Holt, Rinehart & Winston, London

Brookers, J and G Crawshaw 1989, Selling the States, *Travel Tourism Gazette*, No 1838, 12 January, 61–66

Bruns, R 1993 The reservation edge, *Lodging* **18**(7), 18–23

Cahill, M 1992 How flagging sales are changing the flags: changes in hotel franchising in USA, *Lodging* **18**(2), 17–19, 21–2

Chaplin, D 1988 Master plan, *Marketing*, 20 October, 24–30

Chaudry, R 1990 Doing business in Europe, *Restaurants and Institutions* **100**(24), 94–102

Christmas, J 1993 Managing today and preparing tomorrow, *Communications Technology, Bottomline* **8**(3), 20–3, 27

Churchill, D 1993 The franchise affair, *Caterer and Hotelkeeper*, June, 32–4

Clark, C R 1992 Gearing yourself up for better times ahead, *Lodging* **18**(3), 33–4, 36

Commission of the European Communities 1989 *The cooperation between firms in the Community: franchising, commerce and distribution*, Brussels

Commission of the European Communities 1981 *European code of ethics for franchising*, Luxembourg

Connell, J 1992 Branding hotel portfolios, *International Journal of Contemporary Hospitality Management* **4**(1), 26–32.

Cullen, T P and J L Rogers 1988 Quality and price perceptions, *International Journal of Hospitality Management* **7**(2), 151–60

Curtis, S and G Wason 1991–93 The hotel industry in recession, *Insights*, No 4, A91–A96

Dev CS and J R Brown 1990 Franchising and other operating arrangements in the lodging industry: a strategic comparison, *Hospitality and Restaurant Journal* **14**(3), 23–41

Doty, J L 1971 Financing franchise systems, *Cornell HRA Quarterly*, August, 17–22

The Economist 1993 Europe's hotel industry, tough at the top, 12–18 June, 99–102

Emmons, R J 1971 The psychology of franchising, *Cornell HRA Quarterly*, February, 60–7

Fowler, A and D Fowler 1985 *Franchising: a small business guide*, Sphere Reference, London

Futures trends in chain franchising, *Lodging Hospitality* **45**(5), May 1989, Supplement 22,24,26

Go, F 1989 International hotel industry: capitalising on change, *Tourism Management* **10**(3), 195–200

Go, F and J Christensen 1989 Going global, *Cornell HRA Quarterly* **30**(3), 73–9

Gomes, A J 1986 *Hospitality in transition*, American Hotel & Motel Association, Washington, DC

Goymur, D 1992 Booking ahead, *Caterer and Hotelkeeper* **185**(3711), 20–6

Hall, P and R Dixon 1989 *Franchising*, Pitman, London

Hanks, R D, R P Noland and R G Cross 1992 Discounting in the hotel industry: a new approach, *Cornell HRA Quarterly*, February, 15–23

Himestra, S J 1990 Employment policies and practices in the lodging industry, *International Journal of Hospitality Management* **9**(3), 207–21

Hotel's Editors 1991 What's ahead in reservations technology? *Hotels* **25**(10), 93–4

Hotel's Editors 1992 Is your CRS working hard enough?, *Hotels* **26**(8), 71–2

Hotel's Editors 1993 The ABCs of yield management, *Hotels* **27**(4), 55–6

Hotel's Editors 1993 Technology to the revue, *Hotels* **27**(8), 37–8

Horwath & Horwath Consulting 1988 *A portrait of the hotel and tourism industry*, Horwath & Horwath Publications, UK

Housden, J 1984 *Franchising and other business relationships in hotel and catering services*, Heinemann, London

Hunt, S D and J R Nevin 1975 Trying agreements in franchising, *Journal of Marketing* **39**, 20–6

International Hotel Association 1992 Waiting for better times worldwide, *Hotels*, January, 54–6

Izraeli, D 1972 *Franchising and the total distribution system*, Longman, London

James, R M 1987 Pinpoint your product segment, *Lodging*, January 40–1

Kaplan, A 1987 The franchisor–franchisee relationship: stronger partnership greater growth, *Lodging*, January, 47–8

Kay, J 1993 *Foundations of corporate success*, Oxford University Press, Oxford

Kimes, S E 1989 The basics of yield management, *Cornell HRA Quarterly*, November, 14–22

Kostecka, A 1985 Restaurant franchising in the economy, *Restaurant Business*, March, 165–82

Kursh, H 1968 *The franchise boom*, Prentice-Hall, Englewood Cliffs

Lee, D 1985 How they started – the growth of four hotel giants, *Cornell HRA Quarterly*, May, 22–3

Lewis, R C 1990 Advertising your hotel's position, *Cornell HRA Quarterly* **31**(2), 84–91

Lima, T 1987 Chains vs. independents: it appears chains are winning the battle, *Lodging Hospitality*, July 7, 9

Lilley, P 1992 Hotel world, *Travel Trade Gazette*, No 2030, 22 October, 31–6

Lodging Editors 1989 Major chains plan marketing strategies for 1989, *Lodging* **14**(5), 37–9, 60

Lydecker, T 1987 Franchising: who swings the most chain? *Restaurant and Institutions* **97**(8), 30–5, 46

Management companies reach a crossroads, *Lodging Hospitality*, January 1982, p 90

Mandigo, T R 1987 Gauge the franchisors' support systems, *Lodging*, January, 43–6

Martin, F 1989 New segments and rising sales build franchising clout, *Hotels and Restaurants International* **23**(2), 46–8

Martin, F 1992 The global hotel industry: 10 trends and challenges, *Hotels* **26**(4), 3–6

Meldelsohn, M 1970 *The guide to franchising*, 1st edn, Pergamon Press, Oxford

Meldelsohn M 1979 *The guide to franchising*, 2nd edn, Pergamon Press, Oxford

Meldelsohn M 1982 *The guide to franchising*, 3rd edn, Pergamon Press, Oxford

Messenger, S Y and S M Lin 1991 International hotel advertising, *International Journal of Contemporary Hospitality Management* **3**(3), 28–32

Morgan, M S 1991 Travellers Choice: the effects of advertising and prior stay, *Cornell HRA Quarterly* **32**(4), 40–9

*Official Journal of the European Communities*, EEC Regulation 1984/83 on the Application of Article 85 (3) of the treaty to categories of exclusive purchasing agreements, No L173/5, June 1983

Olsen, M D 1993 International growth strategies of major US hotel companies, *EIU Travel & Tourism Analyst*, No 3

Orkin, E B 1990 Forecasting's new meaning in yield management, *Lodging* **15**(9), 39–40

Praster, M 1990 Franchisors fight for competitive edge, *Hotels* **24**(2), 46–8

Reliham, W J 1989 The yield management approach to hotel-room pricing, *Cornell HRA Quarterly* **30**(1), 40–5

Reid, R D and M Sandler 1992 The use of technology to improve service quality, *Cornell HRA Quarterly* **33**(3), 68–73

Ritchie, J R 1994 *Travel tourism and hospitality research: a handbook for managers and researchers*, John Wiley & Son, New York

Rounce, J 1987 International hotel product branding: segmenting the market place, *Travel Tourism Analyst*, February, 13–2

Rowe, M 1990 Surviving the franchisor swap meet, *Lodging Hospitality* **46**(2), 36–8, 40

Rowe, M 1992 Holiday Inn: fat and sassy to lean and mean, *Lodging Hospitality* **48**(7), 24–6

Sasser, N E and R L Banks 1976 Lender attitudes towards hotel financing, *Cornell HRA Quarterly*, February, 29–33

Scoviak, M 1987 Interstate's skilled management, *Hotels and Restaurants International* **21**(2), 47–52

Scoviak, M 1988 Low-risk, high-profit franchises offer global growth opportunities, *Hotels and Restaurants International*, February, 38–47

Seltz, D D 1982 *The complete handbook of franchising*, Addison-Wesley, Reading, MA

Slattery, P 1991 Hotel branding in the 1990s, *Travel & Tourism Analyst* **1**, 23–5

Spiselman, A 1991 Luxury by association: a look at top consortia, *Hotels* **25**(3), 58–60

Stevenson, G 1992 CRS: No reservations about it, *Lodging* **17**(11), 16, 19–20

Tarrant, C 1989 UK hotel industry – market restructuring and the need to respond to customer demands, *Tourism Management* **10**(3), 187–91

Vaughn, Ch L 1979 *Franchising*, Lexington Books, Canada

Wagner, G and M Rowe 1992 Technology for all seasons, *Lodging Hospitality* **48**(6), 26–36

Watkins, E 1990 Technology at your service, *Lodging Hospitality* **46**(3), 66–8, 70

Weinstein, J 1988 Spreading in franchising in the USA, *Restaurants International* **98**(18), 207–8

Wolchuck, S 1992 How Choice uses franchising to grow worldwide, *Hotels* **26**(4), 52–4

Yoakum, J R 1992 How CRS can fill your rooms, *Lodging* **17**(7), 16, 19–20

# CHAPTER 9

# The link between industry structure, independent hotels and consortia

OBJECTIVES

After reading this chapter you should be able to:
- Relate Porter's analysis of industry structure to the hospitality industry.
- Understand the size and importance of the independent hotel sector.
- Understand the nature and types of consortia and how they can assist the independent hotel in competing.

## INDUSTRY STRUCTURE: THE ISSUE OF FRAGMENTATION

The hospitality industry can best be described as fragmented. Over the past several decades the total number of individual units in both the hotel and restaurant segments has increased substantially. The relatively low entry cost into this industry, compared with that of manufacturing, has contributed to this fragmentation by giving many the opportunity to own and operate their own enterprise. This fragmentation is also present because, as a service, the hospitality enterprise must be convenient to the customer when the customer wants it. Consequently, hospitality services must be widely dispersed throughout the marketplace. Unlike concentrated manufacturing operations, which can stock goods for long periods of time and ship them to the customer over great distances, hospitality businesses must be where the customer is. Not only must they be where the customer is, they must also meet the many diverse needs of an increasingly demanding buyer. Thus, for example, one hotel in a specific geographic location may not be able to meet the needs of both the business traveller and the leisure traveller. Likewise, it will be impossible to meet every potential customer's expectations with just one restaurant: thus the fragmented structure of the industry is the consequence of providing services to a customer when and where he or she wants them.

## HOSPITALITY INDUSTRY STRUCTURE: AN ANALYSIS

Prior to the 1950s the industry was dominated by independents carving out their niche in an owner-operated business. It was during the 1950s that a fundamental shift in industry structure began to occur in this stronghold of individualism, with multi-unit operators emerging as a major force on the hospitality scene. In many cases the multi-unit operator was someone who had evolved from independent single-unit operation, having decided to expand from one unit to several. In other instances the multi-unit operation resulted from mergers and acquisitions by large corporations seeking growth in the hospitality industry.

This change in the industry structure has prompted the need for a change in the way these organizations are managed. The skills associated with managing a single unit are not applicable to the demands of overseeing several. The ability to guide the success of several units demands a commitment to strategic thinking upon the part of management. While the industry sructure is shifting to the control of the major public limited companies, independent privately owned firms still dominate the market.

The structure of the industry within which the hospitality unit competes is a key factor in influencing the firm's overall success and survival. The profitability of the industry and therefore that of the firm is based upon the strength of the **five competitive forces** that make up the structure of an industry: existing competitors, potential competitors, suppliers, buyers and substitutes. As profitability is based upon the collective strength of these competitive forces, not all industries or industry segments have the same profit potential.

Analysis of these forces must be of a long-term strategic nature, as the structure is not likely to change appreciably in the short term. In analysing an industry, effects such as economic upturns and downturns, or material shortages, should not be considered if they are short term, and unlikely to alter the structure of the industry. A strategic manager, when conducting an industry analysis, has to distinguish short-term anomalies from long-term structural realities.

To begin any analysis of industry structure it is important to define what we mean by the term **industry**. For the purposes of analysis Porter's definition is appropriate: a group of firms producing products that are close substitutes for each other. Clearly, the hospitality industry encompasses many firms providing a variety of goods and services that may be substituted for each other, depending on the forces driving the consumer's decision. As the hospitality industry is so diverse, the strengths of the various competitive forces vary depending on the industry segment in which a business unit competes. For example, firms that compete only in the budget hotel sector face different strategic issues and profitability potential from multi-concept hotel firms, which compete in numerous sectors. However, while the segments differ in terms of strategic issues they are still driven by the same five competitive forces.

In most industries competition tends to drive down profitability because of structural problems such as overcapacity. As competition intensifies and firms continue to return lower than acceptable returns, they will eventually go out of business as sources of finance dry up. A brief discussion of these five competitive forces and their influence upon firms in the hospitality industry will assist in assessing their importance.

## Existing competitors

In industries that are growing and possess greater demand than capacity, there is usually less intense competition between firms, which are able to sell all of their products. However, most segments in the hospitality industry are experiencing increased competition due to chronic overcapacity. It is becoming increasingly difficult for most firms in the industry to enjoy the returns required by institutional investors, because there are more hotel rooms and restaurant seats than there is a demand for them. This overcapacity forces the firms to lower prices or increase services in order to attract customers, thereby reducing their return on investment. In competitive terms, the advantage is with the largest firms, as they have a much broader base to distribute costs in order to sustain profitability and increase market share, even in periods of slow growth. For instance, the top 100 restaurant chains have increased their share of the market to slightly over 50 per cent: the top three – McDonald's, Pepsico and Burger King – control over one-third of the chain market, all at the expense of smaller competitors. As the food service companies compete for larger pieces of a slowly growing pie, they face increasingly intense rivalry. Discounting – once unheard of in the industry – is now a fact of life affecting even the largest competitor, McDonald's. Another problem brought on by intense industry competition is exit barriers, which have forced marginally profitable firms to remain in the industry because there is no market for used assets which, while not as valuable as the land on which they reside, still constitute a significant investment. Therefore firms accept less than planned growth rather than bear the large losses of company disinvestment.

## Threat of entry of new competitors

While the hospitality industry is not in a growth stage, except for certain segments such as budget hotels and contract catering, it is still an attractive industry for potential competitors compared to other industries. Entry barriers are relatively low, unless one is attempting to build a national chain rapidly to compete against the large established chains. The cash flow aspects of the industry are unique, in that there are few or no credit sales, with the accompanying problems of managing accounts receivable. It is basically a cash-orientated industry. The competitive problem with new entrants into the industry is that unless they purchase existing companies they create new capacity in an industry already suffering from overcapacity. The purchase of Holiday Inns by Bass plc, for instance, simply transferred ownership of an existing firm to another competitor. While the tactic of the new owners may lead to a greater market share, they will not alter the structure of the industry by increasing capacity. Porter cites eight **barriers to entry** that may deter firms from either changing segments or from entering the industry altogether. These barriers may deter a conglomerate from entering the industry as well as deterring a seafood restaurant chain from revamping and becoming, say, a Mexican restaurant chain. Porter's eight barriers to entry are as follows.

Economies of scale

These force a competitor to compete on a large scale immediately, or enter on a small scale and accept price/cost disadvantages. The quick-service restaurant segment is a good example. Firms desiring to compete against the big three – McDonald's, Pepsico and Burger King – must attempt to overcome their enormous marketing advantage by bearing extremely high marketing costs per unit in an effort to wrest market share away from the big three.

Proprietary product differences

In the hospitality industry this is not a significant factor, as imitation of successful product concepts is a fact of life. Hotel chains, for example, have found very little brand loyalty, even with their frequent guest programmes. Because of their high cost and limited success, the move lately has been away from these programmes, which attempt to differentiate service and product.

Brand identity

The nature of service industries means that brand identity is important, as the majority of consumers are risk averse, particularly when there is increasing importance placed on a successful meal experience. For example, research indicates that consumers are motivated to try new restaurants for a limited number of reasons: personal recommendation of friends, good newspaper reviews, advertised specials or boredom with their regular restaurants. New competitors are therefore forced to overcome this natural reluctance on the part of restaurant patrons to visit new concepts without some outside stimulus.

Switching costs

In terms of risk, buyers bear switching costs each time they try a new restaurant or hotel. They are not guaranteed a successful, pleasant encounter, and can be described as mostly risk averse.

Capital requirements

Most major corporations and investor groups possess sufficient capital to enter the hospitality industry. However, given the industry's poor performance over the last few years, fewer firms seem to be attracted to purchasing assets – even depressed assets. The latest entrants are mainly firms from countries such as Japan, which enjoy a currency advantage.

Access to distribution channels
The new entrant needs to secure distribution for its product. A prime distribution channel in the hospitality industry is location. Inability to procure satisfactory locations, owing to their acquisition by competitors or their high cost, is a very real barrier to entry, and may force firms to acquire existing companies in order to obtain favourable locations.

Government policy
Various governmental bodies possess the wherewithal to erect entry barriers through licensing requirements, legal action or procedural processes. Business licences and liquor licences are examples of potential barriers. These can be insurmountable at times, particularly in the case of liquor sales. As firms begin to compete internationally they will confront ever more constraints imposed by host governments.

Expected retaliation
In industries where competition is intense, as in the hospitality industry, new entrants are greeted with strong retaliation by established firms. This propensity to attack not only forces new entrants to bear heavy marketing costs for advertising and promotion, but also eliminates any 'honeymoon period' when the new competitor opens for business .

The barriers to entry to the hospitality industry are not unique, but they require potential competitors to possess a comprehensive knowledge of the industry segment in which they desire to compete. Even existing hospitality firms face these barriers when they attempt to change segments within the industry. Success in one segment is not always easily transferable to another segment.

## Bargaining power of suppliers

In the hospitality industry, smaller companies are in less powerful positions than the firms that supply them their raw materials. Price quotes and credit terms are based primarily upon volume and history of success: a fact that favours the large chains over the smaller chains and independent operators. National and regional firms, with their large volume buying, are able to reduce the bargaining power of the large suppliers.

However, suppliers of raw materials are only one of the three major suppliers to the industry. The other two are capital markets and labour markets. Recently, the hospitality industry has not fared well in both these market areas. Ironically, as profitability is adversely affected by pressures from raw material suppliers and labour markets, as well as by consumer resistance to price increases, the hospitality firm's ability to attract new sources of capital is impaired. The increased cost of capital may raise financial risk to the point where continued operations are threatened.

## Bargaining power of buyers

Buyers attempt to force down prices and receive more service by playing one competitor off against another. A good example is the number of business travellers who possess frequent guest privileges for numerous hotel chains and choose where they will stay based upon incentives currently being offered. While most individual buyers have limited bargaining power, there is a new type of powerful buyer emerging in the industry: the mega travel agencies. These firms are able to bargain with hotel industry firms because of the large volumes of business they book annually. They are growing in importance as more and more corporations look to travel agencies to lower their travel costs, and so they are becoming more powerful than the provider in terms of such things as rates and capacity. Hotel firms, in particular, should choose their partners carefully, in order not to surrender long-term competitive advantage for short-term profitability.

## Threat of substitutes

Firms in the hospitality industry face a variety of substitutes, which vary according to the industry segment in which they compete. Restaurant firms in particular are faced by numerous substitutes. By far the largest substitute for eating in a restaurant is preparation in the home. Strong competition also comes from convenience stores and supermarket delicatessens. The recent surge in the popularity of frozen gourmet dinners has been partly fuelled by the advance of technology, in both the manufacture of the product and the introduction of microwave ovens. The consumer can now prepare and eat types of food that previously could not have been prepared at home.

In the hotel industry, substitution is not as prevalent. For the business segment, increasing room rates may make day trips and teleconferencing more appealing. In the destination resort markets, cruise ships seem to be catching a larger share of the market. With the advancing technology of high-speed mass transportation, business hotels may find themselves faced with declining occupancy as business travellers resort to high-speed short-duration trips in an effort to decrease corporate travel expenses.

The strength and importance of these five competitive forces vary, but they exert significant pressures on the hospitality industry. They comprise the strategic structure of the industry and are not easily changed by individual firms. Therefore, before entering the industry or changing segments, managers must conduct a thorough analysis to determine whether the existing structure is compatible with the firm's strength and weaknesses.

# THE HOSPITALITY INDUSTRY: A STATISTICAL ANALYSIS

Most firms in the hospitality industry are small independent units; it is important that these firms consider their strategic response.

International trends in tourism over the past 40 years have shown an average growth in tourist arrivals of just over 7 per cent. Average growth rate in the Asia and Pacific region over the past ten years has been higher than the world average.

Europe can be considered the axis of world travel, with an average growth rate of 3.7 per cent over the past 10 years. It is by far the largest area in terms of tourist arrivals and tourism receipts. In the last decade it accounted for 60–65 per cent of tourist arrivals and 50–55 per cent of receipts. The relevance of such statistics is that these trends are mirrored within the hospitality industry.

## Worldwide hotel industry

Room supply
In 1993 the worldwide hotel room supply stood at 9.2 million rooms. Over the last 20 years the room supply has grown at an average of 3.5 per cent per year. An examination of product growth by region shows that room supply has decreased in Europe from 49 per cent in 1970 to 39 per cent in 1990. Asia, on the other hand, has increased its room supply from 5 per cent of the total to 15 per cent in 1990. North America's share has remained unchanged at 35 per cent. These figures illustrate the dominance of Europe and significant growth in Asia.

Market structure
The market structure for upper and mid-level hotels shows that North America is dominated by chain hotels, both foreign and domestic. In contrast, Europe is highly fragmented: independent hotels dominate the market with a figure of 70 per cent, while domestic chains constitute 19 per cent and foreign chains 11 per cent. In Asia and the Pacific, independent hotels account for 66 per cent, and foreign chains for 20 per cent. Africa and the Middle East have 53 per cent of independents, and only a small fragment (11 per cent) of domestic chains. The contrast between the Americas and Europe is even more marked in a country such as Italy, where approximately 90 per cent of hotels are in independent ownership.

Regional estimates of the market structure for lower-level hotels are not generally available, but with the exception of North America, this market is dominated by independents. In North America, budget chains have been successful for many years, although in terms of occupancy they have been on a steady decline since 1980. In the UK, budget chains (lodges) became established in the latter half of the 1980s. A further expansion of lower-market chains is expected throughout many European countries and other countries with mature markets during the 1990s. In most places where lower-market chains have been established, performance in terms of room occupancy greatly exceeds the average.

Market segments The two main market segments for most hotels are business and leisure. The average worldwide distribution between business and leisure guests is currently 60/40 per cent. However, this is not representative of all hotel types. For example, in lower-market US chains the leisure sector dominates the market, with more than 68 per cent, while in France and the UK the business sector dominates the market, with between 70 and 80 per cent of market share.

## European Union

Room supply The top three EU countries in hotel room supply are Italy, Germany and Spain, which between them have 61 per cent of total EU hotel rooms and 60 per cent of total hotels. Several key characteristics distinguish the European hotel industry:

- It is highly fragmented and dominated by independents.
- The UK is the most chain orientated. This orientation is evident at both lower and mid/upper level markets.
- The penetration by US-based hotel chains is minimal.

The domination of independent hotels in the mid and upper market is particularly evident in Austria (95 per cent), Italy (92 per cent), Switzerland (89 per cent), Spain (65 per cent), Benelux (64 per cent), Germany (60 per cent), and France (54 per cent). In contrast, Scandinavia, Eastern Europe and the UK are dominated by chains (66 per cent, 60 per cent and 56 per cent respectively).

Market segments and economic factors European countries in general are dominated by hotel guests from outside the host country: 53.4 per cent in 1991. However, when analysed by individual countries, Germany, the UK, Italy and France are dominated by domestic guests, while the remaining countries are dominated by foreign guests. For the lower markets, domestic guests dominate the market in absolute terms. These observations suggest that the hotel industry in these four countries is highly dependent on their domestic economies.

While the performance of the European hotel industry in 1991 was dominated by the impact of the Gulf War, 1992's results were dominated by the condition of both national and global economies, with an upturn seen in 1993–94. The European hotel industry is influenced by the economies of the major European countries, along with other major world economies such as Japan and the USA.

## Major EU countries

France

At the end of 1992, quoted hotel companies in France operated with 1,340 hotels and 115,928 rooms. More hotel rooms were added in France during this period (within the major hotel companies) than in all the other continental countries and the UK together. Most of the expansion came from the French companies Accor and Louvre, which jointly added 10,295 rooms, and accounted for 97.8 per cent of the total net additions to room stock in the country. In contrast to these indigenous firms, foreign chains added no new rooms to their total in net terms in France. The share of room stock owned/operated by publicly quoted companies in the French hotel market in 1992 was 22.3 per cent, up from 20.4 per cent in 1991.

In terms of publicly quoted companies, France is characterized by 57.5 per cent of rooms at the low level of the market: this is the highest proportion of any European country. These rooms are mainly in the budget chains of the domestic companies, such as Accor with Ibis, Urbis, Arcade and Formula 1, and Louvre with Campanile and Première Classe.

Foreign firms, on the other hand, are located at the medium and higher levels of the market. France is also characterized by a high proportion of limited-service and rooms-only hotels. These two segments of the market count for 58.6 per cent of the rooms and are dominated by the domestic chains. The French chains concentrate on achieving high room volumes in their limited-service hotels and, with few non-room facilities, are able to maintain high margins.

Germany

Although hotel chains in Germany aim for primary locations, the hotel market is still largely fragmented, owing to the dominance of the small family-run hotel within the hotel market. The *hotel garni*, serving breakfast only, also features strongly within the German hotel industry.

The first hotel groups to move into Germany did so in the early 1960s. These were chains such as Inter-Continental, Hilton and Sheraton. Domestic chains, such as Steigenberger AG and Maritim, were either non-existent at this time or very limited in their operations. The focus of these international hotel groups was to develop city centre locations targeted at a high market level and mostly operated under management contracts. The chains who followed them were Ramada, Novotel and Holiday Inn, and as a result the boom in hotel construction was from 1963 to 1973. However, it was not until the mid 1970s that German hotel firms had a major impact on the market. At present there is a combination of German and international groups operating within the country.

At the end of 1992, publicly quoted companies in Germany operated 202 hotels, with all but a handful of the hotels in the former West Germany. Germany is distinct from other major Western economies such as the USA, UK and France, because its sole quoted hotel company – Kempinski – has only a minor presence in its domestic hotel market. Over half the hotel rooms in Germany are in major city locations: a high figure for a developed economy. The relatively low exposure to other locations is dominated by Accor, with 67 hotels, and Queens Moat Houses, with 29 hotels. Unlike the UK and France, there is no single dominant city in Germany, which produces a wider geographic spread for foreign firms, international brands and foreign demand. The very high proportion of rooms at the high and medium levels of the market is consistent with the extensive exposure to major city locations, and is indicative of an emphasis on the business market. Most of the exposure at the lower levels of the market is from Accor, which has 50 (Ibis 23, Arcade 17, Urbis 6 and Formula 1, 4).

The high emphasis on full-service hotels is consistent with the paramount importance of the business market to the German hotel industry. It is also consistent with the locational spread and the market level profile. Derived from these features is the high average size of hotels, which at 184 rooms is more than double the average size in the UK and France. The profile of the German hotel industry means that potentially they can attract stronger room occupancies, higher achieved room rates and higher margins than quoted companies in the UK. German hotel facilities are mainly directed at the business traveller, and an increasingly important sector of the industry lies in conferences. Following this, the German hotel product has changed over the years to reflect this significant sector of the market. Most of the hotels built recently have a special emphasis on this sector.

In 1992 there were in Germany 52 hotel associations with 518 hotels and about 88,044 rooms, apartments and suites.

The major cities in West Germany – Berlin, Dusseldorf, Frankfurt, Hamburg and Munich – account for 51.9 per cent of the quoted room stock. The occupancy rates in the country are relatively low, as the figures reflect an average for different kind of hotels, including garni hotels, which dominate the market.

Germany has an unusually high concentration for a developed country of rooms in primary locations. Frankfurt, which is the main financial marketplace and has several trade fairs, is the biggest supplier of quoted room stock, followed by the Bavarian capital Munich. Munich always had a high percentage of international business owing to its history, its trade fairs, and several functions such as the 'Oktober-Fest'.

Germany's hotel market does not concentrate mainly on one destination like the UK, but on several cities. Over half the supplied hotel rooms are in the primary cities. Only recently have secondary and tertiary destinations been developed by hotel firms as feasible locations. Accor, Queens Moat Houses and the newly formed brands of Steigenberger AG – Maxx, Avance and Esprix – are dominating these markets.

In 1992, overnight stays reached the figure of 266.7 million in the former West Germany, an increase of 0.2 per cent over 1991. This figure is based on hotels with nine beds or more, excluding camping facilities.

Since 1990 there has been a decrease in the number of overnight stays by foreigners. In 1992 there was a reduction by 1.4 per cent to 26.9 million. This is partly offset by an increase of 5.5 per cent in domestic overnight stays. Foreign visitors to Germany are mainly from the EU countries and the USA.

Spain

In Spain, 1992 was a year of consolidation for quoted hotel companies, following the large increases in hotel supply in time for the Olympic Games and Expo. At the end of 1992 publicly quoted hotel companies operating in Spain accounted for 80 hotels, with 12,503 rooms. Most expansion in that year came from the domestic group Cofir, which added four more hotels. The overall split between primary and other locations is 46 per cent of rooms in primary cities. Spain has increased the proportion of rooms at the mid-market level from 47 per cent to 54.8 per cent, and these have all been secondary location additions. Spain, like Italy, has no budget hotels in the portfolios of quoted companies.

Italy

At the end of 1992 the major hotel companies in Italy operated 115 hotels and 19,522 rooms. Italy showed the second largest growth of any European country during this period.

From 1987 onwards the hotel sector as a whole lost numerous businesses, decreasing from 38,114 at the beginning of 1988 to 36,166 in 1991. However, rooms over the period 1989–91 rose from 922,084 to 938,141, suggesting growth in the average number of rooms per hotel. The decline in foreign demand in the years 1989 and 1990 represents an important phase in the country, transforming it away from a traditionally receiving country for tourism. In the three-year period 1989–91, demand for accommodation by Italians amounted to 66 per cent of total demand. In terms of growth in this demand category, if 1985 is allocated the base index of 100, the 1991 index was 122, which gives an indication of trends in demand over this period.

There are four regions that absorb about half of the internal demand: Veneto (13 per cent), Trentino-Alto Adige (11.9 per cent), Emilia-Romagna (11.6 per cent), and Tuscany (12.4 per cent). The whole of southern Italy in 1991 accounted for 18.8 per cent.

In the period 1989–91, accommodation demand in Italy by foreigners reduced significantly in terms of both average length of stay and a reduction in arrivals. Demand for accommodation in the coastal zones of Italy fell during the period, while demand in the main towns and cities grew. The latter geographical area accounted for 28.6 per cent of total foreign flow in 1988, 30.6 per cent in 1989 and 31.8 per cent in 1990.

In terms of country of origin, the greatest demand for hotel accommodation comes from the EU, at 61.7 per cent of the total, with 36.2 per cent from Germany, 7.8 per cent from the UK, and 7.6 per cent from France. Demand for accommodation reaches a peak in the summer months, and is at its lowest in January.

Concentration of the major companies is minimal; it has now risen to 6.5 per cent, but most hotels are still independent resort hotels owned by families. More than 4 per cent of bedrooms in Italy are in the major city locations, but the trend is for further expansion in other locations.

**United Kingdom** In 1991 the UK had a supply of approximately 507,000 hotel rooms. Of these, 23.5 per cent or 119,000 rooms were in public limited companies (plc). Over the last few years the UK plc hotels have seen a growth in concentration. The largest ten companies in the UK have increased their room supply from 64,081 rooms in 1986 to 89,382 in 1991, constituting approximately 76 per cent of the total plc hotel rooms and 18 per cent of total UK hotel rooms. The biggest companies are expanding fast, at the expense of smaller companies and independents.

UK hotels are concentrated in England (75 per cent), followed by Scotland (16 per cent), Wales (8.5 per cent) and Northern Ireland (8.5 per cent).

The UK hotel industry is dominated by small hotels. In England in 1994 86 per cent of all hotels had less than 26 rooms and only 2.2 per cent had more than 100 rooms. The equivalent figures for Scotland are 85 per cent and 2.4 per cent. Wales has 89 per cent of its hotels in the 1–30 rooms category; only 1.2 per cent have more than 100 rooms.

One way to analyse the structure of the UK hotel industry is through the various classification schemes in existence. Hotels in the two-star category account for 38 per cent of the total and three-star for 44 per cent (AA classification). Only 0.6 per cent of hotels are in the five-star category, and 3.3 per cent are classified as lodges, which are a form of motel-style accommodation.

Of the non-bed and breakfast hotels (more than eleven rooms), it is possible to identify a number of product categories: 37.5 per cent of the total are seaside hotels, 32 per cent older city hotels, 20 per cent are country house hotels and 4.5 per cent are London hotels .

The UK hotel industry is highly dependent on the domestic market. In 1991, 60 per cent of guests in UK hotels originated from within the UK, followed by North Americans (15.5 per cent), continental Europeans (13 per cent), and Japanese (4.1 per cent). An absolute majority (61 per cent) of hotel guests in UK hotels are business travellers, and only 19 per cent of them are holiday tourists.

# HOTEL CONSORTIA

In analysing the structure of the hotel industry in a number of European countries, we have shown that the traditional pattern of the industry is made up of individually owned hotels. This has been changing in recent years: the pattern has come to resemble more closely that of other industries, with a small number of firms increasing their share of the market, the remainder being shared by a large number of smaller firms, most of them operating single hotels. The independently owned hotel may still be the typical firm in the industry but its continued existence has been increasingly associated with hotel consortia. This section examines the nature of hotel consortia and their benefits for members, including their types and activities. The relationship between hotel consortia, their members and industry structure will be analysed.

The varied nature of hotel provision within the industry has already been extensively documented in this chapter. The term 'industry' can be misleading, suggesting as it does some standard type of hotel; this could militate against a proper understanding of a group of businesses that are often characterized by their diversity – licensed hotel, luxury hotel, country house hotel, motel and so on. The concept of **heterogeneity** is an essential one when examining the provision of hotel facilities, particularly in the European hotel industry. This stems from the low level of ownership concentration amongst hotels, which stresses the heterogeneity of the industry. For instance, by using figures contained in industry data it can be calculated that the hotel units controlled by the 30 largest companies in the UK account for only 5 per cent of the total industry.

This emphasizes the complexity of the hotel industry, which seems to be one of the industry's strengths, in that hotels can alter their form of services in line with expectations of market trends. Not only do hotels have the opportunity to alter the way in which they meet customer demands, but the structure of the industry can allow this to happen. The combination of these two factors, together with other environmental variables such as location, supports the view that the industry is heterogeneous, and its forms of provision will obviously adapt and change over time. There are several forms of hotel ownership, of which the development of group organizations is the most notable.

## Group organizations

While group organizations can grow by conventional corporate expansion, or by the innovative methods of franchising, another method of establishing them is through the development of consortia. Hotel operations in the EU face a severe competitive environment; the smaller independent hotel is likely to have a limited future, or must at best be prepared to face lower financial returns than at present. One of the biggest problems that small independent hotels have is competition from large hotel chains such as Hilton and Hyatt. The only way that smaller operations can compete against the chains' more sophisticated marketing techniques is by joining a consortium. Hotel consortia can create a group image in the market, which may extend to a common name, facilities and standards, and joint promotion. Figures from Huddersfield University's Hotel and Catering Research Centre in the UK show that between 1988 and 1992 the number of independent hotels and rooms in consortia both grew by 26 per cent, to 1,215 and 32,843 respectively.

## Definition

Consortia are not limited to the hospitality industry: there are consortia of solicitors, accountants, builders and so on. The term **consortium** can be defined as a number of bodies that come together for a common purpose. Relating this to the hospitality industry, several definitions of a hotel consortium have been given. One such is that it is an organization of hotels, usually but not necessarily owned autonomously, which combine resources in order to establish joint purchasing and trading arrangements and operate marketing services. These aims will often be achieved by setting up a centralized office, whose activities will be financed through a levy subscription on the number of hotel units.

Some authors define a hotel consortium as a number of independently owned units that voluntarily affiliate, seeking benefits from access to significantly greater resources than would be possible on their own.

A further definition is that a hotel consortium is an organization of hotels that combine their resources to establish corporate management services, such as purchasing, personnel and training, marketing and public relations.

Looking at another definition, which is concerned with standards of service, a hotel consortium can be defined as a collection of hotels with similar standards and voluntary membership, paying a fee for marketing and sales service run exclusively for the benefit of the consortium.

These definitions have similar meanings: independent hotels with the same purpose join their resources together and share the benefits. This reflects the original concept of the consortium: a kind of mutual self-help organization. The concept is particularly attractive to independent hotels, as they can take advantage of the economies of scale created by such organizations. In addition, they gain access to specialist corporate expertise, which is not available within their own hotels.

## Consortium types and activities

Types

As hotel consortia have grown rapidly, it has become increasingly difficult to distinguish between the main types of consortium. Several consortia have changed their form and have begun to offer much wider services to their members. This complexity has been affected by three significant factors:

- A single hotel may belong to more than one consortium, although most consortia now try to restrict this as part of their membership agreements.
- Several chain hotels, either separately or collectively, have membership of consortia, even though consortia were originally created to serve independent hotels.
- The business formats of consortia have become complex in the development of various types of management contract, franchise and joint venture.

Activities

Consortium activities are dependent upon the type of consortium. Nevertheless, most consortium activities seem to be undertaken to increase revenue for their members. This is true of all the consortia involved in marketing and its associated functions. Also, the marketing activity of consortia mirrors the marketing activity of chains in the respect of promotion and distribution channels.

- **Promotion.** Typically, consortia engage in the full range of promotional activities, especially through the establishment of brand names and image, plus logos, print media and other forms of communication.
- **Distribution channels.** Consortia manage distribution channels to encourage hotel sales through travel agencies, tour operators and tourist boards. The main function of a hotel consortium is often to establish and operate a central reservations system.
- **Product and price.** These are two elements of the consortium's activities that it cannot manage in the same way as chains. Consortia usually make an asset out of the individuality of their member hotels, but as these are independently owned and operated, there is little control over product and price. Such control is exercised through the criteria established for membership, which vary from consortium to consortium.

Clearly, the principal activity of hotel consortia is marketing, to increase the revenue of member hotels. It is also possible to conceive of consortia involving themselves in activities such as accounting and financial management, which have hitherto been outside their scope. Strictly, there is no impediment to a hotel consortium's being established to manage any of the corporate functions of hotels, or indeed any combination of corporate functions.

## HOTEL CONSORTIA AND THEIR MEMBERS

Most hotel consortia in the UK do not invite or persuade any hotels to apply for membership. Applicants have to apply themselves in writing to the consortium. All consortia employ similar procedures for membership application, which consist of four basic stages:

1 A formal application letter must be sent to the consortium. Each applicant will receive an application form for completion. This requests details of the hotel's facilities, ownership, management, hotel gradings, achievements and awards currently received.
2 Application forms are received by the board of the consortium, and an inspection time frame is set.
3 Successful applicants receive confirmation of acceptance and a contract, together with invoices for the initial first-year membership and annual marketing fees.
4 The hotel's signed contract is returned with payment for services to commence in the coming year.

One interesting issue of joining a consortium is the inspection process that relates to the standard of quality control within the consortium. This is dealt with later in this chapter.

### Relationships

The relationship between a hotel consortium and its member hotels is an important area. Three main features can be identified:

- the degree of formality;
- multiple ownership;
- corporate members.

**Degree of formality**

Hotel consortia differ in their formality. Many of the smaller consortia are member controlled: they agree on their collective behaviour and are overseen by a committee of elected members. These consortia present the loosest connection between members, and the least formal tie. In contrast, many of the larger consortia are limited companies and thus more formal businesses. These differences in formality will affect factors such as objectives, and the influence that members can exert on the consortium (and vice versa). They also mean that hotel consortia cannot be thought of as a single kind of organization. There is not the homogeneity of operation among consortia that exists, for instance, with management contracting and franchising.

Multiple
membership

The relationship between hotel consortia and their members is further complicated by hotels that hold membership of more than one consortium. A more comprehensive corporate development has been achieved by several independent hotels through their membership of different types of consortium. This strategy of multiple membership extends the corporate advantage to a wide range of functions, and can allow independent hotels to behave in terms of marketing, purchasing, personnel and training as if they are a hotel chain.

Corporate
members

The original appeal of hotel consortia to customers was that they comprise independently owned and managed hotels. Some consortia, however, comprise both hotels that are independently owned and managed and hotels that are owned and managed by another hotel chain. Preferred Hotels is an example of a consortium that admits only independent hotels to membership. Others, such as Best Western and Consort Hotels, admit both independent and chain hotels. The growth of corporate members in a consortium allows them to gain the benefits of membership and retain their competitive edge over independent hotels, as they have highly supportive marketing departments within their own companies. It is in an effort to reduce this gap that a growing number of independent hotels have taken membership of more than one marketing consortium.

These three features of the relationship between hotel consortia and their members are crucial to consortium operation, particularly the degree of formality, which can affect the objectives of a hotel consortium. This will also have some influence on quality control mechanisms.

## Benefits and costs

Before an independent hotel decides to join a consortium, the costs have to be weighed against the benefits; member hotels have many very different reasons for joining consortia. Nevertheless, the common denominator is that each hotel is looking for extra business to be generated, normally from markets to which the hotel would not have access. The benefits that consortia offer to member hotels are different from hotel to hotel and from consortium to consortium, but most hotels join for three basic reasons:

- to increase bookings;
- to improve purchasing;
- to get together with like-minded hoteliers.

The membership literature of six leading hotel consortia in the UK – Best Western, Consort Hotels, Minotels, Guest Accom, Small Luxury Hotels of the World, and Pride of Britain – shows that they offer many common benefits, even though the details and emphasis vary slightly:

- a full-time professional marketing unit, which researches and follows up the type of business most appropriate to members;
- participation in various marketing schemes, such as Go as you Please, motoring programmes, promotions to the business and conference trade, coach tour operators and travel agencies;
- a central reservations service;
- appearance in the consortium's guide and traveller's handbooks;
- discounts on a wide range of commodities and services through central purchasing;
- referral business from the consortium's hotels in the UK, Europe or even further afield;
- press exposure via PR activities organized by the consortium;
- professional advice on all aspects of marketing member hotels;
- The retention of member hotels' independence.

Obviously all consortia offer their member hotels the opportunity to compete effectively with the hotel chains, and two of the most significant benefits of membership seem to be marketing and purchasing discount schemes. The value of the benefits offered to members is reflected in the membership fee, which varies considerably from consortium to consortium. Some fee structures are complicated, and depend on the number of bedrooms; others are related to the length of membership. A consortium that charges more for membership tends to provide a wider range of benefits. For example, the Leading Hotels of the World consortium offers its members not just marketing and central reservations systems but huge purchasing discounts and a range of other facilities including individual and local promotions. Even though consortium membership fees seem to be a large amount of money, they seem to provide good value, with hotel members getting a substantial return on their investment. Most consortia try to maintain a high level of membership fee, as they are careful to maintain their image and quality standards.

## INTERNATIONAL HOTEL CONSORTIA

Just as there are national and international hotel chains, so there are national and international hotel consortia. The environmental pressures and internal needs that cause consortia to move from operating solely in one country to operating in the international arena are the same that drive chains to do so. Examples of this internationalization include the Australian consortium Flag International, which is planning to set up a group in Europe; the expansion of Minotels into North and South America; and the merger of Prestige with Small Luxury Hotels of the World. Although hotel consortia and chains have similar reasons for becoming international, the relative importance of these influences is different:

- International hotel consortia tend to comprise hotel properties that have a history of attracting an international clientele. Such hotels therefore need to belong to a consortium that will assist, promote and market them to the existing international client base.
- International hotel consortia enable independent hoteliers to promote themselves to customers who they previously may not have been able to reach individually.
- Consortia create a critical mass sufficiently large to support increasingly essential marketing tools, such as an international sales office and central reservations systems.
- Consortium membership enables independents to employ a brand image strategy to compete with the large chain operators
- There is a limit to the number of hotels that meet the membership criteria of each consortium, and if the organization is to grow it must move into the international marketplace.

## Features

A feature of consortia is the fiercely independent nature of many of the member hotels. It would be possible, for instance, for these owners to invite hotel management contractors to operate the properties on their behalf. Such a contract would give the hotel all the advantages of chain membership and relieve the owner of the actual management of the property. That owners do not choose this option, but prefer consortium membership, indicates their commitment to managing their own hotels.

All basic types of international consortium can be classified into four categories:

- **Full consortia.** These organizations provide not only marketing expertise and services but also assistance in human resources and purchasing.

- **Marketing consortia.** These provide marketing expertise. An example of this type of consortium is Small Luxury Hotels of the World.
- **Reservation systems.** These provide a central reservations system, usually based around a single freephone telephone number. Utell is an example of this catagory.
- **Referral consortia.** These are affiliations by hotels and their reservation systems. In this case it is often chains rather than independent hotels that affiliate with airlines, such as JAL World and Golden Tulip Worlwide Hotels.

As hotel consortia have grown internationally it has been increasingly difficult to distinguish between these four types. Utell, for instance, originated as a reservations system; during the mid 1980s it began to provide corporate marketing services to its members.

## Size and scale

The internationalization of consortia is becoming a major trend. Looking ahead means looking globally beyond national and regional boundaries, and voluntary chains or associations are doing this by seeking members in new geographic areas.

## Activities

Essentially, international consortia engage in marketing on behalf of their members. In many respects this marketing activity mirrors that of chains, but there are some significant differences in that the focus is on promotion and distribution. The similarities relate largely to the marketing activities of **promotion** and **place** (distribution channels): two of the four P's of the marketing mix.

Most consortia engage in the full range of promotional activities, including the definition of a brand image. The problem that confronts consortium directors is that because the organization is made up of independent hotels, the characteristics of the properties may vary quite widely. This is why many consortia establish a brand around a specific image rather than detailed product characteristics. They also promote as an advantage the fact that although their hotels belong to a brand, they offer individuality and uniqueness. Other promotional activity includes the development and delivery of advertising campaigns, the operation of sales offices, the production and distribution of brochures and other print material, and the management of sales conferences and visits.

## Functions

In addition to these very important **external marketing** activities, the main function of the international hotel consortium is often to set up and operate a central reservations system. Another feature of consortium management is the importance of **internal marketing**. Membership of the consortium needs to be marketed: existing members need to be satisfied that membership is of continuing value, and new members need to be attracted to the consortium, to allow further scale economies and growth. New members need to get the best out of membership while complying with the consortium's policies. Like hotel management contractors, consortia have to satisfy their clients that the service they provide is worthwhile. To demonstrate this they establish clear reporting systems, which enable members to identify the effectiveness of their membership. These can include monthly reservation reports, detailing a wide range of information such as telephone call volume, conversion rates, and costs per reservation, as well as regular sales reports.

## QUALITY CONTROL AND MEMBERSHIP CRITERIA

The issue of quality control within large and small consortia differs. These differences relate back to the criteria and standards for membership, and the relationship between the consortium, its members and new applicants.

### Large hotel consortia

In general, large hotel consortia monitor their quality first through their criteria for membership. They all have their own particular criteria, which they use to define themselves in the marketplace and to select the right applicants for membership. Independent hotels will know from the criteria of the various consortia which one is appropriate for their organization, and which they may be able to join. These strict membership criteria are the most significant factor in the quality assurance aspects of a large consortium. By establishing such criteria, consistency is achieved within the organization, and operational standard procedures should be regarded as a part of creating and maintaining a quality image.

To define standards, research is required. Market research on guests' needs and expectations is probably the most important factor in deciding the quality levels of large hotel consortia. Knowing what customers need and expect will allow a consortium's marketing to reach specific levels, products and customer groups. Once a consortium has determined its quality levels, it can translate them into definite product specifications in terms of standards for membership, which are important in maintaining quality and keeping member hotels in the system.

These standards are embodied in a standard checklist, used in the inspection process for new applicants and existing members. This usually covers tangible or material components, such as the layout, decor and design of rooms, facilities, equipment and materials to be used in the room. Strictly speaking, quality standards should be more concerned with the degree and level of services offered by individual hotels, but the tangible material components are easier to identify and control.

The criteria and quality standards for membership of large hotel consortia are usually established by boards consisting mainly of consortium executives, plus some elected members. To ensure that standards are maintained, large consortia check the performance of new applicants and existing members by means of standard inspection processes. Four types of inspector are employed:

- consortium inspectors;
- independent inspectors;
- representatives of other member hotels in the form of visiting guests;
- consultant companies.

These four forms of inspection are operated on different occasions, once for new applicants and then annually for existing members. The inspection is very detailed. One organization, for instance, assesses hotels on a 1,000-point scale: any member hotel is automatically placed on probation unless it achieves 800 points, and is required to undertake corrective action if it fails to achieve 850 points. New applicants are rejected if their scores are less than 850 points. Such inspections are very effective, and only eligible independent hotels are accepted as consortium members. Once accepted they also need to be aware of the quality of their operation at all times. Another aspect of this process is that differences exist between the inspection of new applicants and existing members by the consortium, probably because the consortium must ensure that new applicants are able to maintain quality standards and corporate identities.

Most large hotel consortia have only one standard checklist that they use on every inspection process, for new applicants, existing members, different grades of member and different types of member. Consortia with this approach are working to a minimum acceptable standard, which usually emphasizes the facilities of the hotels in question.

Large hotel consortia employ standard inspection procedures quite effectively. It is very important that the process is continuous and consistent. The large consortia's performance checks are based solely on the output of their members' hotels, and not on crucial processes within those hotels, such as staff performance. This may just be a function of size: the large number of hotels to be checked impose time and cost restraints on the inspection process.

Hotel consortia, by their very nature, are unable to correct or manage any properties of their member hotels. However, they can do two things to correct poor standards:

- apply strict selection procedures for new applicants; and

- put members that do not meet quality standards on probation before (if necessary) asking them to leave.

Of course, in a service operation, true quality control goes beyond such membership criteria to address the characteristics of human behaviour. While all large consortia would agree that staff training courses help to control quality standards, only a few put this into practice, offering on average two courses per hotel member per year. In general, consortium quality standards concentrate on the tangible areas of layout, decor and facilities, not staff performance.

## Small hotel consortia

We have implied that some of the large consortia are neglecting the issue of quality in its fullest sense, but at least they do all impose strict membership criteria. This is not so for all the small hotel consortia; yet membership criteria are essential tools for any consortium to define itself in terms of market position and corporate identity. A few small consortia perform market research in order to design quality levels and set quality standards based on customer needs and expectations; others establish their membership standards on the basis of what they themselves believe is the best. Unfortunately, good service has nothing to do with what the service provider believes it is: it has only to do with what the *customer* believes it is.

Why is research not being performed? There are several possible reasons. Perhaps consortium management are not aware of the need to do this; or perhaps they believe that their experiences and perceptions of customer quality standards are sufficient. Like the large consortia, small hotel consortia also check performance against quality standards. As for the large consortia, inspections are based on standard checklists, which are primarily concerned with tangible material components. However, small consortia normally perform the inspection process only once, before admitting new members. Existing members are inspected only if there are guest complaints, or after major alterations, and such inspections are often more informal. Hence the quality control procedures are not continuous; nor are they consistent. Small hotel consortia seem to be more concerned about the quality of new applicants than that of existing members. However, like large consortia, they can ensure that quality standards are maintained through their selection procedures for new applicants, and a probationary period for members that fail to meet the required standards.

Most small consortia operate a probationary period of up to a year; a few consortia allow their members until the end of their membership term to correct any mistakes. As well as providing these longer probationary periods, small consortia have more of a tendency to compromise with their members. This is very significant, because a degree of compromise might affect the quality management of hotel consortia, their corporate identity and their members, particularly for those that do not expel members until the end of their membership term.

Hence the degree of formality within a hotel consortium has an effect on the organization's quality control. Large consortia employ standard checklists, and use them to set minimum acceptable standards, accepting hotels that are above the minimum standard and rejecting those that are below. Is this approach appropriate? We can identify a number of advantages and disadvantages.

Advantages:
- Uniform standards are applied within the consortium.
- Minimum quality standards are assured.
- The checking system is easily applied and controlled.
- Customer perceptions and expectations can be accurately anticipated.
- Advertising and promotion can be targeted accordingly.

Disadvantages
- It may be difficult to apply a uniform system to different hotel types.
- It may create a confusing identity, if there is a wide range of grades within the same consortium.
- It may make it difficult to obtain maximum value from advertising and promotion spending, because of the range of grades within the consortium.

Both large and small consortia believe that a quality organization results from a collection of quality member hotels, but they develop this view from different perspectives. Large organizations believe that control from the consortium can influence the quality of the member hotels. Member hotels of small consortia believe in the direct approach: control from the consortium cannot influence quality. It seems that only the large hotel consortia fully recognize the importance of quality control, and tend to operate it on a formal basis.

## Trends

Just as other business formats are growing in complexity, so are consortia. In an increasingly sophisticated marketplace equally sophisticated marketing is needed to sustain occupancy and reach new customers. Individual properties have neither the expertise nor the level of investment required to develop reservation systems, national and promotional campaigns nor the other activities that a consortium can provide. A consortium offers the opportunity for independent hoteliers to join together to operate in the global marketplace.

**SUMMARY**

This chapter related Porter's analysis of industry structure to the hospitality industry, and highlighted the competitive pressures within the industry. One important element to consider is the size and structure of the hotel industry and, in taking this view, the importance of the independent hotel sector. Independent hotels have to compete with the major chains, and one option is for them to join a consortium. The chapter concluded with an analysis of the nature and types of consortium and how they can assist the independent hotel in competing with the major chains.

**FURTHER READING**

Accor 1993 *Accor plc Annual General Meeting*, 4 June, France

Barclays De Zoete Wedd 1993 *The hotel sector: focus on the UK*, Barclays De Zoete Wedd Research, London.

Barclays De Zoete Wedd 1993 *BZW conference: prospects for the UK hotel industry*, Barclays De Zoete Wedd, London.

Baum, C 1992 Consortia expand sales: reservation efforts, *Hotels*, July, 88–94

Best Western Special Issue 1990 *Hotel and Motel Management*, 24 September

Byrne, A 1993 International hotel consortia. In A Pizam and P Jones (eds) *The international hospitality industry*, London: Pitman, pp. 126–32

Gledhill, B 1993 QMH shock, *Caterer and Hotelkeeper*, 8 April, 9

Gordon, R 1993 Strategic alliances for Forte, *Caterer and Hotelkeeper*, 21 October, 23

Horwath Consulting 1992a *United Kingdom hotel industry 1992*, London: Horwath Consulting

Horwath Consulting 1992b *European hotel industry 1992*, London: Horwath Consulting

Horwath International 1992 *Worldwide hotel industry 1992*, New York: Horwath International

Horwath International 1993 *Worldwide hotel industry 1993*, New York: Horwath International

Huddersfield University 1992 *International Hotel Groups Directory 1992*, London: Hotel Portfolio Research

Krutick, J S 1991 *The European hotel industry: the race is on*, New York: Salomon Brothers

Latham, J 1992 In: C P Cooper and A Lockwood (eds) *Progress in tourism recreation and hospitality management*, Vol 4, London: Bellhaven Press, pp. 267–81

Mars and Company Consultancy Ltd 1992 Unpublished internal report, London

Mercury, S R L 1992 *Fourth report on Italian tourism*, Rome: Italian Ministry of Tourism and Performing Arts

Mintel 1992 *Hotels 1992*, London: Mintel International Group Ltd

Pannell Kerr Forster Associates 1992 *Eurocity Survey 1992*, London: Pannell Kerr Forster Associates

Pannell Kerr Forster Associates 1993 *Eurocity Survey 1993*, London: Pannell Kerr Forster Associates

Queens Moat Houses plc 1993 *Queens Moat Houses plc Annual Report and Accounts 1992*, Interim Report 1993, 29 October, London

Salomon Brothers 1993 *5th Annual European Hotel Industry Investment Conference*, The Dorchester, London

Slattery P and S Johnson 1991 *Quoted hotel companies: the world markets*, London: Kleinwort Benson Securities

Slattery, P and S Johnson 1992 *Quoted hotel companies: the European markets*, London: Kleinwort Benson Securities

Slattery, P and S Johnson 1993 *Quoted hotel companies: the European markets*, London: Kleinwort Benson Research

Slattery, P, A Roper and A Boer 1985 Hotel consortia: their activities, structure and growth, *Service Industries Journal* **5**(2), 192–9

# CHAPTER 10

# Strategic trends and developments

**OBJECTIVES**

After reading this chapter you should be able to:
- Identify aspects within the general environment that will affect the hospitality industry.
- Consider an economic and political overview of Europe in 1994 with trends to the year 2000.
- Discuss trends in hotel financing.
- Consider the global hotel investment marketplace.

## THE GENERAL ENVIRONMENT

Since 1950 there has been a tremendous growth in international tourism. According to figures from the World Tourism Organization, arrivals rose from 25.3 million in 1950 to over 500 million in 1994. Tourism, including its infrastructure and related supply-side industries such as aviation and hotels, has become one of the world's largest single industries, as well as the most international. It is a generator of employment and an earner of foreign currency in both the developed and developing countries of the world. It is increasingly an industry that attracts the involvement of major corporations as well as retaining the interest of both government and government-funded agencies, and specifically national tourist boards.

During the period 1950–92 the average annual increase in international arrivals has been about 7 per cent and tourism is now considered to be one of the top three industries worldwide. Growth has not been even, however, in times of recession: in the early 1970s and early 1980s there was temporary stabilizing of tourism demand. These periods were followed by economic recovery and a corresponding revival in international tourism. The overall performance of tourism has been closely linked with the state of the world economy and in particular the economies of the major generating countries. International tourism is not only at the mercy of economic performance and the inevitable cycles but is also subjected to a range of events such as:

- the Chernobyl disaster,
- terrorist activity, and
- the fall in value of the US dollar, all in 1986.

International tourist arrivals in Africa and the Middle East during this period were down significantly, which caused a consequent shift in destination choice by many Americans in favour of countries in the Pacific and the North American continent.

The Gulf War in 1991 created a virtual cessation of travel to the Gulf and nearby countries, with cancellations increasing dramatically and occupancies down in all sectors of the travel industry. The conflict in the former Yugoslavia from 1992 caused the removal of an increasingly popular tourist destination, following a number of years of impressive growth. It is almost inevitable that similar major conflicts, disasters and upheavals will occur in the future, but their location and timing will often be beyond the reach of commentators and are best seen with hindsight.

The global experience of almost uninterrupted growth has not been shared equally by all destinations. Indeed, in many countries the real and perceived potential of inbound tourism is seen as supporting a nation's balance of payments, and so they have developed tourism on a massive scale, generating increases in tourist arrivals and spending at rates well above the average rates of increase. Many countries in the East Asia and Pacific region, such as Singapore, Thailand, Malaysia, Korea, Australia and Indonesia, are examples of this, mainly at the expense of Europe and North America: in the 30 years to 1990 the region's share of arrivals has increased tenfold and receipts fivefold. This increase in share is that of an expanding market, and represents remarkable growth in a highly competitive environment.

In the future, global growth is likely to be depressed by slow-growing market segments, especially short cross-border trips, and by the very meagre performance of some big origin countries, most notably Germany in the 1990s, and the USA. Travel from a number of major origin countries, especially in Europe, may be increasingly constrained by ceiling limitations to travel (linked essentially to annual leave entitlements). By the year 2005 travel from seven of the fifteen largest origin countries (in terms of spending) could be significantly restricted by these ceiling effects.

The tourism industry has changed considerably in the 1980s. As already mentioned, the market has grown rapidly, albeit at different rates around the world. There has been increasing demand for quality and value for money rather than low prices. Increases in leave entitlements have stimulated the demand for short holidays and weekend trips, both domestically and internationally. The market has become more segmentated and fragmented, and there has been a growth in leisure rather than business-related travel, particularly independent travel rather than escorted tours. Finally, the types of firm involved in the tourism business have changed from enthusiastic amateurs to major publicly owned companies with a professional attitude to management. Over the past decade, the numbers of small privately owned firms and even reasonably large companies involved only in travel have diminished. Today, most of the large companies are either publicly owned or are divisions of large corporations.

## THE CONSUMER

In addition to the obvious influence of prices and income on the demand for travel, social and work patterns and consumer tastes also influence the overall growth of the travel industry. Social change tends to impact slowly on the tourism business, but there have been a number of important changes over the past decade, which are likely to continue through the 1990s and beyond. These include:

- a move towards healthier living;
- a shift towards more active rather than passive recreational pursuits;
- the growing importance attached to the quality of life;
- an interest in the natural environment, its flora and fauna;
- a growing interest in exploring other cultures.

Working hours and leave entitlements affect travel demand, even if the traveller has the income needed to indulge travel interests: they impose ceilings that prevent demand from growing unconstrained. Travel growth in a given market does not continue to grow exponentially: as the limits to travel become more important and a market matures, growth takes on the shape of an S-curve. Consumer tastes and preferences also change. For example, it used to be possible for a hotelier in most Western markets to cater to market stereotypes, such as the family on holiday or the businessman on a brief trip. Such traditional market segments are now much less reliable. The population of the Western world is ageing: life expectancy has practically doubled in the last century, and age has become a more important factor in determining consumer behaviour as different age groups develop different interests and consumption patterns. The hotelier therefore has constantly to adapt to changing market characteristics and demand patterns. Competition is intensifying, long-haul travel, (barring external shocks) looks set to become cheaper relative to short-haul, and consumer tastes are constantly changing. Down-market resorts, such as the traditional sun and sea destinations in Europe, have suffered because of consumers' more sophisticated demands. Independent travel is increasing at the expense of organized packages, and the methods of selling and distributing the hotel and travel product are changing as new computerized systems are introduced.

Clearly, market segmentation is becoming a vital issue in the hotel trade. The principal market segments that international hotel corporations seek to attract depend to some degree on the hotels' locations and the standards of service they provide. The incompatibility of different market segments, such as business travellers, conference delegates and leisure travellers, was identified by the airlines long before the hotel industry recognized the issue, either as a problem or as a growth opportunity. In fhe 1960s, international carriers discovered that it was becoming increasingly difficult to serve and satisfy different categories of passenger with the same product, particularly if each passenger was paying a different price for what appeared to be a common service level. This became especially apparent with business and holiday passengers occupying identical seats and enjoying the same level of service, but paying substantially different fares. The difficulties encountered by the airlines in combining different market segments within the same cabin space ultimately led to the introduction of the business-class cabin, to separate corporate travellers from travellers with discounted tickets.

Following the airlines' lead, in 1975 the Hyatt Regency Hotel in Atlanta created executive floors, named Regency Club. This concept of de luxe accommodation spread rapidly; in such floors, furniture and fixtures are of a quality superior to those found elsewhere in the hotel, and extensive additional amenities are provided in the bedrooms and bathrooms. The feeling of exclusivity is cultivated through such amenities and services as an executive floor private elevator, lounges, upgraded guest room size and furnishings, upgraded bathrooms, and the maintenance of a guest history containing information concerning the guest's preferences for rooms, number of visits and billing. Service levels are also a critical component for the executive floor. As a result of the high staff-to-guest ratios, the executive floor must be operated as a hotel within a hotel. Typically it would have its own manager, concierge, check-in and check-out.

Segmentation offers the public a wider and clearer recognition of brand images, although market maturity and diversity are partially the cause of brand segmentation. The strongest push appears to be coming from the hotel companies, their franchisees and developers, because segmentation is a means of meeting the companies' and developers' business needs:

- the need to maintain company growth in the face of a saturated market;
- the need to rationalize or unify an inconsistent chain; and
- the need to respond to developers' objectives by matching the hotel concept to the sites available.

## DEMOGRAPHIC TRENDS

As living standards improve, the developed world's population is living longer and becoming more affluent. The proportion of the world's population in active work is declining, and the proportion of the population in healthy and relatively prosperous retirement rising. This has important implications for the travel and accommodation industries. Life expectancy in Europe and North America has almost doubled in the past century and is continuing to extend in Europe. For example, in 1973, 12 per cent of the population in Europe was aged over 65; by the end of the century that figure will have risen to 17 per cent. By the year 2000 about 100 million Europeans will be aged 55 and over, and this will represent a healthy and relatively wealthy segment that has grown up expecting to be able to travel internationally.

These demographic trends can be seen in the total population and in the major cities. The growth in the size of the world's major cities and their relative rankings is illustrated in Table 10.1. Such information gives an indication of where demand for hotel development might take place to the year 2000. Developers should keep a keen eye on potential growth locations in developing countries such as Brazil or India. There is nothing new in such changes: the difference is in the pace of change. In the sixteenth century Florence was the financial capital of Europe, and Constantinople was one of the world's largest cities. In the year 2000 none of the megacities will be in Europe.

**Table 10.1 World megacities**

| 1600 | 1800 | 1950 | 2000 |
|------|------|------|------|
| Peking (China) | Peking (China) | New York (USA) | Mexico City |
| Constantinople (Turkey) | London (UK) | London (UK) | São Paulo |
| Agra (Moguls) | Canton (China) | Shanghai (China) | Tokyo |
| Cairo (Egypt) | Constantinople (Turkey) | Rhein/Ruhr (Germany) | Calcutta |
| Osaka (Japan) | Paris (France) | Tokyo (Japan) | Bombay |
| Canton (China) | Hangchow (China) | Peking (China) | New York |
| Yedo (Japan) | Yedo (Japan) | Paris (France) | Seoul |
| Kyoto (Japan) | Naples (Italy) | Tieutzin (China) | Shanghai |
| Hangchow (China) | Soochow (China) | Buenos Aires (Argentina) | Rio de Janeiro |
| Lahore (Moguls) | Osaka (Japan) | Chicago (USA) | Delhi |
| | | Average population | |
| 0.44 million | 0.60 million | 7.46 million | 16.91 million |

Source: Pannell Kerr Forster Associates, 6th Annual European Hotel Industry Investment Conference, November 1994, London. Organized and sponsored by Pannell Kerr Forster Associates, Salomon Brothers, Jones Lang Wootton.

In addition, the combination of attitude change, health and prosperity will ensure that the over-55 segment will become an ever more important part of the travel and accommodation market. These trends in demographic structure are being mirrored in North America and the Asia/Pacific regions, which represent one of the most important markets in the world travel and tourism industry. The hotel sector is increasingly recognizing the need to cater specifically for the over-55 travellers, who are willing to travel off-peak, willing and financially able to be more adventurous in their choice of destination, and keen to travel for short periods as well as to take longer breaks.

At the same time population growth rates are slowing in many countries. So the largest industrial nations, for example – Russia, the USA, Japan, Germany, France, the UK and Spain – had a total population of 870 million in 1980. This is projected to increase by 12.3 per cent between 1980 and the year 2000, but their share of the population of the world's 30 largest countries will decline by almost 17 per cent over the same period. Thus while leisure time and the ability and willingness to travel will increase, the distribution of the world's travelling public is likely to change and diversify, and attention will have to be paid to the new emerging markets.

## CONSUMER DYNAMICS

In considering the consumer, five aspects can be identified that will affect developments in the hospitality industry:

- rising affluence;
- rising discretionary time;
- rising travel experience;
- the changing nature of demand;
- global deregulation and transport competition.

### Rising affluence

The recession in the industrialized countries in the early 1990s was severe, and along with the effects of the Gulf War was a factor depressing the world travel market in the short term. Over the longer term, however, the major economies of the world will continue to grow during the latter part of the 1990s. In turn this means that the majority of consumers in industrialized countries will become more affluent, and their propensity to spend their discretionary income on holidays and travel will continue to increase. Long-term growth in affluence on a global scale will have two important consequences:

- consumers will travel more frequently;
- price *per se* will become less important as a determinant of the travel decision process.

This does not mean that price will not matter – it indeed will still be crucial, but in the sense that **value for money** rather than cheapness will be the central issue. The pressure on product providers will be to meet the consumer's threshold values of quality and levels of service while remaining price competitive.

## Rising discretionary time

Societies that are more affluent tend to have more leisure time, although there are important and persistent national differences: Japan and the USA, for example, are characterized by short employee holidays. In comparison, within Europe a variety of interrelated trends, such as the ageing populations, and the increasing instances of early retirement, will see a rise in average free time available in industrialized countries. In absolute terms, time is an influencing factor and consumer behaviour will increase in importance. However, because discretionary income tends to rise more quickly than does discretionary time, there will be an increasing emphasis on the quality of leisure time. Consumers will be demanding value for time as well as value for money.

## Rising travel experience

In considering the industry, evidence suggests that the experience of overseas travel is cumulative: the more you do the more you want to do. The international travel market of 500 million trips includes an increasing number of relatively experienced and therefore relatively confident travellers, whose desire for reassurance from their holiday product is diminishing. In contrast, rising affluence is bringing into the international travel market consumers from countries that until recently had few if any overseas holidaymakers. The international market will therefore be characterized by the increasingly stark contrast between a core of experienced and confident travellers and an inflow of new and unconfident ones.

## The changing nature of demand

A valuable source of information on demand trends in the UK hotel industry is the British Hotel Guest Survey, run every year since 1982. The survey tracks a wide range of market trends and developments that impinge upon the hotel industry. One aspect to consider in relation to business travellers is exactly who the customer is. Many of these travellers are subject to some form of corporate policy, and so it is inevitably a department or individual at head office that determines choice. In addition, in terms of behaviour a majority of such travellers tend to be **satisfiers** rather than **optimizers**: when such a traveller has found a hotel of acceptable standard, they tend to return to it rather than shop around for another that might be better. Hotel brands and hotel classification schemes are both factors that can influence the choice of a hotel. Business travellers nowadays attach increasing importance to brands rather than to star ratings.

## Global deregulation and transport competition

Although it is impossible to foresee exactly what the structure of the world transport market will be in ten years' time, it seems inevitable that consumers will be presented with an increasing variety of choice on major transport routes, and that ultimately competition will continue to drive the real price down. The latest EU agreement on the liberalization of air transport is the most far-reaching so far, and despite a poor record of implementation, over time it should gain practical as well as rhetorical acceptance at European level. Given the state of the global airline industry it is unrealistic to expect deregulation to send airfares tumbling. However, the longer-term dynamics are clear: air transport will become more competitive, and it is likely that fares will continue to decline more. This will have two direct effects:

- The proportion of expenditure on holidays accounted for by travel will continue to decline. This means that consumers will be encouraged to travel further and more frequently.
- The difference between the wholesale and retail prices of travel will diminish as competitive pressures on transport providers force the retail price down closer to marginal cost. It is inevitable that the discount available to bulk purchasers will be squeezed. In effect, the sustainable price differential between packaged products and independently arranged trips will diminish, undermining one of the most fundamental competitive levers that the packaged product has to offer.

The trends in all this suggest that there will be increasing congestion in the travel market. The key message of this analysis of consumer and structural dynamics is that fundamental pressures from both the demand and the supply sides are affecting the established concept of a packaged holiday product, and influencing the competitive balance between packaged and non-packaged travel.

The issue of congestion is important, as distribution of tourists away from the premier attractions is now a serious problem in some countries. Venice, for example, is considering a number of initiatives to control visitor flows and the consequential environmental damage. Although such problems are not yet so acute in the UK, it is certainly true that, as in other countries, some attractions are massively over-subscribed at peak times while others remain half empty. As concern over environmentally responsible and sustainable tourism grows in the future, there is likely to be increasing pressure on government and other administrative bodies to initiate policies reconciling the conflicting demands of tourists with those of the environment in the local community.

## STRATEGIC ISSUE OF HOTEL BRANDING

Product differentiation and branding within the hotel industry had its beginnings in the USA, notably with Holiday Inns, but has now extended to companies such as Forte, Accor and Choice International. Prompted by growing market sophistication and intensive competition between various chains and their better understanding of what the public wants, the hotel industry has followed these companies' leads and has committed itself to supplying an ever widening spectrum of varied new product lines. Segmentation has been stimulated by recognition of the increased marketing potential of product branding aimed at specific markets.

Growth is desirable for all businesses, and it is imperative for publicly held hotel companies, but after the great flush of construction in the late 1980s many companies found expansion increasingly difficult. The market at the existing level of rates was in many places saturated; however, by launching new chains and new product lines the hotel firms have created a new vehicle for growth. Hotel chain operators have continued to broaden market appeal through segmentation, creating subchains with different names and price levels. In addition, product fragmentation has become popular: new product lines or variations have been launched in the hope that they would fit the needs and wants of emerging or growing markets. Although a hotel offers only one basic service – accommodation – other peripheral services that contribute to the improved quality of the core service may or may not be offered for sale, such as meals and alcoholic beverages, entertainment and recreational amenities. This multiplicity of services contributes to the complexity of management, not only because it extends the scale of problems but also because each service can and does interact with others.

The level of service offered by hotels is generally reflected by their pricing structure and classification, broadly identified as luxury, upscale, basic full service and economy. This product branding has been one of the most powerful marketing tools of the century. It started with the developments of brands in consumer products such as Coca Cola, Mars and Marlboro, and has seen them become rapidly internationally recognized brands. Hotel product branding is also becoming important: the industry shares three essential characteristics with consumer products:

- standard specifications;
- consistent quality; and
- consistent marketing.

In the hotel industry, consistency of product is reflected in the internal specification of rooms, external appearance and design of the property, and the range of services offered to the customer. Brand consistency is achieved by standardization – an especially important feature of the hotel industry, particularly if international markets are involved. The knowledge in the mind of the customer that he or she will get a standard product, regardless of the country or region of location, has become an important part in the marketing of hotels.

The advent of computer reservations systems has permitted the development of consistent marketing around the world, and has helped to enforce the power of hotel brands to retain the travelling clientele. Thus a customer in one country can reserve more or less the same room in any other country free of charge from the hotel in which he or she is lodged at the time the booking is made. Alternatively the travel agent who arranges a client's itinerary can select, through a CRS, a standard product to meet the client's known preferences regardless of which region or country the client is going to.

US hotel companies, for instance, have decided that the ability to deliver consistently a high quality/value ratio would make or break their business. Each of the new hotel product brands launched by large companies offers a promise of specific services and makes it harder for the hotel managers to give too much product and services for the price charged. Product branding has been more or less forced on the hotel chains. The lack of new sites for hotel construction in many cities has meant that acquisitions were the only way to expand in desirable centres. In turn, this has meant inheriting a mixture of properties, different hotel grades, that somehow needed to be brought under one corporate umbrella. At the same time, hotel corporations began to recognize that product branding is a necessary step in an increasingly competitive environment, in which the products on offer had become almost indistinguishable from one chain to the next. The days of the versatile hotel that can be all things to all people appears to be over. Today all the US major companies boast at least two, and the majority three, hotel brands, typically in the luxury, mid-market and budget sectors. This approach has also been adopted by a number of the larger European chains such as Forte and Accor.

As hotel chains have expanded throughout the world, and domestic and international travellers have become an accepted part of everyday life, demand for and competition between hotels has heightened, particularly among the major corporations. At the same time, hotel operating costs have continued to rise, encouraging hotel operators to reduce staffing levels, adopt more widespread use of computerized accounting and management systems, and improve energy management and internal controls. The economies of hotel operations require high levels of occupancies and rooms on a year-round basis. For the majors this has meant attracting a broad market base, but experience has demonstrated that different market segments are not always compatible. At the same time as the mass market splintered into many fragments of more demanding customers, international hotel corporations encountered more competition. This obliged hotel firms to focus their marketing initiative so as to be perceived by customers as specialists rather than general practitioners.

## CUSTOMER BASE

Hospitality managers today are subject to the twin issues of being customer driven and market focused. The rationale for being customer driven is **customer share**: that is, a company's highest priority should be given to retaining the customer. Such an approach is backed up with statistics illustrating the relative advantage of keeping an existing customer rather than going out and creating new ones. In the hospitality world of market focus, the predominant measure is **market share**. Here the idea is to grow the company by growing market share. Both ideas are simple and appealing, and both are short sighted. There are more ambitious goals, which combine the thinking about the customer and the market, but with superior results, by increasing the hotel company's share of customers' spending.

Hospitality firms that focus on customer share of total spending ultimately benefit in four ways:

- They upgrade and constantly improve their product or service offerings and in doing so allow the business to grow by tapping into earned customer loyalty.
- They create new extensions or enhancements to products or services, growing the hospitality business by adding new dimensions.
- They get close to their customers, with the prospect of increased customer spending.
- They make improvements in internal processes and systems that can lead to faster, leaner and higher quality operations overall.

It is this customer share focus that encourages the firm to build and grow a lasting relationship with each individual customer, based on providing them with a unique and competitively superior value product or service. This value proposition stems from a combination of customized product, communication and service delivery, in effect treating each customer as a unique segment of one. For most hospitality firms this is a big change in business philosophy, and could trigger a massive shift of resources.

The traditional manager concentrates on reaching the market and making the sale. Communications are broadly directed at possible customers. The service philosophy is to react, and to respond (hopefully quickly) once a consumer raises his hand. In contrast, the customer share competitor puts primary emphasis on developing a relationship with the individual customer once the initial sale has been made. The customer and supplier (hotel, travel agent, tour operator, airline) share information in a way that allows communication to be customized to the client's individual needs. Mutually discovered knowledge about the customer's needs allows for a proactive service philosophy to take the initiative even before the customer recognizes a need.

Customer share management becomes a prime source of competitive advantage. Focus on it permits growth in mature markets, and permits product development, channel extension and improved service delivery. It also allows comparison across account teams, sales reps, districts, regions and marketing efforts, and permits statistical process control. It is therefore possible to classify customers, to establish requirements for share gain, and to concentrate on most hospitality firms' best prospect, the current customer.

## The basics

First, the hospitality firm should look carefully at its core service or product, to analyse how it could be improved. Ironically, one of the greatest obstacles to this exercise is customer satisfaction measurements. These only rate the quality of what is provided, not what *could* be provided, and so they could become a diversion from continuous improvement and increased customer spending. Such an approach shows how customer share management requires customer focus to maximize customer life cycle value and customer share. Managers target marketing efforts based on net future value and share. They also customize communication that is targeted, timed and personalized.

The relationship built up with the customer spurs the firm to constant and continuous improvement and redefining of the hospitality business.

## Discovery and delivery

There are two essential steps to increasing the firm's customer share:

- understanding the customer better than the customer does;
- understanding the firm and its products.

These two steps are **discovery** and **delivery**. The whole process generates new ideas and becomes a systematic process to build the firm's capabilities. It begins with an audit that forces the sales and marketing team to diagnose the firm's relationship, in terms of successes and failures, with its customers. The points a firm should consider are:

- What is our share of the customer's purchases? Are we viewed as a vendor or as a partner?
- Have we consistently realized opportunities to extend our business?

- Do we sell only when asked, or do we search for new ways to provide value?
- Do we understand the customer's future aspirations?
- Are we aligned, or are we a roadblock to the customer's requirements?

In the hospitality industry, customer delivery requires a database of users *and* non-users. It also requires an in-depth understanding of product competition, dissatisfactions, the customer's purchase pathway, and propensity to a loyal repurchase. Discovery begins with understanding the strategic and economic drivers of the customer. Then the manager transforms that knowledge into ideas, products and services that benefit the firm and the customer, with the creation of a partnership. Unlike the traditional approach, the firm is not selling individual predetermined products or services, but is thinking about the customer's needs first and then linking them in new ways to the firm's current or potential customers. This is a continuous dynamic process, which involves in-depth analysis and rigorous data gathering.

## How discovery works

The discovery team focuses the company's sales and marketing people outward on the customer and gives them the time, training and support to learn all they can about the customer. They can then bring that information back to be put to use improving the operation. Delivery involves considering the firm, analysing its systems and processes in order to streamline and improve its capabilities, and then connecting the system with customers.

## Moving from discovery to delivery

In the name of better service, firms have been bombarding customers with needs assessment forms, performance feedback questionnaires and endless surveys on lifestyles and tastes. Such information can be useful, but as it is also available to competitors, many firms have found it of limited advantage. In any case, a customer who tells you that everything is fine does not help you to know what you can do better. To stay ahead of the competition, customer-share-driven firms go beyond asking customers what they want: they go out and discover what customers need even if they are not yet aware of it. Unlike other customer service schemes that have come and gone, discovery is a process that requires considerable investment and training, time and effort. It is this aspect that makes it such a competitive advantage, because it resides in the knowledge and creative capabilities of a firm's sales force: competitors cannot duplicate it. The ultimate reward of the discovery process is not only that it increases customer share but that it also adds tremendous value to the hospitality firm, because new products and ideas win new capabilities and growth.

In the 1990s, the key marketing capability will be maximizing share of the most profitable customers. This makes marketing more effective by targeting the firm's best prospects, and it links diverging individualized customer needs with flexible customizable products and services. Historically, this approach has seen a shift from order takers to business partners:

- requires a rebalance in the vendor–customer relationship;
- broadens sales requirements and definitions of value;
- creates new opportunities for exclusive supply.

In summary, competitors may be taking this approach even if the customers are satisfied, but the central issue is how the firm is working to get more out of the business. Measuring customer satisfaction is important, but it only identifies how they feel about the business. By targeting customer share, managers will discover the right balance of investments to drive the customers to act, and actions (not feelings) lead to growth and profits. Discovery not only builds customer share: it can actually change the way a firm positions itself, and it is this that is the central pay-off in taking this approach.

## EUROPEAN ECONOMIC AND POLITICAL OVERVIEW

The European hospitality industry is subject to a multitude of global economic and political influences. Historical analysis supports the close link between the economic cycle and the well-being of the hotel sector. Equally, economic issues in the European hotel markets are influenced by events occurring in other major world economies, such as Japan and the USA. The global nature of the hospitality industry ensures that trends in the global economy are just as relevant as those in the domestic European markets. The major determinant of the hotel sector's performance in 1994 was the pace of global economic recovery. International recession had a profound effect on the industry in the early 1990s: while there has been some recovery, major country economic growth remains de-synchronized. If one considers the period 1980–94, one can see differences in annual gross domestic product growth rates in the major industrialized countries: while GDP has continued to grow in 1994 in the USA and UK, this positive trend has been partially offset by continued weak performance in continental Europe. The figures presented in Table 10.2 illustrate that, for the period 1992–95, the low point for GDP growth rates was forecast for 1993, with some European countries moving out of recession at a faster rate during the period 1994–95. The low point for GDP growth rates in the UK was 1992.

Table 10.2  European GDP growth

|  | 1992 (%) | 1993F (%) | 1994F (%) | 1995F (%) |
|---|---|---|---|---|
| West Germany | 1.2 | −1.7 | 2.2 | 2.5 |
| France | 1.2 | −1.3 | 2.3 | 3.1 |
| UK | −0.4 | 2.0 | 3.5 | 3.5 |
| Italy | 0.7 | −0.7 | 2.0 | 2.8 |
| Spain | 0.8 | −1.0 | 1.6 | 2.6 |
| Portugal | 1.1 | −1.0 | 1.2 | 2.1 |
| Switzerland | −0.3 | −0.9 | 1.9 | 2.5 |
| Netherlands | 1.3 | 0.4 | 2.0 | 2.5 |
| Belgium | 0.9 | −1.4 | 1.4 | 2.7 |
| Denmark | 1.3 | 1.4 | 3.7 | 2.5 |
| Sweden | −1.9 | −2.1 | 2.3 | 1.9 |

Source: Salomon Brothers, 6th Annual European Hotel Industry Investment Conference, November 1994, London. Organized and sponsored by Pannell Kerr Forster Associates, Salomon Brothers, Jones Lang Wootton.
F = Forecast

Germany's economy, however, improved in 1994, achieving approximately 2.2 per cent growth for the year. Looking further afield, Japan has bottomed out to show modest growth in 1994. The prospects for industrial economic growth are improving, but the performance of the Japanese and continental European economies remained downbeat in 1994. Inflation has remained muted in virtually all industrial countries, and European unemployment is still at a high level. Favourable trade policy developments have boosted optimism about the medium-term outlook for global growth. Within Europe, although the move towards a wide-band exchange rate mechanism has offered an opportunity for countries to reduce their massive fiscal deficit, short-term interest rates moves in this direction have so far been minimal. So far only the UK

Table 10.3  General government surplus (+)/deficit (−) as a percentage of GDP

|  | 1980 (%) | 1985 (%) | 1992 (%) | 1993 (%) | 1994 (%) | 1995F (%) |
|---|---|---|---|---|---|---|
| Italy | −6.9 | −13.8 | −10.8 | −9.8 | −9.4 | −9.3 |
| Sweden | −4.0 | −3.8 | −7.1 | −14.0 | −12.0 | −11.0 |
| Belgium | −9.2 | −8.8 | −6.8 | −7.2 | −5.6 | −4.8 |
| Germany | −3.6 | −2.4 | −6.4 | −6.4 | −6.3 | −4.3 |
| UK | −5.3 | −1.5 | −6.1 | −7.2 | −5.0 | −3.3 |
| Spain | −2.6 | −6.9 | −4.5 | −7.3 | −7.0 | −6.2 |
| France | 0.0 | −3.1 | −3.9 | −5.6 | −5.1 | −4.9 |
| Denmark | −2.9 | −2.0 | −2.5 | −4.6 | −5.2 | −3.2 |
| Japan | −4.1 | −1.0 | +1.3 | −2.4 | −4.4 | −4.4 |
| USA | −1.3 | −3.1 | −4.5 | −3.5 | −2.6 | −2.1 |

Source: Salomon Brothers, 6th Annual European Hotel Industry Investment Conference, November 1994, London. Organized and sponsored by Pannell Kerr Forster Associates, Salomon Brothers, Jones Lang Wootton.
F = forecast.

authorities have adopted measures that will substantially reduce the deficit: a point illustrated in Table 10.3.

The various world economies are at different stages of the cycle. With the USA, Canada and Australia well into the upturn (1995), the UK, France and Germany are experiencing a gradual recovery. Japan is nearing the end of the slump but has not yet reached the bottom. Generally, Spain will continue to experience economic recovery in 1995. However, such an analysis does not illustrate how deep any slump will be or how long or how brisk recovery will be.

## Inflation

Average inflation in the European Union dropped to 2.9 per cent in 1994 and 2.8 per cent in 1995, a 30-year low. Inflation in most European countries has already fallen close to the low point of the past twenty years. The trends in consumer price inflation rates for the period 1963–95 are illustrated in Table 10.4.

**Table 10.4 Consumer price inflation rates in selected European countries, 1963–95**

|  | 1963–72[a] (%) | 1973–82[a] (%) | 1983–92[a] (%) | 1993 (%) | 1994F (%) | 1995F (%) |
|---|---|---|---|---|---|---|
| European Union | 4.6 | 11.7 | 5.2 | 3.5 | 2.9 | 2.8 |
| West Germany | 3.2 | 5.2 | 2.2 | 4.2 | 3.0 | 2.2 |
| France | 4.4 | 11.1 | 4.4 | 2.1 | 1.7 | 1.9 |
| UK | 5.0 | 14.2 | 5.6 | 3.0 | 2.4 | 2.9 |
| Italy | 4.2 | 17.0 | 7.4 | 4.2 | 3.9 | 4.0 |
| Spain | 6.8 | 16.6 | 7.7 | 5.7 | 4.6 | 4.5 |
| Portugal | 6.4 | 20.8 | 15.0 | 6.5 | 5.6 | 4.4 |
| Netherlands | 5.4 | 7.1 | 2.0 | 2.6 | 2.8 | 2.3 |
| Belgium | 3.8 | 8.0 | 3.5 | 2.5 | 2.5 | 2.6 |
| Denmark | 6.3 | 10.5 | 3.9 | 2.0 | 2.0 | 2.5 |
| Sweden | 4.9 | 9.9 | 6.5 | 4.7 | 2.3 | 3.0 |

*Source:* Salomon Brothers, 6th Annual European Hotel Industry Investment Conference, November 1994, London. Organized and sponsored by Pannell Kerr Forster Associates, Salomon Brothers, Jones Lang Wootton.
F = forecast. [a] Period averages

Slow growth, low capacity use and disinflationary pressure from external trade should ensure that European inflation remains low during the period 1994–96. However, the inflation slowdown has largely been a result of Europe's severe recession, and with unemployment rates and budget deficits both rising, doubts are growing about the durability of low inflation in the second half of the 1990s. Sharp fiscal tightening and/or faster productivity gains are needed to sustain low inflation expectations. However, if a monetary or fiscal stimulus is used, it is likely that inflation will tend to rise. Ultimately, voters will select policies that help to set

**Table 10.5 Major nationwide elections in Europe, 1995–98**

| Date | Country | Type of election |
|---|---|---|
| March 1995 | Finland | Parliament |
| May 1995 | France | President |
| Autumn 1995 | Portugal | Parliament |
| Autumn 1995 | Belgium | Parliament |
| Spring 1996[a] | UK | Parliament |
| Spring 1997 | Spain | Parliament |
| Autumn 1997 | Greece | Parliament |
| End 1997 | Ireland | Parliament and President |
| Spring 1998 | France | Parliament |

*Source:* Pannell Kerr Forster Associates, 6th Annual European Hotel Industry Investment Conference, November 1994, London. Organized and sponsored by Pannell Kerr Forster Associates, Salomon Brothers, Jones Lang Wootton.
[a] The UK elections will be held before their April 1997 deadlines.
*Note:* In most cases, parliamentary dates represent legal deadlines, but elections could occur before these deadlines.

inflation's course, and in the period 1995–98 will have ample opportunity to do so (Table 10.5).

General elections are likely in a number of the EU member states within the next two to four years, and these elections could elicit a protest vote against slow growth and high unemployment. Worries about voter impatience could prompt the abandonment of fiscal restraint among Europe's governments.

## Interest rates

Despite the recent exchange rate mechanism crisis and Germany's anti-inflationary policies, short-term interest rates have declined significantly and are at an historical low level. In addition, a move to a wider ERM banding relieved some of the currency strains within the EU. Equally, within the EU, interest rates are also affected by trends in US and Japanese interest rates. Interest rate yield curves in most European markets will steepen or preserve their current steep shapes. Another aspect that will undoubtedly influence voter intention throughout Europe is the burden of taxes and other government levies. As indicated in Table 10.6, the range is considerable, and for comparative purposes figures for the USA and Japan are included.

**Table 10.6 Burden of taxes and other government levies (1992 government levy ratio)[a]**

| | Total (%) | Of which: tax ratio (%) | Share of total tax revenue | |
|---|---|---|---|---|
| | | | Direct taxes (%) | Indirect taxes (%) |
| Sweden | 50.6 | 35.7 | 56.1 | 43.9 |
| Denmark | 48.8 | 46.3 | 63.2 | 36.8 |
| Netherlands | 46.9 | 28.6 | 56.4 | 43.6 |
| Austria | 45.0 | 30.2 | 46.9 | 53.1 |
| France | 43.7 | 22.4 | 39.7 | 60.3 |
| Germany[b] | 43.7 | 25.1 | 48.3 | 51.7 |
| Belgium | 42.9 | 27.9 | 57.5 | 42.5 |
| Italy | 40.8 | 25.9 | 56.6 | 43.4 |
| Portugal | 38.7 | 26.3 | 41.4 | 58.6 |
| Greece | 36.0 | 25.1 | 24.3 | 75.7 |
| Ireland | 35.7 | 30.3 | 45.8 | 54.2 |
| Spain | 35.4 | 22.0 | 53.0 | 47.0 |
| UK | 33.4 | 26.9 | 46.6 | 53.4 |
| USA | 30.7 | 21.4 | 60.4 | 39.6 |
| Japan | 29.3 | 20.5 | 60.8 | 39.2 |

*Source:* Salomon Brothers, 6th Annual European Hotel Industry Investment Conference, November 1994, London. Organized and sponsored by Pannell Kerr Forster Associates, Salomon Brothers, Jones Lang Wootton
[a] Taxes and social security contributions as a percentage of GDP, based on the national scheme
[b] Salomon Brothers' estimate for 1994 and 1995 German tax shares are 45% and 46% respectively

In summary, therefore, Europe in 1995 faces three challenges:

- In the near term the objective has to be to restore growth in terms of gross domestic product.
- In the medium term, the need is to restore balance in terms of low inflation and reduced unemployment; to increase efficiency and competitiveness; and to restore fiscal stability.
- Over the long term there is the issue of integration within the EU. There is already a debate within the Union as to whether its membership should be widened in terms of numbers or deepened in terms of federal control. Equally, the strains and problems of the European exchange rate mechanism and a single European currency may see such policies abandoned.

In facing these challenges, three choices will have to be addressed:

- It may mean a return to high and uneven inflation, along with currency instability.
- Policies will need to be adopted to resolve these problems, and depending on the political party in power, there may be a return to high taxes and regulated markets.
- Finally, the adoption of fiscal discipline and market liberalization may in the end produce a successful single market.

The answers to these choices will be reflected in the voting patterns of ordinary men and women in the major nationwide elections in Europe, scheduled over the period to 1998. These economic and political factors will now be related to a case study on the London hotel market.

## CASE STUDY: KEY ECONOMIC AND POLITICAL FACTORS INFLUENCING THE LONDON HOTEL MARKET*

| | |
|---|---|
| 1978–80 | The strength of sterling against other world currencies, exacerbated by the introduction of VAT, reduced the attractiveness of London to foreign investors and also tourists, with a resultant negative effect on hotel income performance. |
| 1980–85 | Increasing hotel occupancies, combined with significant real growth in average achieved room rates, led to steady improvement in the performance and profitability of London hotels. The resulting increase in capital values produced a strong speculative market in hotels with growth potential. |
| 1986 | Political events, terrorist events and environmental disasters reduced the volume of tourist arrivals, especially from the USA. In addition, sterling's strength against the dollar caused a significant reduction in demand for hotel rooms and a corresponding decline in income. |
| 1987–89 | Performance improved in this period as the UK economy continued to grow, although the strengthening of sterling against the dollar in 1988 again acted as a constraint on overall operating results. In 1989, total tourist arrivals to the UK reached a record 17.7 million: of these some 9.5 million visited London. This tourist demand, coupled with strong business demand, resulted in many London hotels achieving record profitability. Foreign investors, particularly the Japanese and Scandinavians, became major investors in the London property investment market. The hotel investment market flourished, with record transaction prices achieved. |
| 1990–91 | Hotel performance began to slow during 1990 owing to the deepening recession and the rumblings of the Gulf crisis. During 1991 the Gulf War constrained international travel and economic recession in most markets. These factors had a damaging effect on London hotel performance. Owing to emerging problems in emerging markets, many foreign investors withdrew from the London property investment arena. During this period there were almost no significant hotel transactions. |
| 1992 | Despite a deepening UK recession and an increase in global recession, there was some slight recovery in investment demand after the difficulties of 1991, owing to |

* *Source*: Pannell Kerr Forster Associates, *London Trends 1994*.

the weakening of sterling and the perceived bottoming-out of the property investment market. Two major transactions in London included the sale of the Gloucester and the Athenaeum by Rank plc.

## Turning points of room occupancy and average room rate in London hotels

The early 1990s saw the London hotel market in the doldrums, although it started to move into the recovery stage during 1993, with a rise in room occupancy and slight growth in average achieved room rate. The trends for 1994 have been positive and in terms of historic behaviour can be related to the last economic downturn of 1981–83. For all hotels in London, occupancies hit a low in mid-1981, averaging 66 per cent, and it was not until August 1983 that occupancy levels returned to the long-term average performance of 75 per cent. To reach this level took about two years. In the most recent downturn, room occupancy for all hotels bottomed out in November 1991 at just under 65 per cent. Again, the recovery has taken two years, with the 75 per cent level achieved in December 1993.

During the previous recession, the quality hotels led the market out of recession as early as May 1981. There was a lag of 14 months before the average room rate showed any sign of improvement during the 1981–83 downturn, although tourist hotels had to wait until March 1983 before rates started to rise. In the recent recession, the five-star hotel market showed an improvement in occupancy from September 1991, but the average room rate showed signs of recovery in late 1993 and into 1994. Since October 1993, the average room rate for all hotels has shown modest growth over the previous year. As a pointer to the future, it is possible to analyse the pattern of recovery during the recessionary period 1981–83. Once occupancies had reached 75 per cent in 1983, coming out of recession, the growth in average room rate in the following year was about 13 per cent, equivalent to 8 per cent in real terms. In the succeeding year (1985), the rate grew by a further 19 per cent, 13 per cent in real terms, as occupancies in the region of 80 per cent were attained. Assuming a similar pattern of recovery this time, it might be anticipated that by the beginning of 1995 the average rate will have grown by around 11 per cent, taking account of inflation. By 1997, the enhancement in rate should have continued, with occupancies around 80 per cent. Comparisons between the two recessionary periods suggest that such operational figures are attainable. Should occupancies approach 80 per cent in the period 1994–95 , there should not be the need for the deep discounting policies that characterized the first three years of the 1990s.

## GLOBAL INVESTMENT MARKETPLACE

### Introduction

Investment media such as equities, gilts and commercial property have undergone extensive performance measurement in recent years, providing existing and potential investors with useful, comparative information. In assessing these performance measurements, many have analysed historical performance as an indicator to future performance over the long term, and have theorized, for example, that commercial property performance is inherently cyclical.

**Table 10.7 Global hotel investment market place, autumn 1994 (transaction analysis)**

|  | Europe | Asia/Pacific | North America |
|---|---|---|---|
| Number of transactions | 16 | 48 | 36 |
| Total value ($m) | 530 | 1,596 | 1,100 |
| Average price per room ($) | 149,000 | 145,000 | 77,500 |
| Average hotel size | 222 | 227 | 400 |

Note: Lot size $10m plus. Sales over last 12 months
Source: HVS International

Following the sharp decline in asset values and market liquidity bought about by the recession of the early 1990s, the global market in 1994 entered a new cycle. In the USA values and activity showed a strong recovery, and the UK is following in its wake. Europe, however, is lagging further behind, with the market remaining both depressed and illiquid, but with the possibility of recovery when one takes into consideration the USA and the UK. Table 10.7 illustrates the global hotel investment marketplace in the 12 months prior to autumn 1994. It is interesting to note the bias towards the Asia and Pacific region, and the figures reflect the economic growth potential in the three regions identified.

A new kind of asset manager could emerge in Europe as a buffer between hoteliers desperate to expand and funds nervous about investment in the sector. Interest has been expressed in US real estate investment trusts (REITS), which attracted $1.5 billion into hotels during the 12 month period to November 1994. The whole of Europe managed only half that amount during the same period (Figure 10.1).

UK based funds were so keen to be involved in this form of investment as the USA moved out of recession that they accounted for 10 per cent of these issues. While tax differences have affected the development of REITs in the UK, it is possible that other forms of trust could evolve to help the industry expand. Such an approach could spread holdings across different firms and types of hotel, an approach that would probably gain the support of institutions. There is a need in Europe for a new approach to finance, as operators rely almost solely on debt finance from banks. It is the banks that are proving reluctant to fund development, despite widescale recovery in the hotel industry. Countries other than the UK are much less reticent in hotel investment. Investment from Asian countries, particularly Singapore, has been focused on London, explained perhaps by its fast rate of recovery.

One reason for the surge of money from South-East Asia is that there is

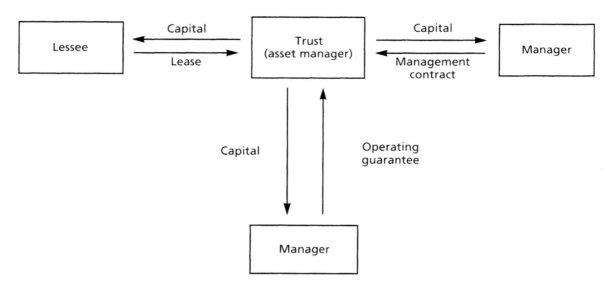

**Fig. 10.1 The basic structure: multi-tenant**

*Source:* Pannell Kerr Forster Associates, 6th Annual European Hotel Industry Investment Conference, November 1994, London. Organized and sponsored by Pannell Kerr Forster Associates, Salomon Brothers, Jones Lang Wootton

virtually no investment market there. In Hong Kong hotels are equivalent to offices. The Ritz Carlton in 1994 sold for $580,000 per room compared with an average below $150,000 for European deals and $77,500 in the USA. Investors in South-East Asia are taking a keen interest in the hotel industry. In Jakarta, Indonesia, during 1994, there were 56 hotel projects under way, comprising a total of 24,000 rooms. Many are sponsored by cash-rich conglomerates, which see hotels as a low-risk way into potential tourism growth. However, some hotel operators have agreements giving investor owners the right to terminate tenancies without cause. Hoteliers face the problem that where Asians invest, they demand a say in management. This is why vacant possession is more attractive than buying into a business. Paris and London are the prime targets, although companies will pay substantial sums in order to fill geographical gaps in their chains. However, such investment is fickle, and could slow if vendors ask unreasonable prices.

## The USA

The USA, having shown the earliest signs of economic recovery, has experienced a sharp reversal in sentiment towards the hotel sector. While hotel values rose on average by 15 per cent in the USA during 1993, there was a wide disparity in performance between regions. Current market indicators point to an even stronger increase in hotel values in 1994. This rebound has occurred largely as a result of sharply improved business confidence, combined with low interest rates, the availability of equity, and the ability to purchase quality properties at prices well below replacement cost. The pace of recovery has been boosted by the realization among hotel investors that the window of opportunity for investment will only be shortlived. In sharp contrast to only two years ago, potential buyers now greatly outnumber sellers. The period 1988–91 saw four years of uninterrupted decline in hotel values. The year 1992 saw the initial stages of a recovery followed by a firmer upswing in 1993. The macroeconomic industry precursors to this recovery can be detailed under four points:

- economic growth;
- occupancy trends;
- supply;
- availability of capital.

**Economic growth**

The demand for hotel rooms is closely tied to economic growth. A close analysis of GDP, which is a broad measure of economic growth, is a good indicator of both business and leisure travel trends. Recovery in real GDP growth commenced in 1991: June 1994 saw 4 per cent growth, and in the second quarter of 1994 growth was recorded at an annualized figure of 3.7 per cent.

**Occupancy trends**

Occupancy has seen a gradual but steady increase since 1991, the year in which the economy started to pull out of recession. Average rates still remain under pressure, although they seem to be on the increase.

**Supply**

Overbuilding in the mid-1980s followed by severe recession in the early 1990s brought a halt to the supply pipeline, at least for the short term. Given that existing hotel values remain below replacement cost in the vast majority of instances, new development on a significant scale is some way off. Existing hotels will therefore benefit directly from rising room night demand without any dilutions through short-term supply increases.

**Availability of capital**

The low interest rate environment in the USA has encouraged investors to look at other sectors offering comparative yield advantages. The hotel sector has been an obvious candidate. The number of significant hotel transactions in the USA doubled from 21 in 1991 to 42 in 1993. Hotel transaction rates improved in 1994, but the market is now entering a phase of stock shortage, with relatively few hotel owners actually wanting to sell, further stimulating the price recovery. Yields are now falling, not only as a result of strong competition for profit, but also because investors' confidence in future operating performance is higher. The figure of 42 sales in 1993 includes sales of hotel properties for a transactional price in excess of $10 million. Geographically, California continues to be the preferred state for hotel investment, with eleven major sales recorded in

1993. Other states with multiple sales include Florida, Illinois, Hawaii and Georgia.

The profile of hotel buyers continues to be dominated by operators, both domestic and overseas, many of whom are aligned with a separate source of capital, and there is an increasing number of sophisticated, knowledgable buyers in the marketplace. They are obtaining high-quality property, often at extremely favourable prices, and the general consensus would appear to be that the recent past has represented the greatest opportunity in the US hotel industry since the 1930s. During 1995 there was an increased availability of both debt and equity capital for hotel acquisitions. Increased availability of third-party debt financing for the acquisition of existing hotels should decrease through the alliance of buyers and seller financing, and increased overall market activity, assuming that low mortgage interest rates continue. In the foreseeable future there should be a continued imbalance between the large number of qualified buyers looking for products and the limited number of quality hotels on the market.

## United Kingdom

The UK has also seen a marked increase in both demand for investment and market activity, although this is mainly confined to London during the period 1993–95. With the recovery under way in 1993, the most encouraging trend in London during 1995 was the depth of investment demand for quality hotels. This produced competitive bidding, and prices were being realized at significantly higher levels than 12 months prior to this period. Notwithstanding this turnaround, hotel values are still below their 1989 peak. Hoteliers in 1995 reported good recovery in occupancy, although average rates remained under pressure. The upturn in investment is primarily the consequence of foreign buyers, mainly from the Far East, looking to position themselves in the market while it is perceived to be in a recovery phase. This is compounded by a relative lack of available products, with the vendors stubbornly holding out for a required price level.

London hotel investment

Over the entire period 1977–92, London prime hotel total returns averaged just under 22 per cent p.a.; by comparison UK consumer prices rose by an average of 7.7 per cent p.a. For the same period, capital values increased at an average rate of just over 13 per cent p.a. During 1986–90, a period of rapid property value escalation, prime hotel capital values increased by approximately 21 per cent. Income return in the form of net operating profit increased by 7.5 per cent p.a over the entire period 1977–92. From 1986 to 1990, the principal period of capital growth, income return increased by just over 6 per cent p.a. Investment in the London hotel market is determined by prevailing international and political factors, their impact on demand and the supply of quality hotel rooms. During the period just discussed, the number of quality hotel rooms in London has increased by only 0.4 per cent. The quality hotel room supply has fluctuated over the period under review, owing to the opening of hotels, and the increase or decrease of room supply due to major refurbishments or closures for a limited period. Owing to strict planning policy, a shortage of suitable sites, and variable prices, new hotel development has been restricted. Over the period identified, six new quality hotels opened but only one was newly built, the remainder being conversions of existing buildings. The restrictions on supply in this sector have had a positive impact on the value of prime hotel properties in London, as demand continues to exist from major operators not represented in the capital.

## Europe

The European economy is clearly lagging behind those of the USA and UK in the economic cycle. The UK entered the recession in 1990 while most European economies enjoyed economic growth, albeit on a declining level, through till 1992. During these difficult economic times throughout Europe hotel performance was down, and the traditional buyers of European hotels suffered from a lack of liquidity. As a result there has been a dearth of hotel transactions during the past two years, as vendors have been unwilling to lower asking prices to levels that the more economically motivated buyers are willing to pay. These market conditions throughout Europe are only too familiar for those involved in the US and UK markets in recent years. Based on the cyclical nature of the hotel investment markets demonstrated in these two countries, it can be said that the depressed market for Europe hotel transactions is about to change in 1994–95. The question is how soon and how strong a recovery can be expected.

Following in the tracks of the UK, where recovery commenced in 1992, Europe is now showing signs of recovery, as indicated in various trends and particularly forecasts of GDP growth for 1994–95. Of course, hotel demand is also highly correlated with the economic conditions of the primary source markets for international hotel demand, and this factor also bodes well for future growth. The USA and UK – both key demand sources within the major European cities – are well on the way to full recovery. Another principal feeder, Japan, also looks to have turned the economic corner. Indeed Ciga (purchased in 1994 by ITT Sheraton), the Italian luxury hotel group, recently announced an increase in occupancy across its chain of 9.3 percentage points for the first seven months of 1994. Three further factors suggest a recovery in liquidity and values:

342 Strategic trends and developments

- Unlike the USA, most major European cities have not been plagued by excessive new supply. Planning controls are generally strict in the historic capitals of Europe: therefore as economic recovery occurs the improvement is likely to be felt rather quickly by European hotels.
- Many if not most of the major international hotel chains are already looking to take advantage of recent downturns to position or reposition themselves in the European markets through new acquisitions. As sellers become more realistic and buyers more frustrated, this will inevitably lead to greater transaction activity and rising values.
- There is a general consensus among investors that commercial property rents and yields, which tend to lead the hotel sector, have generally stabilized and are poised for growth in 1995.

Having mentioned the positives it should also be mentioned that the revival may be somewhat dampened by two factors:

- the rise of the yield curve in the financial markets during the first half of 1994, increasing the cost of long-term funds;
- the fragility of European consumer confidence, fuelled by the fact that Germany is expected to struggle out of recession and will therefore lag behind the overall trend.

A clear pattern showing the cyclical nature of property investment has again emerged in the hotel industry. This is seen by the economic recovery stimulating an increase in both room demand and investor liquidity, followed by an upturn in investment activity as buyers compete for positions while a window of opportunity is perceived. This results in value being squeezed higher, as already seen in the USA and UK. As the economic recovery in Europe becomes more solid, so the cyclical trend will be repeated in the hotel markets. However, given that European hotel values have not declined to the extent of those in the USA, the upturn may not be as pronounced.

European city hotel ownership profiles

Direct hotel investment continues to be a specialist investment medium undertaken by some hotel operating firms and favoured by wealthy individuals, but on the whole shunned by serious institutional investors. The ownership pattern and structure of quality hotels in the major European cities reflects to an extent the historic development of the hospitality industry and its future investment trends.

Direct management, in which the manager owns the assets, continues to dominate the European hotel market, mirroring a particular phenomenon of the European hotel industry, where family ownership has dominated for generations. From these family-owned hotel chains have emerged some of Europe's largest hotel companies. With the globalization and expansion of the hotel industry stimulated by improvements to air travel, many of the family-established hotel companies sought to manage properties on behalf of owners through the vehicle of management contracts. Management contract structures are most evident where recent hotel development has taken place, particularly in Brussels and Amsterdam. Since their inception, when the major operating companies dominated contract terms, a more recent trend is where owners have been able to negotiate favourable terms, as operators compete for representation in key European cities.

In Germany, for instance, the emerging structural pattern of hotel ownership in Frankfurt has seen leases becoming more prevalent. This structure, which follows the lease rent agreement common in the commercial property arena, is becoming more acceptable, though still not as common in the hotel sector. German institutions, which are more content with the lease structure, are investors in their domestic hotel industry. The emergence of leases in other cities such as London, however, has not to date encouraged institutional investment. Franchising is less common; the quality hotel sector is nevertheless represented in new hotel markets such as Frankfurt. With limited finance available, owners hold a strong negotiating position with those franchisors who are keen to increase their European representation. Owners obtain a cost-effective marketing gain, and if the current climate of liquidity continues to persist, their franchises may be anticipated to expand within the quality hotel sector. This trend may reinforce continued ownership of European hotel property by owner–operators and limit the expansion of operators through lease and management contracts. However, if operators do not invest in property to establish quality examples and create critical mass for their franchise systems, it will be very difficult to create a successful consistent brand.

Private owners, ranging from wealthy individuals to large family-controlled international companies, dominate the international market. Private sector ownership, which dominates in London, is primarily made up of publicly quoted companies. Many began as private concerns and most still manage the asset directly. A number are increasingly utilizing vehicles such as sale and leaseback, which serve to delete their direct ownership of the asset for accounting purposes, although new policies suggest that this will be limited in the future. The long-term trend in Europe is therefore towards the US and Asian situation, where the asset and its management are frequently separated, as seen in the restructuring by the Marriott chain in 1992. In the traditional markets of London, Madrid and Milan, domestic owners dominate. In Paris the ownership profile is more mixed, as hotel ownership was dominated historically by individuals; consequently when these properties were placed on the market, much interest was shown by international investors, and the ownership nationality became more diverse. In Frankfurt domestic investors dominate owing to the keenness of institutions and individual consortia to invest in hotels. In the major European capitals, hotel ownership nationally has reflected to an extent the geographic changes in world buying power. Domestic nationals initiated the hotel ownership in the 1970s, with revenues from oil-wealthy Arab investors invested in the industry. The 1980s saw an influx of Japanese and Scandinavian funds in particular, but also Asian investors, whose interest has dominated during the early 1990s.

Owing to limited sources of finance in many European cities and a finite supply of quality hotels due to a shortage of feasible development sites, hotel operators have, through necessity, become more flexible to investor needs. The emergence of management structures such as leases and performance-linked management contracts in the newer hotel markets of Brussels and Frankfurt, and the increase in the more traditional markets of London and Madrid, is evidence of this response. This increased awareness will serve to broaden the investor base in the hotel industry, as shown in Frankfurt, where the German institutions are more common investors in the hotel sector. The hotel industry will continue to be one of the most global sectors of the property industry, with owners and operators continually reviewing new markets for product representation and investment opportunities. Investment demand received a boost during 1993 with further interest rate falls, but is generally still strongly focused on low-risk well-let properties with good income security. Cross-border buying activity remained relatively depressed except in the UK, although the cash-rich German open-ended funds are increasingly turning their attention to the Benelux countries.

The market for Europe's major office developments continues to suffer from the continent's lingering economic recession. However, while speculative development activity has virtually ground to a halt, occupiers in some instances are now actively exploiting low rental levels and increasing vacancy rates. In consequence there have been some notable local variations in property market activity in a number of countries. Trends in 1994–95 seem to indicate further price readjustment in virtually all areas as markets continue to take account of ongoing imbalances and reduced economic activity. As markets bottom out, however, there have been clear opportunities during 1994–95 for investors and occupiers alike, ahead of an economic upswing, to do business at extremely attractive prices. It is expected that Dutch and German investors will be in the vanguard of this activity, with co-investment from the UK also in evidence. The level of hotel investment activity varied widely across Europe during 1993 and 1994: there was increased interest in those countries moving out of recession and in those where a major over-supply was not created in the booming economic cycle of the late 1980s. Most investor interest was and is currently focused on London, where South-East Asian, Middle Eastern and domestic purchasers believe that the hotel property market has bottomed, with favourable exchange rates, historically low interest rates and property values making investment attractive. A number of London hotel transactions occurred during 1993 and 1994.

France, Germany and Spain are still in the recessionary phase during this period and activity has been limited despite a substantial reduction in interest rates.

## A VISION OF THE HOTEL INDUSTRY TO THE YEAR 2020

In considering trends in the hotel industry to the year 2020 a number of Iissues need to be addressed:

- How will a guest book a room?
- How will the hotel room be priced, sold and administered?
- How will the guest be serviced in the hotel?
- What pressures will we experience from suppliers and which can we apply?
- What will be the core business of a hotel?
- What are the implications for the prioritization of investment, in particular as it relates to information technology?

New technology is expected to play a crucial role in the success and location of future hotel development. Massive refurbishment may also be required to bring existing buildings up to the standards demanded by business travellers. Hoteliers currently concentrate on the way this technology will revolutionize booking methods. Booking rooms from your TV or office personal computer will affect the demand for services from travel agents. Such an approach will also revolutionize hotel development. Rooms will become an extension of the working environment, which will mean providing a range of electronic equipment rarely seen today outside offices and some homes. A generation is growing up that will be tomorrow's business travellers. They will expect services such as interactive TV, which provides both entertainment and video conferencing as standard. Travellers will also stay in touch with head office via the videophone, which will also act as a fax and copier – particularly when international calls are as cheap as local ones. This will cut the need for support staff, and other staff reductions will come from contracting out services such as laundry. Operators who spend most of their time predicting the impact of IT on room booking should realize that it could have a significant effect on the pattern of new development.

Within the hospitality industry, emphasis is increasingly and directly related to individual customers by developing the product they need, delivering that product with skilled staff, and having the systems to coordinate the operation. Much of this focus is on marketing, which can be regarded as understanding, predicting and meeting changing consumer tastes. The central role of the marketing function is to impart knowledge, understanding and anticipation of customer tastes to the rest of the firm, and in this sense make individual managers marketeers within their own functional role This has led to new marketing requirements for reaching individual customers and responding to their needs. These changes are made possible by technology that facilitates direct supplier-customer contact and delivery, and are related to Porter's analysis in Figure 10.2.

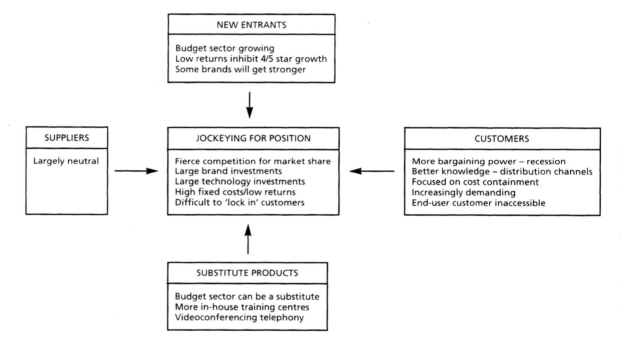

**Fig. 10.2 Forces influencing competition in the hospitality industry**

*Source:* Pannell Kerr Forster Associates, 6th Annual European Hotel Industry Investment Conference, November 1994, London. Organized and sponsored by Pannell Kerr Forster Associates, Salomon Brothers, Jones Lang Wootton

## Technology

The level of investment in new computer technology and the development of extensive databases is considerable, as the hospitality industry becomes increasingly global in terms of markets and competition. While such systems were originally developed by the airline industry, they are increasingly seeking to expand their coverage on non-airline travel services such as hotels and car rentals. It is expected that more reservations will be made from home or from the office, especially for domestic travel, and the largest slice of the budget of hospitality organizations will be allocated to direct marketing through computerized database applications. Hospitality product suppliers have some fairly straightforward expectations in respect to this new technology:

- to know more about what existing and potential customers want;
- to reach these customers and tell them what is on offer;
- to satisfy customers so that they both come back and spread the good word;
- to operate profitably.

From the consumers' point of view the objectives are to simplify and speed up the travel decision process. They look for a system that will help them to:

- make individual choices from a broad menu of travel and activity options;
- receive timely and accurate destination and travel information;
- simplify access into the travel information labyrinth;
- resolve concerns and confirm expectations;
- save money.

From this perspective, a database marketing support program responds to trends and contributes to the achievement of the organization's objectives. It will consist of three main elements:

- the product database;
- the customer database; and
- the booking and reservation system to tie them all together.

## The product database

Many destinations have developed or are developing a computerized product database, which is an important asset. Such a product inventory system provides descriptive and timely information on many facilities, attractions, accommodation, services, special events and programmes. Because it provides phone numbers and contacts for use by consumers and for agents it facilitates the marketing and utilization of the industry's products and services. One aspect that is of particular importance for this product database is its ability to capture consumer data. This provides the foundation for expansion into a wide range of customer database marketing.

## Customer database

An increase in targeted marketing requires an increase in customer data. Forecast trends suggest that those who have not taken advantage of what computer technology can offer to individual customers will be at a competitive disadvantage. A customer database can be used to identify who the customers are: not just the visitors themselves, but those that influence the visitors. Data can be collected not only on past visitors but also on non-visitors, whose travel habits and characteristics indicate that they could be future visitors. A number of factors influence the visitors, including travel agents, tour operators and hotel chains. It is therefore particularly important to view destination database development through the eyes of consumers, providing them with what they want, when and where they want it.

## Database structure

In understanding existing visitors, certain traditional information is provided for in the customer record. It includes customer demographics, travel patterns and activity profile, expenditure data, past trip evaluation and satisfaction, and transaction history. This record is kept current and accurate through frequent updating and customer contact. This traditional information is valuable, but it is only the first step in using customer databases. What is also needed is the information to reach new visitors through the use of database technology to address a number of priorities.

The first priority is to concentrate on **existing market segments**, because these are the types of customer who have already expressed the highest interest in the destination in terms of purchase behaviour. **Potential market segments** are those with similar characteristics to existing market segments; these customers have indicated the purchase of similar products to what the destination offers. It is not necessary to persuade them to visit an unknown destination but only to travel to the specific destination. **Expanded potential market segments** comprise travellers who seek similar products to what the destination offers but do not now visit the region. Potential market segments for additional or enhanced products are those potential visitors if additional or enhanced products are offered. These might be new types of resort, convention conference facilities, new recreation resources or infrastructure improvements. These segments need to be convinced to try out new products that the region is now known for.

To reach potential new customers it is important to find people like the existing visitors, and hence it is important to gather information about existing visitors, to lead the firm to databases of persons with similar characteristics. One example of this approach is at ITT Sheraton. Over the past few years the company has invested $70 million in a new reservations system that gives it market information and provides an ability to understand its customer base. It also gives it a facility to do database marketing. In February 1993, for instance, ten properties in Hawaii identified a downturn in demand for April, May and June. The traditional approach to that downturn would have been probably to increase advertising in Sunday magazine travel sections. Instead ITT chose to mail a targeted offer to 650,000 people who travelled to Hawaii. It gained $3 million in revenue for those hotels during that period.

## Use of databases in marketing

Market planning   Information is the basis of planning: with it, the firm can target market to maximum effect, but without it can only guess or aim and hope. Both product and customer databases are core elements of an information management programme that tell the firm what it has and who may want to buy it. It provides marketing direction and the ability to monitor effectiveness.

Selling   Because the product database is both comprehensive and accessible, it allows staff to not only provide information, but to generate customer interest and to sell. Such an approach allows staff to highlight the strong points of a hotel or resort and convey their own knowledge and enthusiasm, and so such an approach is a powerful selling tool.

Repeat customer development   Both hotels and airlines have seen the benefit of establishing a loose but structured association with their repeat visitors. As the frequent-fly clubs, hotel clubs and the like have shown, such an association can offer a number of marketing opportunities. Clubs generate a sense of loyalty in many of their members, and at the same time act as a defence against others who may be trying to persuade visitors to go elsewhere. One example of such a destination area club is Club France. This is considered by the French Government tourist office to be a great marketing asset. It is now at a stage where with the help of the private sector the benefits are substantial and the members are prepared to pay $65 per year for the privilege of belonging.

Relational database marketing applications   The prime purpose of this approach is to link the customer information in the hotel's or airline's database with other databases which allow the organization to reach more customers. What is involved is a comparison of the firm's database with others that share the same characteristics as the hotel's or airline's current visitors. Relational database work is one of the most productive ways to expand the breadth of the firm's customer database. It may find a new group of people that the firm has not tried to reach in the past but who are now revealed as good prospects.

An example of this use of technology will now be shown with a case study on Utell International.

## CASE STUDY: UTELL INTERNATIONAL

Utell International is closely involved in the management, development and maintenance of some very large hotel databases. This includes hotel directories, such as the HTI editions, Jaguar, the electronic imaging and database system on Sabre, and Utell's own live database of detailed reservation information for 6,500 hotels worldwide. The company does not own or have franchise management agreements with its members, nor does it seek to brand them. It acts purely as a third-party reservation and marketing consultant. The sales and marketing activities that it undertakes are reflected in the numbers of reservations that each member hotel achieves. It represents a range of hotels from five star to two star, independent as well as small and large chains, and resorts situated all over the world. Travel agents are the company's prime customers, and account for 95 per cent of all the reservations that Utell books. Its aim is to ensure that the travel agent can make a booking by whichever means they prefer, whether it be the telephone or one of the several automated systems around the world. In line with this, Utell has developed large global distribution networks, including connections to many different multi-access third-party and videotext systems used today by travel agents worldwide.

The core of Utell's business is a vast database of hotel information. The development and management of this is fundamental to the company's success as a reservations provider. The nature of the operation is that because of its size and quality it is able to sell and promote its product as a one-stop shop to travel agents, providing quality service, reliable information and secure delivery of bookings. Because of its size and coverage it is an attractive partner for the CRS systems. The database contains a range of information including rates, selling policies, forms of guarantee, availability of room, location, property description, amenities and pictures, maps and destination information. In taking this approach the benefit for the hotel is that it can provide information on yield management, last room availability, management information for the hotel and management information for the travel agent.

### The challenge for the Utell database

While the larger business city centre hotels are already well served by the CRS, the need is to provide a service to the whole accommodation industry, including small and medium-sized properties. However, investment in technology within the smaller hotels is not usually repaid by the amount of business generated. That is why these properties are often excluded from the system, and so an incomplete picture is gained by the travel agent who is working particularly in the leisure market. Because these smaller hotels are not automatically linked up to the database, owing to prohibitive costs, they find it hard to penetrate their own markets let alone the global hotel market. However, in trying to expand Utell's market to smaller hotels, it is important to consider the issue of quality control. Such smaller lesser-known properties still need to meet basic required standards and provide complete, accurate and up-to-date information. Another issue is one of bypassing the system. If the travel agent, for instance, goes direct to the hotel, they can normally get a better price not in the system, while the hotels would be still trying to cut out the travel agent and get the client to come direct, thereby limiting costly commissions. It is these practices that undermine the use of any automated system and prevent maximization of room rate yield. Finally, Utell needs to address the issue of training. Because this is essentially a new form of booking, investment is needed in retraining and promoting the use of the Utell system rather than the traditional approach of using the telephone, fax or telex for booking accommodation.

**SUMMARY**

This chapter drew together four key areas that have strategic implications for the development of the hotel industry: changing consumer and demand patterns; an economic and political overview of Europe; the hotel investment market; and trends to the year 2020. The chapter took both a global and a regional approach in considering the social and political issues affecting the hotel industry. The hotel investment market was considered in terms of both investor trends and investor requirements: the European, Asia/Pacific and North American markets were analysed. The final section of the chapter focused on trends in technology that will affect the global hotel industry to the year 2020.

**FURTHER READING** Barley, P 1994 Looking for trouble, *Marketing Business*, September, 21–4

Boston Consulting Group 1994 Discovering how to maximize customer share, *Marketing Business*, September, 12–16

Gregory, S R and G G Fenich 1994 Service: the marketing stepchild – a hospitality scenario, *Hospitality & Tourism Educator* **6**(3), 55–8

Hospitality Valuation Services International 1994 *The Hotel Valuation Journal*, Summer/Autumn, London

Jones Lang Wootton 1993 *Hotel Investment Review*, London: Jones Lang Wootton International Hotels, London

Lawson, D 1994 Room for investment, *Property Week*, 1 December, 20–2

Pannell Kerr Forster 1993 *5th Annual European Hotel Investment Conference*, 28 October, The Dorchester, London

Pannell Kerr Forster 1994 *6th Annual European Hotel Investment Conference*, 2 November, The Royal Lancaster, London

Pannell Kerr Forster 1995 *London trends*, London: Pannell Kerr Forster Associates

Pannell Kerr Forster 1995 *Eurocity survey*, London: Pannell Kerr Forster Associates

Pannell Kerr Forster 1995 *The UK Hotel Industry Conference*, 7 March, London

Pannell Kerr Forster 1995 *Institutional Investment in the UK Hotel Industry*, Pannell Kerr Forster Associates, London

PATA 1993 *PATA Destination Database Conference*, USA

Slattery, P, G Feehely and M Savage 1995 *Quoted hotel companies: the world markets 1995*, London: Kleinwort Benson Securities

Sussmann, S 1992 Destination management systems: the challenge for the 1990s. In C Cooper and A Lockwood (eds) *Progress in tourism, recreation and hospitality management*, vol. 4, London: Belhaven Press

Sussmann, S and T Rashad 1994 Geographic information systems in tourism marketing. In C Cooper and A Lockwood (eds) *Progress in tourism, recreation and hospitality management*, vol. 6, Chichester: John Wiley

Witt, S F and L Moutinho (eds) 1994 *Tourism marketing and management handbook*, 2nd edn, Hemel Hempstead: Prentice-Hall

# INDEX